mate venus

Takako Shigematsu

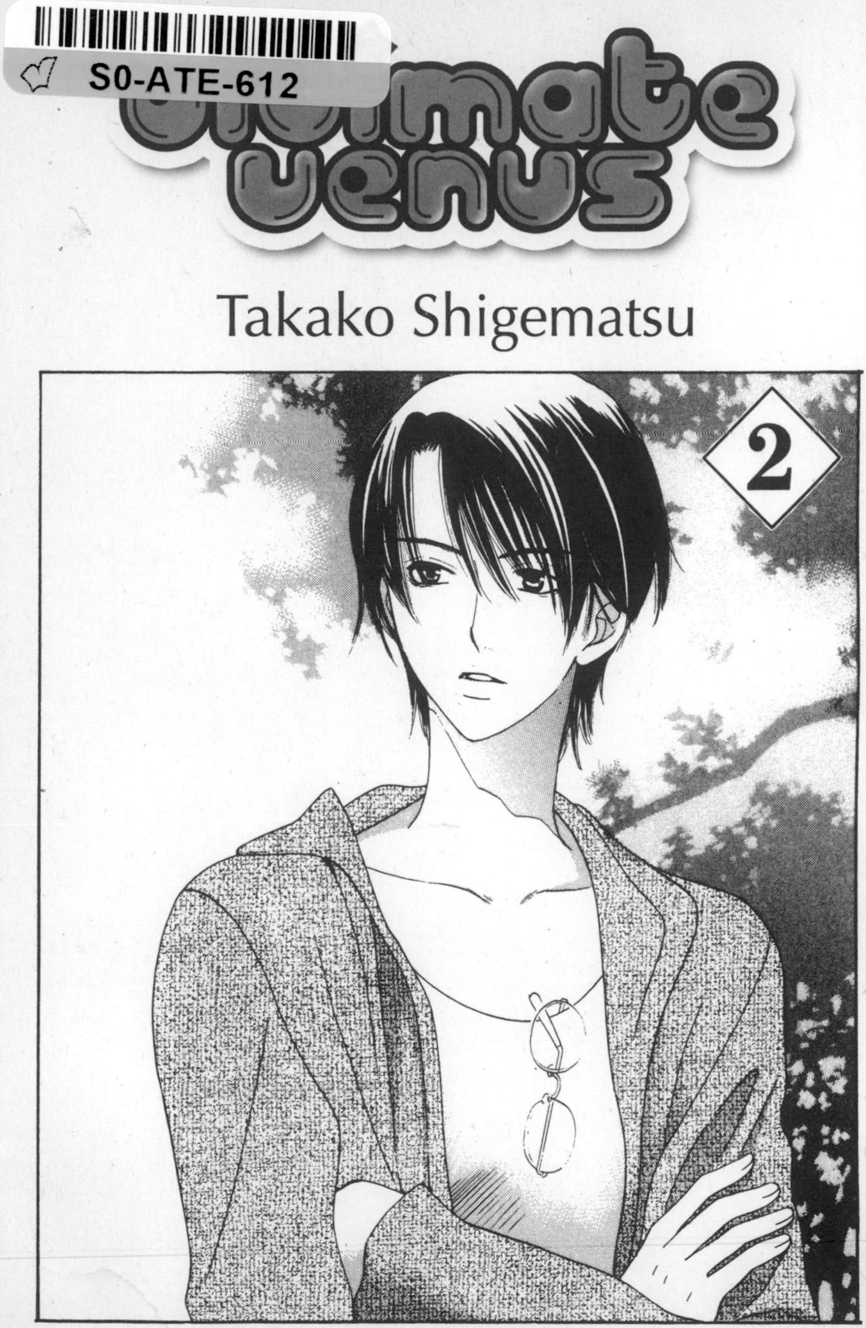
2

Translation –Christine Schilling
Adaptation – Brynne Chandler
Lettering & Retouch – Erika T.
Production Assistant – Suzy Wells
Editorial Assistant – Mallory Reaves
Production Manager – James Dashiell
Editor – Brynne Chandler

A Go! Comi manga

Published by Go! Media Entertainment, LLC

Kyukyoku Venus Volume 2
© TAKAKO SHIGEMATSU 2007
Originally published in Japan in 2007 by Akita Publishing Co., Ltd., Tokyo.
English translation rights arranged with Akita Publishing Co., Ltd.
through TOHAN CORPORATION, Tokyo.

Visit us online at www.gocomi.com
e-mail: info@gocomi.com

ISBN 978-1-933617-89-3

First printed in September 2008

1   2   3   4   5   6   7   8   9

Manufactured in the United States of America

ultimate venus

by

Takako Shigematsu

Volume 2

go!comi

VOLUME : 2
CONTENTS

* Story so far*

When Yuzu Yamashita's mother passed away, she thought she was all alone in the world. Then she met Hassaku Kagami and found out she has a grandmother who is president of the multinational Shirayuki Group, and lives in a castle! Once Yuzu is in line to be the family heir, her life is filled with bizarre dangers, like an attempted kidnapping! Complicating things even more is her classmate, Iyo Hayashibara – the former heir. Though he treats her like an enemy, when Yuzu's in trouble he comes to her rescue...making it nearly impossible for her to tell friend from foe.

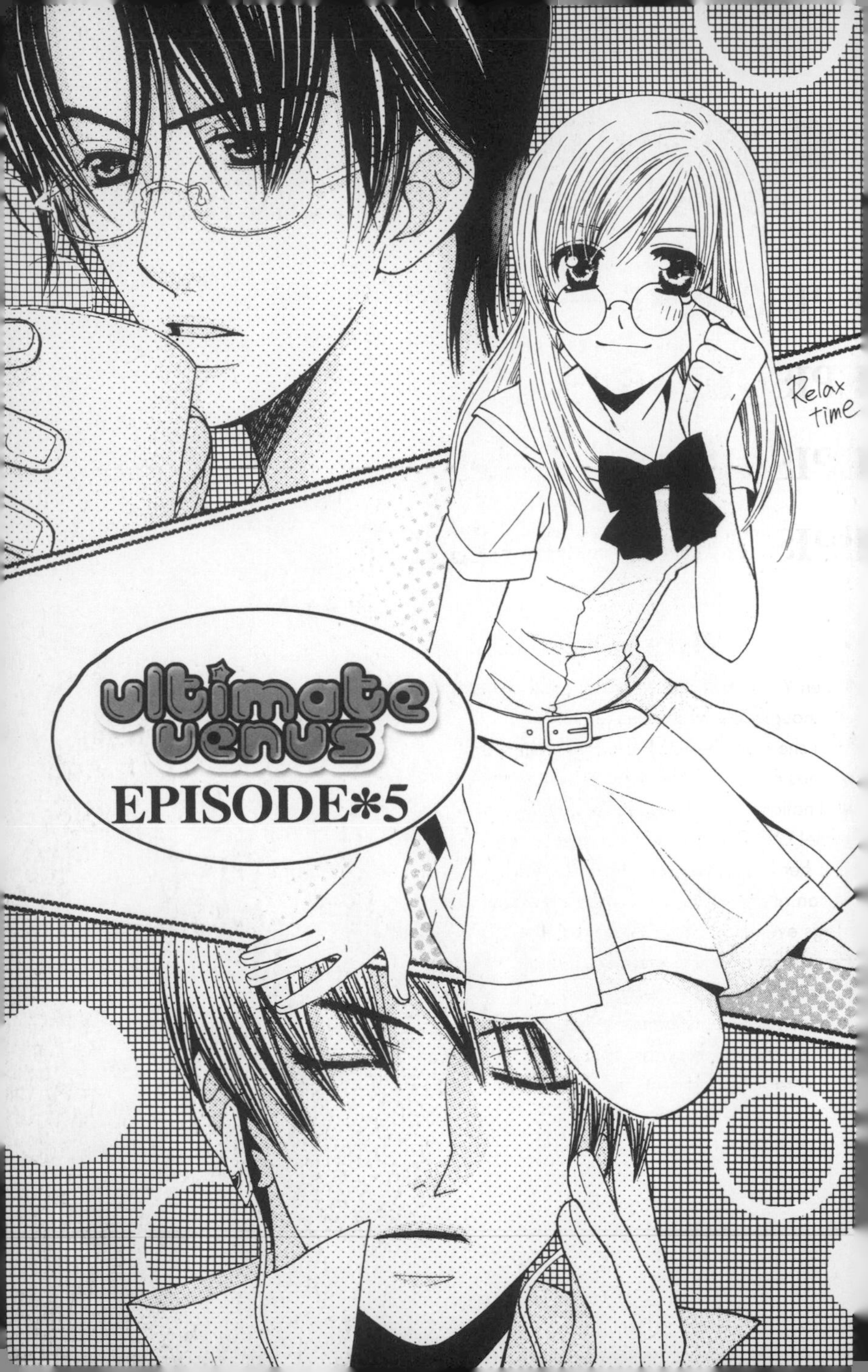
Relax time
ultimate venus
EPISODE*5

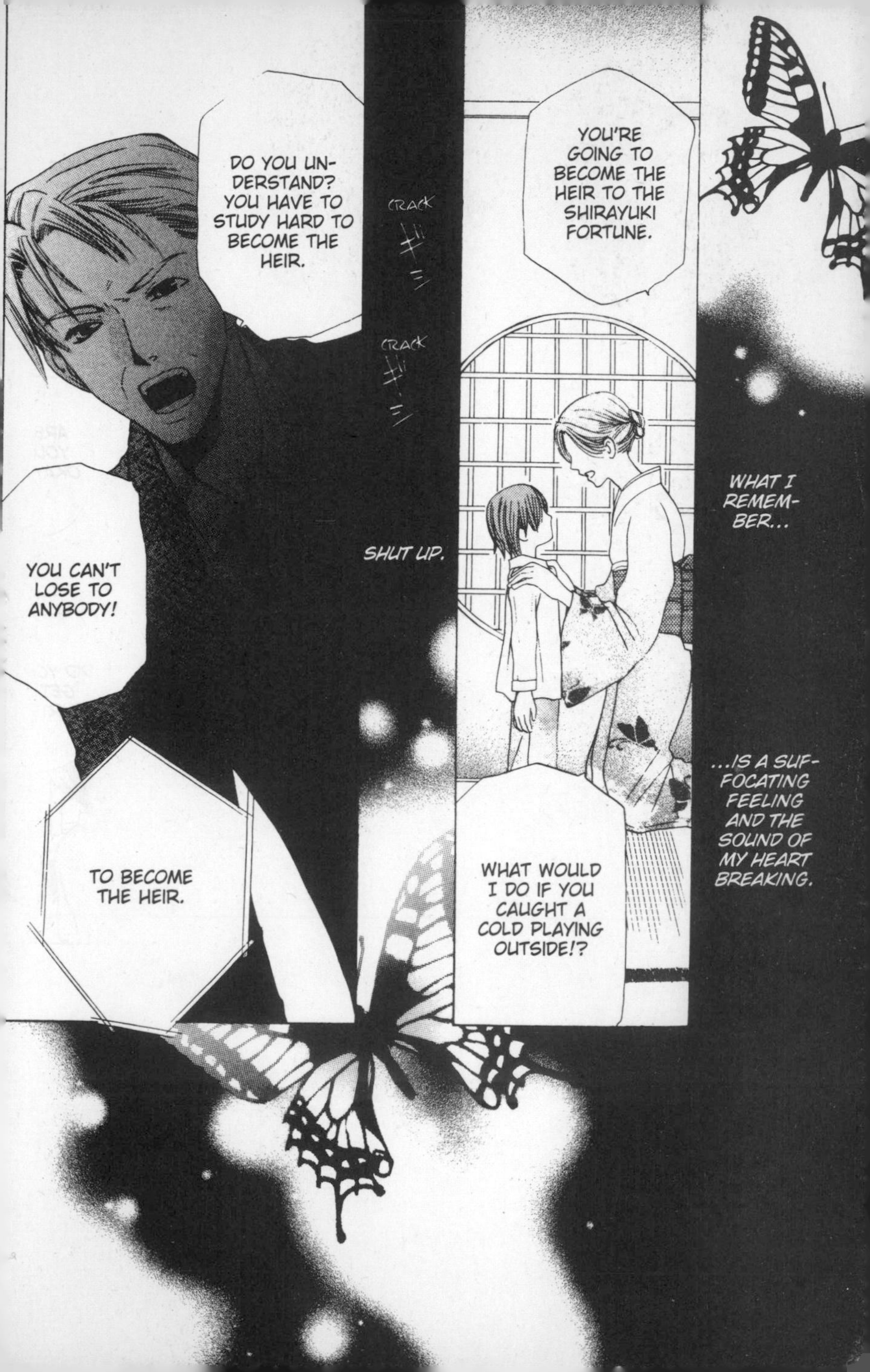
WHAT I REMEMBER...
...IS A SUFFOCATING FEELING AND THE SOUND OF MY HEART BREAKING.
YOU'RE GOING TO BECOME THE HEIR TO THE SHIRAYUKI FORTUNE.
WHAT WOULD I DO IF YOU CAUGHT A COLD PLAYING OUTSIDE!?
CRACK
CRACK
SHUT UP.
DO YOU UNDERSTAND? YOU HAVE TO STUDY HARD TO BECOME THE HEIR.
YOU CAN'T LOSE TO ANYBODY!
TO BECOME THE HEIR.

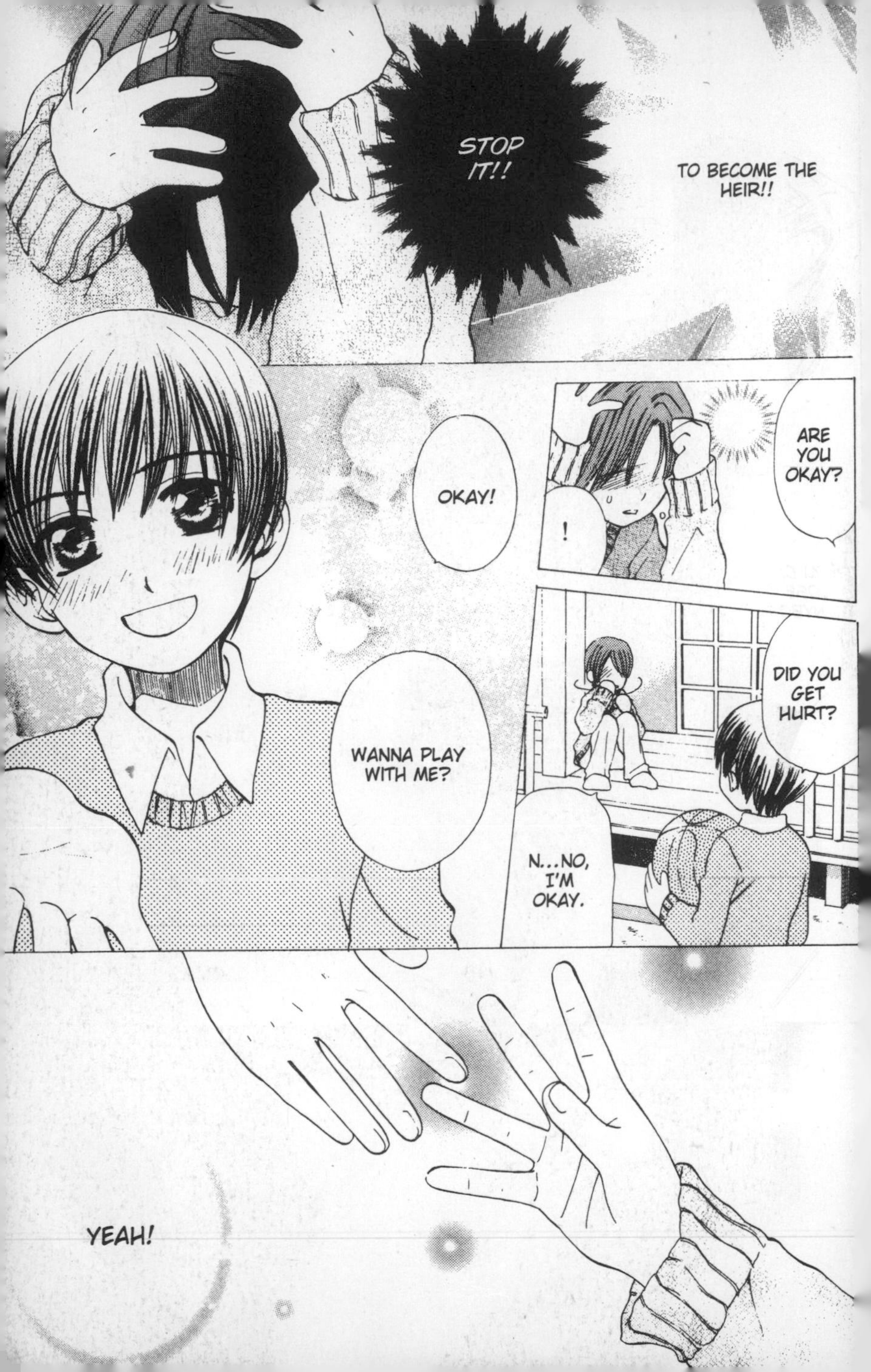
TO BECOME THE HEIR!!
STOP IT!!
ARE YOU OKAY?
!
DID YOU GET HURT?
N...NO, I'M OKAY.
OKAY!
WANNA PLAY WITH ME?
YEAH!

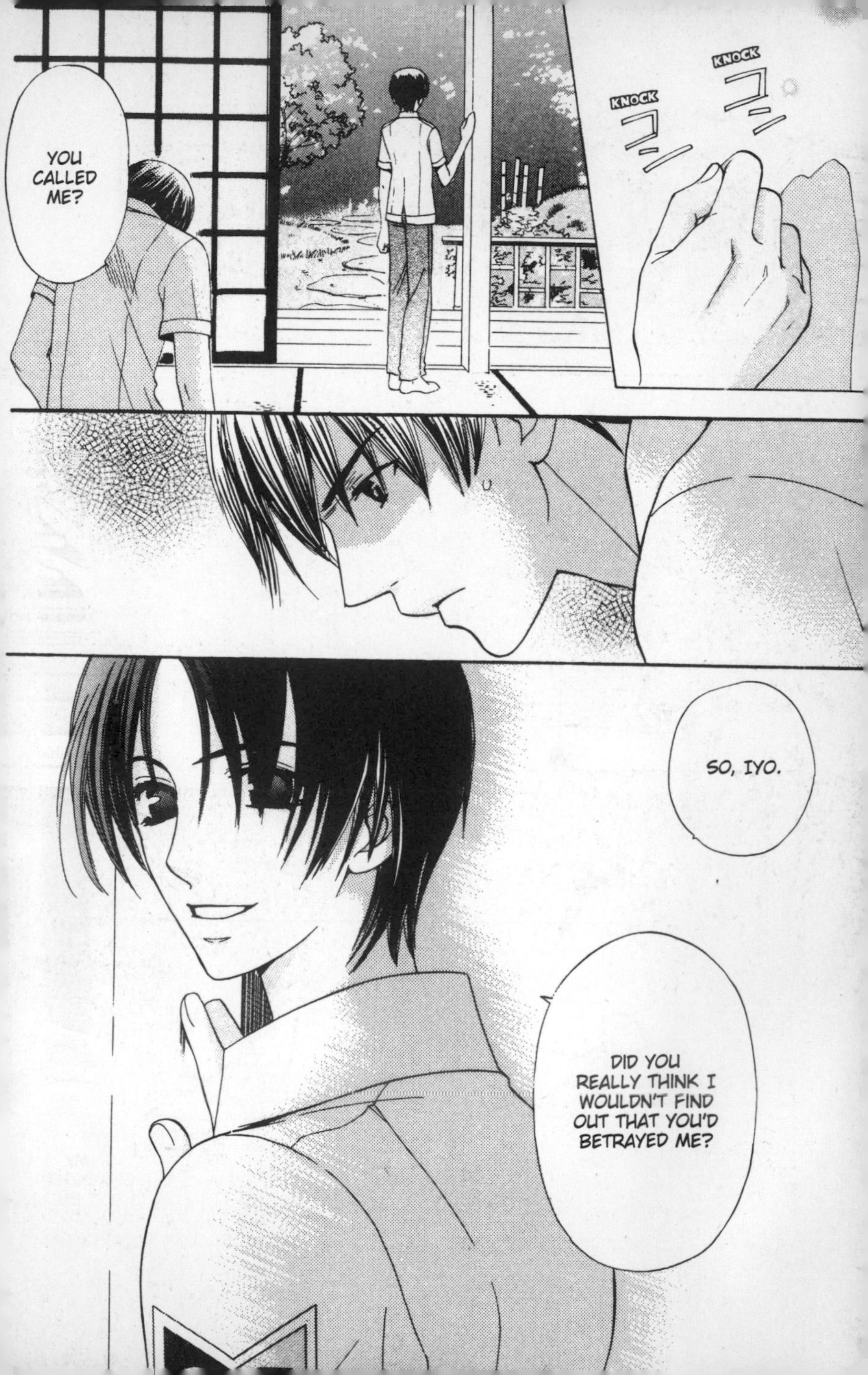
KNOCK
KNOCK
YOU CALLED ME?
SO, IYO.
DID YOU REALLY THINK I WOULDN'T FIND OUT THAT YOU'D BETRAYED ME?

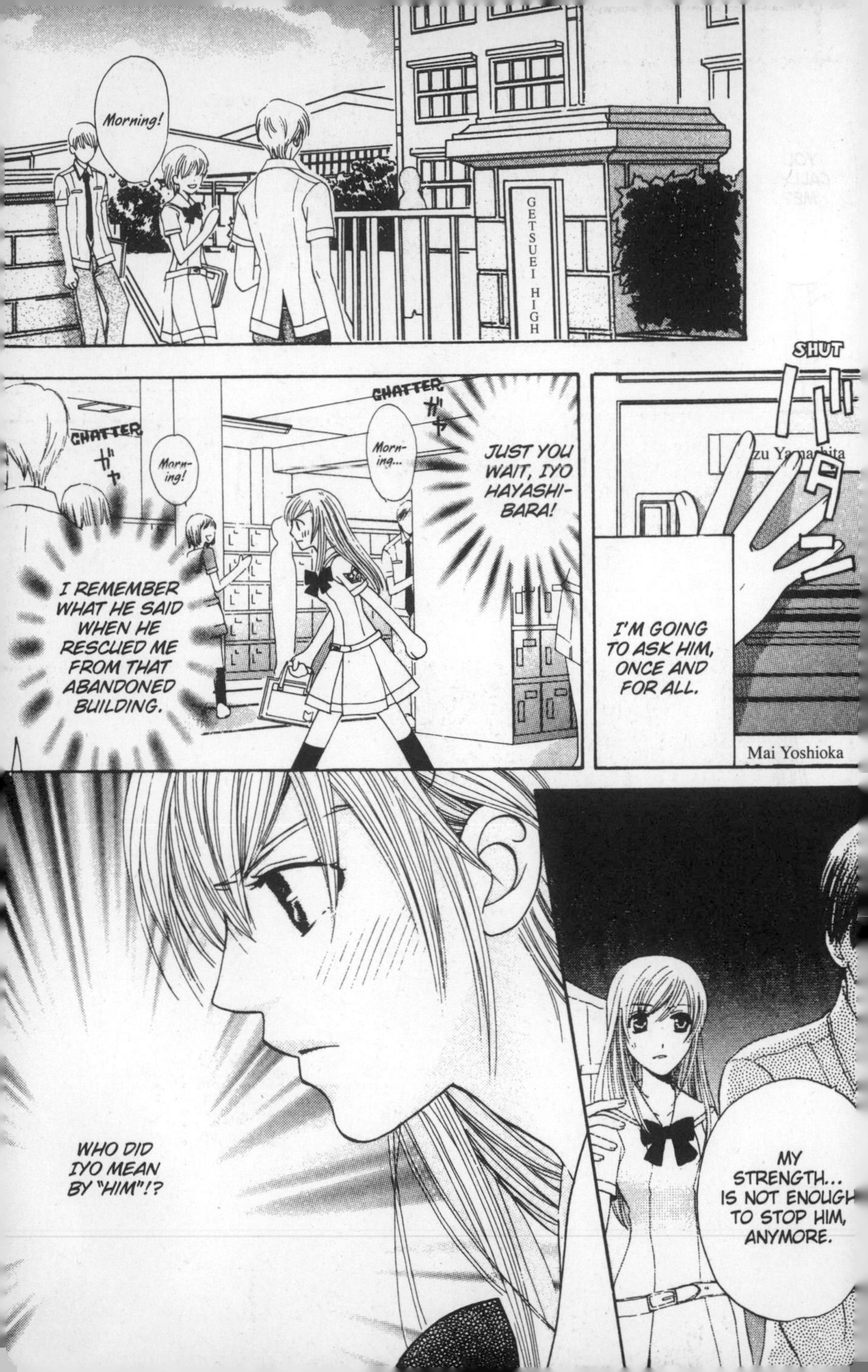
Morning!
GETSUEI HIGH
SHUT
I'M GOING TO ASK HIM, ONCE AND FOR ALL.
Mai Yoshioka
CHATTER
JUST YOU WAIT, IYO HAYASHI-BARA!
Morn-ing...
CHATTER
Morn-ing!
I REMEMBER WHAT HE SAID WHEN HE RESCUED ME FROM THAT ABANDONED BUILDING.
MY STRENGTH... IS NOT ENOUGH TO STOP HIM, ANYMORE.
WHO DID IYO MEAN BY "HIM"!?

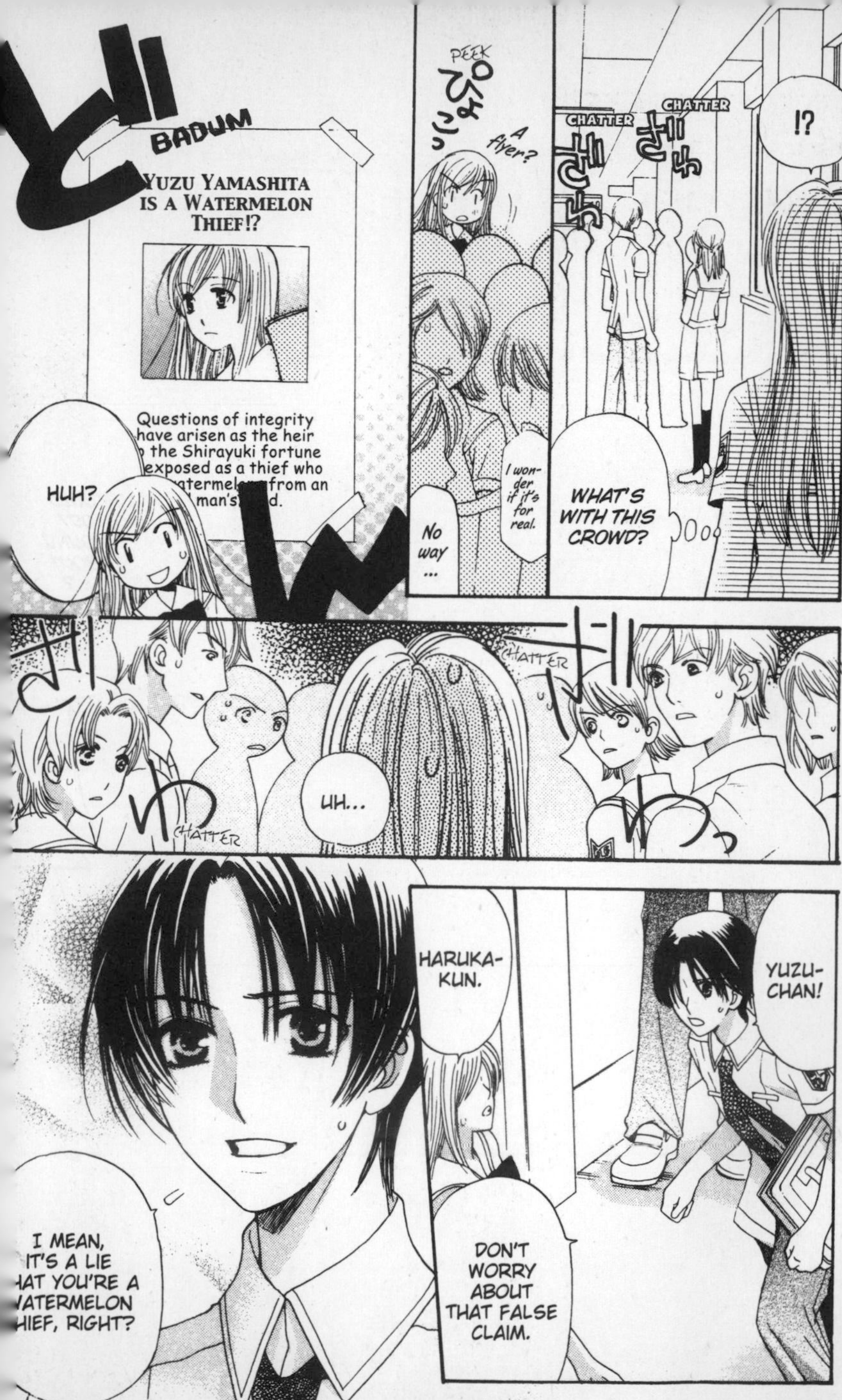
!?
CHATTER
CHATTER
WHAT'S WITH THIS CROWD?
PEEK
ぴょこっ
A flyer?
I wonder if it's for real.
No way...
BADUM
YUZU YAMASHITA IS A WATERMELON THIEF!?
Questions of integrity have arisen as the heir
o the Shirayuki fortune
exposed as a thief who
HUH?
CHATTER
UH...
CHATTER
YUZU-CHAN!
HARUKA-KUN.
DON'T WORRY ABOUT THAT FALSE CLAIM.
I MEAN, IT'S A LIE HAT YOU'RE A VATERMELON HIEF, RIGHT?

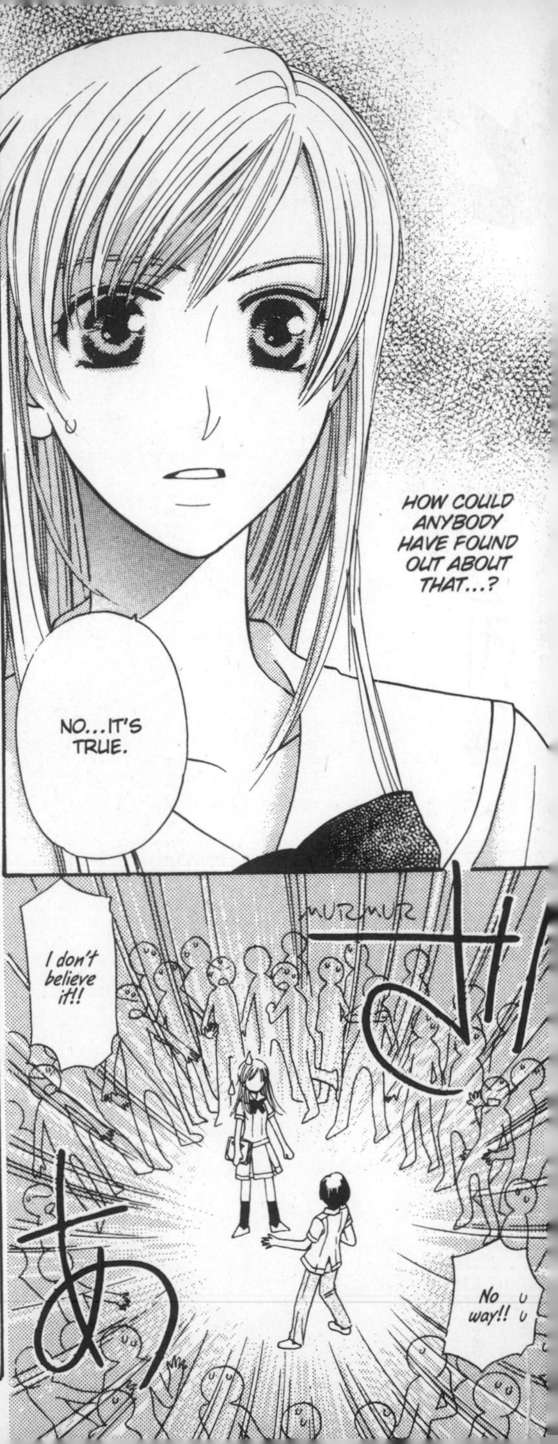
HOW COULD ANYBODY HAVE FOUND OUT ABOUT THAT...?
NO...IT'S TRUE.
MURMUR
I don't believe it!!
No way!!

GREETINGS

Hello and nice to meet you. Thank you very much for picking up "Ultimate Venus" volume 2!

I took a lot of breaks during the writing of this volume. What am I to do? It feels like when I try to write about the past two or three months, all I've done is play video games all the time.

...I'm an example of a naughty adult.

But, I'd still be happy if you read through to the very end.

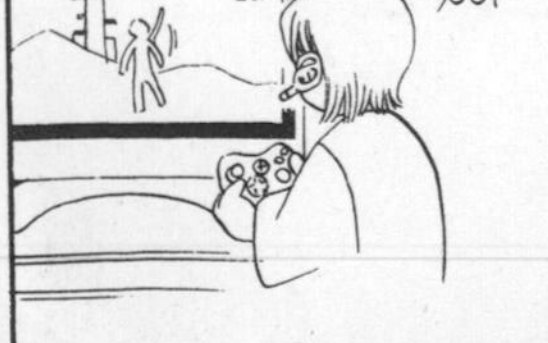
BEEP BOOP

↑ A Naughty Adult

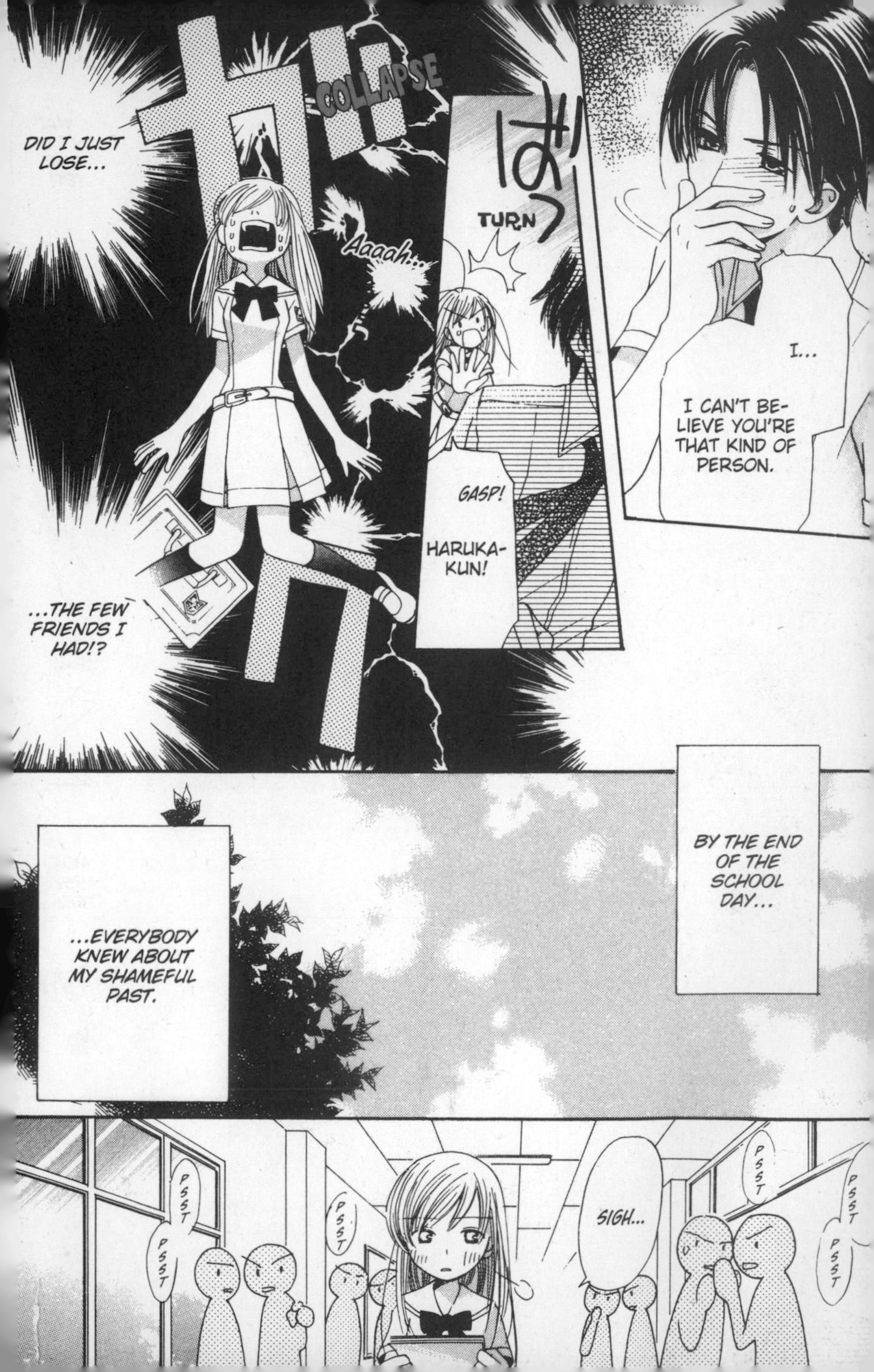
I...
I CAN'T BE-LIEVE YOU'RE THAT KIND OF PERSON.
ばっ
TURN
GASP!
HARUKA-KUN!
COLLAPSE
DID I JUST LOSE...
Aaaah...
...THE FEW FRIENDS I HAD!?
BY THE END OF THE SCHOOL DAY...
...EVERYBODY KNEW ABOUT MY SHAMEFUL PAST.
PSST
PSST
PSST
SIGH...
PSST
PSST
PSST

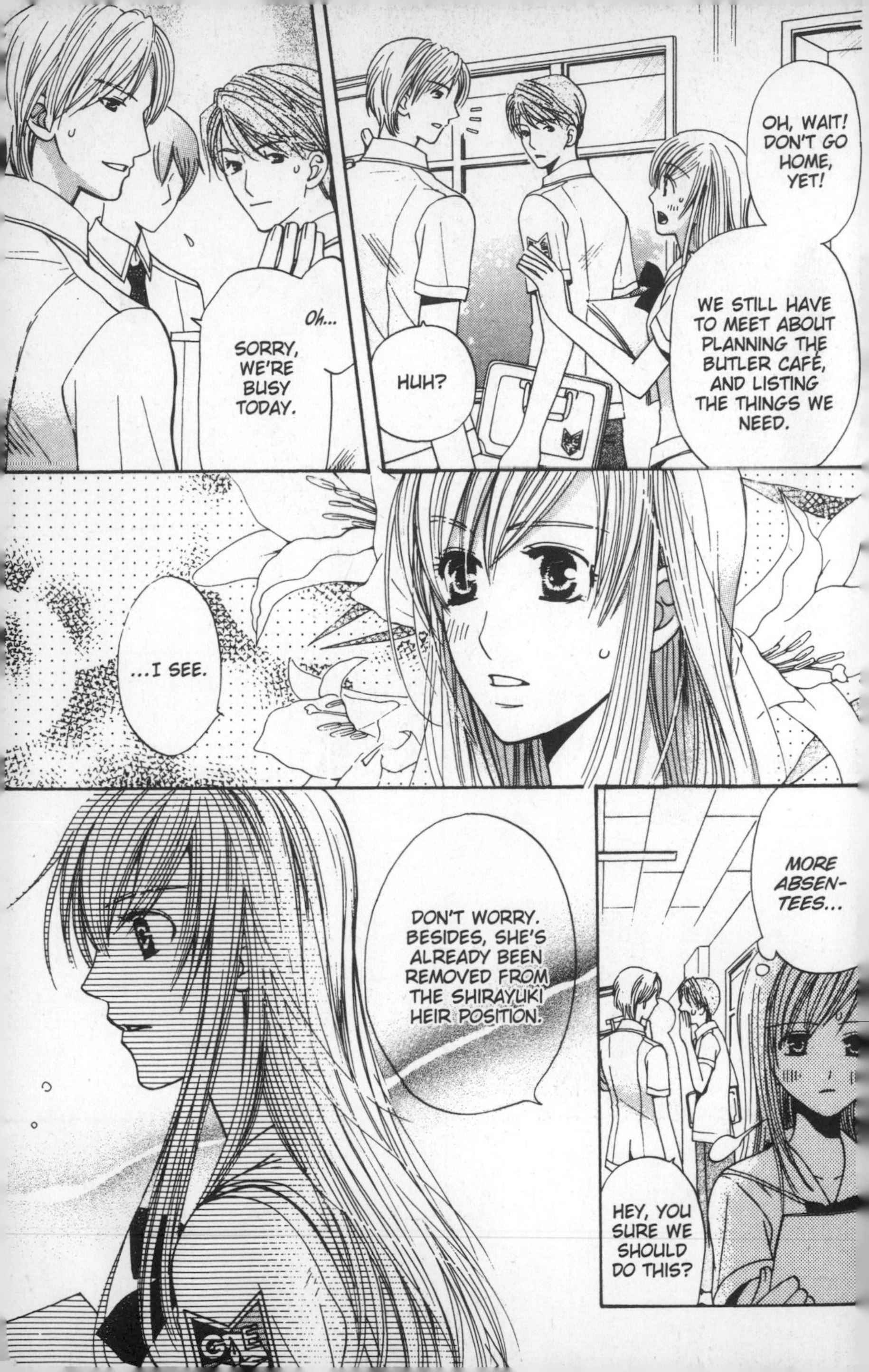
OH, WAIT! DON'T GO HOME, YET!
WE STILL HAVE TO MEET ABOUT PLANNING THE BUTLER CAFÉ, AND LISTING THE THINGS WE NEED.
HUH?
Oh...
SORRY, WE'RE BUSY TODAY.
...I SEE.
MORE ABSEN-TEES...
HEY, YOU SURE WE SHOULD DO THIS?
DON'T WORRY. BESIDES, SHE'S ALREADY BEEN REMOVED FROM THE SHIRAYUKI HEIR POSITION.

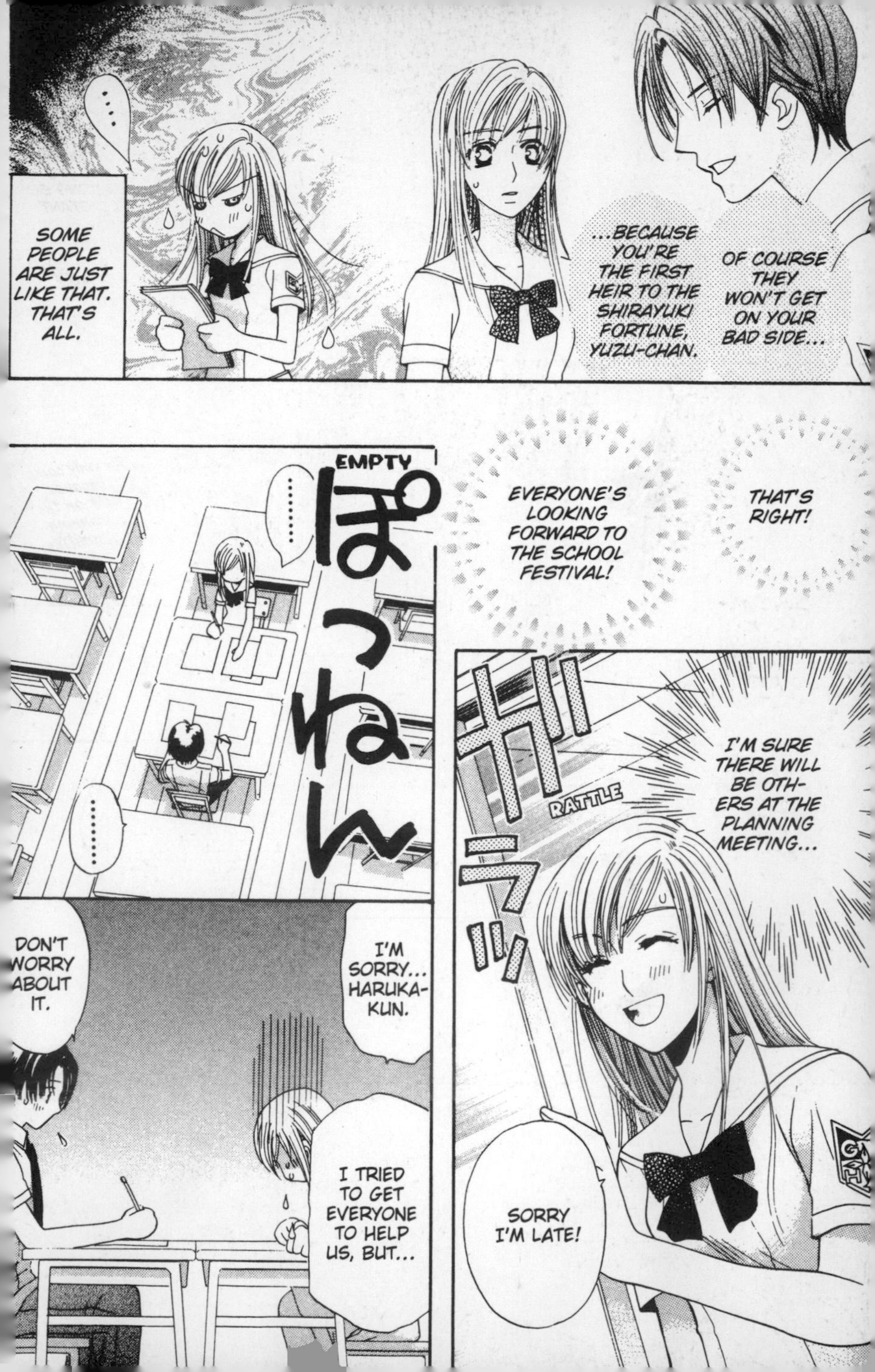
OF COURSE THEY WON'T GET ON YOUR BAD SIDE...
...BECAUSE YOU'RE THE FIRST HEIR TO THE SHIRAYUKI FORTUNE, YUZU-CHAN.
....
SOME PEOPLE ARE JUST LIKE THAT. THAT'S ALL.
THAT'S RIGHT!
EVERYONE'S LOOKING FORWARD TO THE SCHOOL FESTIVAL!
ガラッ
RATTLE
I'M SURE THERE WILL BE OTH-ERS AT THE PLANNING MEETING...
SORRY I'M LATE!
ぽつねん
EMPTY
......
......
I'M SORRY... HARUKA-KUN.
I TRIED TO GET EVERYONE TO HELP US, BUT...
DON'T WORRY ABOUT IT.

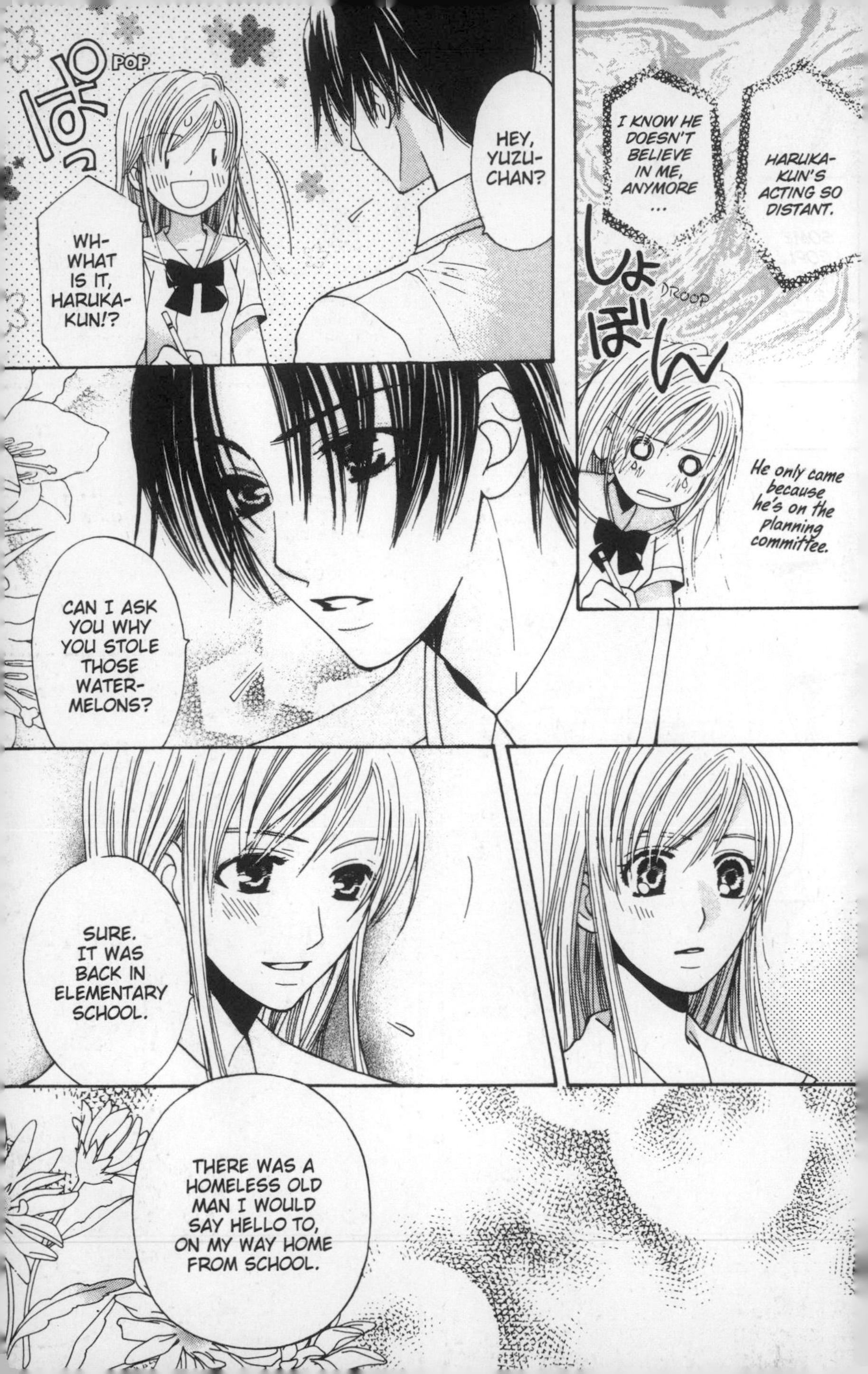
HARUKA-KUN'S ACTING SO DISTANT.
I KNOW HE DOESN'T BELIEVE IN ME, ANYMORE ...
しょぼん
DROOP
He only came because he's on the planning committee.
HEY, YUZU-CHAN?
ぱっ
POP
WH-WHAT IS IT, HARUKA-KUN!?
CAN I ASK YOU WHY YOU STOLE THOSE WATER-MELONS?
SURE. IT WAS BACK IN ELEMENTARY SCHOOL.
THERE WAS A HOMELESS OLD MAN I WOULD SAY HELLO TO, ON MY WAY HOME FROM SCHOOL.

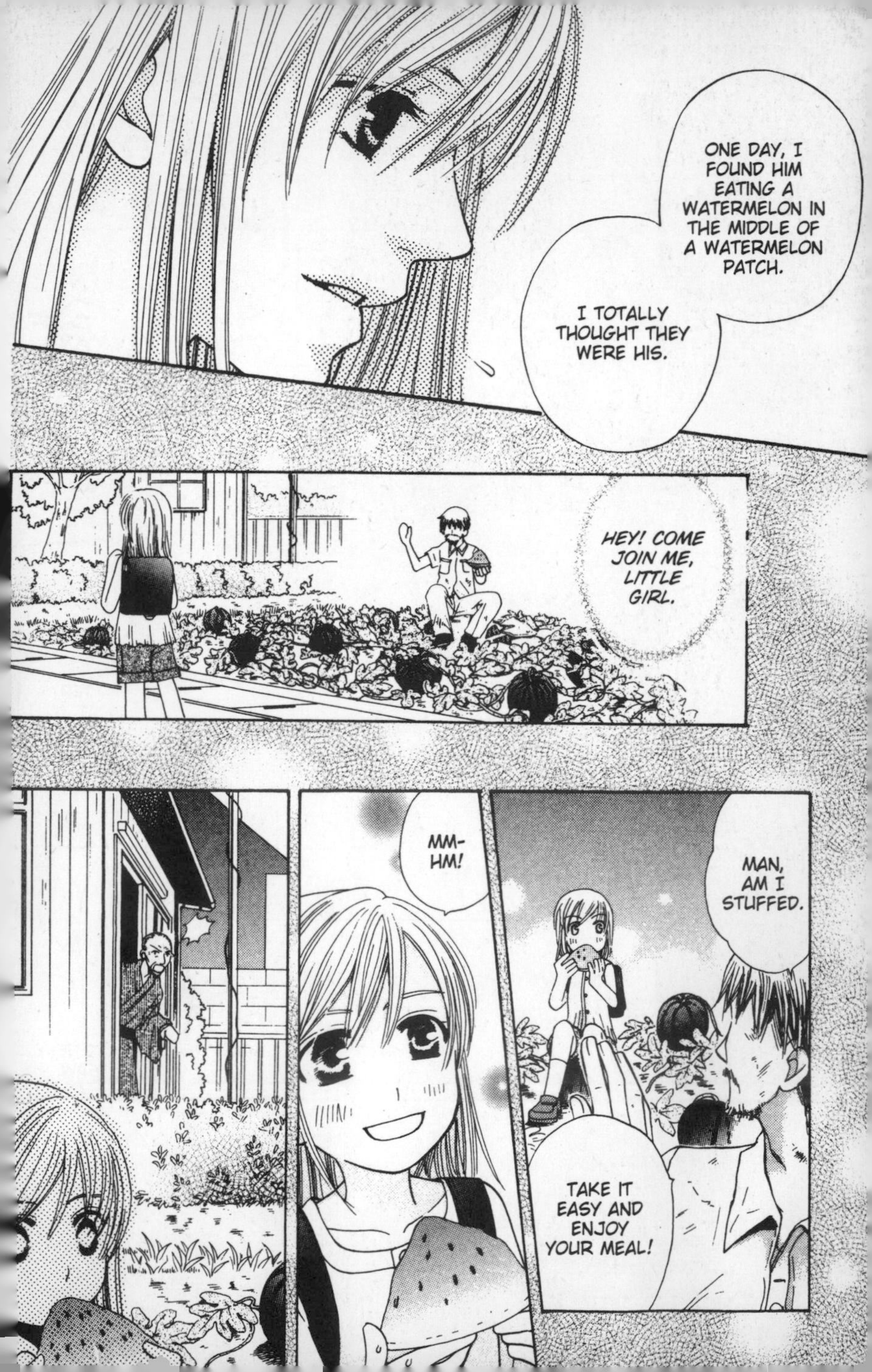
ONE DAY, I FOUND HIM EATING A WATERMELON IN THE MIDDLE OF A WATERMELON PATCH.
I TOTALLY THOUGHT THEY WERE HIS.
HEY! COME JOIN ME, LITTLE GIRL.
MAN, AM I STUFFED.
TAKE IT EASY AND ENJOY YOUR MEAL!
MM-HM!

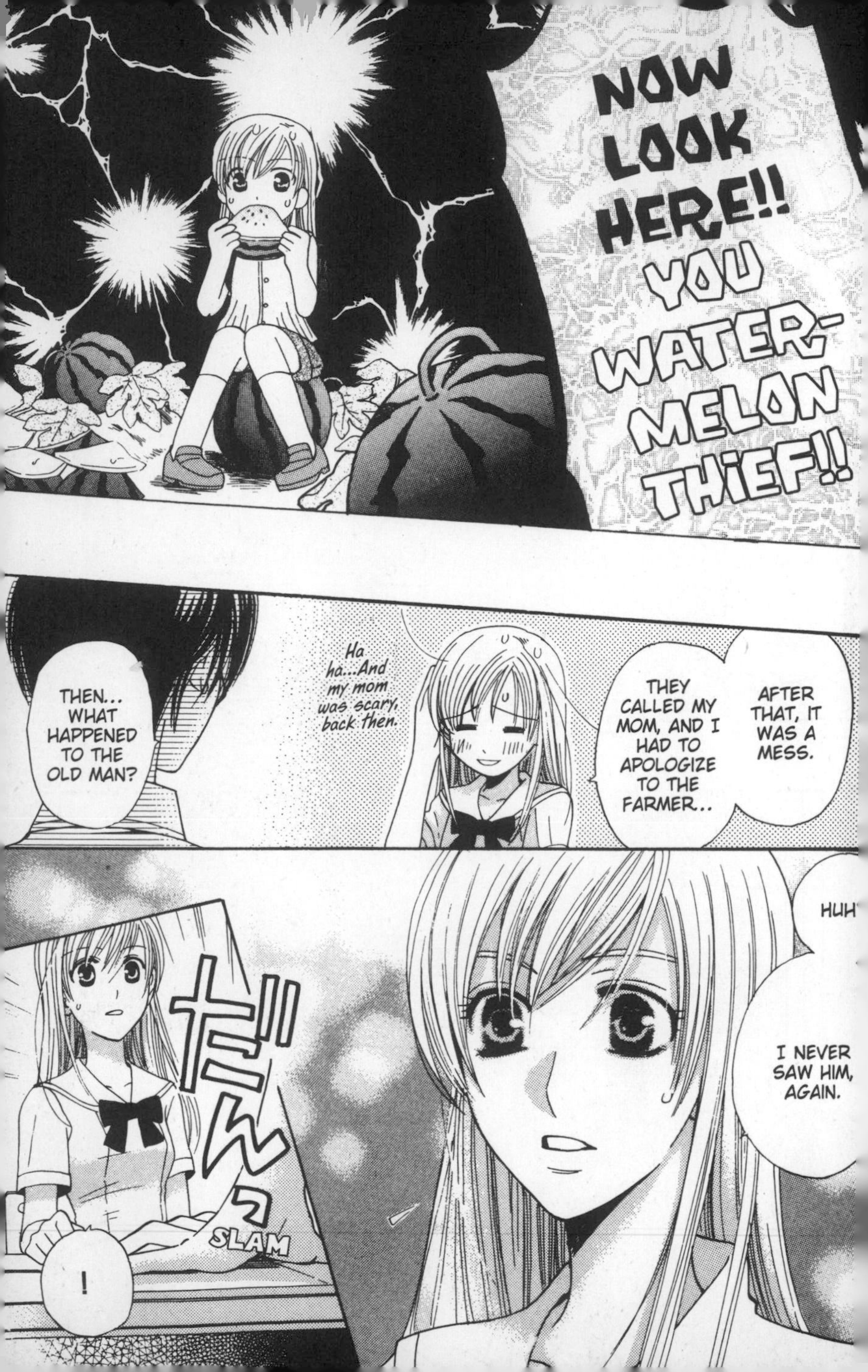
NOW LOOK HERE!! YOU WATER-MELON THIEF!!
AFTER THAT, IT WAS A MESS.
THEY CALLED MY MOM, AND I HAD TO APOLOGIZE TO THE FARMER..
Ha ha...And my mom was scary, back then.
THEN... WHAT HAPPENED TO THE OLD MAN?
HUH
I NEVER SAW HIM, AGAIN.
SLAM
!

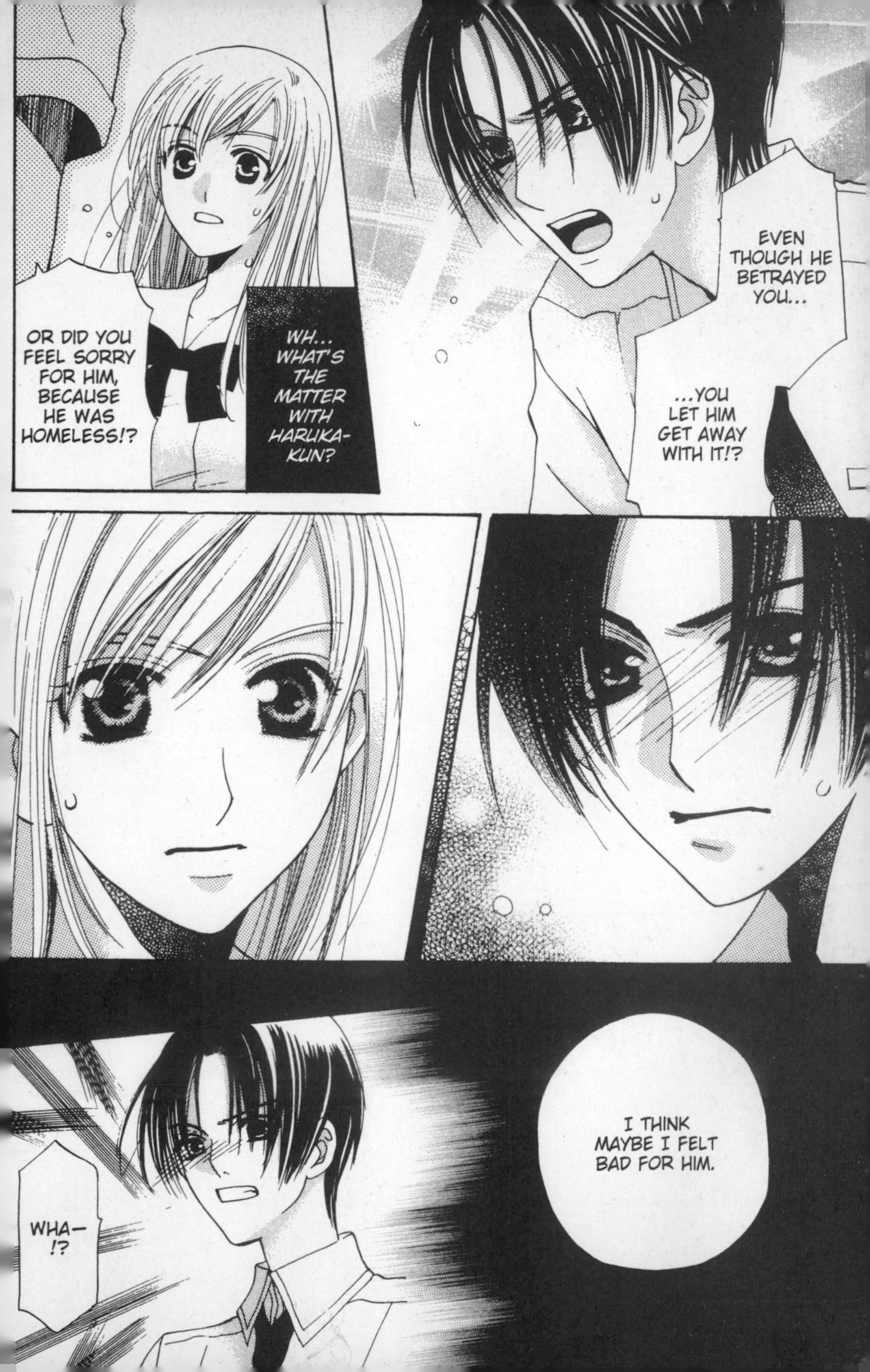
EVEN THOUGH HE BETRAYED YOU...
...YOU LET HIM GET AWAY WITH IT!?
WH... WHAT'S THE MATTER WITH HARUKA-KUN?
OR DID YOU FEEL SORRY FOR HIM, BECAUSE HE WAS HOMELESS!?
I THINK MAYBE I FELT BAD FOR HIM.
WHA—!?

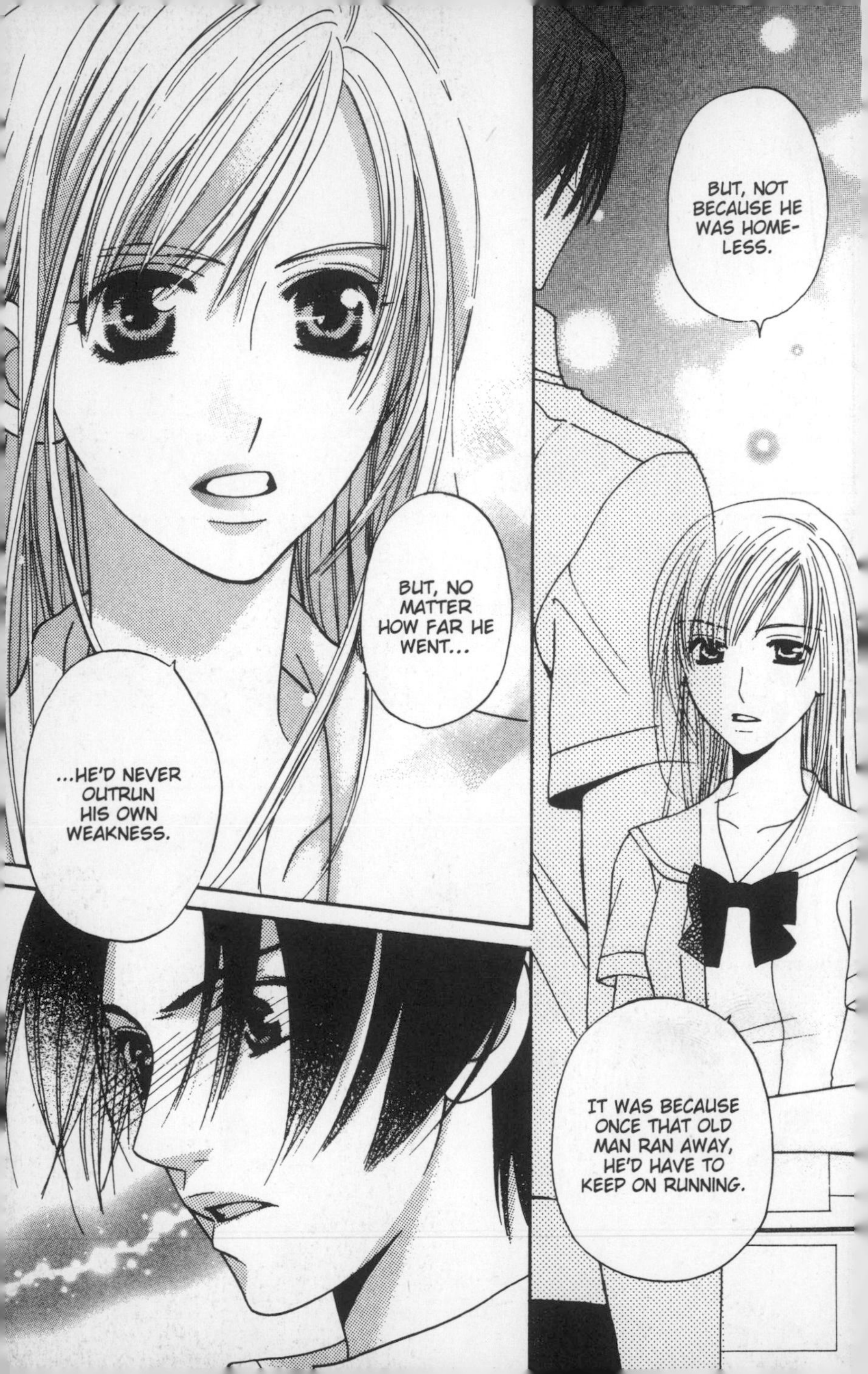
BUT, NOT BECAUSE HE WAS HOME-LESS.
IT WAS BECAUSE ONCE THAT OLD MAN RAN AWAY, HE'D HAVE TO KEEP ON RUNNING.
BUT, NO MATTER HOW FAR HE WENT...
...HE'D NEVER OUTRUN HIS OWN WEAKNESS.

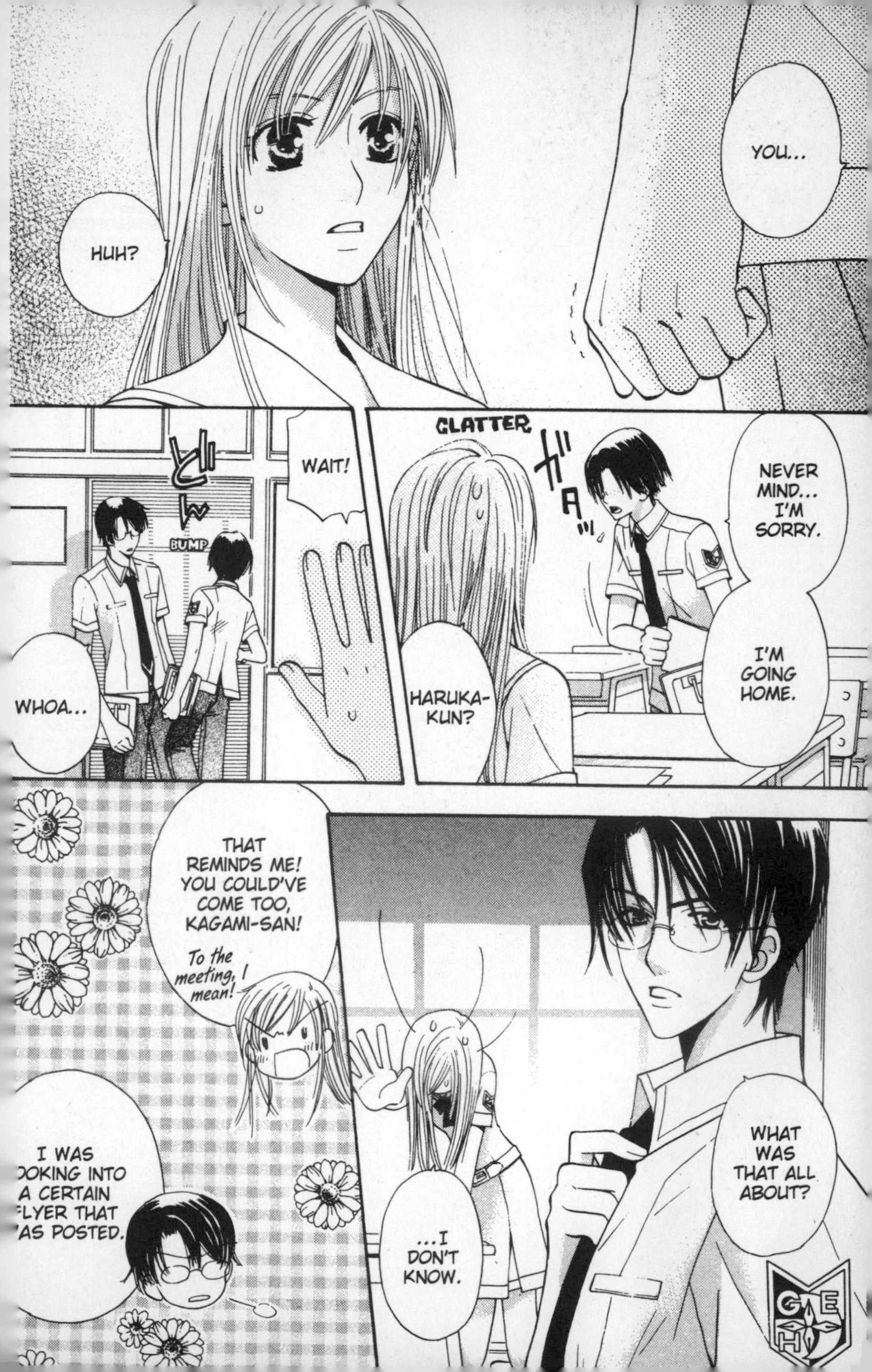
YOU...
HUH?
CLATTER
NEVER MIND... I'M SORRY.
I'M GOING HOME.
HARUKA-KUN?
WAIT!
BUMP
WHOA...
WHAT WAS THAT ALL ABOUT?
...I DON'T KNOW.
THAT REMINDS ME! YOU COULD'VE COME TOO, KAGAMI-SAN!
To the meeting, I mean!
I WAS OOKING INTO A CERTAIN FLYER THAT AS POSTED.

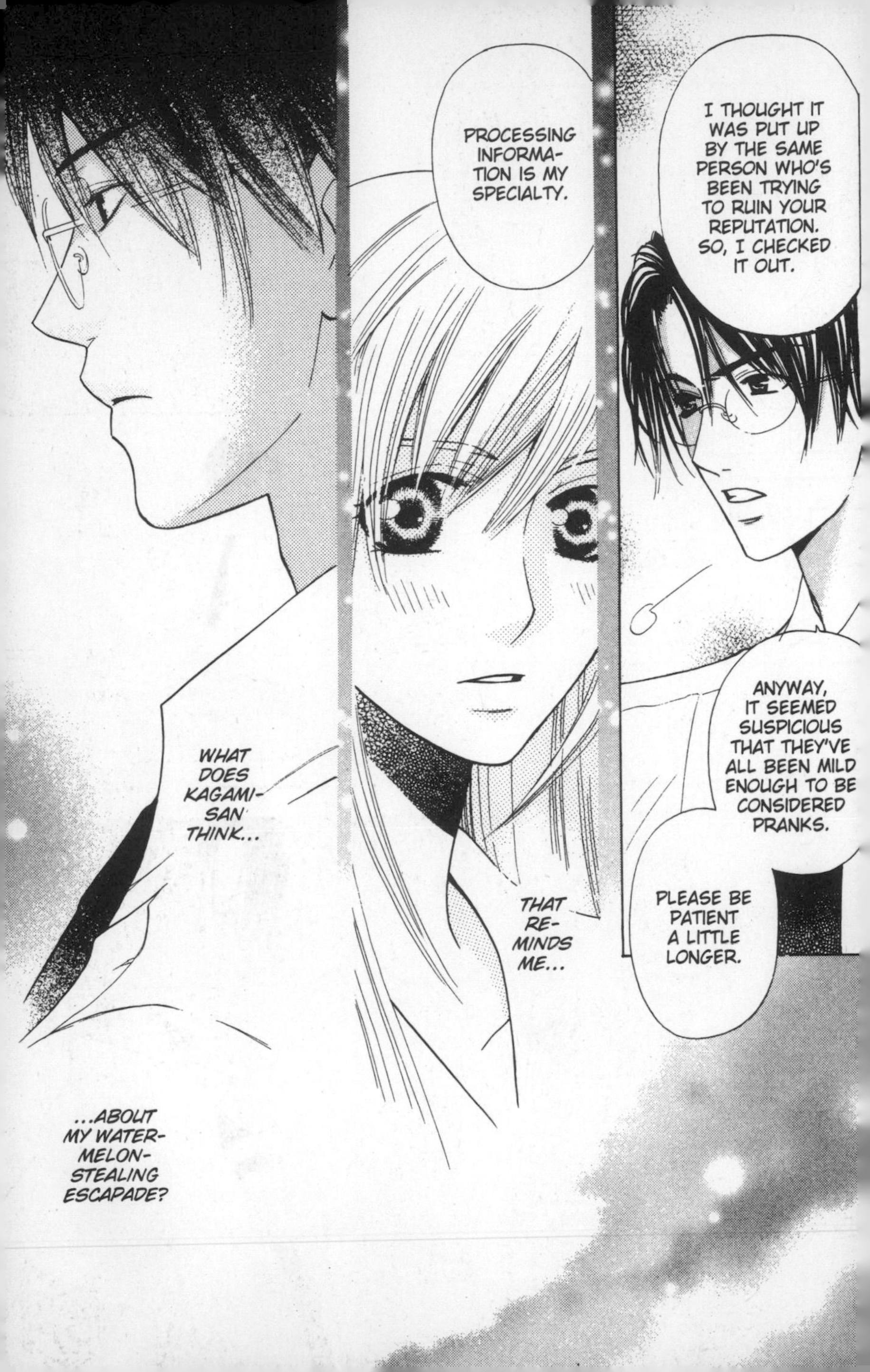
I THOUGHT IT WAS PUT UP BY THE SAME PERSON WHO'S BEEN TRYING TO RUIN YOUR REPUTATION. SO, I CHECKED IT OUT.
ANYWAY, IT SEEMED SUSPICIOUS THAT THEY'VE ALL BEEN MILD ENOUGH TO BE CONSIDERED PRANKS.
PLEASE BE PATIENT A LITTLE LONGER.
PROCESSING INFORMATION IS MY SPECIALTY.
THAT REMINDS ME...
WHAT DOES KAGAMI-SAN THINK...
...ABOUT MY WATERMELON-STEALING ESCAPADE?

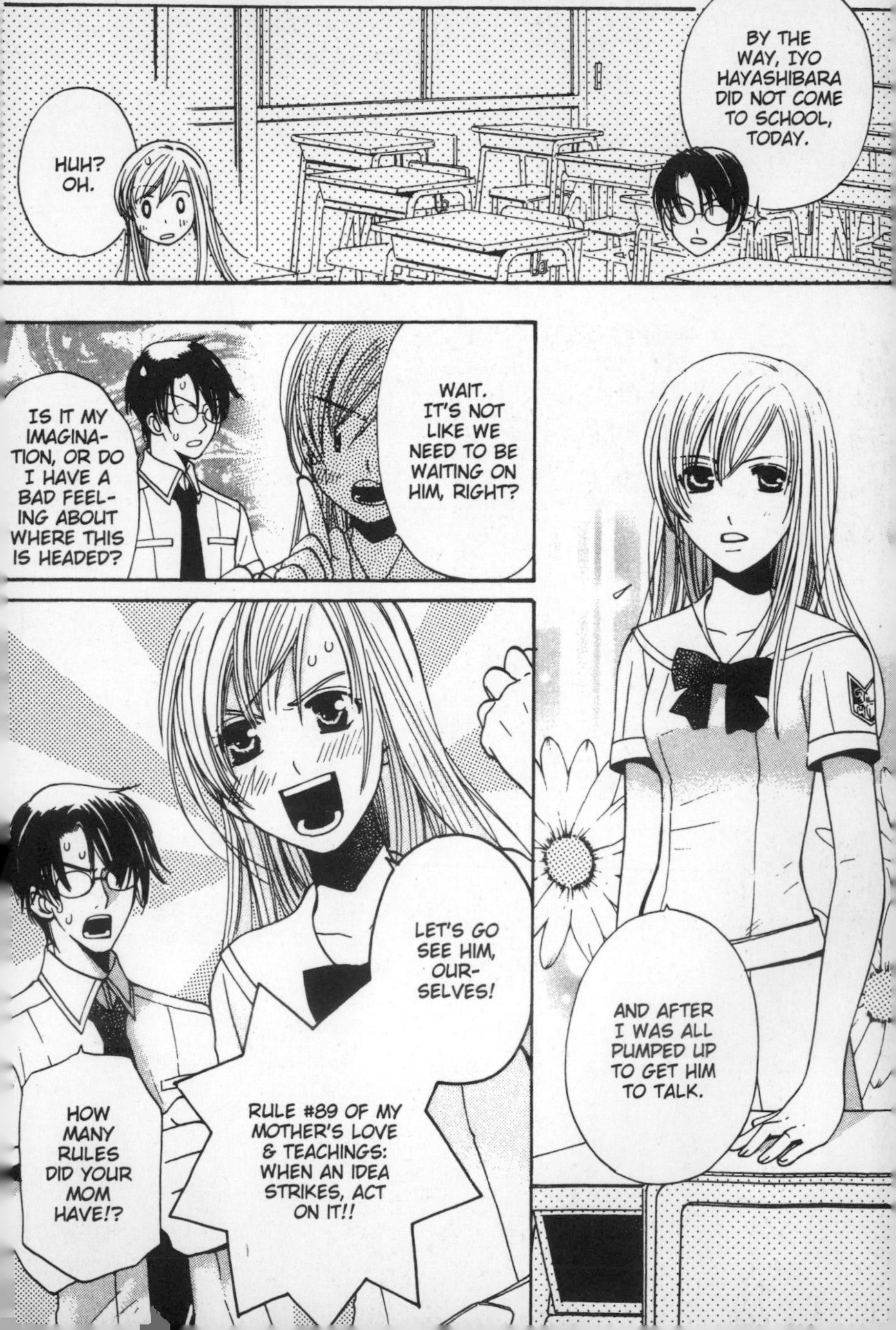
BY THE WAY, IYO HAYASHIBARA DID NOT COME TO SCHOOL, TODAY.
HUH? OH.
AND AFTER I WAS ALL PUMPED UP TO GET HIM TO TALK.
WAIT. IT'S NOT LIKE WE NEED TO BE WAITING ON HIM, RIGHT?
IS IT MY IMAGINATION, OR DO I HAVE A BAD FEELING ABOUT WHERE THIS IS HEADED?
LET'S GO SEE HIM, OURSELVES!
RULE #89 OF MY MOTHER'S LOVE & TEACHINGS: WHEN AN IDEA STRIKES, ACT ON IT!!
HOW MANY RULES DID YOUR MOM HAVE!?

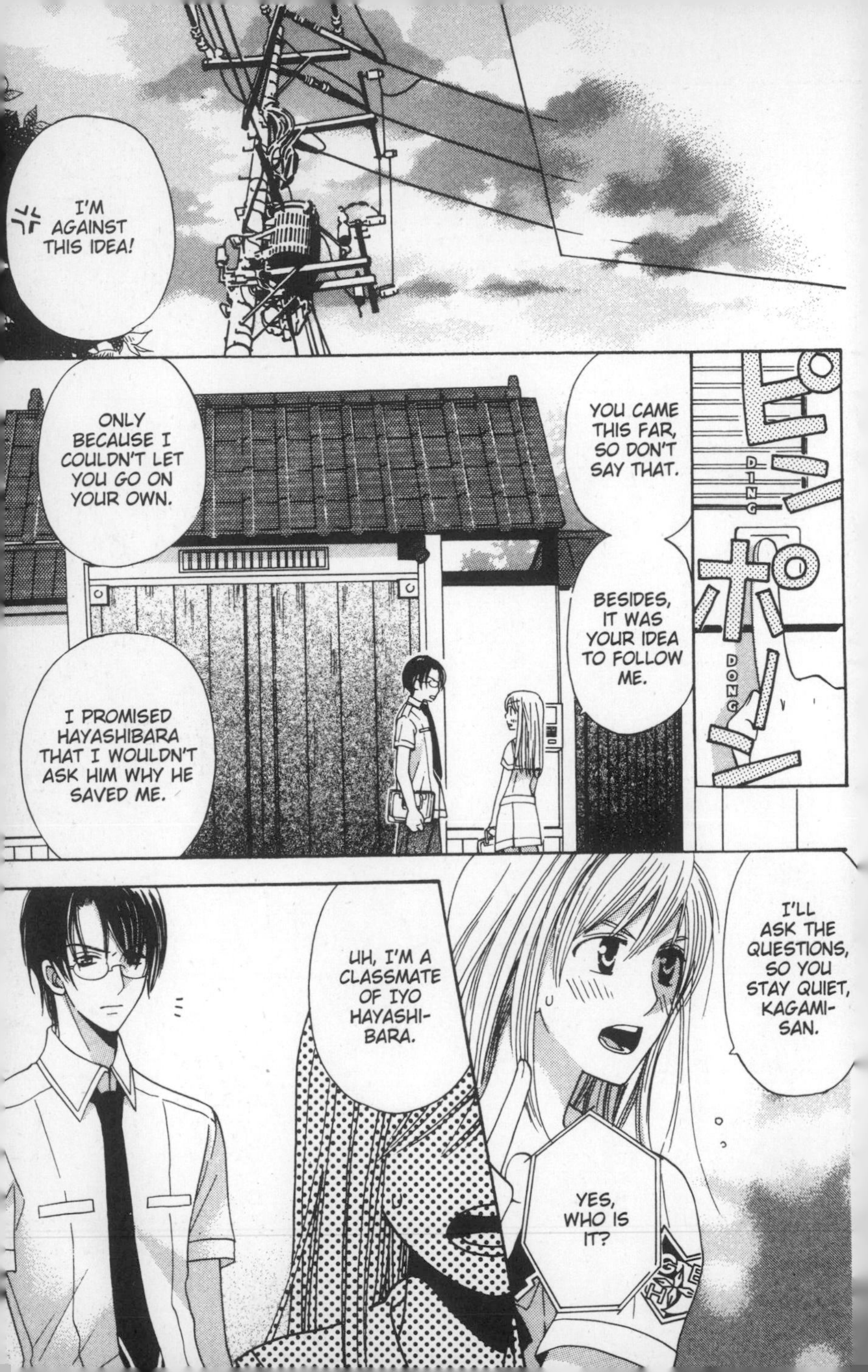

I'M AGAINST THIS IDEA!
DING
DONG
YOU CAME THIS FAR, SO DON'T SAY THAT.
ONLY BECAUSE I COULDN'T LET YOU GO ON YOUR OWN.
BESIDES, IT WAS YOUR IDEA TO FOLLOW ME.
I PROMISED HAYASHIBARA THAT I WOULDN'T ASK HIM WHY HE SAVED ME.
I'LL ASK THE QUESTIONS, SO YOU STAY QUIET, KAGAMI-SAN.
YES, WHO IS IT?
UH, I'M A CLASSMATE OF IYO HAYASHIBARA.

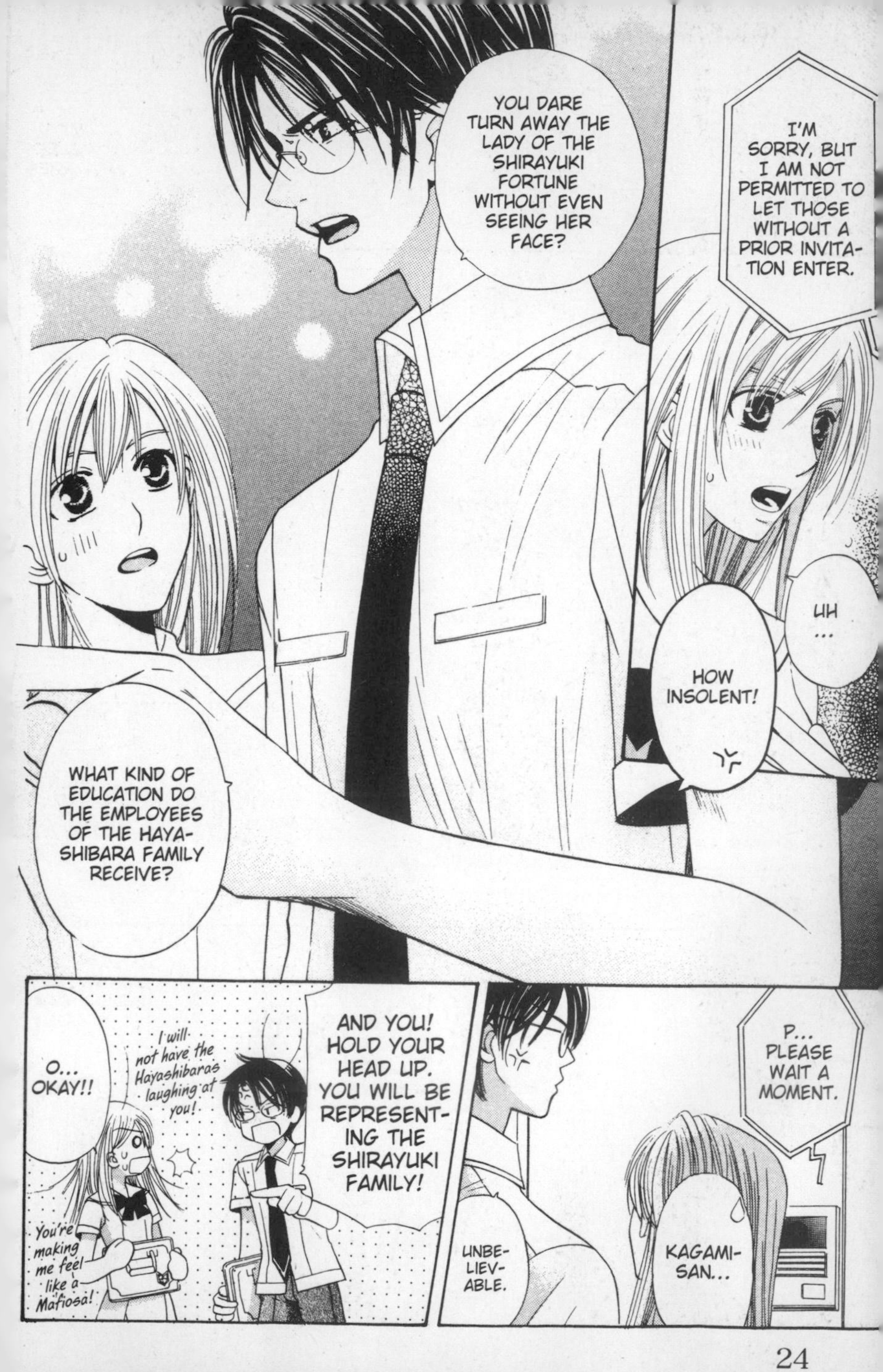
I'M SORRY, BUT I AM NOT PERMITTED TO LET THOSE WITHOUT A PRIOR INVITATION ENTER.
UH ...
HOW INSOLENT!
YOU DARE TURN AWAY THE LADY OF THE SHIRAYUKI FORTUNE WITHOUT EVEN SEEING HER FACE?
WHAT KIND OF EDUCATION DO THE EMPLOYEES OF THE HAYASHIBARA FAMILY RECEIVE?
P... PLEASE WAIT A MOMENT.
KAGAMI-SAN...
UNBELIEVABLE.
AND YOU! HOLD YOUR HEAD UP. YOU WILL BE REPRESENTING THE SHIRAYUKI FAMILY!
I will not have the Hayashibaras laughing at you!
O... OKAY!!
You're making me feel like a Mafiosa!

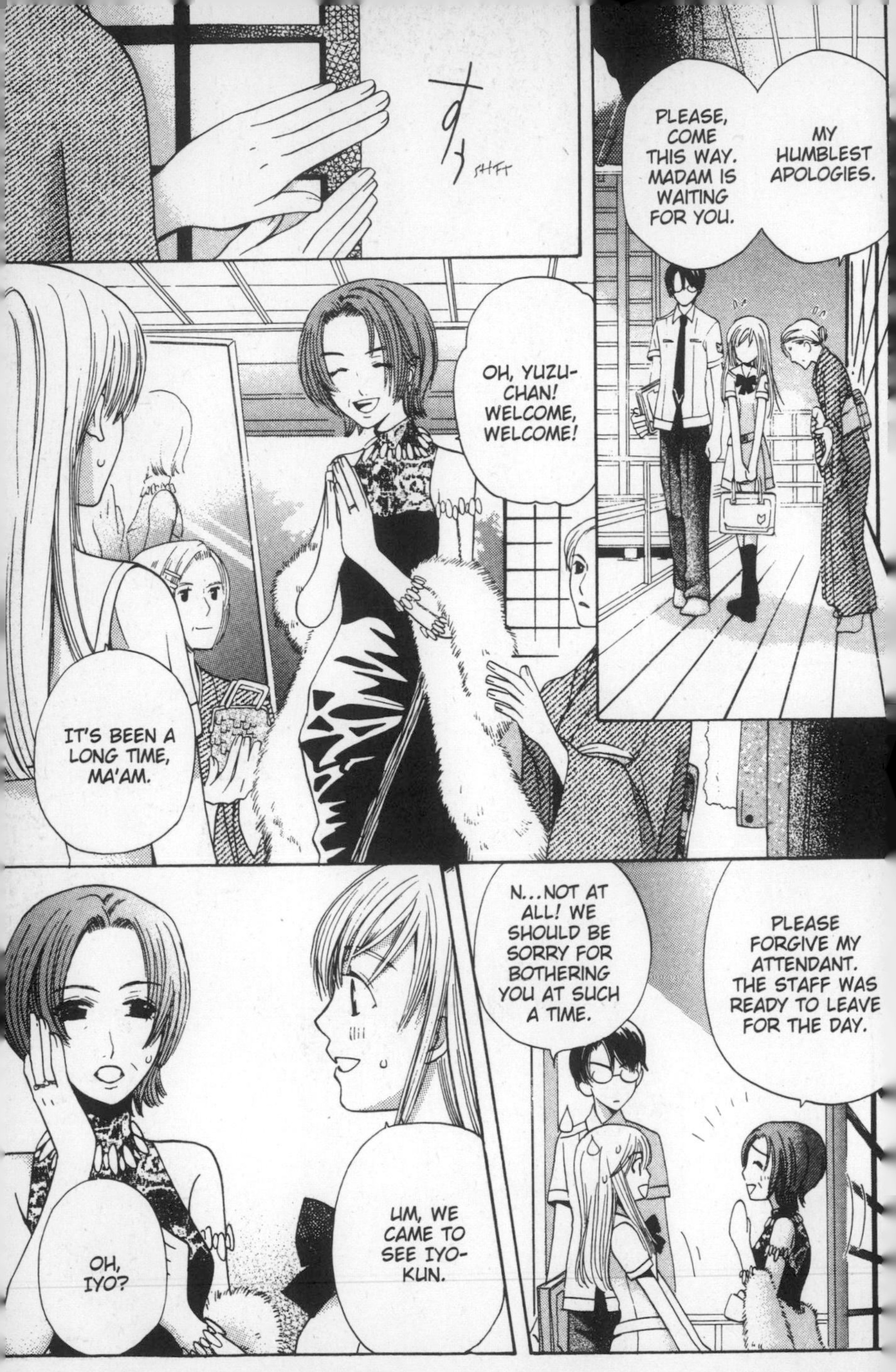
MY HUMBLEST APOLOGIES.
PLEASE, COME THIS WAY. MADAM IS WAITING FOR YOU.
SHFF
OH, YUZU-CHAN! WELCOME, WELCOME!
IT'S BEEN A LONG TIME, MA'AM.
PLEASE FORGIVE MY ATTENDANT. THE STAFF WAS READY TO LEAVE FOR THE DAY.
N...NOT AT ALL! WE SHOULD BE SORRY FOR BOTHERING YOU AT SUCH A TIME.
UM, WE CAME TO SEE IYO-KUN.
OH, IYO?

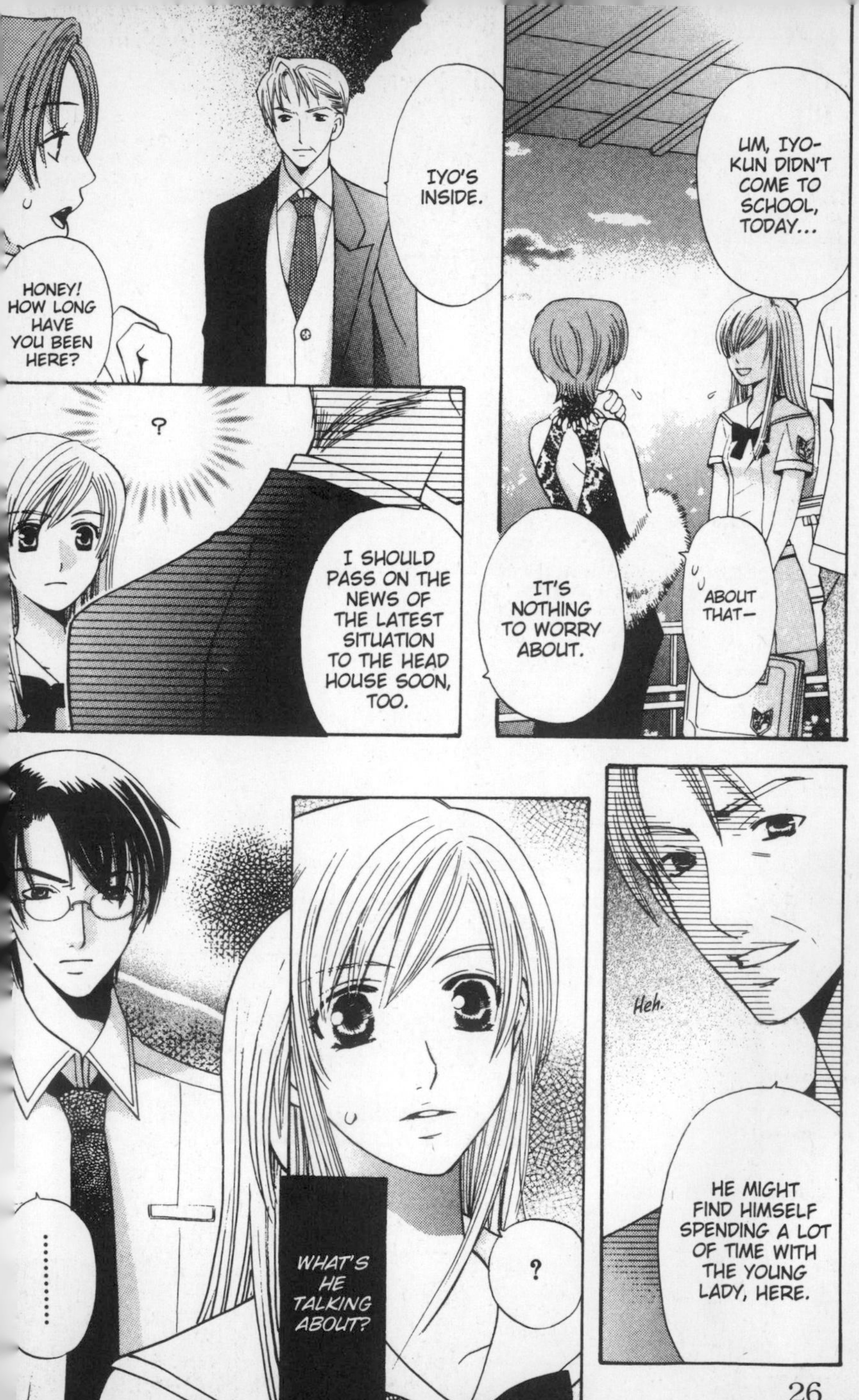
UM, IYO-KUN DIDN'T COME TO SCHOOL, TODAY...
ABOUT THAT—
IT'S NOTHING TO WORRY ABOUT.
IYO'S INSIDE.
HONEY! HOW LONG HAVE YOU BEEN HERE?
I SHOULD PASS ON THE NEWS OF THE LATEST SITUATION TO THE HEAD HOUSE SOON, TOO.
?
Heh.
HE MIGHT FIND HIMSELF SPENDING A LOT OF TIME WITH THE YOUNG LADY, HERE.
?
WHAT'S HE TALKING ABOUT?
......

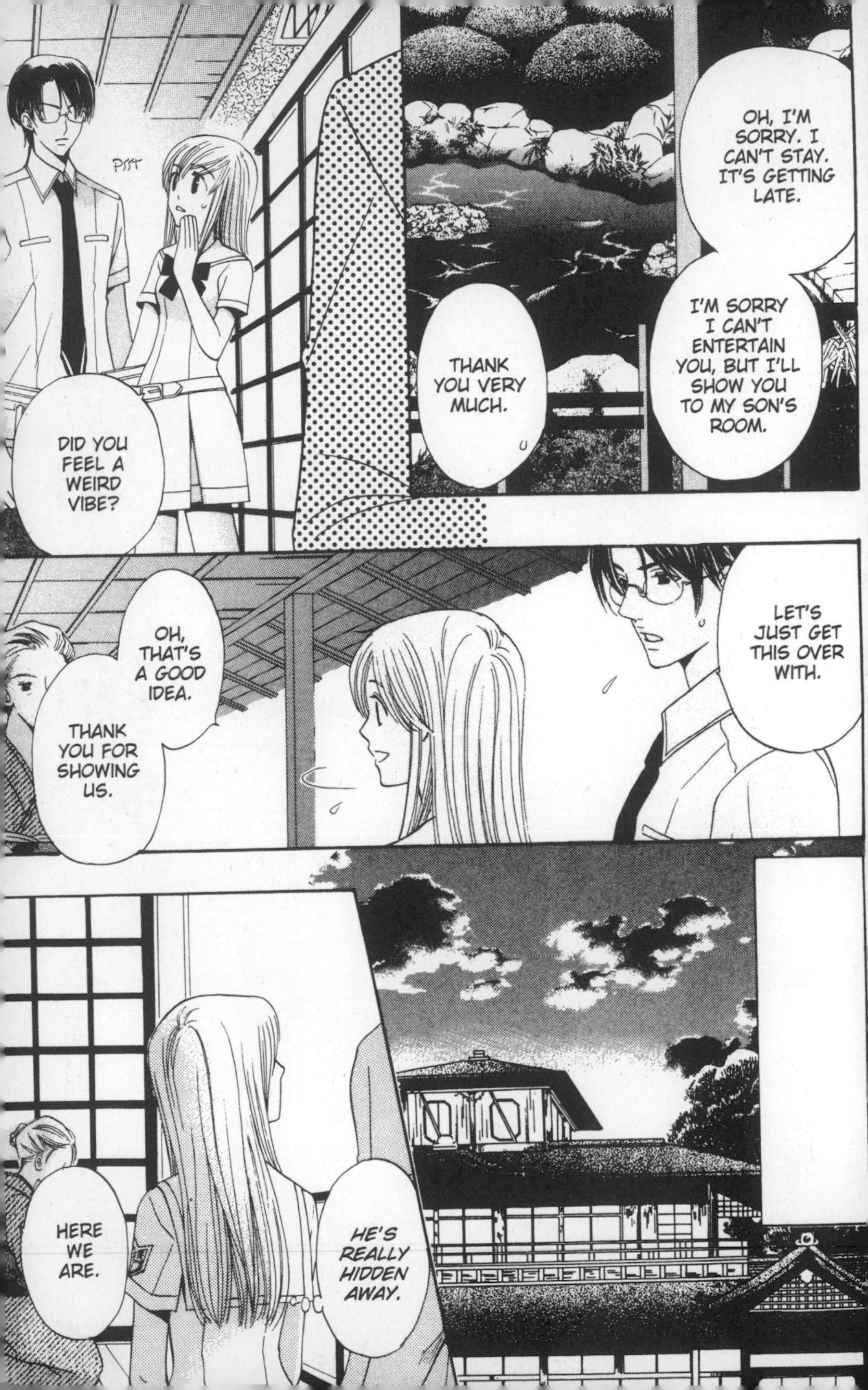
OH, I'M SORRY. I CAN'T STAY. IT'S GETTING LATE.
I'M SORRY I CAN'T ENTERTAIN YOU, BUT I'LL SHOW YOU TO MY SON'S ROOM.
THANK YOU VERY MUCH.
PSST
DID YOU FEEL A WEIRD VIBE?
LET'S JUST GET THIS OVER WITH.
OH, THAT'S A GOOD IDEA.
THANK YOU FOR SHOWING US.
HE'S REALLY HIDDEN AWAY.
HERE WE ARE.

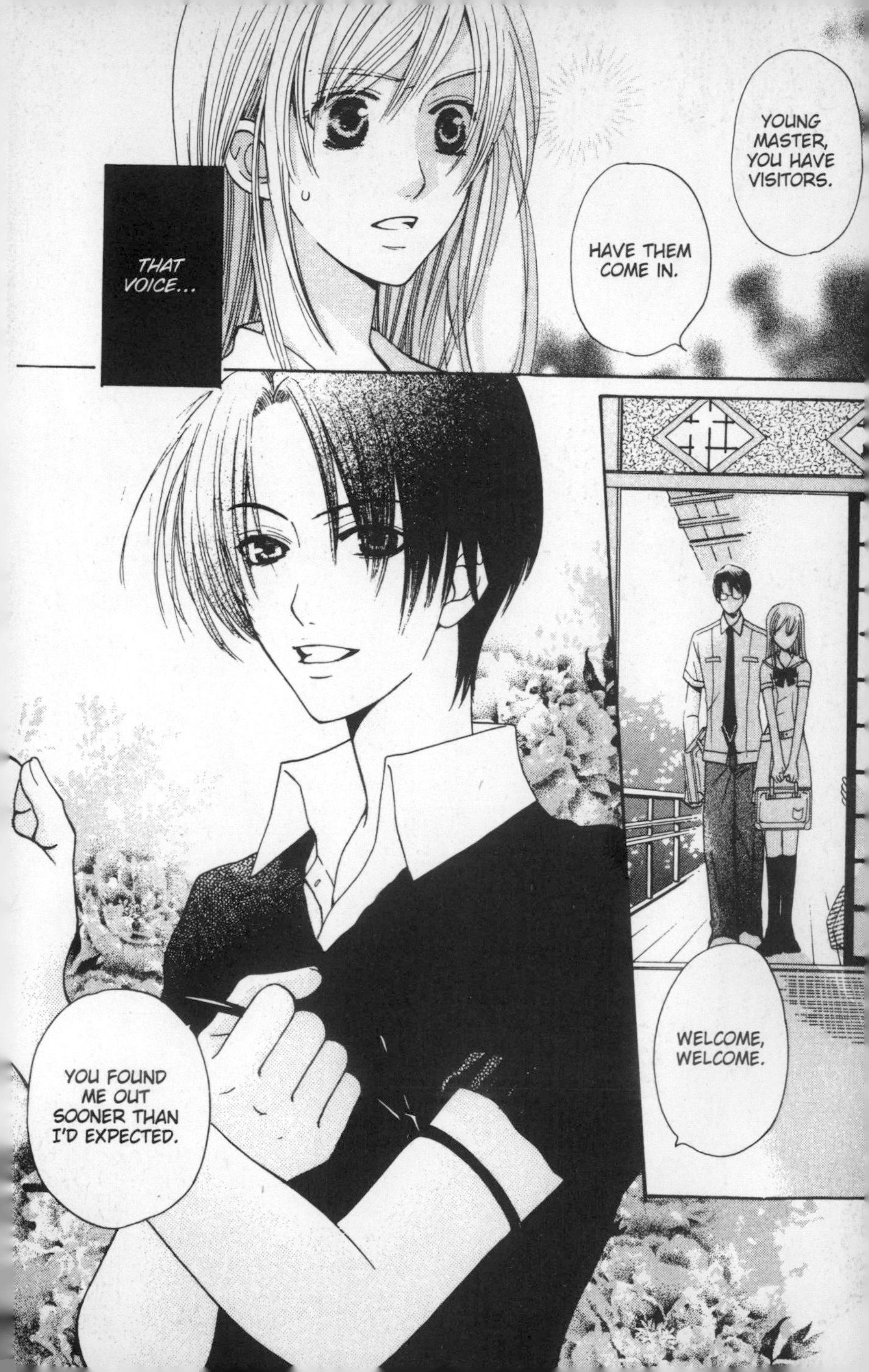
YOUNG MASTER, YOU HAVE VISITORS.
HAVE THEM COME IN.
THAT VOICE...
WELCOME, WELCOME.
YOU FOUND ME OUT SOONER THAN I'D EXPECTED.

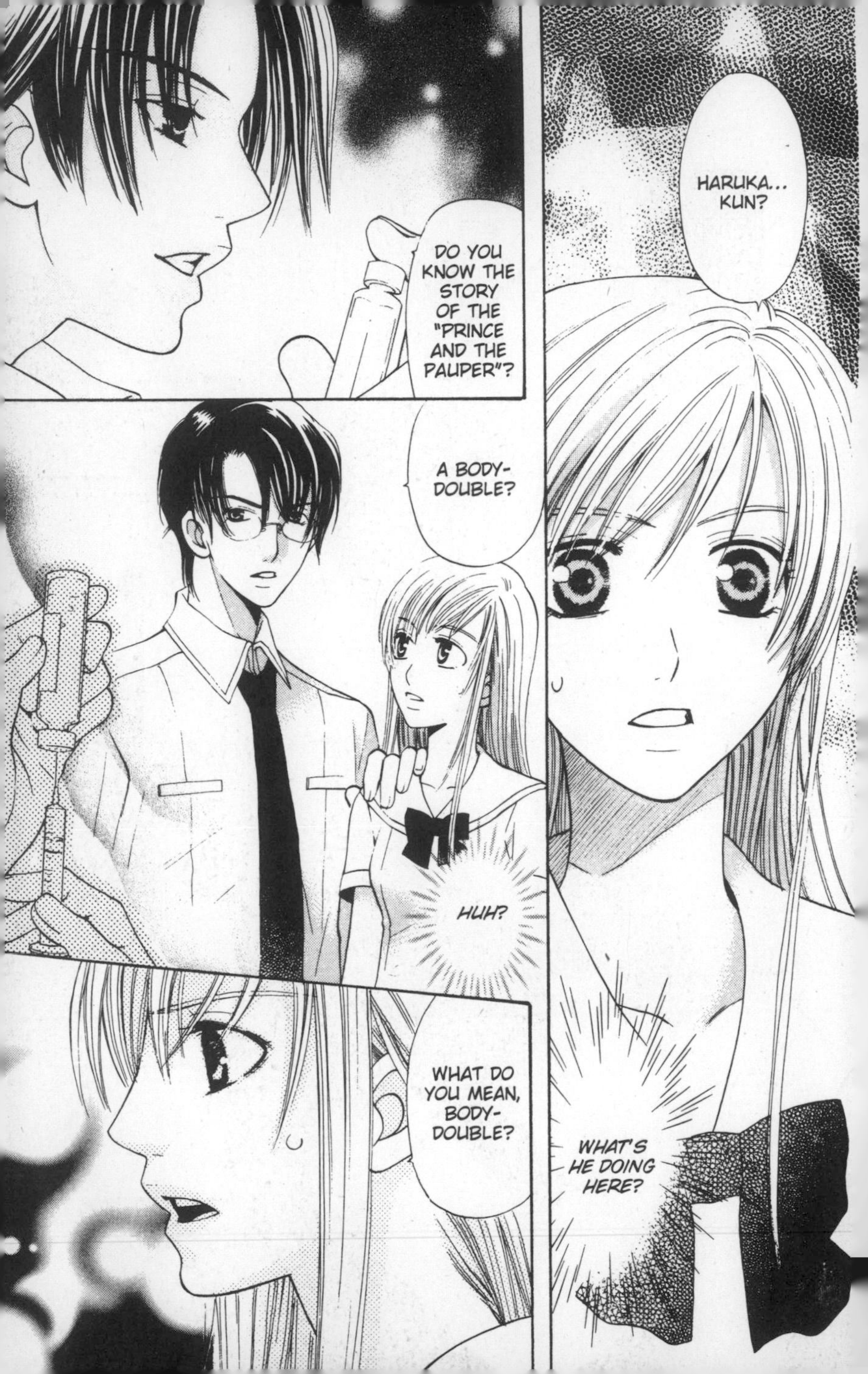
HARUKA... KUN?
WHAT'S HE DOING HERE?
DO YOU KNOW THE STORY OF THE "PRINCE AND THE PAUPER"?
A BODY-DOUBLE?
HUH?
WHAT DO YOU MEAN, BODY-DOUBLE?

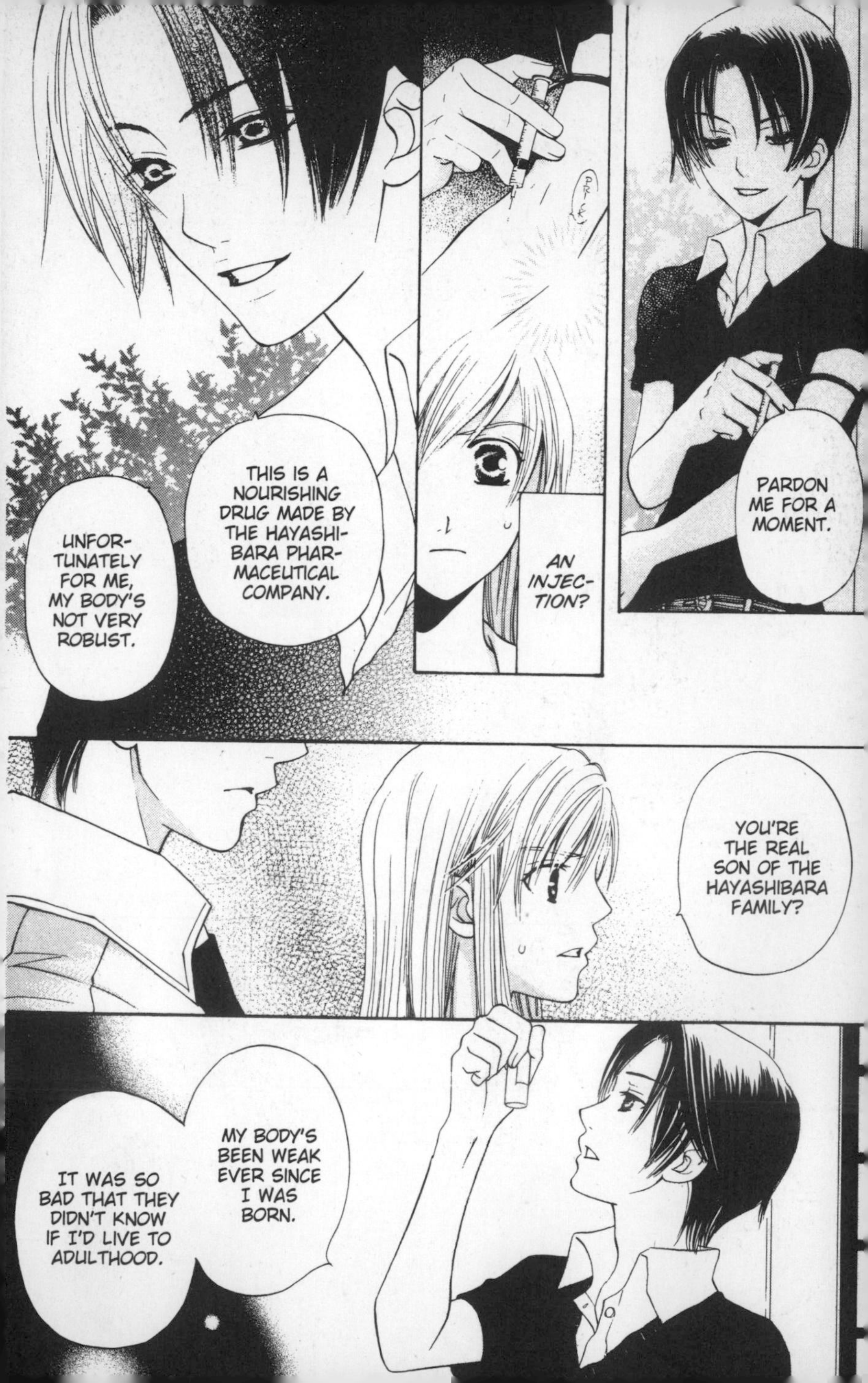
PARDON ME FOR A MOMENT.
PRICK
AN INJECTION?
THIS IS A NOURISHING DRUG MADE BY THE HAYASHIBARA PHARMACEUTICAL COMPANY.
UNFORTUNATELY FOR ME, MY BODY'S NOT VERY ROBUST.
YOU'RE THE REAL SON OF THE HAYASHIBARA FAMILY?
MY BODY'S BEEN WEAK EVER SINCE I WAS BORN.
IT WAS SO BAD THAT THEY DIDN'T KNOW IF I'D LIVE TO ADULTHOOD.

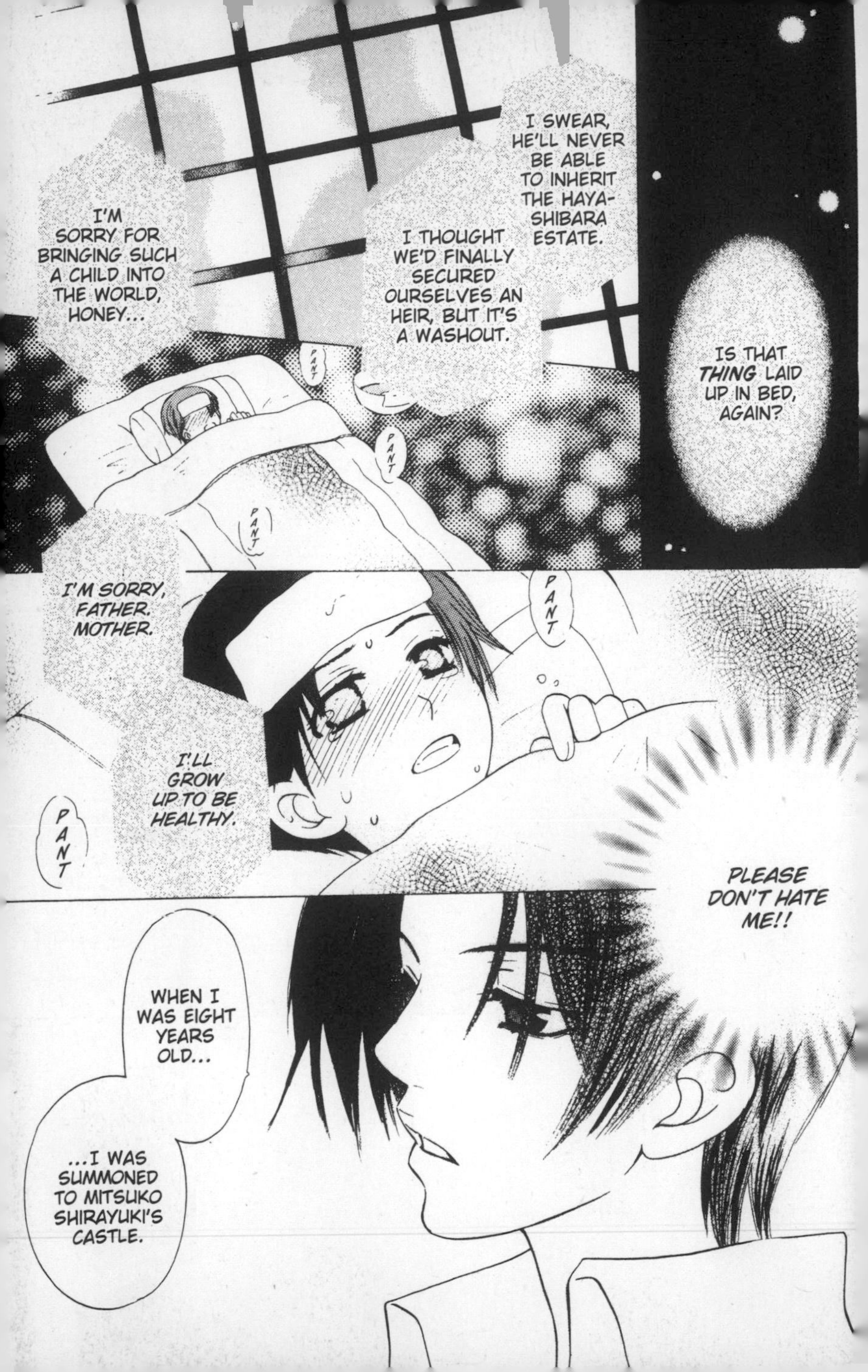
IS THAT THING LAID UP IN BED, AGAIN?
I SWEAR, HE'LL NEVER BE ABLE TO INHERIT THE HAYA-SHIBARA ESTATE.
I THOUGHT WE'D FINALLY SECURED OURSELVES AN HEIR, BUT IT'S A WASHOUT.
I'M SORRY FOR BRINGING SUCH A CHILD INTO THE WORLD, HONEY...
PANT
PANT
PANT
PANT
I'M SORRY, FATHER. MOTHER.
I'LL GROW UP TO BE HEALTHY.
PANT
PLEASE DON'T HATE ME!!
WHEN I WAS EIGHT YEARS OLD...
...I WAS SUMMONED TO MITSUKO SHIRAYUKI'S CASTLE.

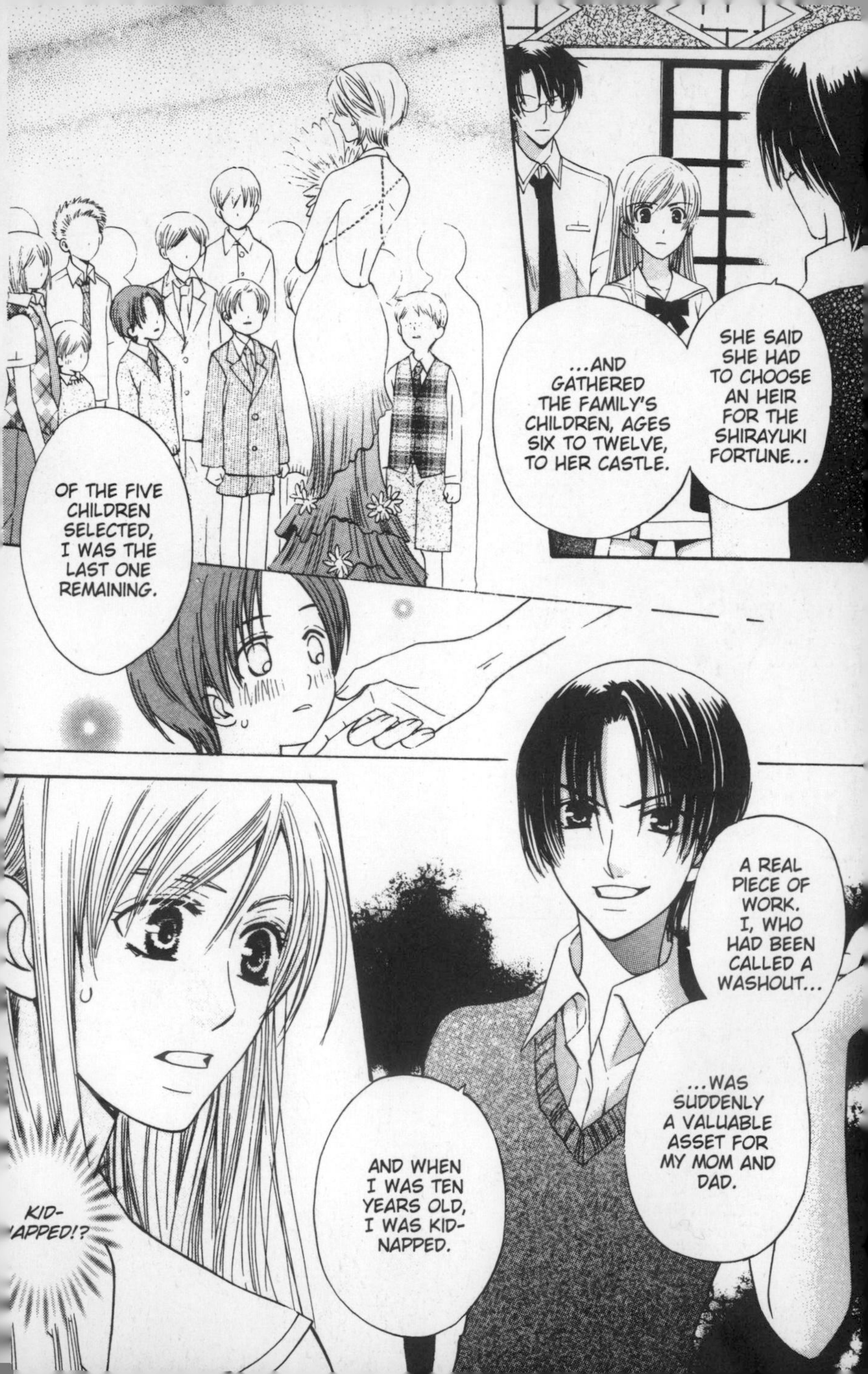
SHE SAID SHE HAD TO CHOOSE AN HEIR FOR THE SHIRAYUKI FORTUNE...
...AND GATHERED THE FAMILY'S CHILDREN, AGES SIX TO TWELVE, TO HER CASTLE.
OF THE FIVE CHILDREN SELECTED, I WAS THE LAST ONE REMAINING.
A REAL PIECE OF WORK. I, WHO HAD BEEN CALLED A WASHOUT...
...WAS SUDDENLY A VALUABLE ASSET FOR MY MOM AND DAD.
AND WHEN I WAS TEN YEARS OLD, I WAS KID-NAPPED.
KID-NAPPED!?

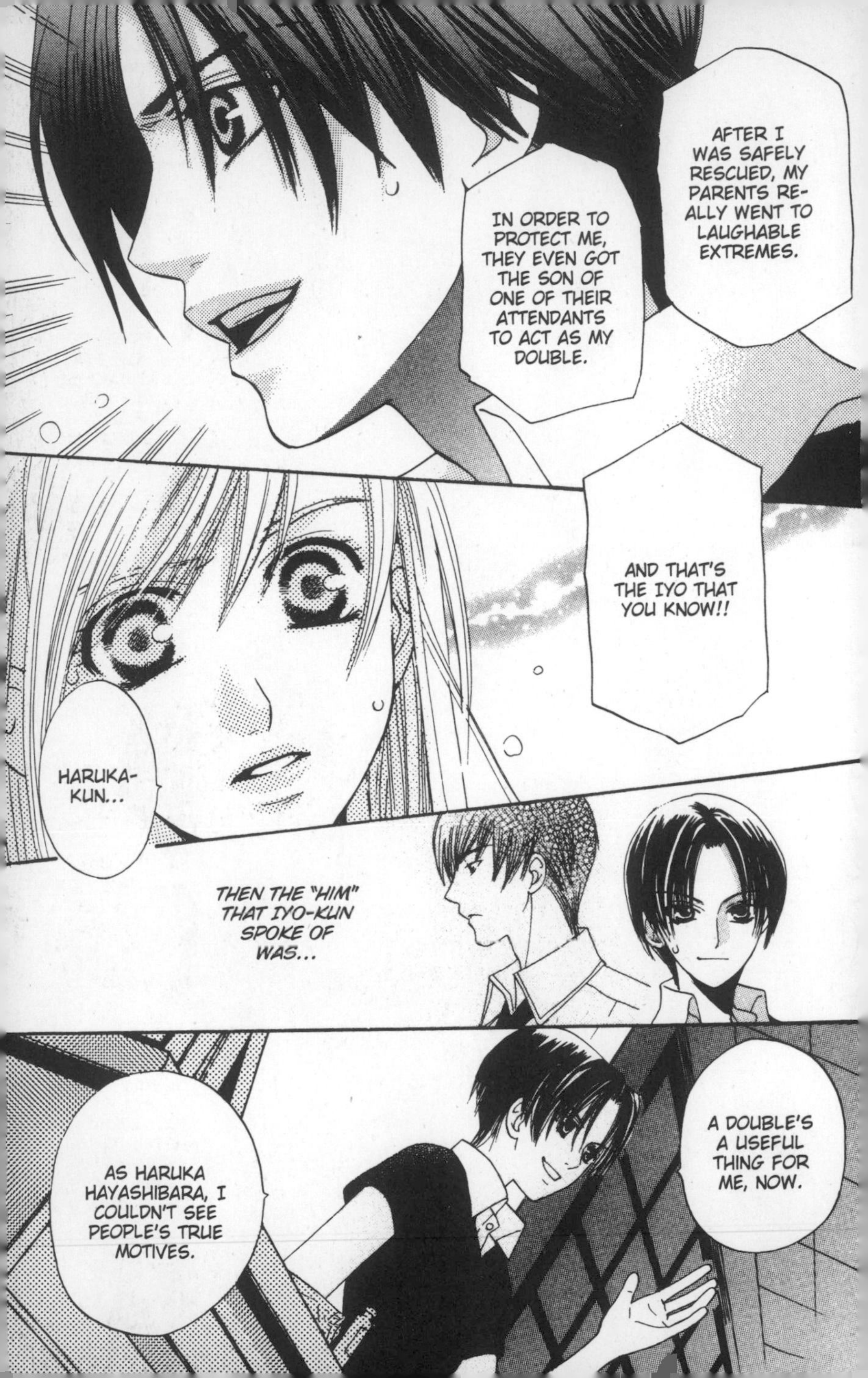
AFTER I WAS SAFELY RESCUED, MY PARENTS REALLY WENT TO LAUGHABLE EXTREMES.
IN ORDER TO PROTECT ME, THEY EVEN GOT THE SON OF ONE OF THEIR ATTENDANTS TO ACT AS MY DOUBLE.
AND THAT'S THE IYO THAT YOU KNOW!!
HARUKA-KUN...
THEN THE "HIM" THAT IYO-KUN SPOKE OF WAS...
A DOUBLE'S A USEFUL THING FOR ME, NOW.
AS HARUKA HAYASHIBARA, I COULDN'T SEE PEOPLE'S TRUE MOTIVES.

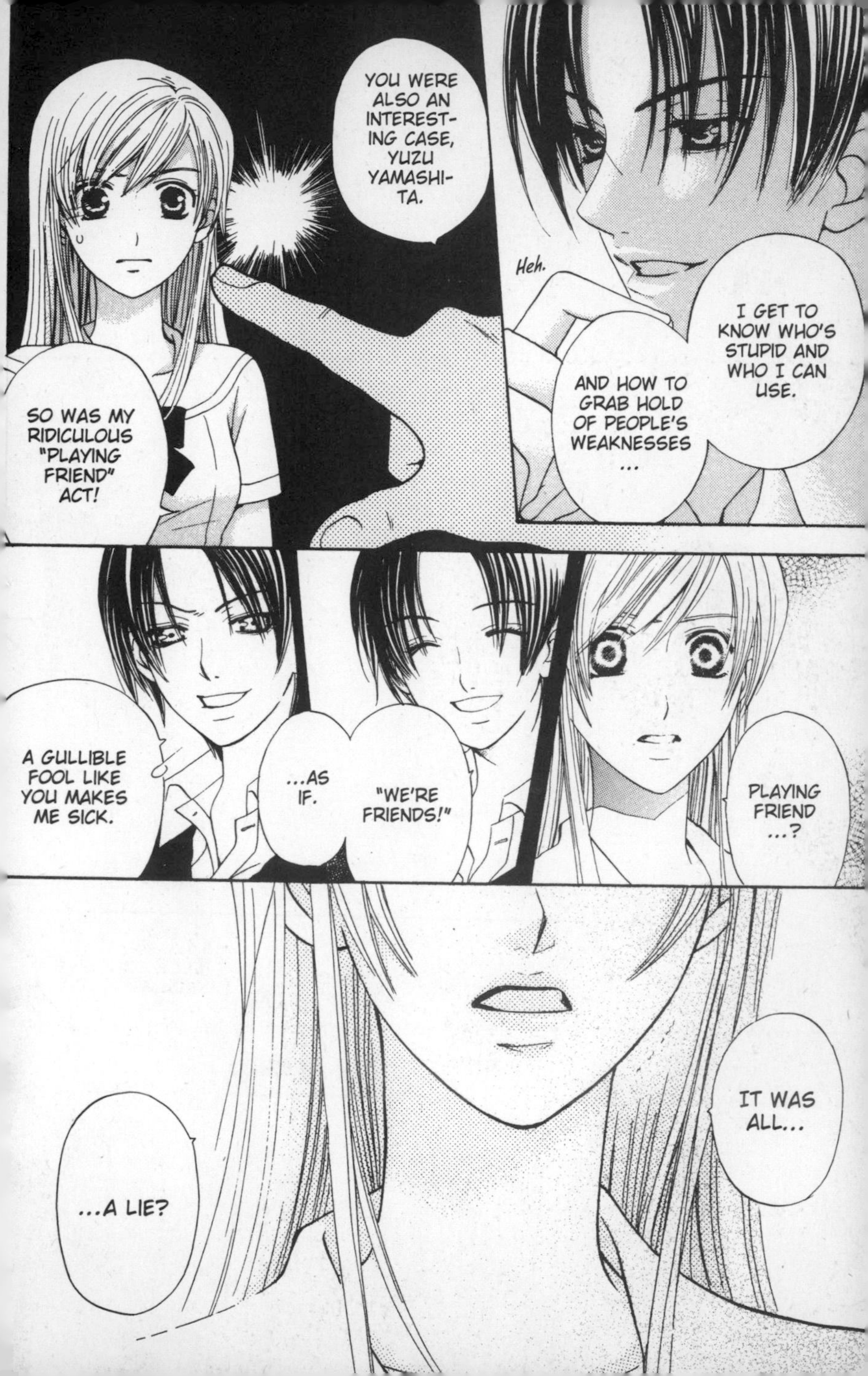
Heh.
I GET TO KNOW WHO'S STUPID AND WHO I CAN USE.
AND HOW TO GRAB HOLD OF PEOPLE'S WEAKNESSES ...
YOU WERE ALSO AN INTEREST-ING CASE, YUZU YAMASHI-TA.
SO WAS MY RIDICULOUS "PLAYING FRIEND" ACT!
PLAYING FRIEND ...?
"WE'RE FRIENDS!"
...AS IF.
A GULLIBLE FOOL LIKE YOU MAKES ME SICK.
IT WAS ALL...
...A LIE?

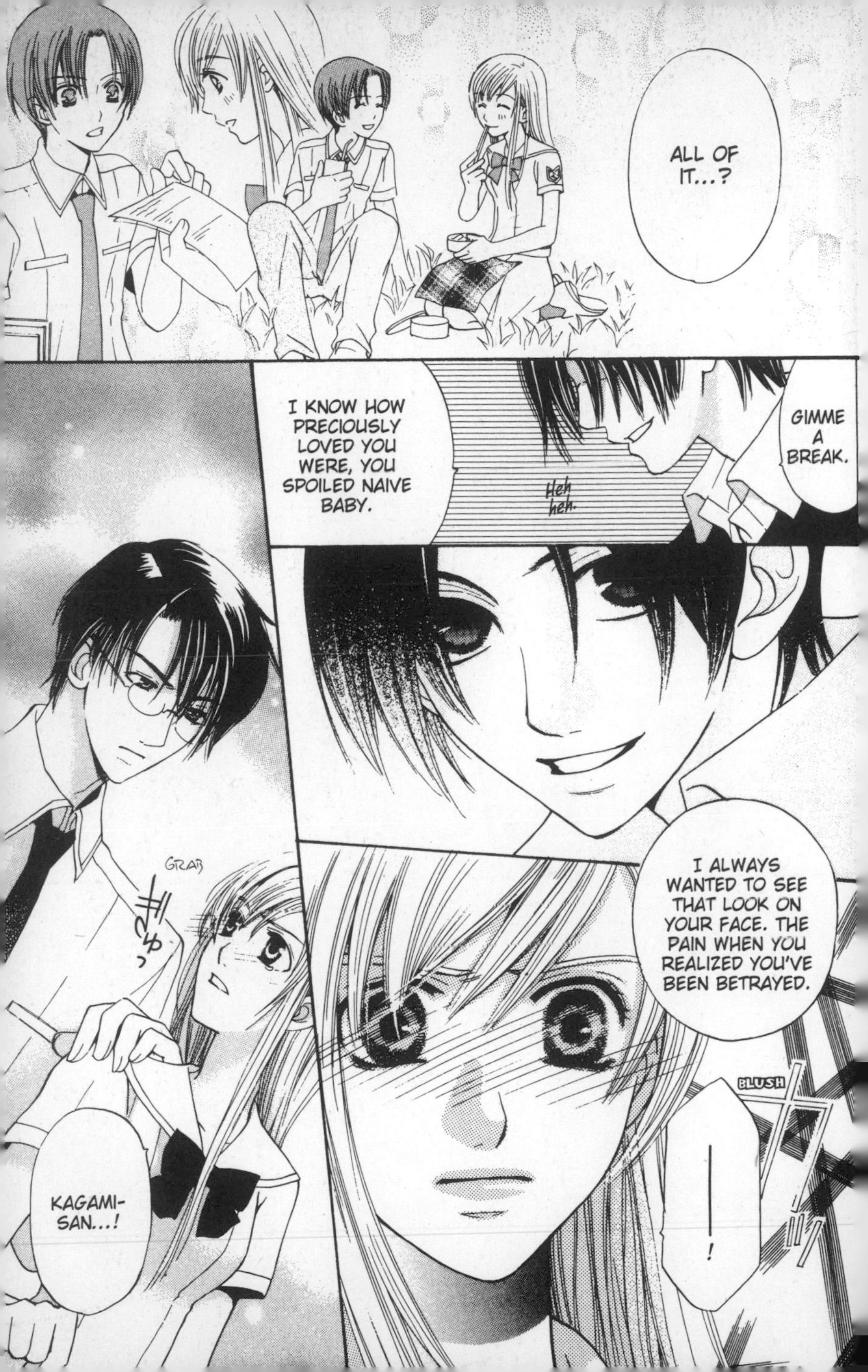
ALL OF IT...?
GIMME A BREAK.
Heh heh.
I KNOW HOW PRECIOUSLY LOVED YOU WERE, YOU SPOILED NAIVE BABY.
I ALWAYS WANTED TO SEE THAT LOOK ON YOUR FACE. THE PAIN WHEN YOU REALIZED YOU'VE BEEN BETRAYED.
BLUSH
...!
GRAB
KAGAMI-SAN...!

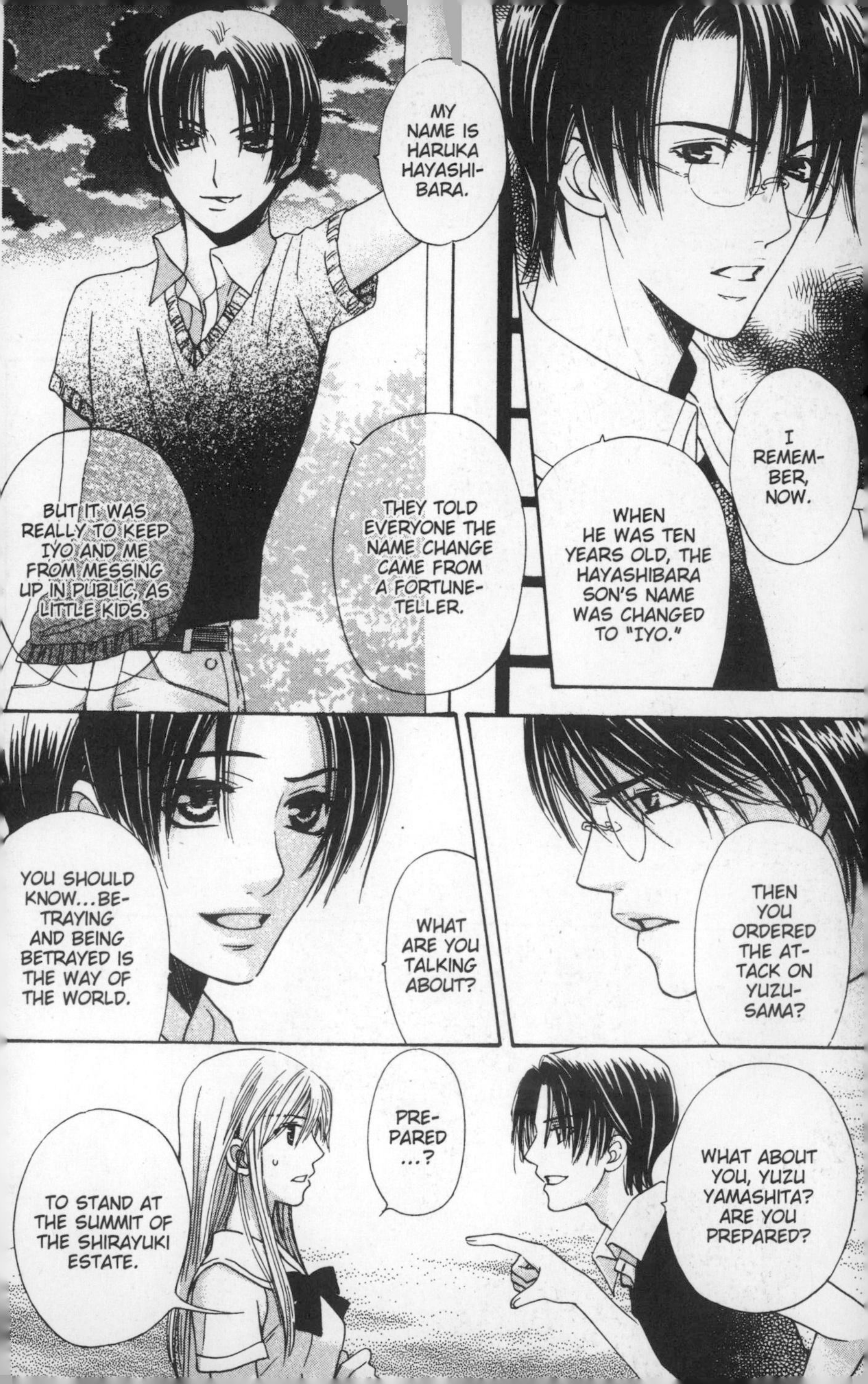
I REMEMBER, NOW.
WHEN HE WAS TEN YEARS OLD, THE HAYASHIBARA SON'S NAME WAS CHANGED TO "IYO."
MY NAME IS HARUKA HAYASHIBARA.
THEY TOLD EVERYONE THE NAME CHANGE CAME FROM A FORTUNE-TELLER.
BUT IT WAS REALLY TO KEEP IYO AND ME FROM MESSING UP IN PUBLIC, AS LITTLE KIDS.
THEN YOU ORDERED THE ATTACK ON YUZU-SAMA?
WHAT ARE YOU TALKING ABOUT?
YOU SHOULD KNOW...BETRAYING AND BEING BETRAYED IS THE WAY OF THE WORLD.
WHAT ABOUT YOU, YUZU YAMASHITA? ARE YOU PREPARED?
PREPARED ...?
TO STAND AT THE SUMMIT OF THE SHIRAYUKI ESTATE.

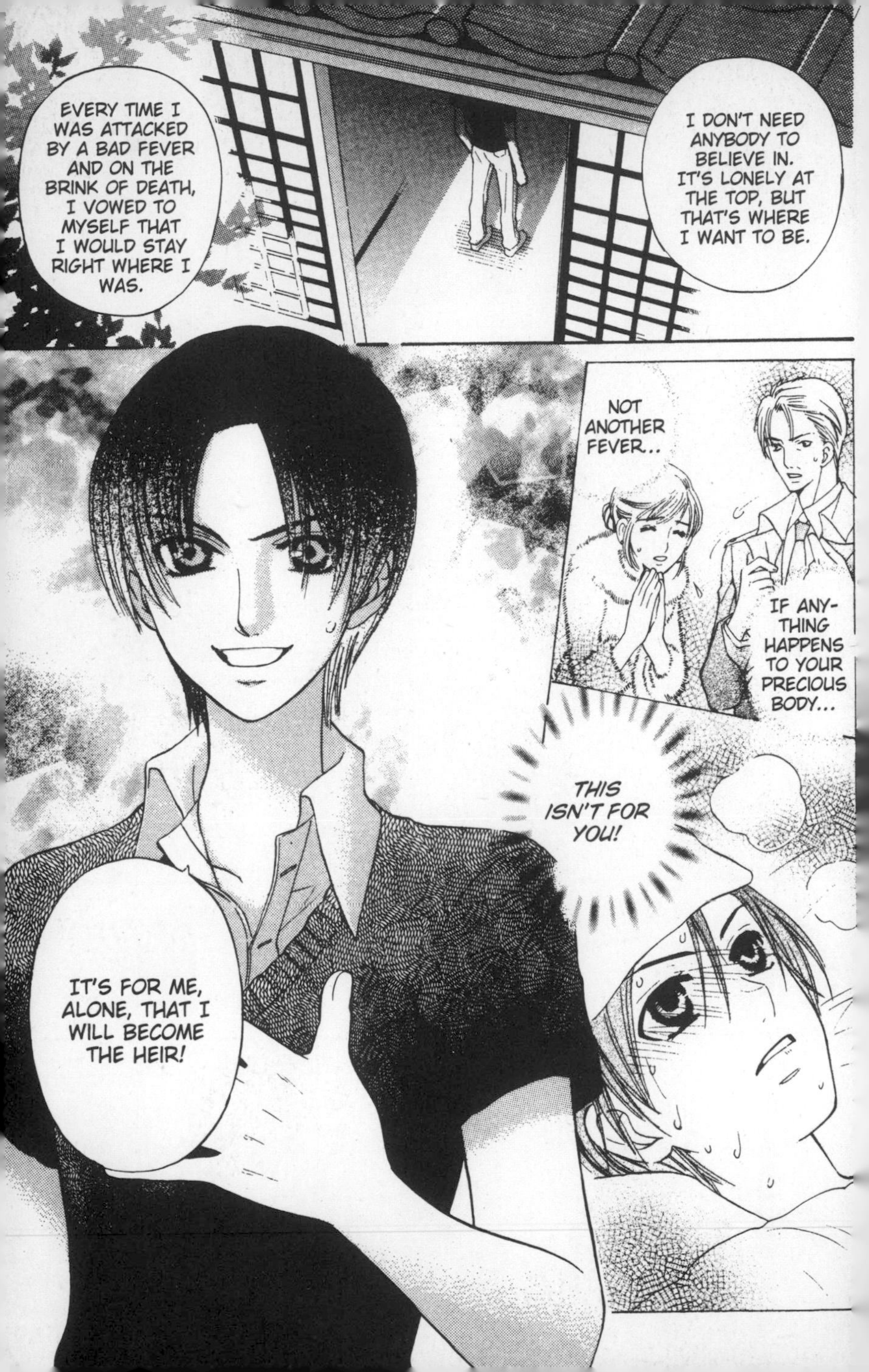
I DON'T NEED ANYBODY TO BELIEVE IN. IT'S LONELY AT THE TOP, BUT THAT'S WHERE I WANT TO BE.
EVERY TIME I WAS ATTACKED BY A BAD FEVER AND ON THE BRINK OF DEATH, I VOWED TO MYSELF THAT I WOULD STAY RIGHT WHERE I WAS.
NOT ANOTHER FEVER...
IF ANYTHING HAPPENS TO YOUR PRECIOUS BODY...
THIS ISN'T FOR YOU!
IT'S FOR ME, ALONE, THAT I WILL BECOME THE HEIR!

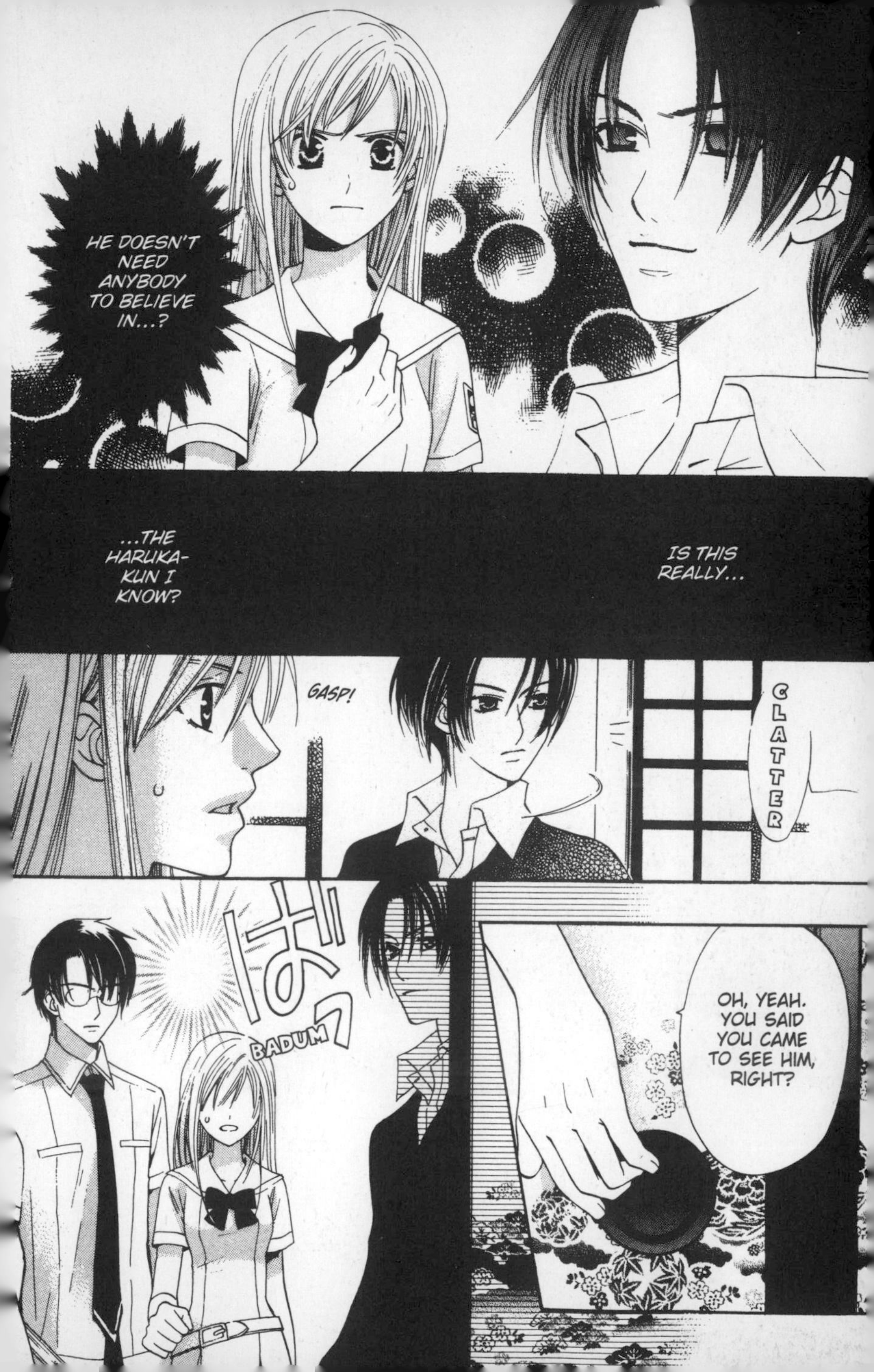
HE DOESN'T NEED ANYBODY TO BELIEVE IN...?
IS THIS REALLY...
...THE HARUKA-KUN I KNOW?
CLATTER
GASP!
OH, YEAH. YOU SAID YOU CAME TO SEE HIM, RIGHT?
BADUM

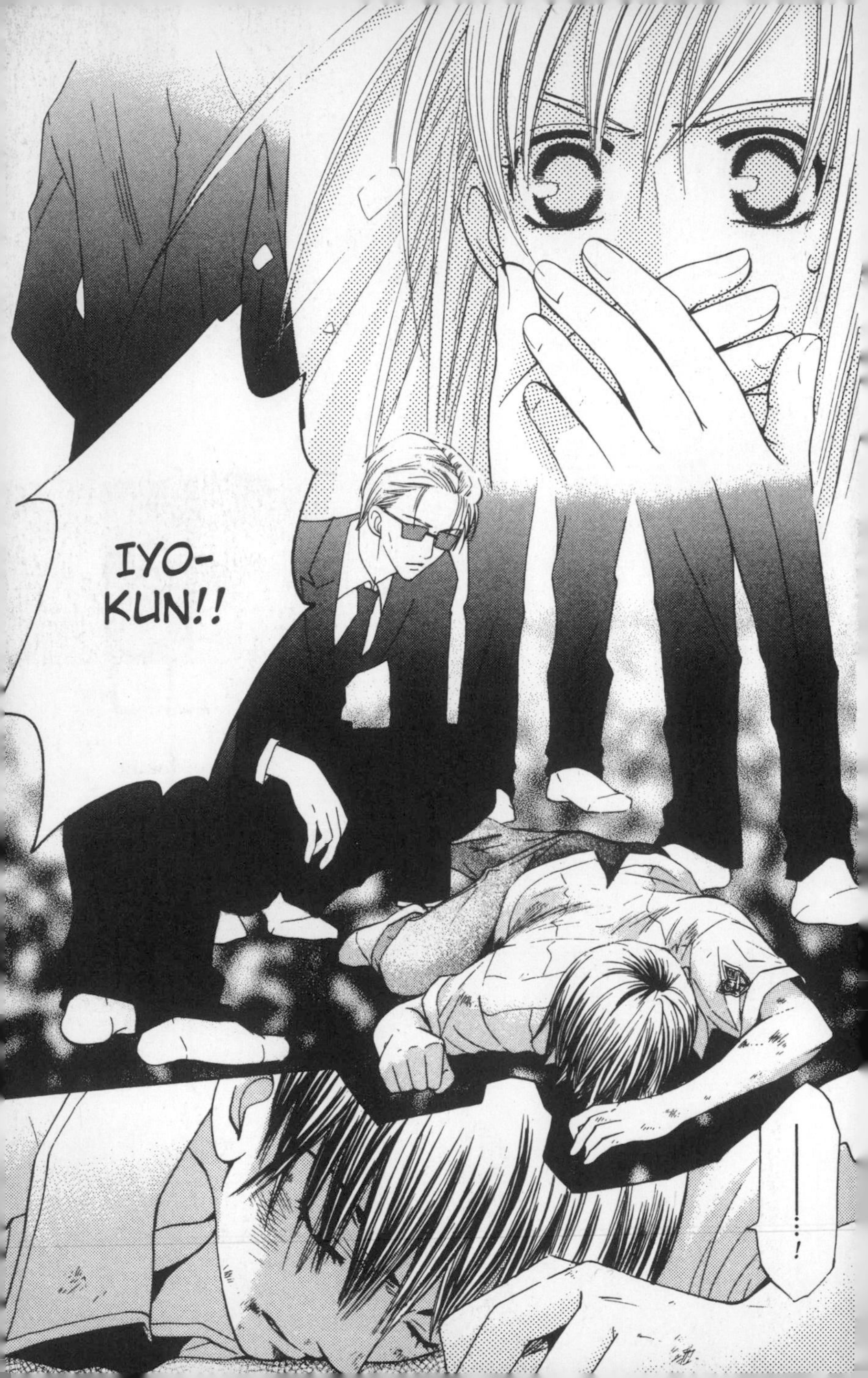
IYO-
KUN!!
......!

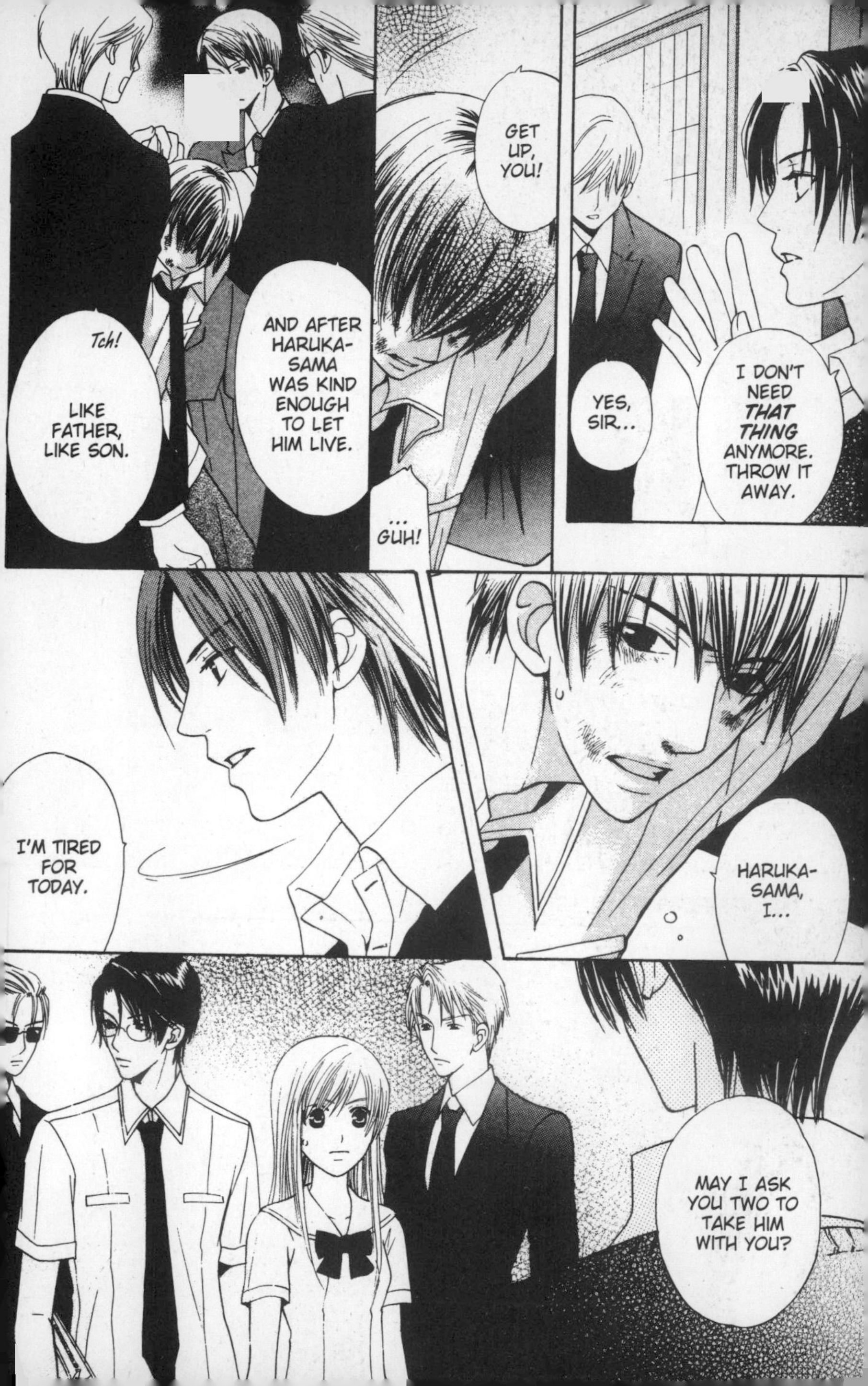
I DON'T NEED *THAT THING* ANYMORE. THROW IT AWAY.
YES, SIR...
GET UP, YOU!
... GUH!
AND AFTER HARUKA-SAMA WAS KIND ENOUGH TO LET HIM LIVE.
Tch!
LIKE FATHER, LIKE SON.
HARUKA-SAMA, I...
I'M TIRED FOR TODAY.
MAY I ASK YOU TWO TO TAKE HIM WITH YOU?

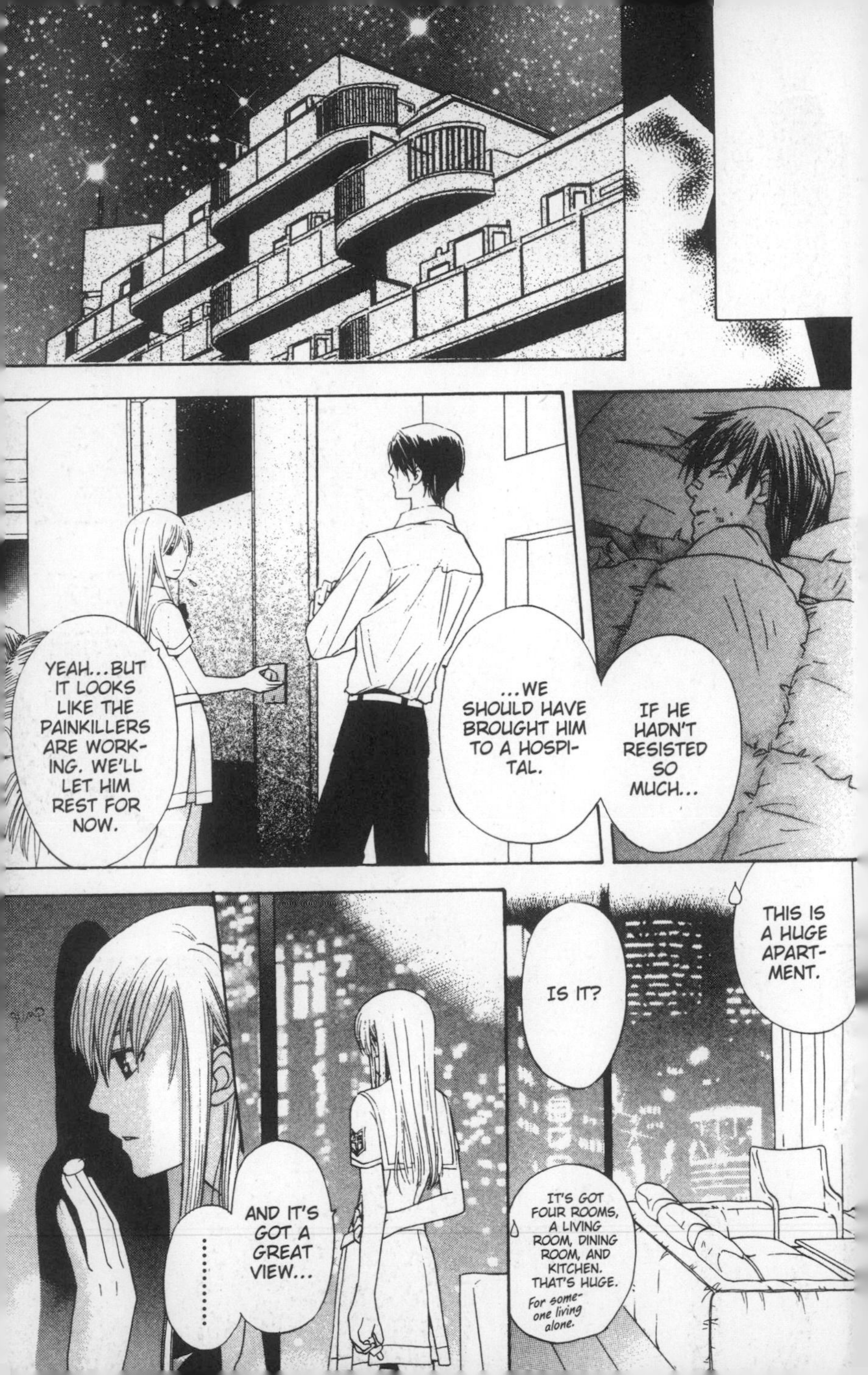
IF HE HADN'T RESISTED SO MUCH...
...WE SHOULD HAVE BROUGHT HIM TO A HOSPITAL.
YEAH...BUT IT LOOKS LIKE THE PAINKILLERS ARE WORKING. WE'LL LET HIM REST FOR NOW.
THIS IS A HUGE APARTMENT.
IS IT?
IT'S GOT FOUR ROOMS, A LIVING ROOM, DINING ROOM, AND KITCHEN. THAT'S HUGE.
For someone living alone.
AND IT'S GOT A GREAT VIEW...
......

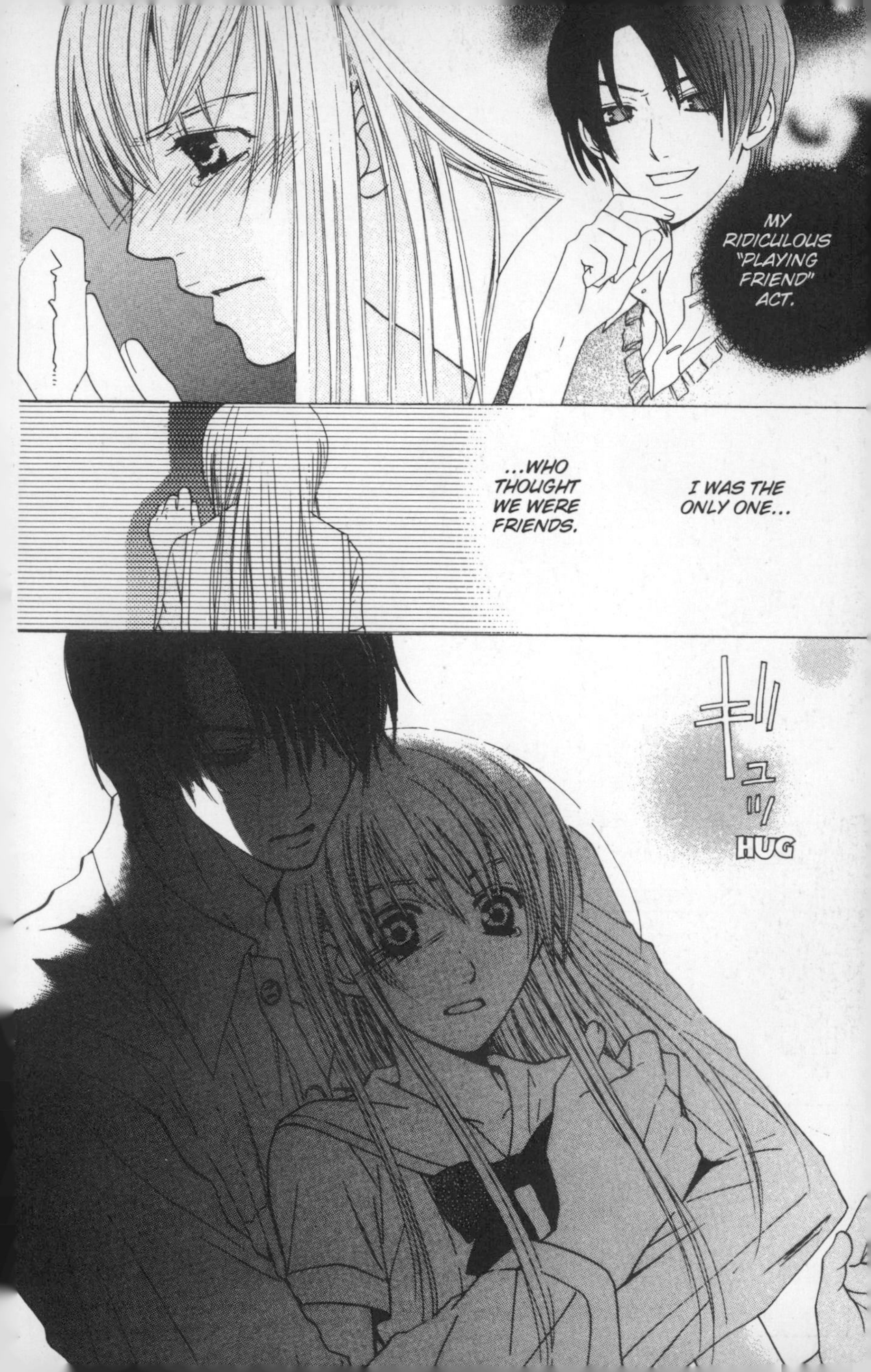
MY RIDICULOUS "PLAYING FRIEND" ACT.
I WAS THE ONLY ONE...
...WHO THOUGHT WE WERE FRIENDS.
キュッ
HUG

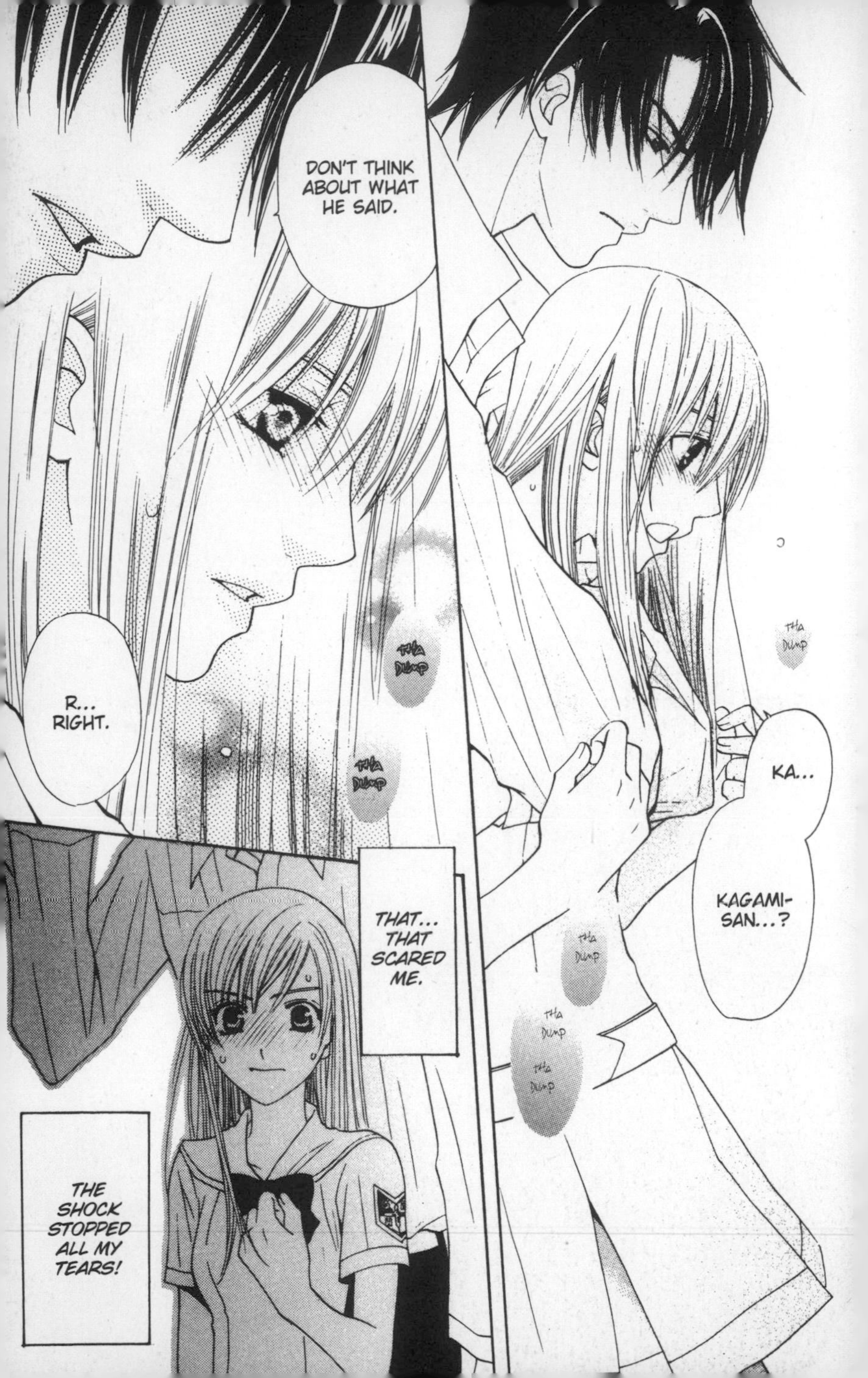

KA...
KAGAMI-SAN...?
THA DUMP
THA DUMP
THA DUMP
THA DUMP
DON'T THINK ABOUT WHAT HE SAID.
THA DUMP
THA DUMP
R... RIGHT.
THAT... THAT SCARED ME.
THE SHOCK STOPPED ALL MY TEARS!

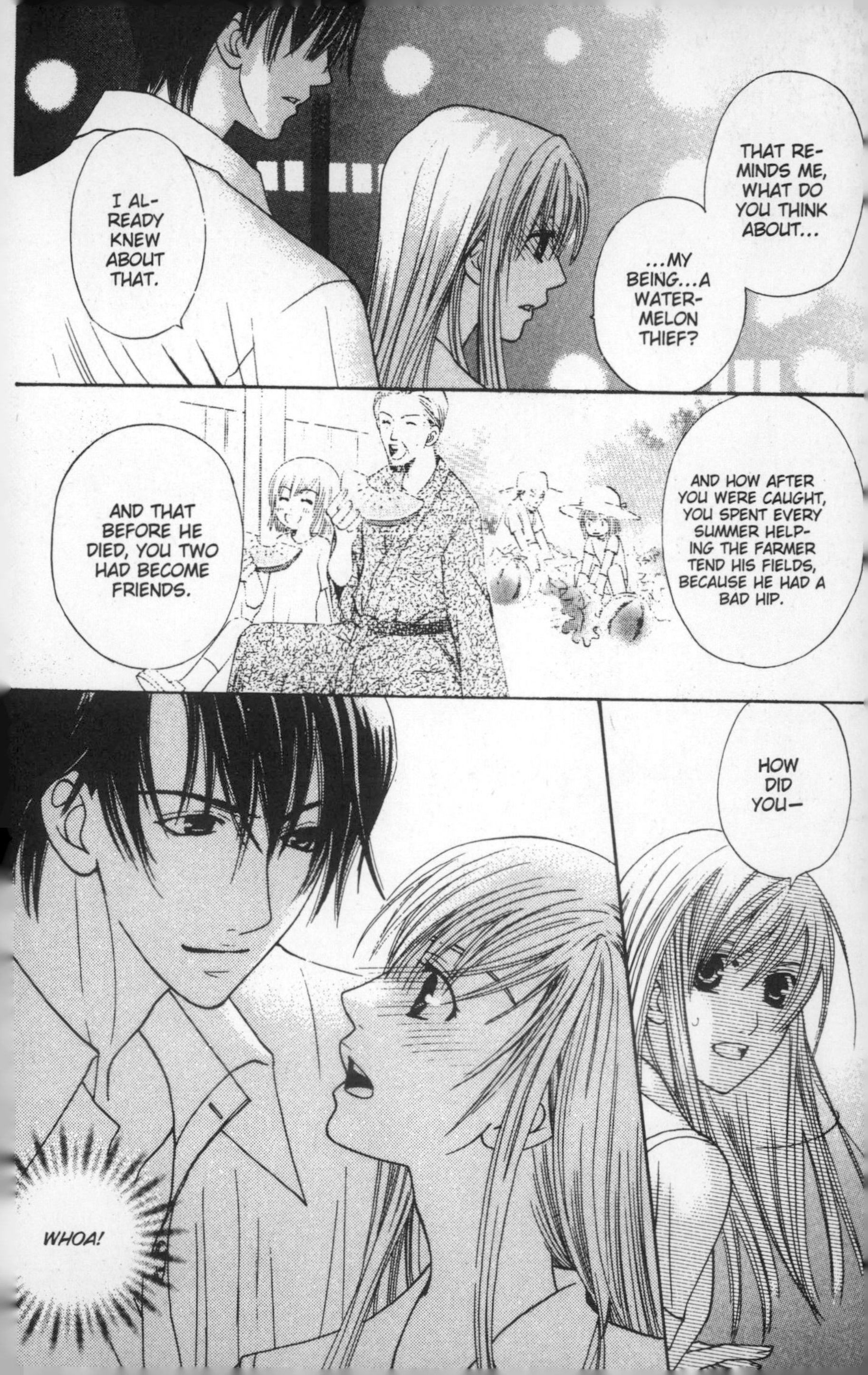
THAT RE-MINDS ME, WHAT DO YOU THINK ABOUT...
...MY BEING...A WATER-MELON THIEF?
I AL-READY KNEW ABOUT THAT.
AND HOW AFTER YOU WERE CAUGHT, YOU SPENT EVERY SUMMER HELP-ING THE FARMER TEND HIS FIELDS, BECAUSE HE HAD A BAD HIP.
AND THAT BEFORE HE DIED, YOU TWO HAD BECOME FRIENDS.
HOW DID YOU—
WHOA!

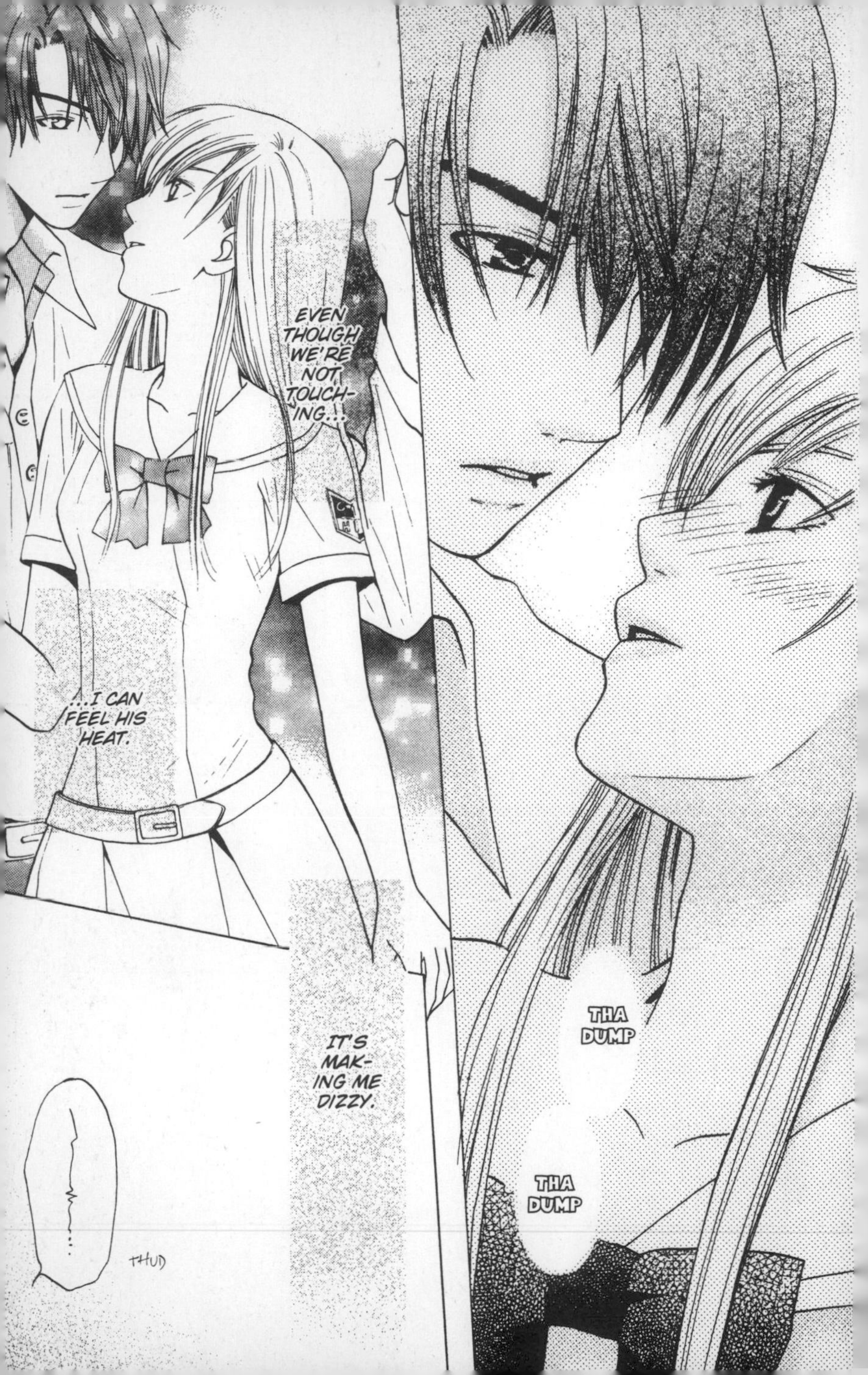
THA DUMP
THA DUMP
EVEN THOUGH WE'RE NOT TOUCHING...
...I CAN FEEL HIS HEAT.
IT'S MAKING ME DIZZY.
......
THUD

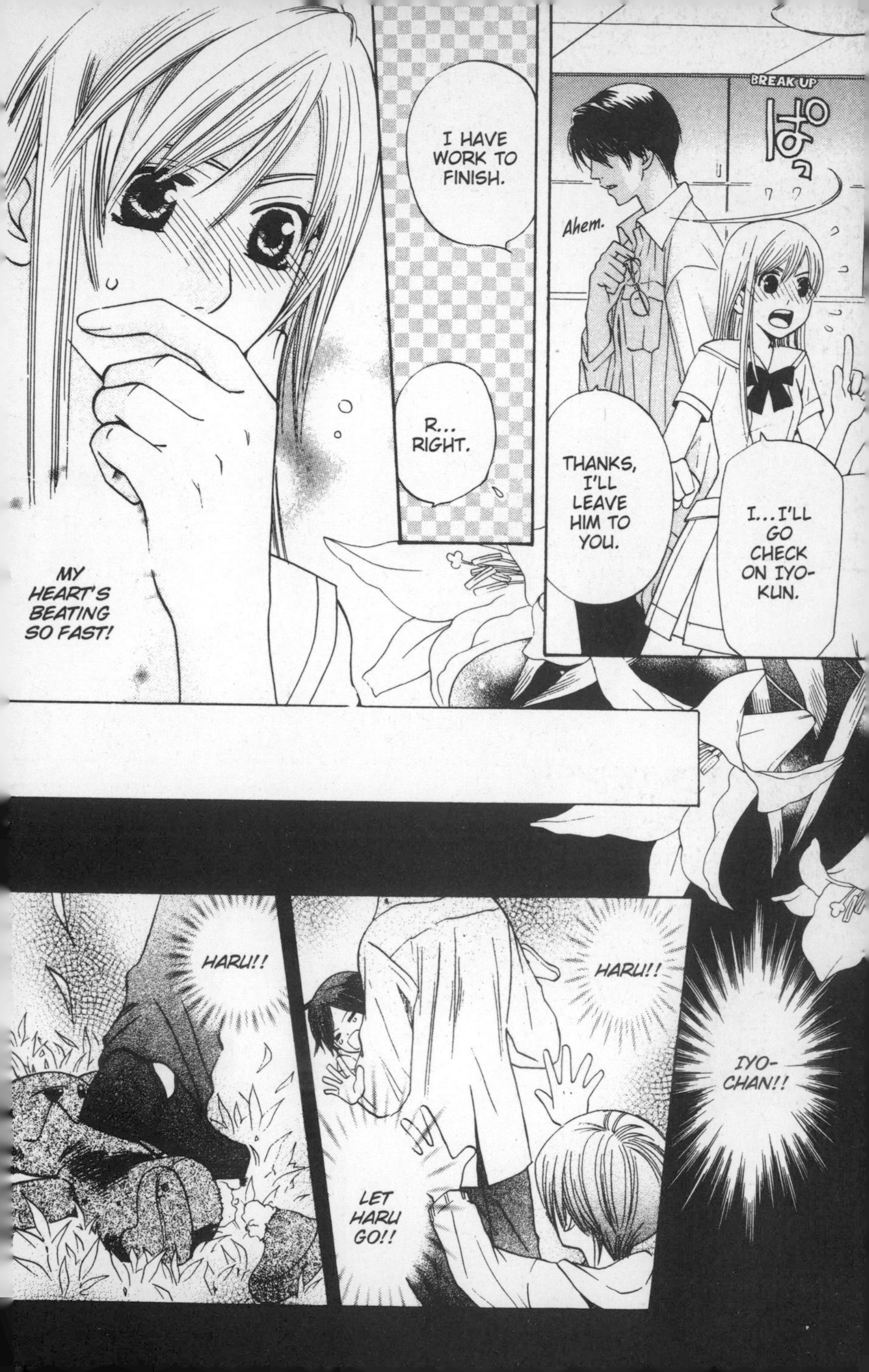
BREAK UP
ぱっ
Ahem.
I...I'LL GO CHECK ON IYO-KUN.
THANKS, I'LL LEAVE HIM TO YOU.
I HAVE WORK TO FINISH.
R... RIGHT.
MY HEART'S BEATING SO FAST!
IYO-CHAN!!
HARU!!
LET HARU GO!!
HARU!!

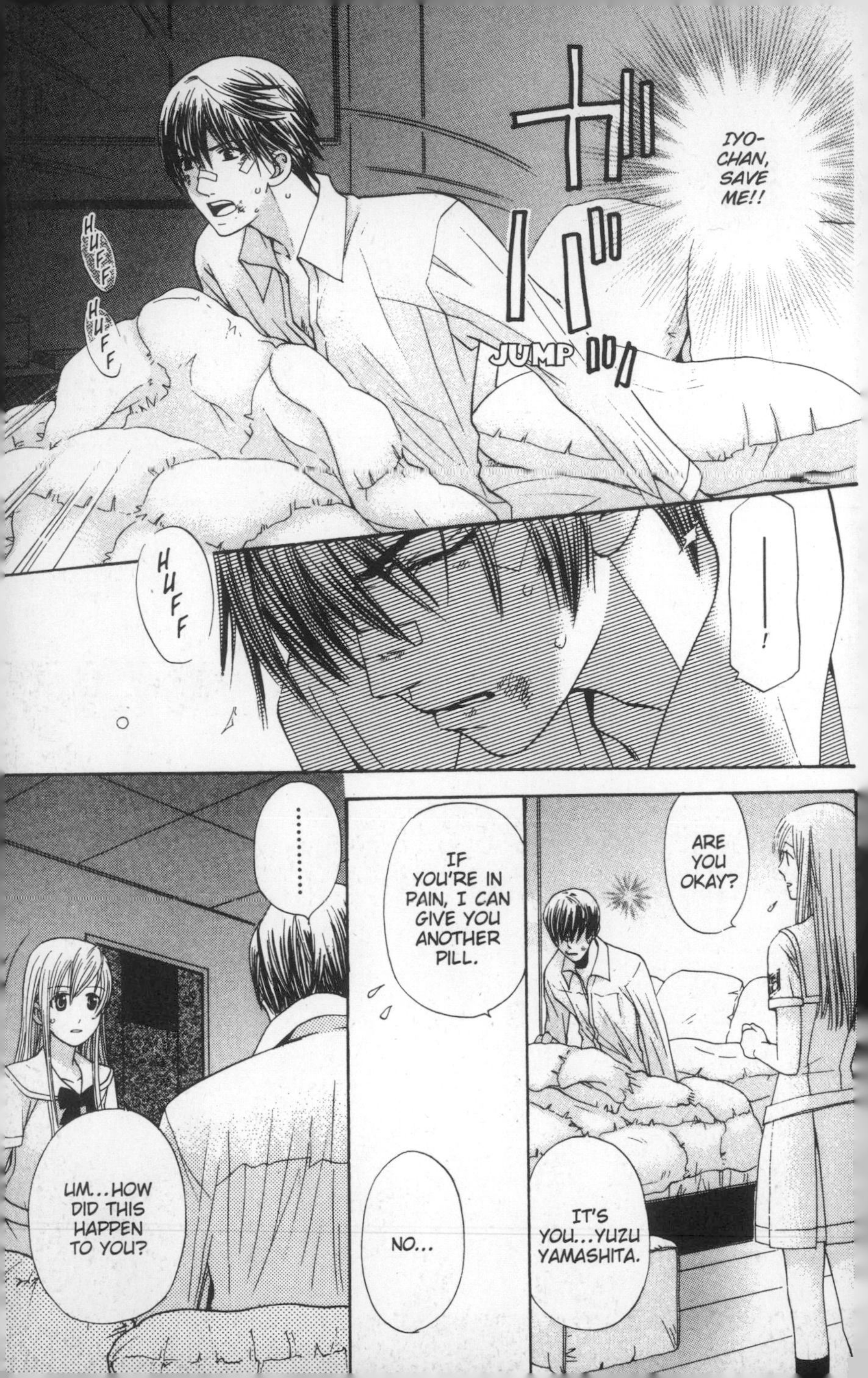
IYO-CHAN, SAVE ME!!
JUMP
HUFF HUFF
HUFF
!
HUFF
ARE YOU OKAY?
IT'S YOU...YUZU YAMASHITA.
IF YOU'RE IN PAIN, I CAN GIVE YOU ANOTHER PILL.
NO...
......
UM...HOW DID THIS HAPPEN TO YOU?

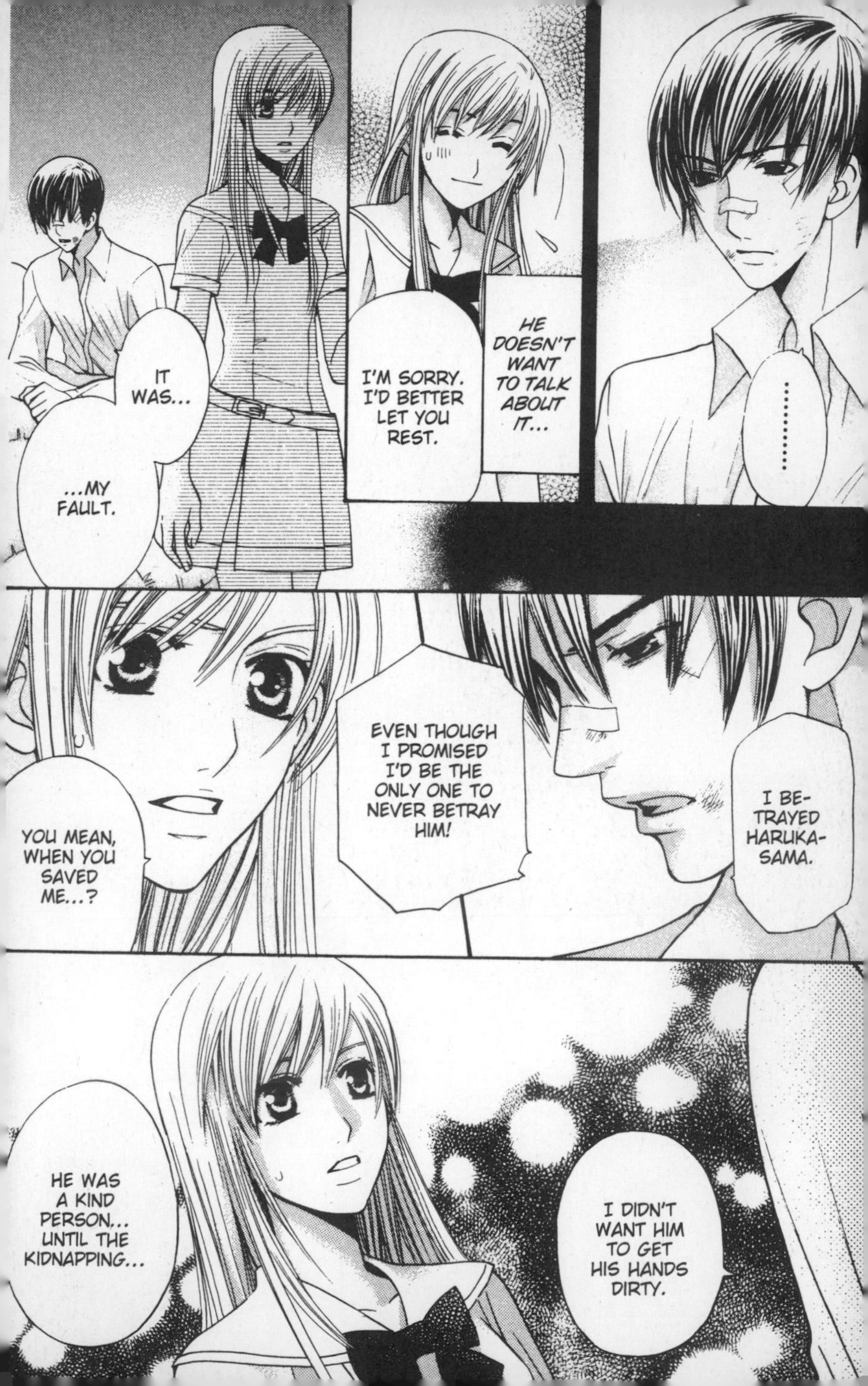
......
HE DOESN'T WANT TO TALK ABOUT IT...
I'M SORRY. I'D BETTER LET YOU REST.
IT WAS...
...MY FAULT.
I BE-TRAYED HARUKA-SAMA.
EVEN THOUGH I PROMISED I'D BE THE ONLY ONE TO NEVER BETRAY HIM!
YOU MEAN, WHEN YOU SAVED ME...?
I DIDN'T WANT HIM TO GET HIS HANDS DIRTY.
HE WAS A KIND PERSON... UNTIL THE KIDNAPPING...

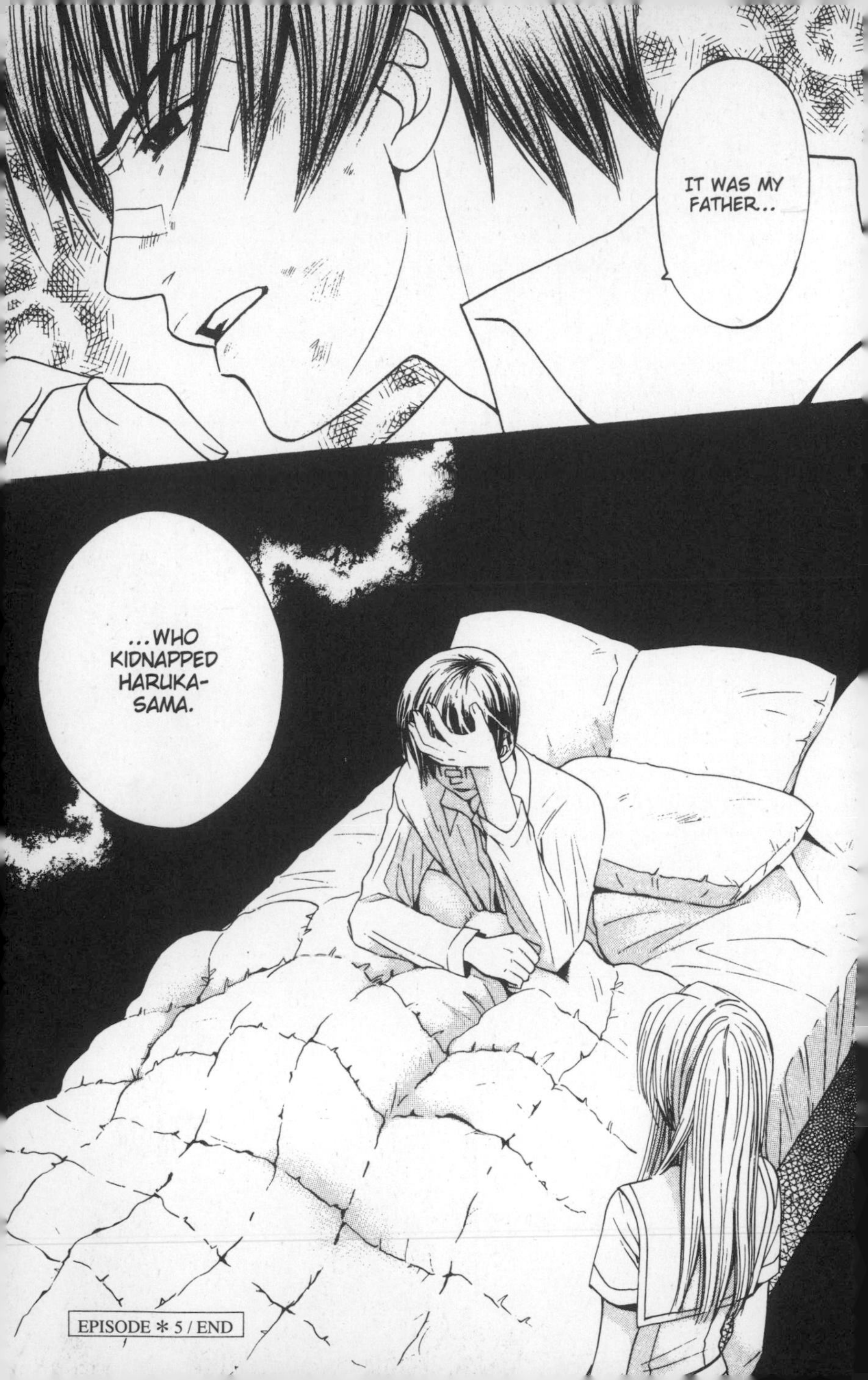
IT WAS MY FATHER...
...WHO KIDNAPPED HARUKA-SAMA.
EPISODE ✻ 5 / END

This past year, I've gotten into seeing a lot of theatre productions. They're mostly musicals, but every time I go, I'm moved in a whole new way and it really invigorates me.
It gets me thinking about what I was missing out on while I wasn't into going.
Along with theatre-going, I'm also reading more Western works...
But when work gets out of hand, I let it slip by the wayside. It's like I'm only

pretending to mature as I take one step forward, and two steps back. Someday, I'd like to see a production on Broadway. But, I can't say for sure if such a grand dream will come true... ○○
I hope it does.

Since I've been having so much writer's block, I told my assistants H-san and T-san "I'll leave one page to you, so please spend the day drawing something," but they just brushed me off. It's embarrassing, but I thought I'd let out some of my frustrations in this afterword.

Well, please enjoy the rest of the story~~

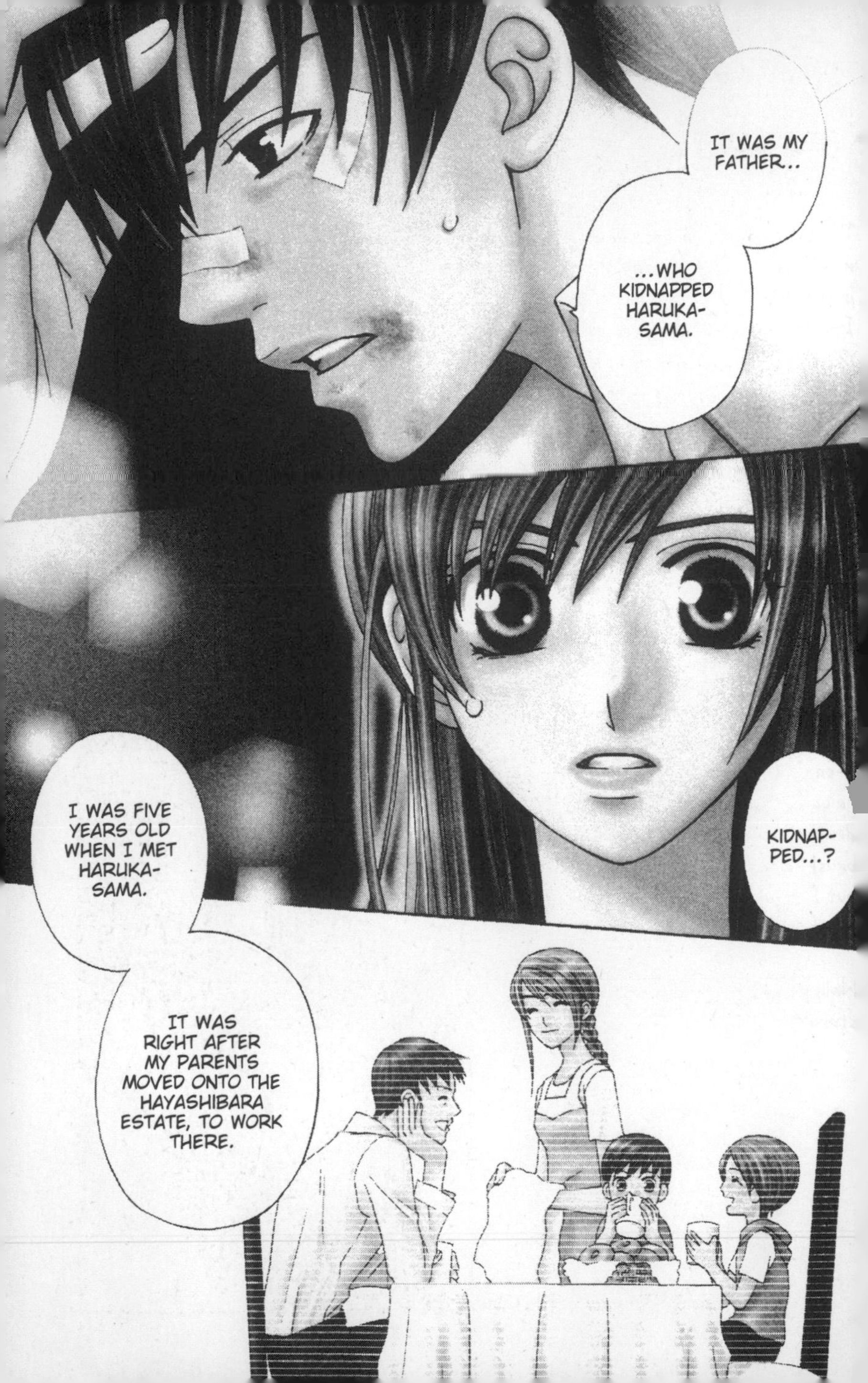
IT WAS MY FATHER..
...WHO KIDNAPPED HARUKA-SAMA.
KIDNAP-PED...?
I WAS FIVE YEARS OLD WHEN I MET HARUKA-SAMA.
IT WAS RIGHT AFTER MY PARENTS MOVED ONTO THE HAYASHIBARA ESTATE, TO WORK THERE.

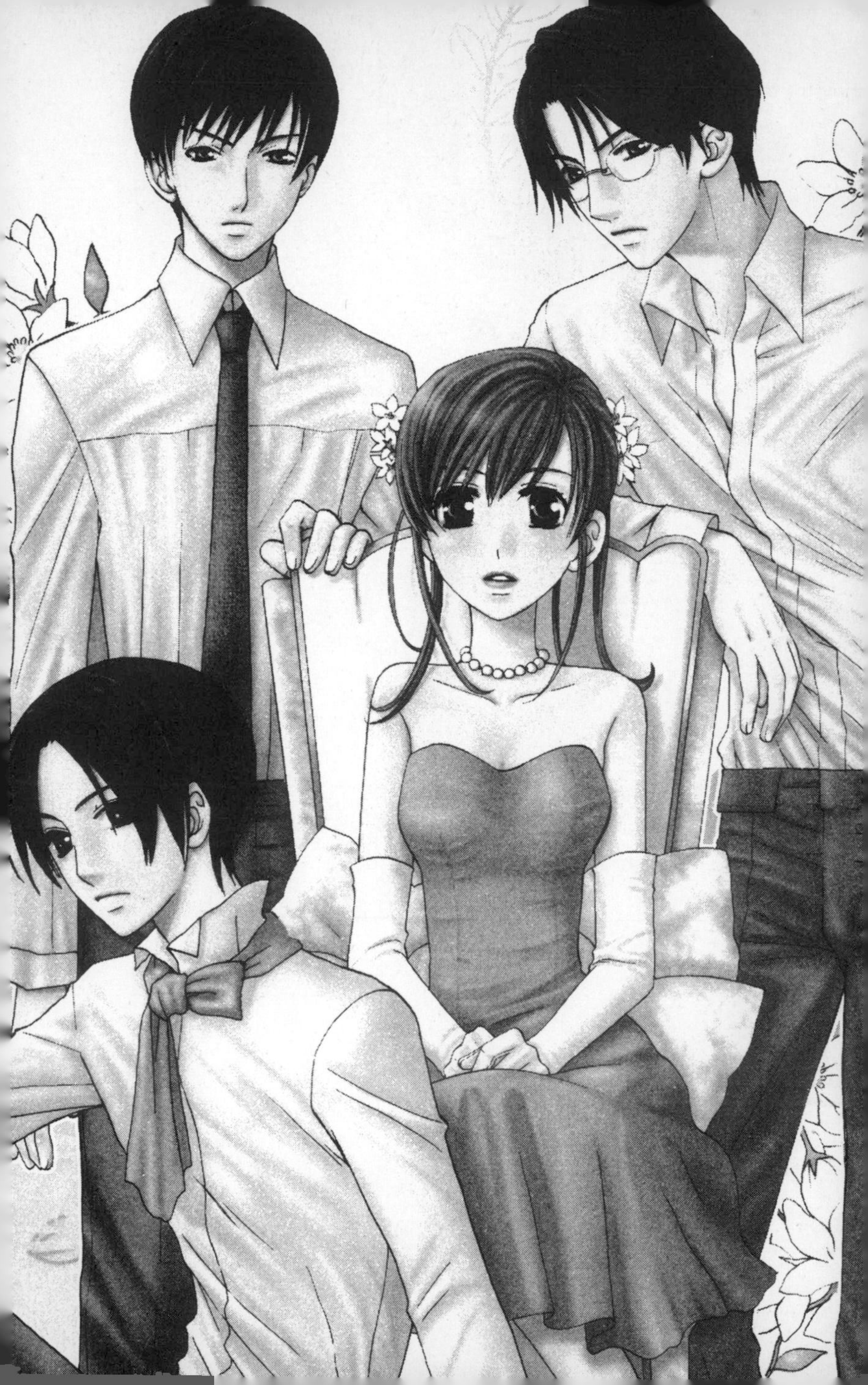

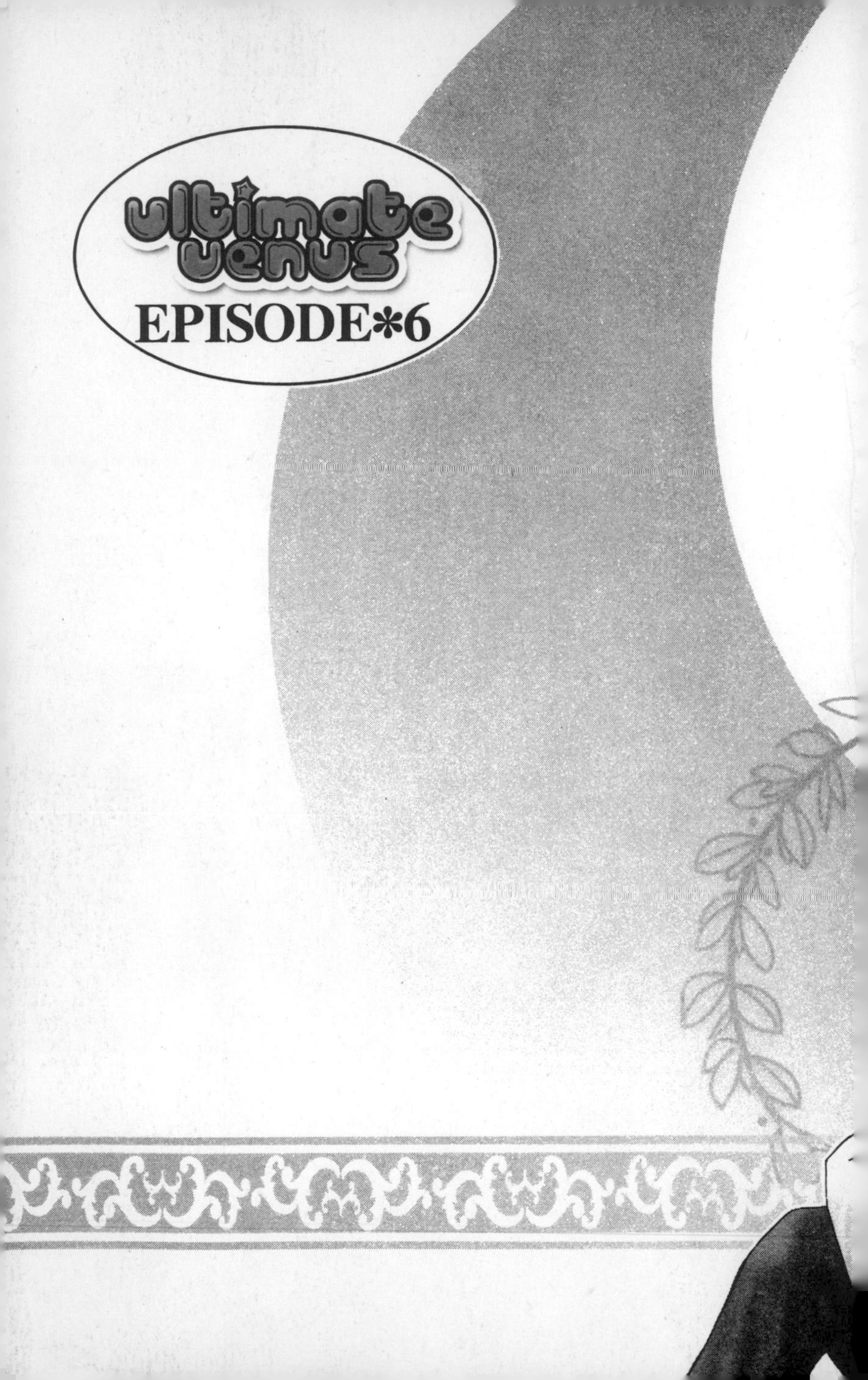
ultimate venus
EPISODE*6

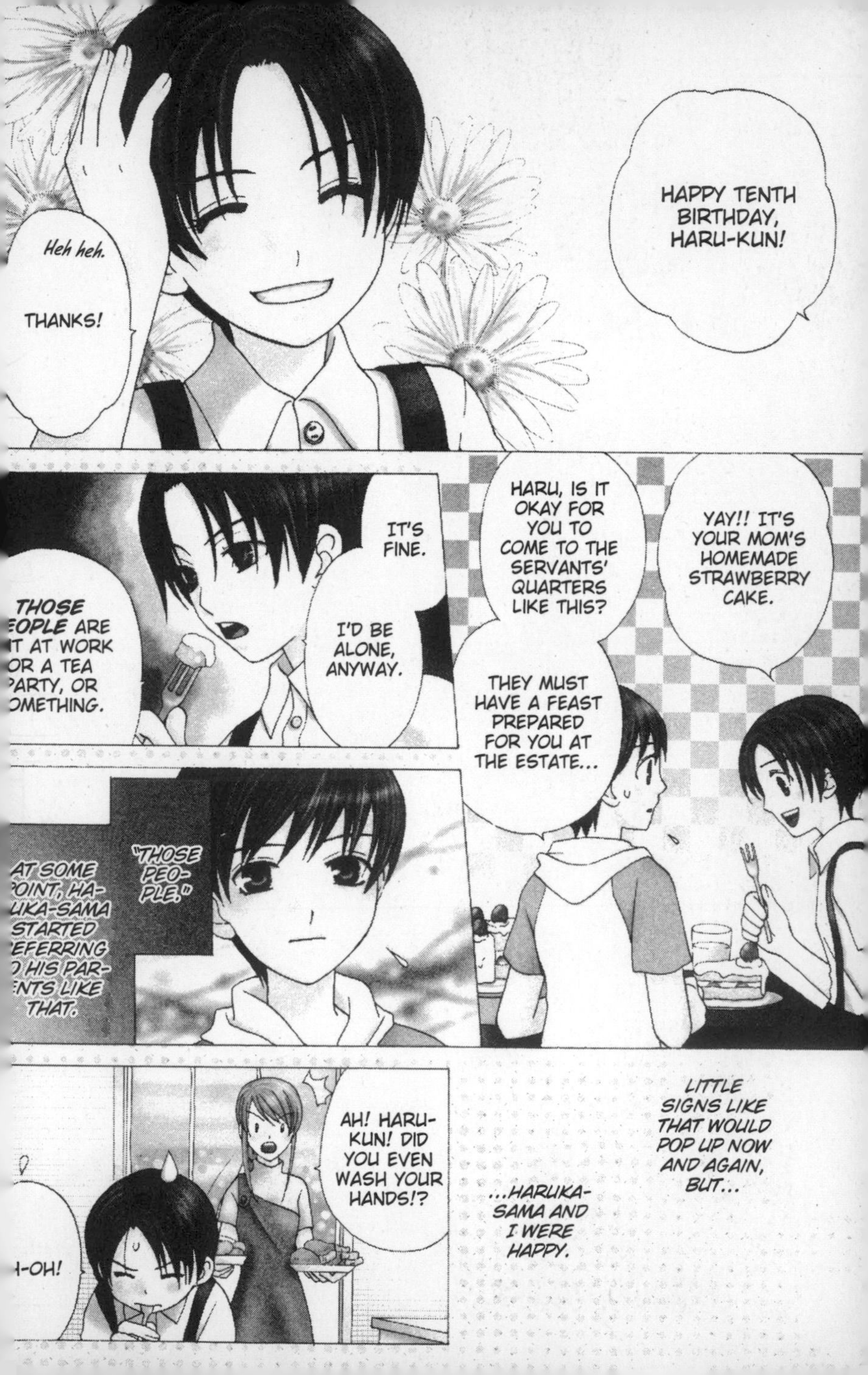
HAPPY TENTH BIRTHDAY, HARU-KUN!
Heh heh.
THANKS!
YAY!! IT'S YOUR MOM'S HOMEMADE STRAWBERRY CAKE.
HARU, IS IT OKAY FOR YOU TO COME TO THE SERVANTS' QUARTERS LIKE THIS?
THEY MUST HAVE A FEAST PREPARED FOR YOU AT THE ESTATE...
IT'S FINE.
I'D BE ALONE, ANYWAY.
THOSE EOPLE ARE T AT WORK OR A TEA PARTY, OR OMETHING.
"THOSE PEO-PLE."
AT SOME POINT, HA-UKA-SAMA STARTED EFERRING O HIS PAR-ENTS LIKE THAT.
LITTLE SIGNS LIKE THAT WOULD POP UP NOW AND AGAIN, BUT...
...HARUKA-SAMA AND I WERE HAPPY.
AH! HARU-KUN! DID YOU EVEN WASH YOUR HANDS!?
H-OH!

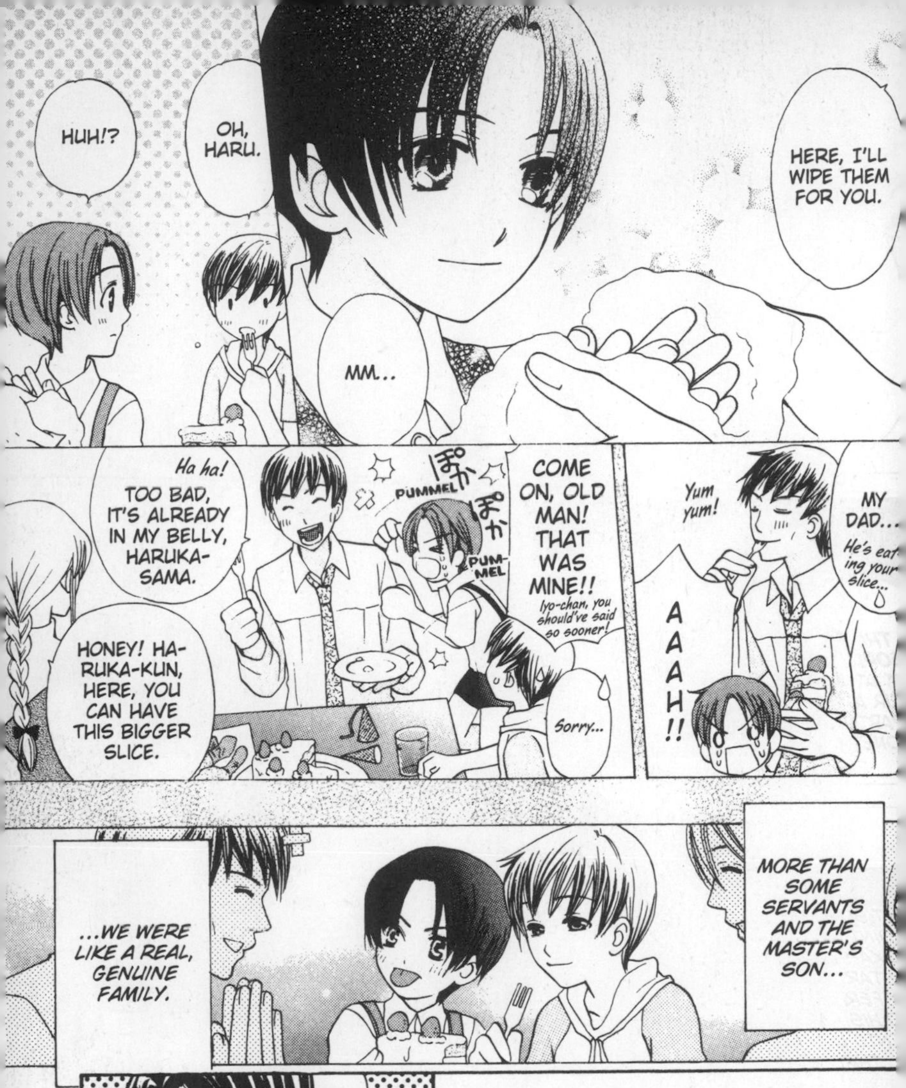
HERE, I'LL WIPE THEM FOR YOU.
MM...
OH, HARU.
HUH!?
MY DAD... He's eating your slice...
Yum yum!
AAAAH!!
COME ON, OLD MAN! THAT WAS MINE!!
Iyo-chan, you should've said so sooner!
ぽか ぽか
PUMMEL PUMMEL
Ha ha!
TOO BAD, IT'S ALREADY IN MY BELLY, HARUKA-SAMA.
HONEY! HARUKA-KUN, HERE, YOU CAN HAVE THIS BIGGER SLICE.
Sorry...
MORE THAN SOME SERVANTS AND THE MASTER'S SON...
...WE WERE LIKE A REAL, GENUINE FAMILY.

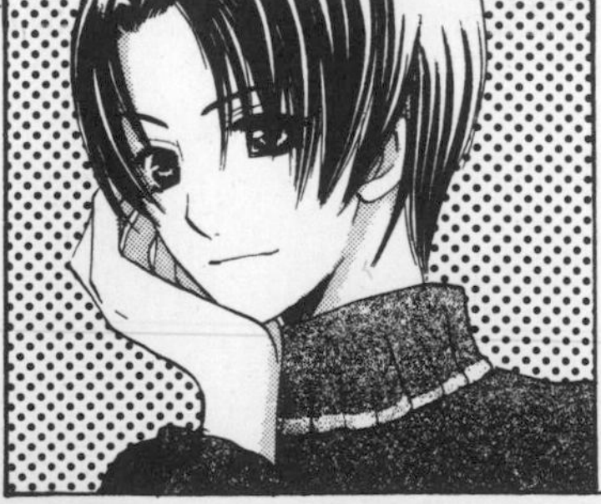

Haruka Hayashibara (age 15)

Birthday: November 11th

Blood Type: A

Hobbies: Online games. Chess.

Favorites: Sweets

When he was a child, his body was weak, so he became an indoor type. Has no physical strength.

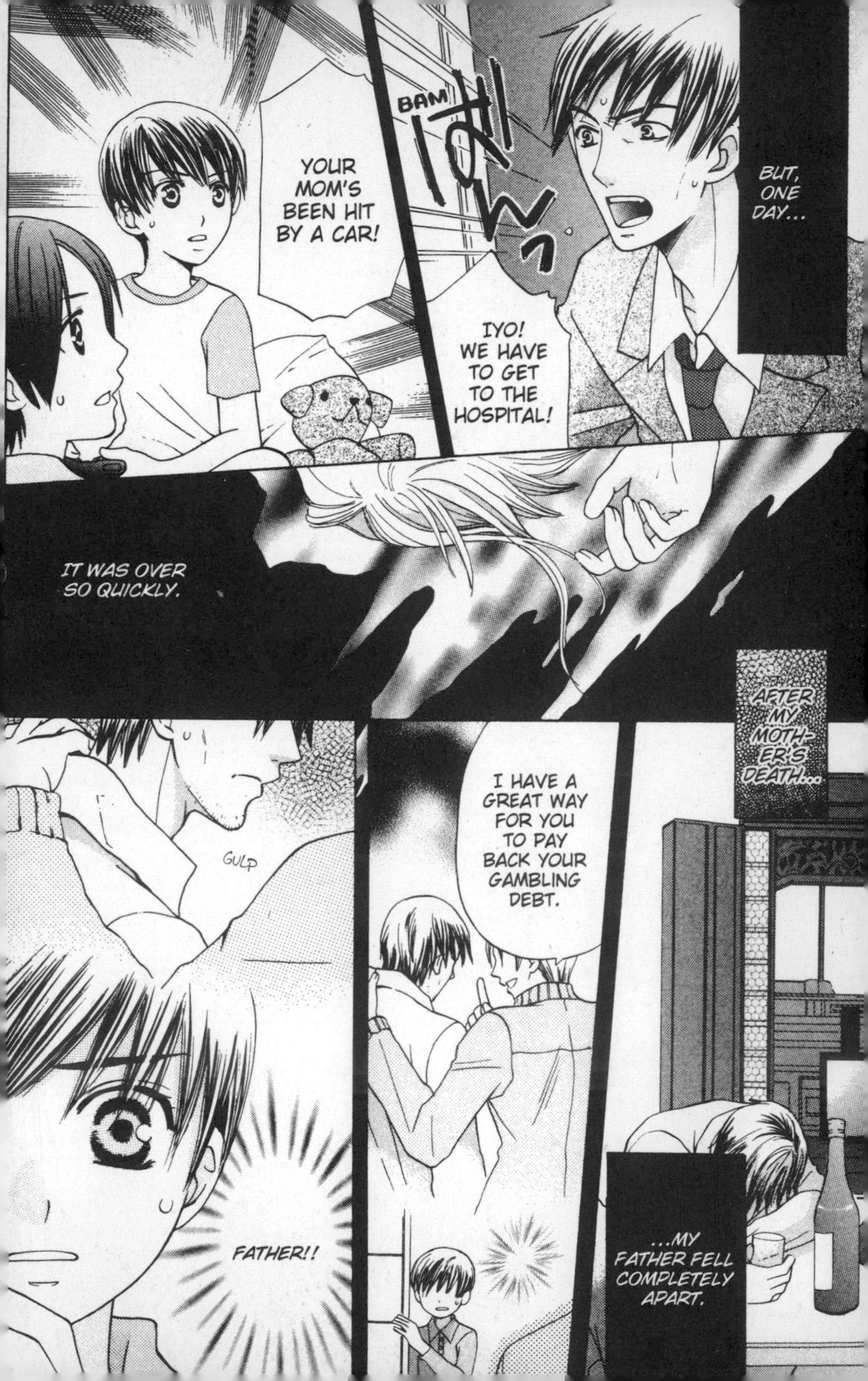
BUT, ONE DAY...
BAM
IYO! WE HAVE TO GET TO THE HOSPITAL!
YOUR MOM'S BEEN HIT BY A CAR!
IT WAS OVER SO QUICKLY.
AFTER MY MOTHER'S DEATH...
...MY FATHER FELL COMPLETELY APART.
I HAVE A GREAT WAY FOR YOU TO PAY BACK YOUR GAMBLING DEBT.
GULP
FATHER!!

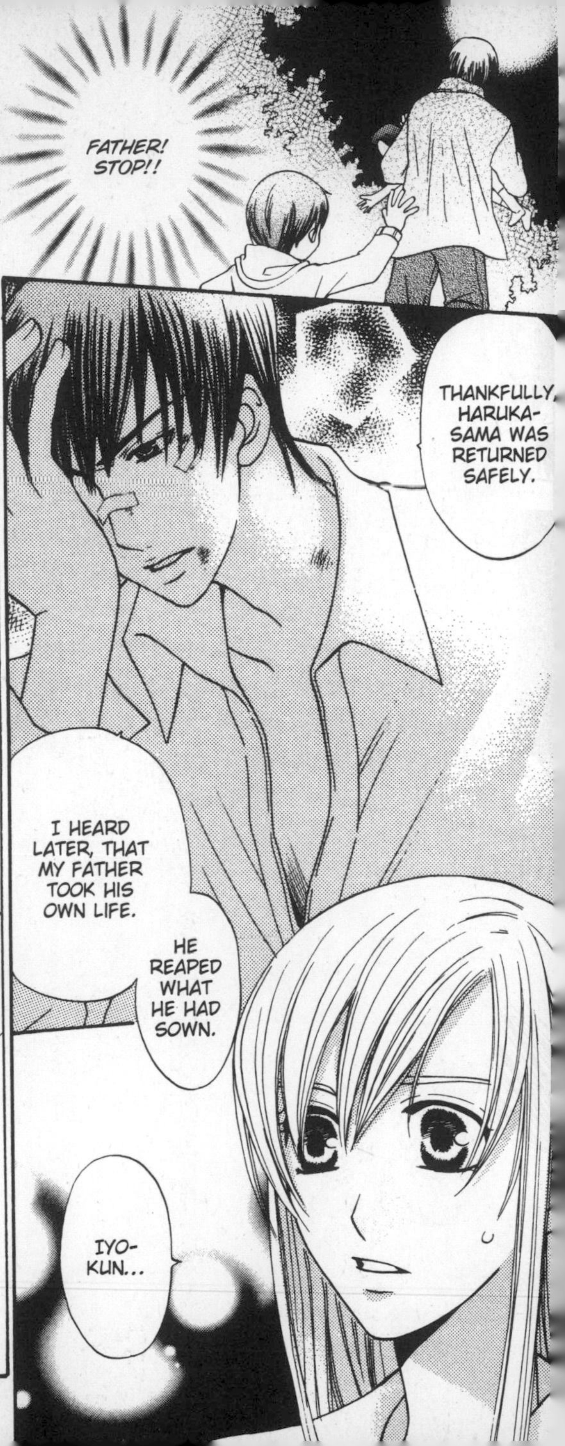
FATHER! STOP!!
THANKFULLY, HARUKA-SAMA WAS RETURNED SAFELY.
I HEARD LATER, THAT MY FATHER TOOK HIS OWN LIFE.
HE REAPED WHAT HE HAD SOWN.
IYO-KUN...

GAME DAYS ①

Around December of 2006, I bought an XBOX 360.
I was moved by that futuristic machine...
And I got really into my first online challenges!!
I hadn't really (okay, **not at all**) been into playing action games, but right now all I will play is "Lost Planet."
So, even when I go out with friends...

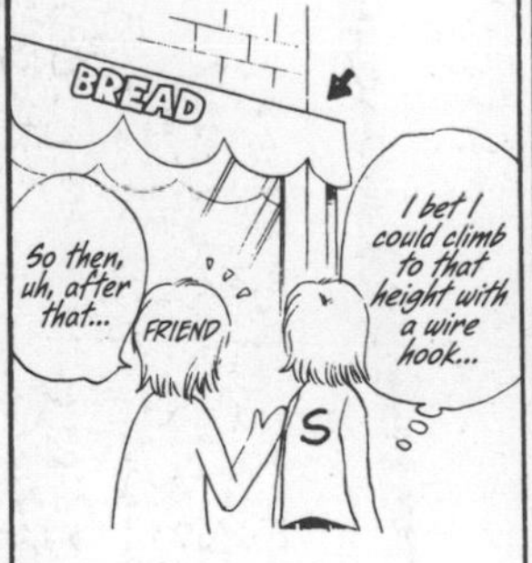
BREAD
I bet I could climb to that height with a wire hook...
So then, uh, after that...
FRIEND
S

I'm getting more detached, thanks to it.
But if I did that, I'd lose all my friends, so for now I gotta put up with it.

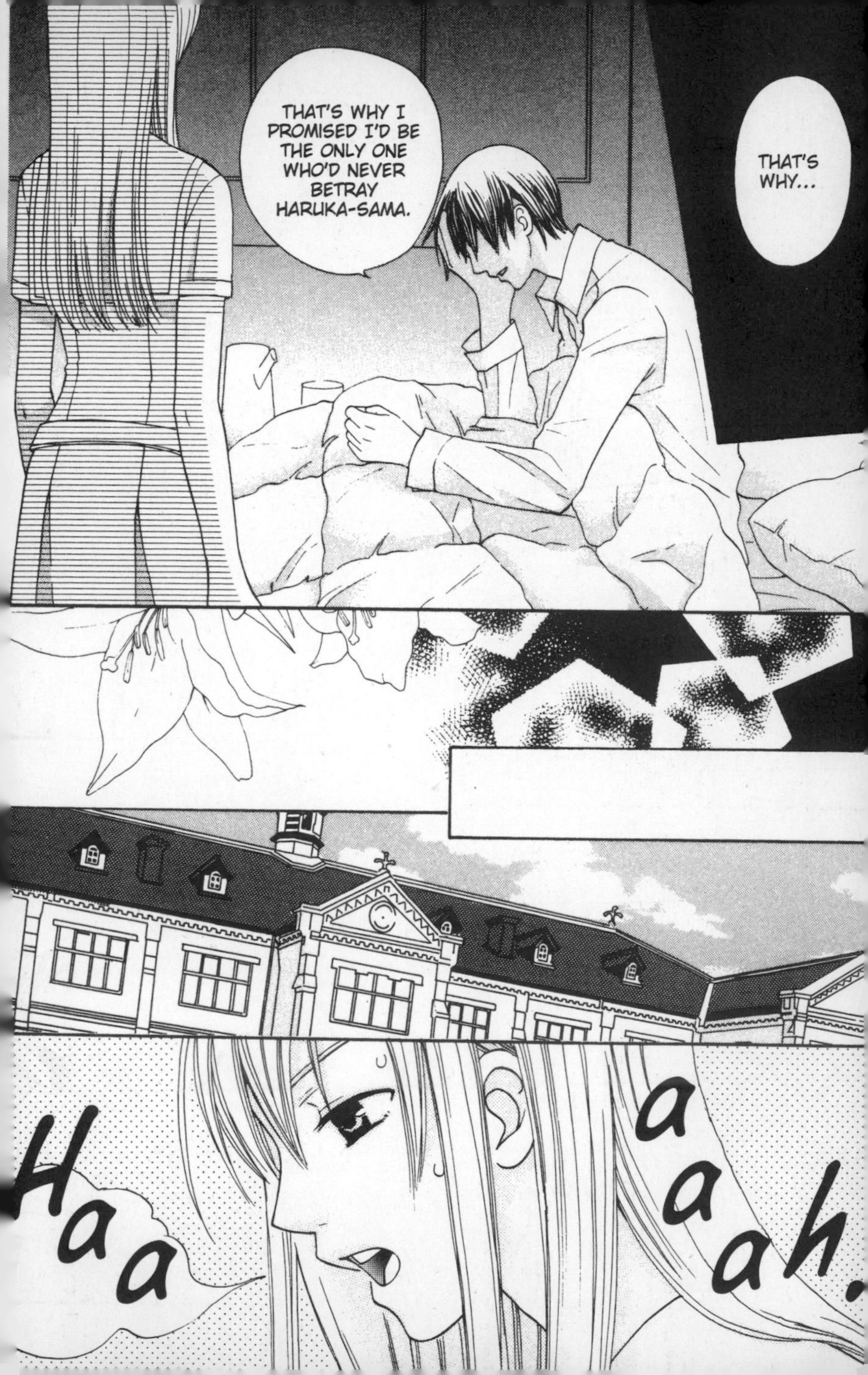
THAT'S WHY...
THAT'S WHY I PROMISED I'D BE THE ONLY ONE WHO'D NEVER BETRAY HARUKA-SAMA.
Haaaaah.

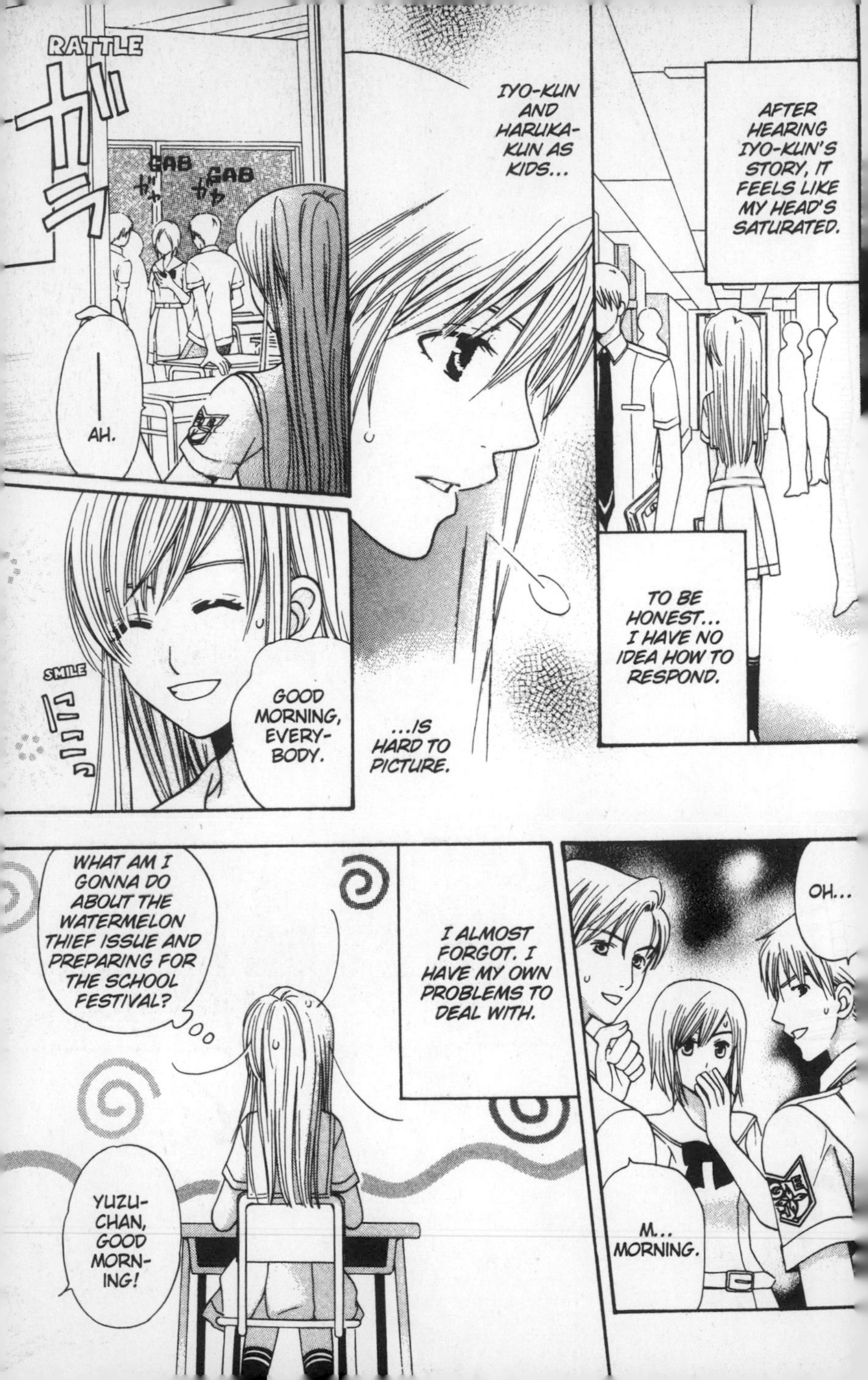
AFTER HEARING IYO-KUN'S STORY, IT FEELS LIKE MY HEAD'S SATURATED.
TO BE HONEST... I HAVE NO IDEA HOW TO RESPOND.
IYO-KUN AND HARUKA-KUN AS KIDS...
...IS HARD TO PICTURE.
RATTLE
GAB
GAB
AH.
SMILE
GOOD MORNING, EVERYBODY.
OH...
M... MORNING.
I ALMOST FORGOT. I HAVE MY OWN PROBLEMS TO DEAL WITH.
WHAT AM I GONNA DO ABOUT THE WATERMELON THIEF ISSUE AND PREPARING FOR THE SCHOOL FESTIVAL?
YUZU-CHAN, GOOD MORNING!

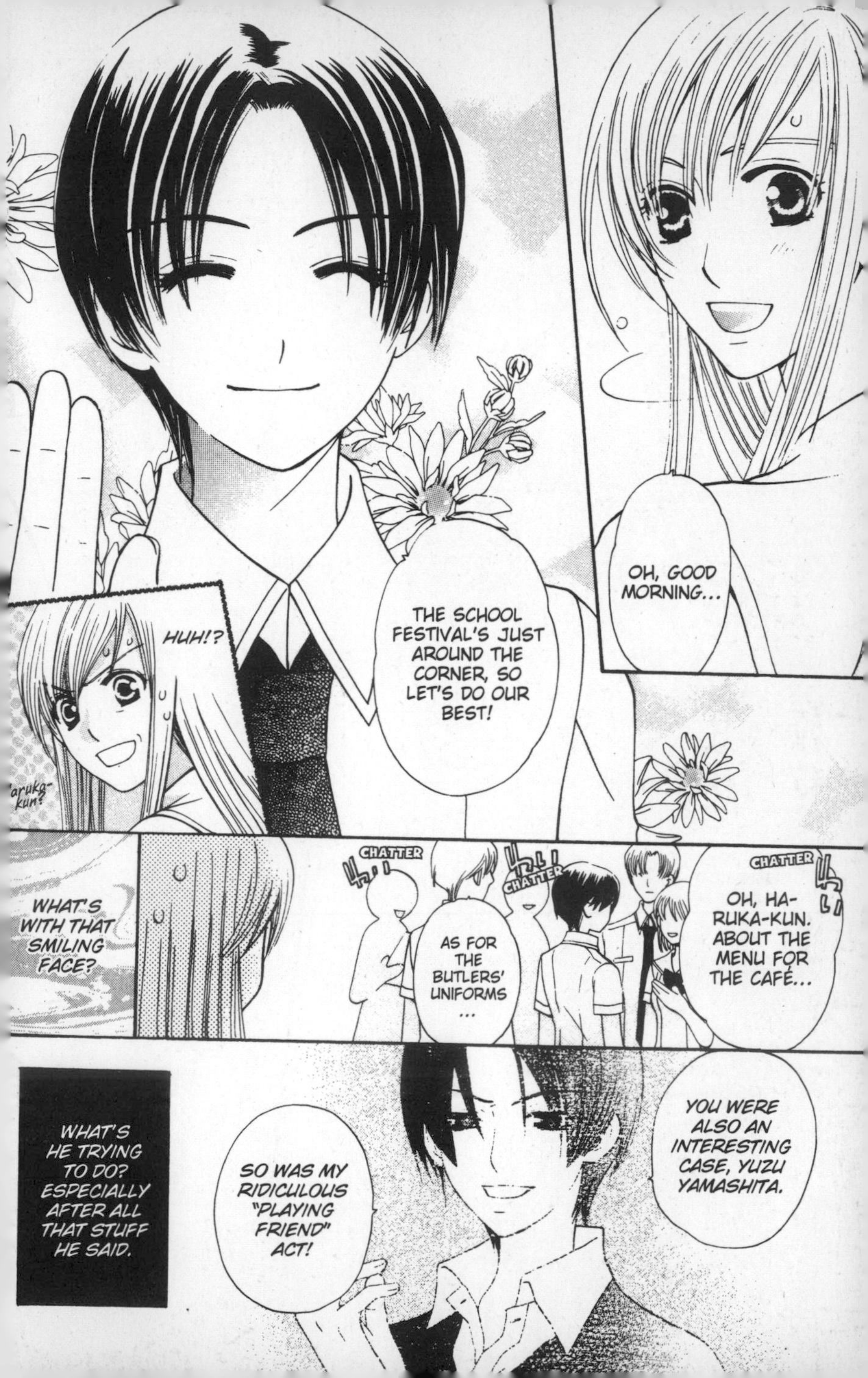

OH, GOOD MORNING...
THE SCHOOL FESTIVAL'S JUST AROUND THE CORNER, SO LET'S DO OUR BEST!
HUH!?
aruka-kun?
CHATTER
OH, HA-RUKA-KUN. ABOUT THE MENU FOR THE CAFÉ...
CHATTER
CHATTER
AS FOR THE BUTLERS' UNIFORMS ...
WHAT'S WITH THAT SMILING FACE?
YOU WERE ALSO AN INTERESTING CASE, YUZU YAMASHITA.
SO WAS MY RIDICULOUS "PLAYING FRIEND" ACT!
WHAT'S HE TRYING TO DO? ESPECIALLY AFTER ALL THAT STUFF HE SAID.

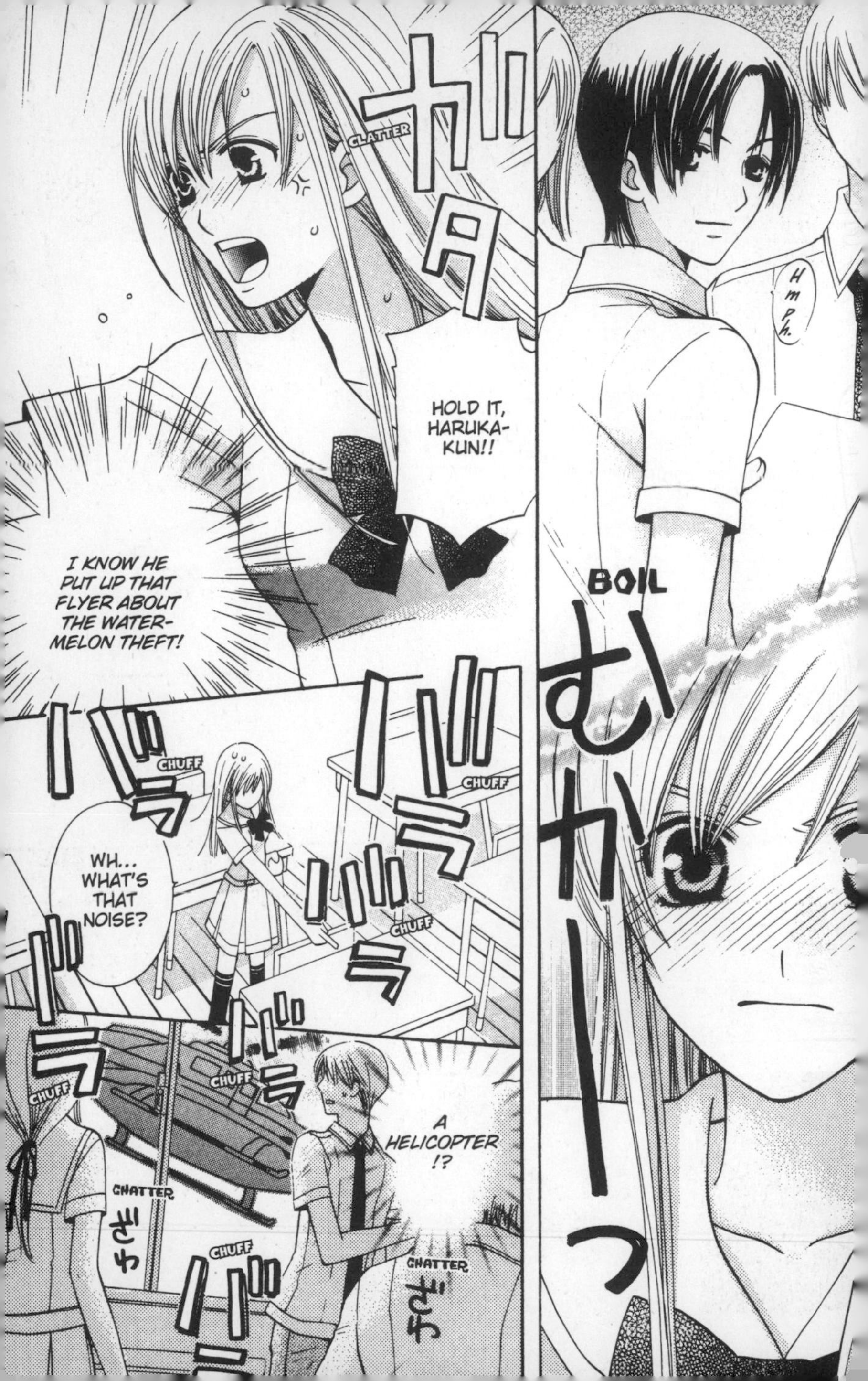
Hmph.
BOIL
CLATTER
HOLD IT, HARUKA-KUN!!
I KNOW HE PUT UP THAT FLYER ABOUT THE WATER-MELON THEFT!
CHUFF
CHUFF
WH... WHAT'S THAT NOISE?
CHUFF
CHUFF
CHUFF
A HELICOPTER !?
CHATTER
CHUFF
CHATTER

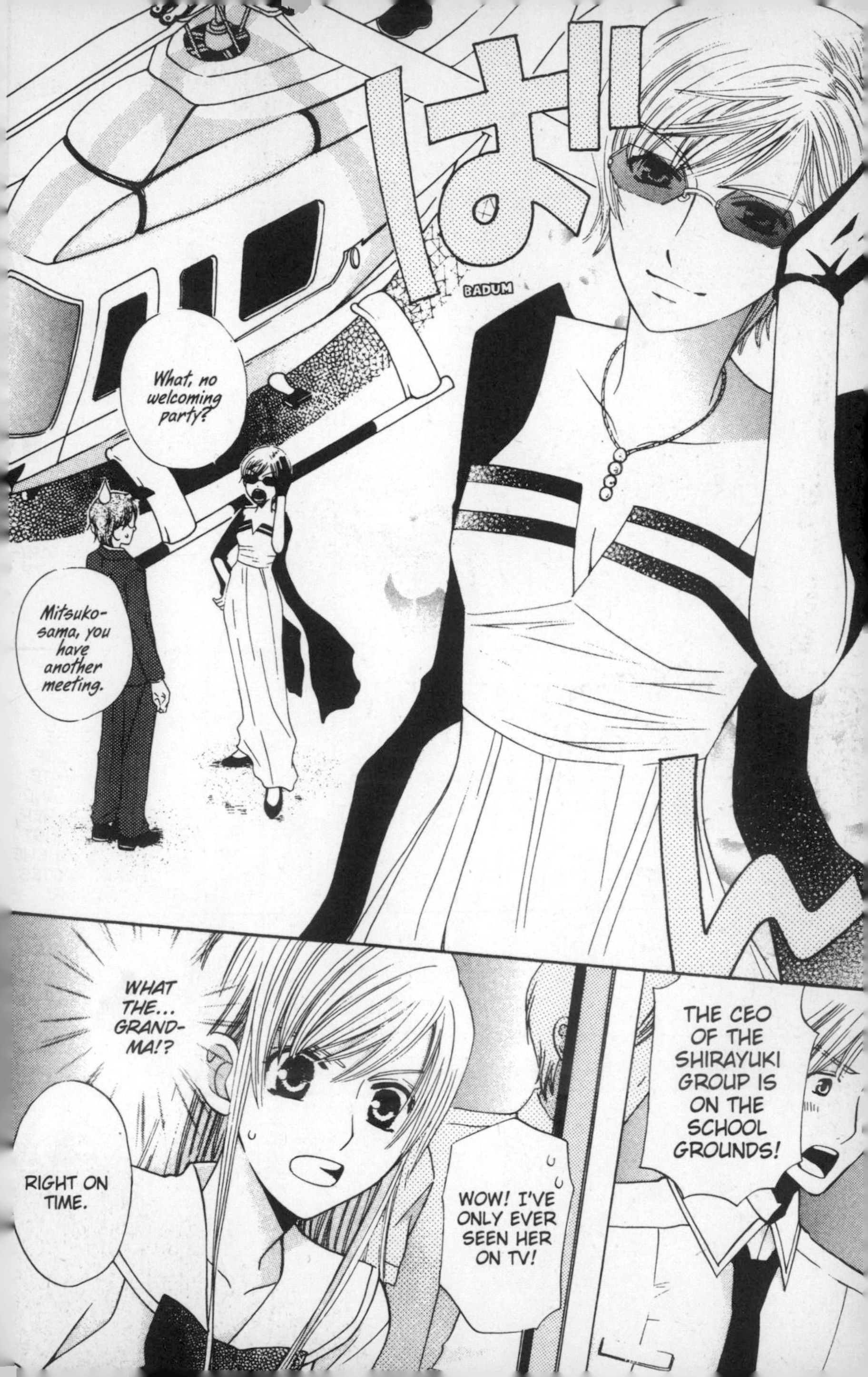
BADUM
What, no welcoming party?
Mitsuko-sama, you have another meeting.
THE CEO OF THE SHIRAYUKI GROUP IS ON THE SCHOOL GROUNDS!
WOW! I'VE ONLY EVER SEEN HER ON TV!
WHAT THE... GRAND-MA!?
RIGHT ON TIME.

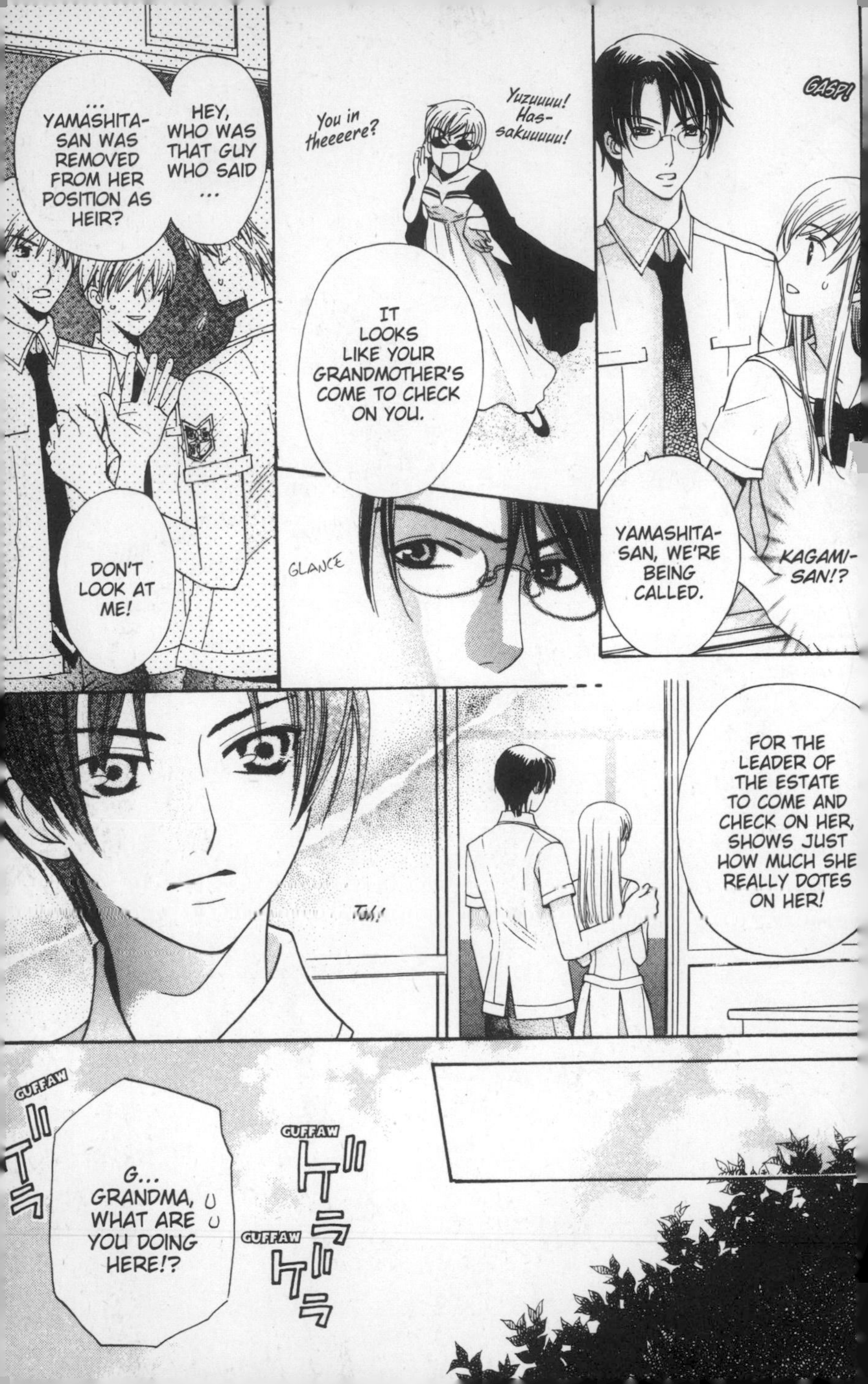

GASP!
YAMASHITA-SAN, WE'RE BEING CALLED.
KAGAMI-SAN!?
Yuzuuuu! Has-sakuuuuu!
You in theeeere?
IT LOOKS LIKE YOUR GRANDMOTHER'S COME TO CHECK ON YOU.
GLANCE
HEY, WHO WAS THAT GUY WHO SAID ...
... YAMASHITA-SAN WAS REMOVED FROM HER POSITION AS HEIR?
DON'T LOOK AT ME!
FOR THE LEADER OF THE ESTATE TO COME AND CHECK ON HER, SHOWS JUST HOW MUCH SHE REALLY DOTES ON HER!
TUG!
GUFFAW
GUFFAW
GUFFAW
G... GRANDMA, WHAT ARE YOU DOING HERE!?

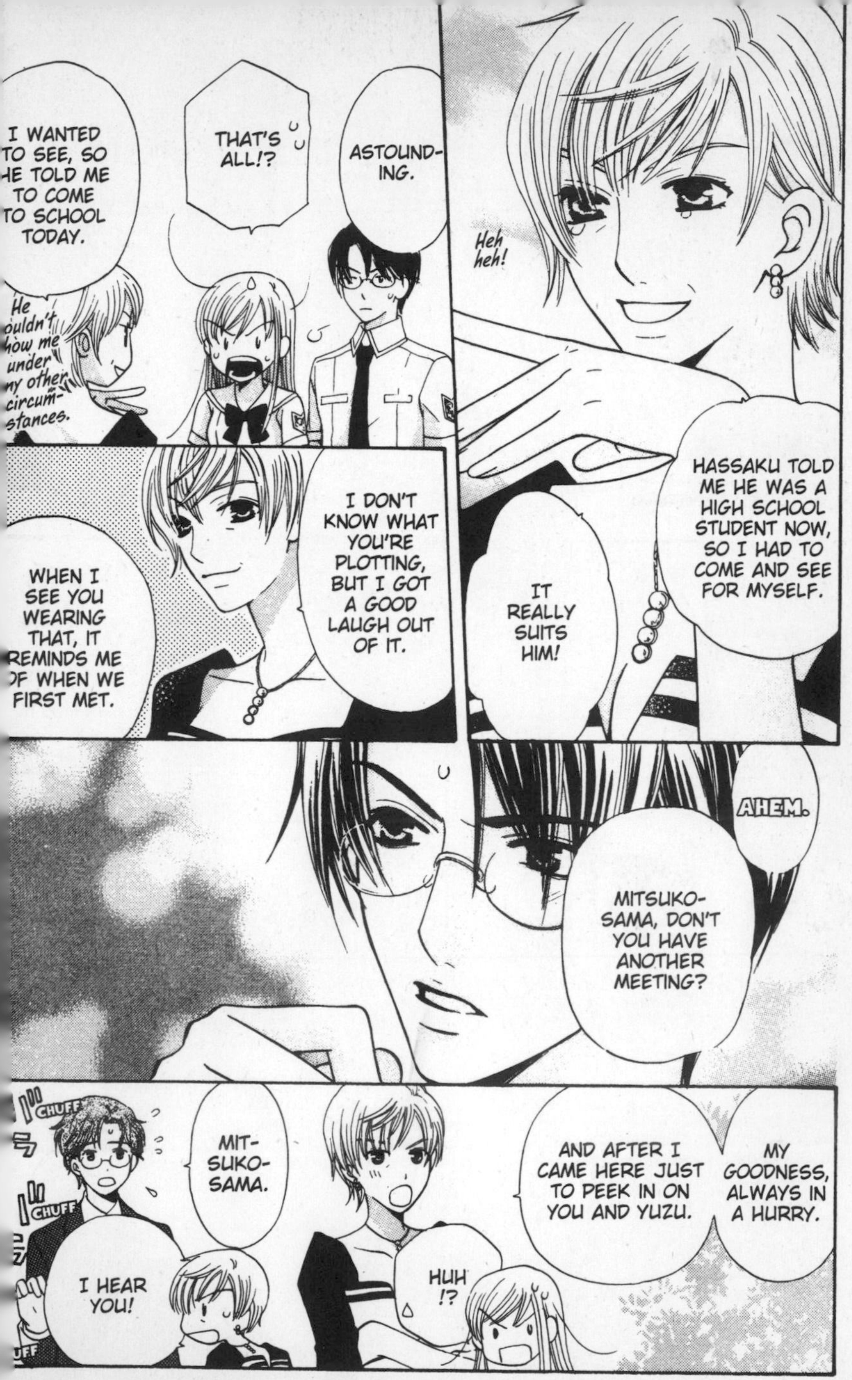
Heh heh!
HASSAKU TOLD ME HE WAS A HIGH SCHOOL STUDENT NOW, SO I HAD TO COME AND SEE FOR MYSELF.
IT REALLY SUITS HIM!
ASTOUND-ING.
THAT'S ALL!?
I WANTED TO SEE, SO HE TOLD ME TO COME TO SCHOOL TODAY.
He ouldn't how me under ny other circum-stances.
I DON'T KNOW WHAT YOU'RE PLOTTING, BUT I GOT A GOOD LAUGH OUT OF IT.
WHEN I SEE YOU WEARING THAT, IT REMINDS ME OF WHEN WE FIRST MET.
AHEM.
MITSUKO-SAMA, DON'T YOU HAVE ANOTHER MEETING?
MY GOODNESS, ALWAYS IN A HURRY.
AND AFTER I CAME HERE JUST TO PEEK IN ON YOU AND YUZU.
MIT-SUKO-SAMA.
HUH!?
I HEAR YOU!
CHUFF
CHUFF

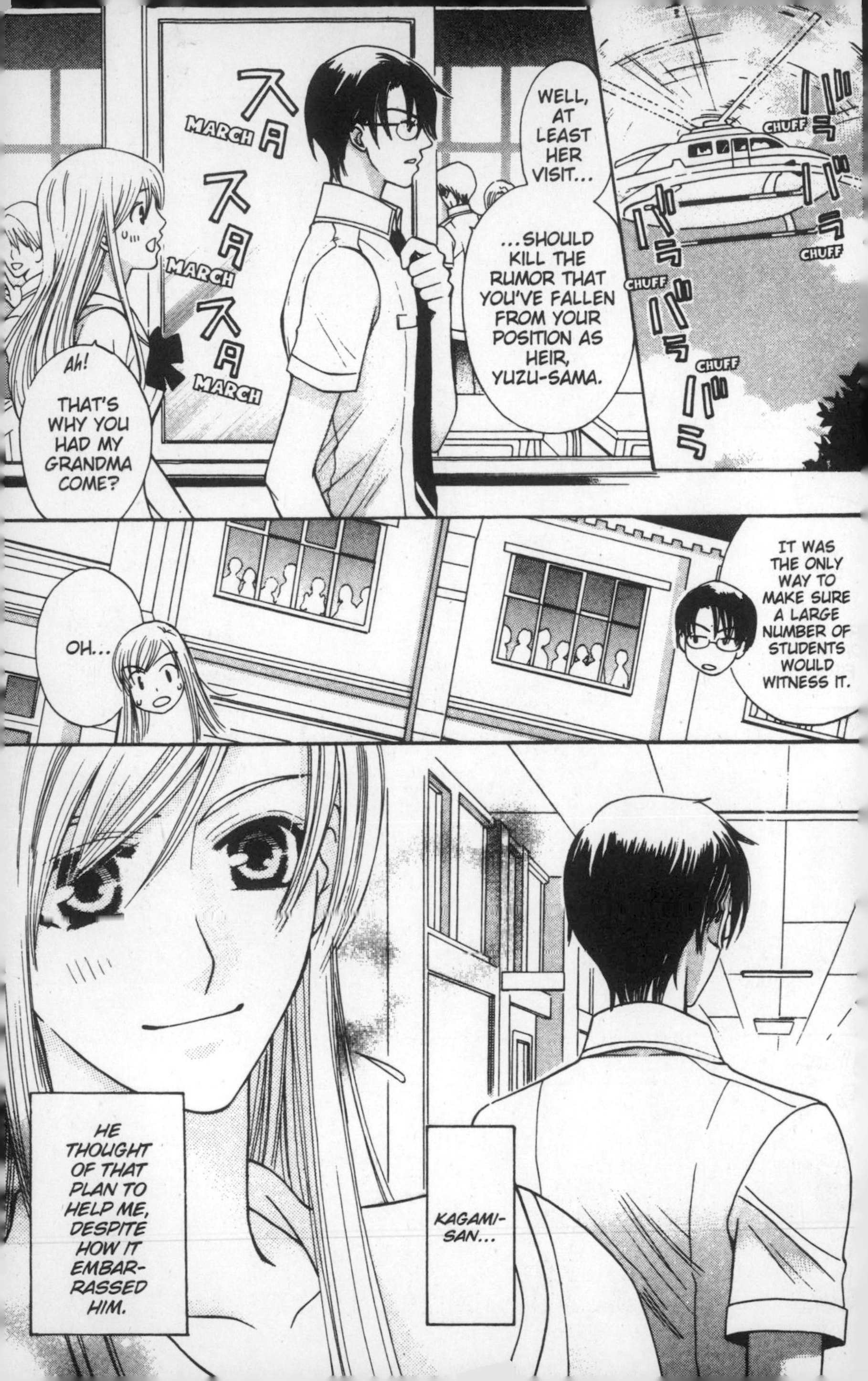
CHUFF
CHUFF
CHUFF
CHUFF
WELL, AT LEAST HER VISIT...
...SHOULD KILL THE RUMOR THAT YOU'VE FALLEN FROM YOUR POSITION AS HEIR, YUZU-SAMA.
MARCH
MARCH
MARCH
Ah!
THAT'S WHY YOU HAD MY GRANDMA COME?
IT WAS THE ONLY WAY TO MAKE SURE A LARGE NUMBER OF STUDENTS WOULD WITNESS IT.
OH...
KAGAMI-SAN...
HE THOUGHT OF THAT PLAN TO HELP ME, DESPITE HOW IT EMBARRASSED HIM.

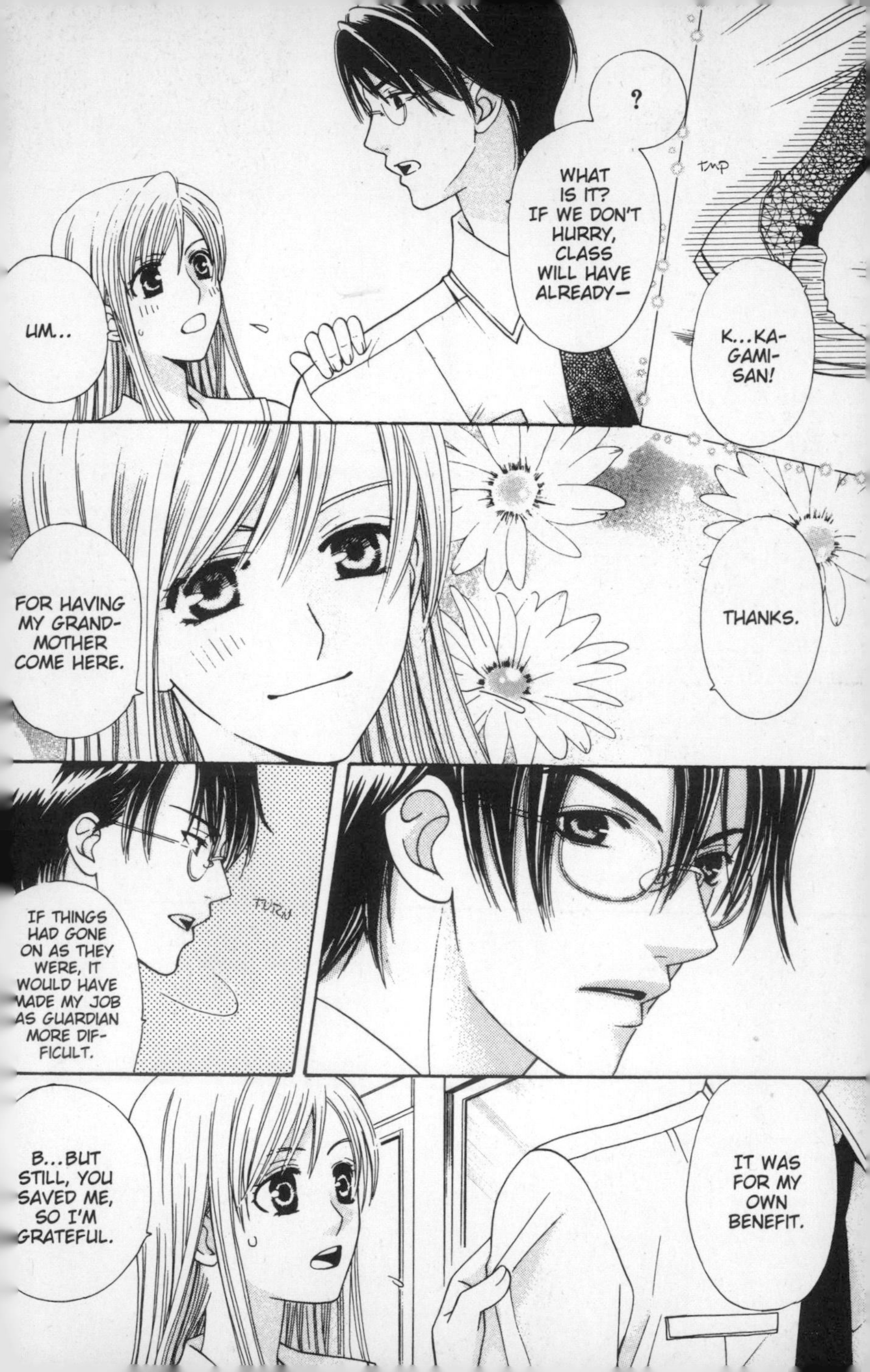
tmp
K...KA-GAMI-SAN!
?
WHAT IS IT? IF WE DON'T HURRY, CLASS WILL HAVE ALREADY—
UM...
THANKS.
FOR HAVING MY GRAND-MOTHER COME HERE.
TURN
IF THINGS HAD GONE ON AS THEY WERE, IT WOULD HAVE MADE MY JOB AS GUARDIAN MORE DIF-FICULT.
IT WAS FOR MY OWN BENEFIT.
B...BUT STILL, YOU SAVED ME, SO I'M GRATEFUL.

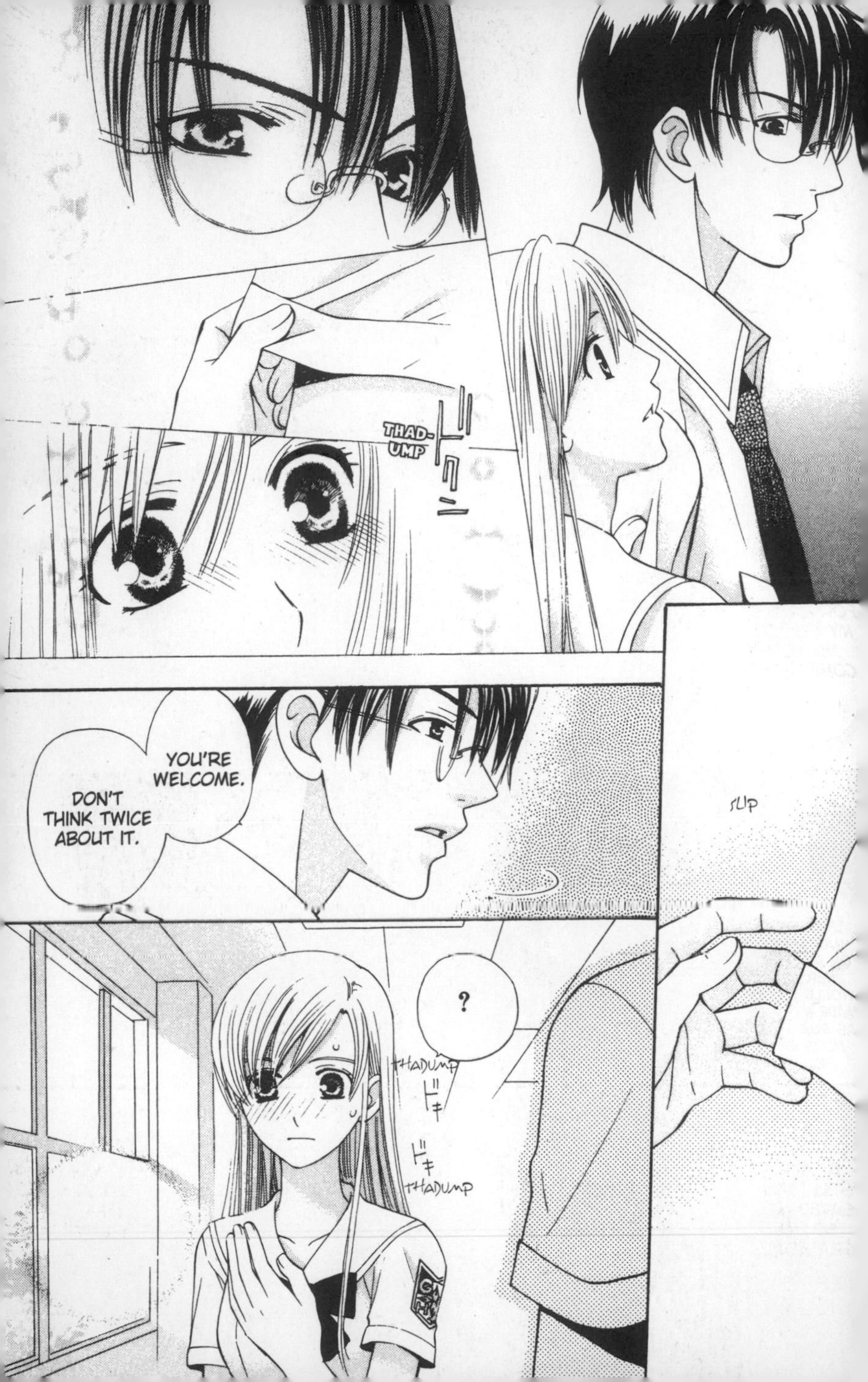
THAD-UMP
ドクン
SLIP
YOU'RE WELCOME.
DON'T THINK TWICE ABOUT IT.
?
THADUMP
ドキ
ドキ
THADUMP

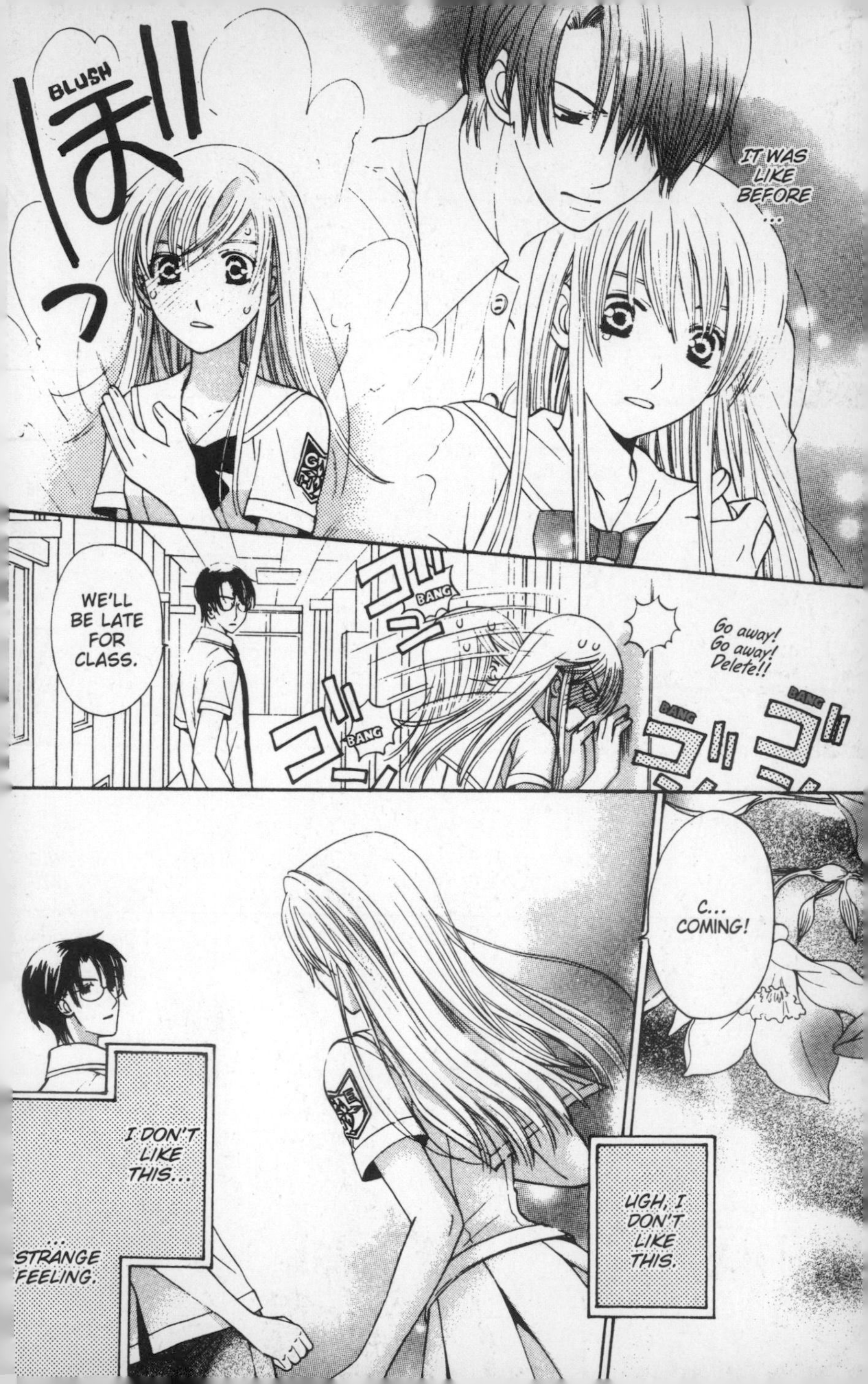
IT WAS LIKE BEFORE...
BLUSH
ぼっ
Go away! Go away! Delete!!
BANG
BANG
BANG
BANG
WE'LL BE LATE FOR CLASS.
C... COMING!
UGH, I DON'T LIKE THIS.
I DON'T LIKE THIS...
...STRANGE FEELING.

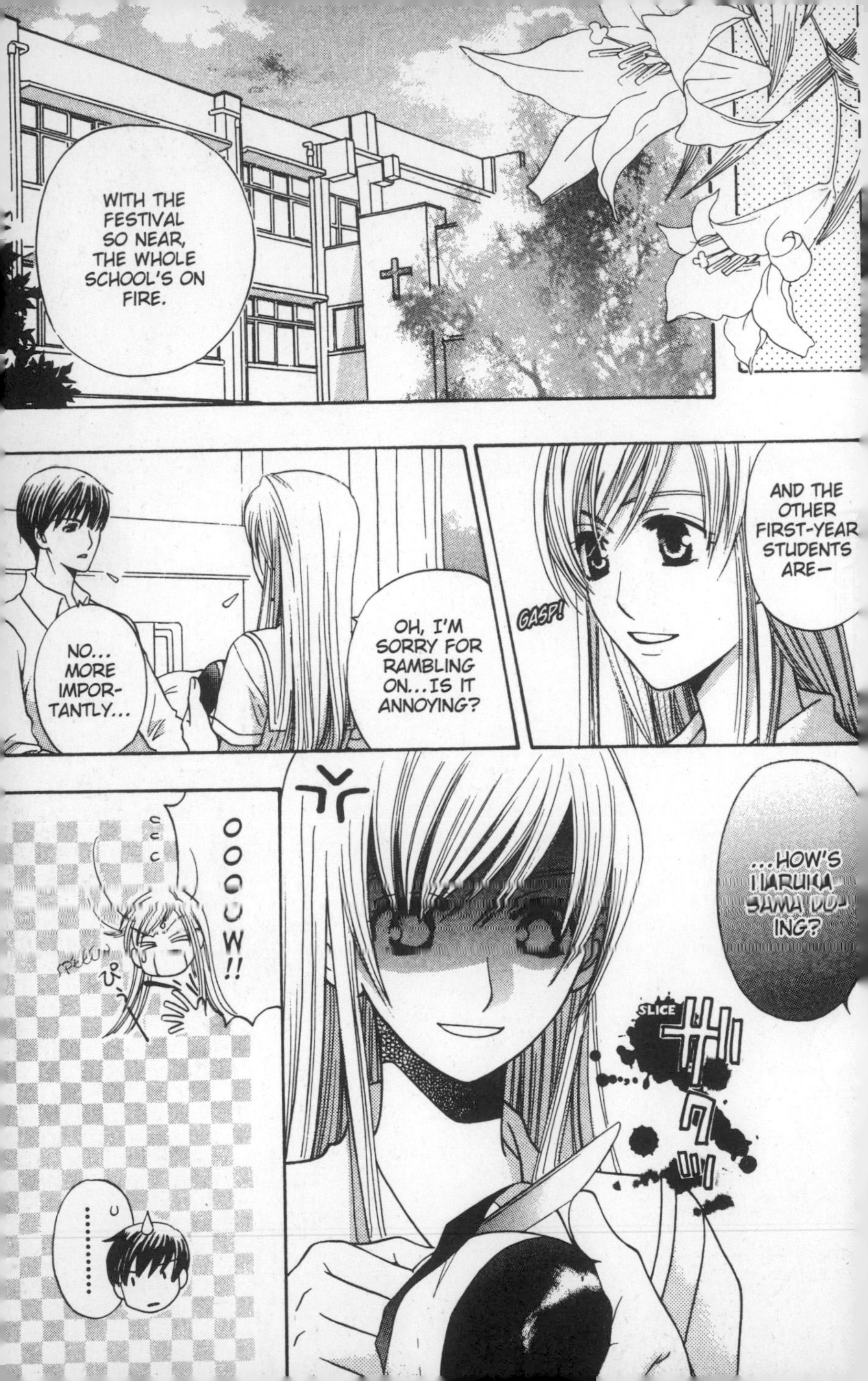
WITH THE FESTIVAL SO NEAR, THE WHOLE SCHOOL'S ON FIRE.
AND THE OTHER FIRST-YEAR STUDENTS ARE—
GASP!
OH, I'M SORRY FOR RAMBLING ON...IS IT ANNOYING?
NO... MORE IMPORTANTLY...
...HOW'S HARUKA-SAMA DOING?
SLICE
OOOOUW!!
......

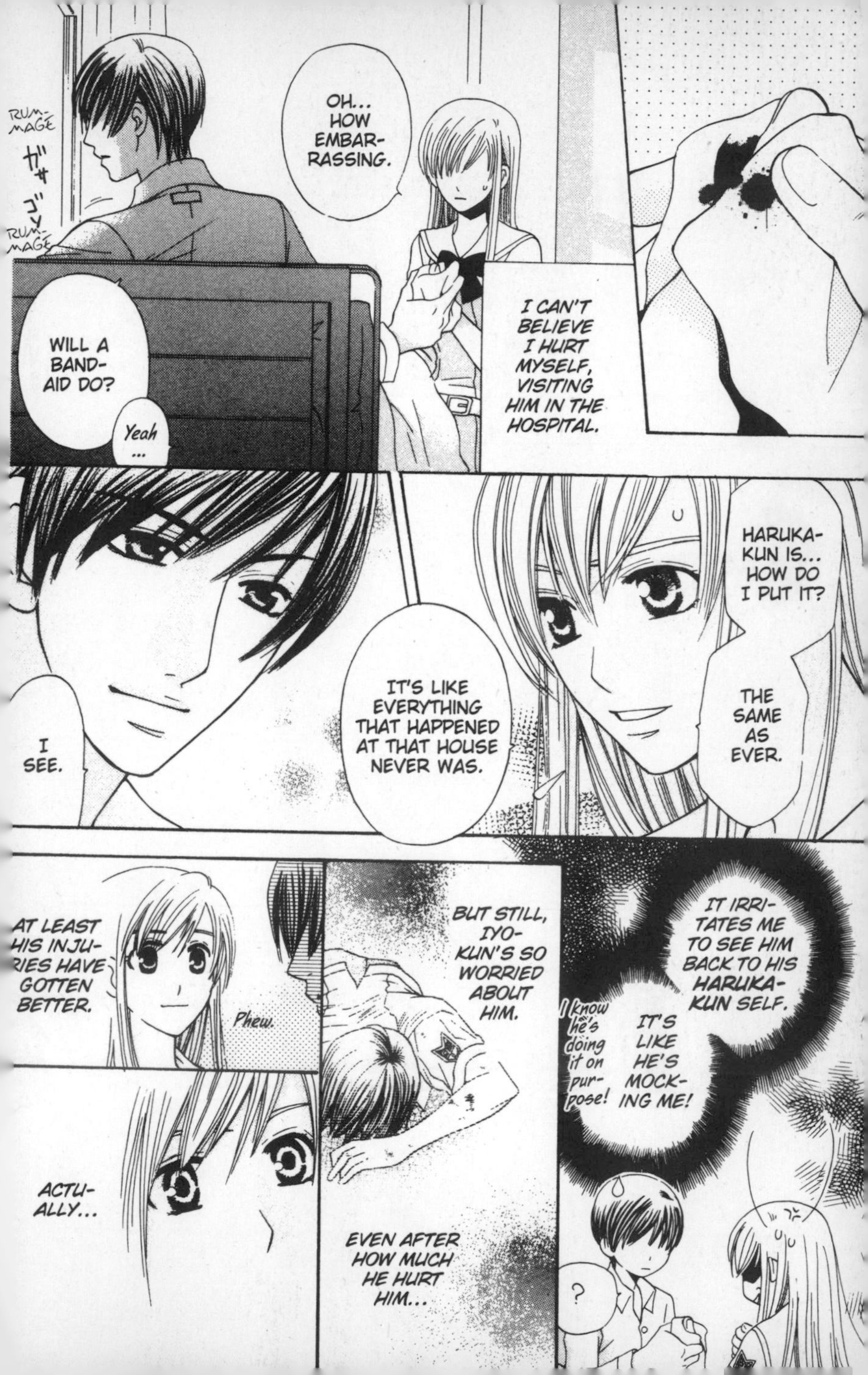
OH... HOW EMBARRASSING.
RUMMAGE
RUMMAGE
I CAN'T BELIEVE I HURT MYSELF, VISITING HIM IN THE HOSPITAL.
WILL A BAND-AID DO?
Yeah ...
HARUKA-KUN IS... HOW DO I PUT IT?
THE SAME AS EVER.
IT'S LIKE EVERYTHING THAT HAPPENED AT THAT HOUSE NEVER WAS.
I SEE.
IT IRRITATES ME TO SEE HIM BACK TO HIS HARUKA-KUN SELF.
IT'S LIKE HE'S MOCKING ME!
I know he's doing it on purpose!
?
BUT STILL, IYO-KUN'S SO WORRIED ABOUT HIM.
EVEN AFTER HOW MUCH HE HURT HIM...
AT LEAST HIS INJURIES HAVE GOTTEN BETTER.
Phew.
ACTUALLY...

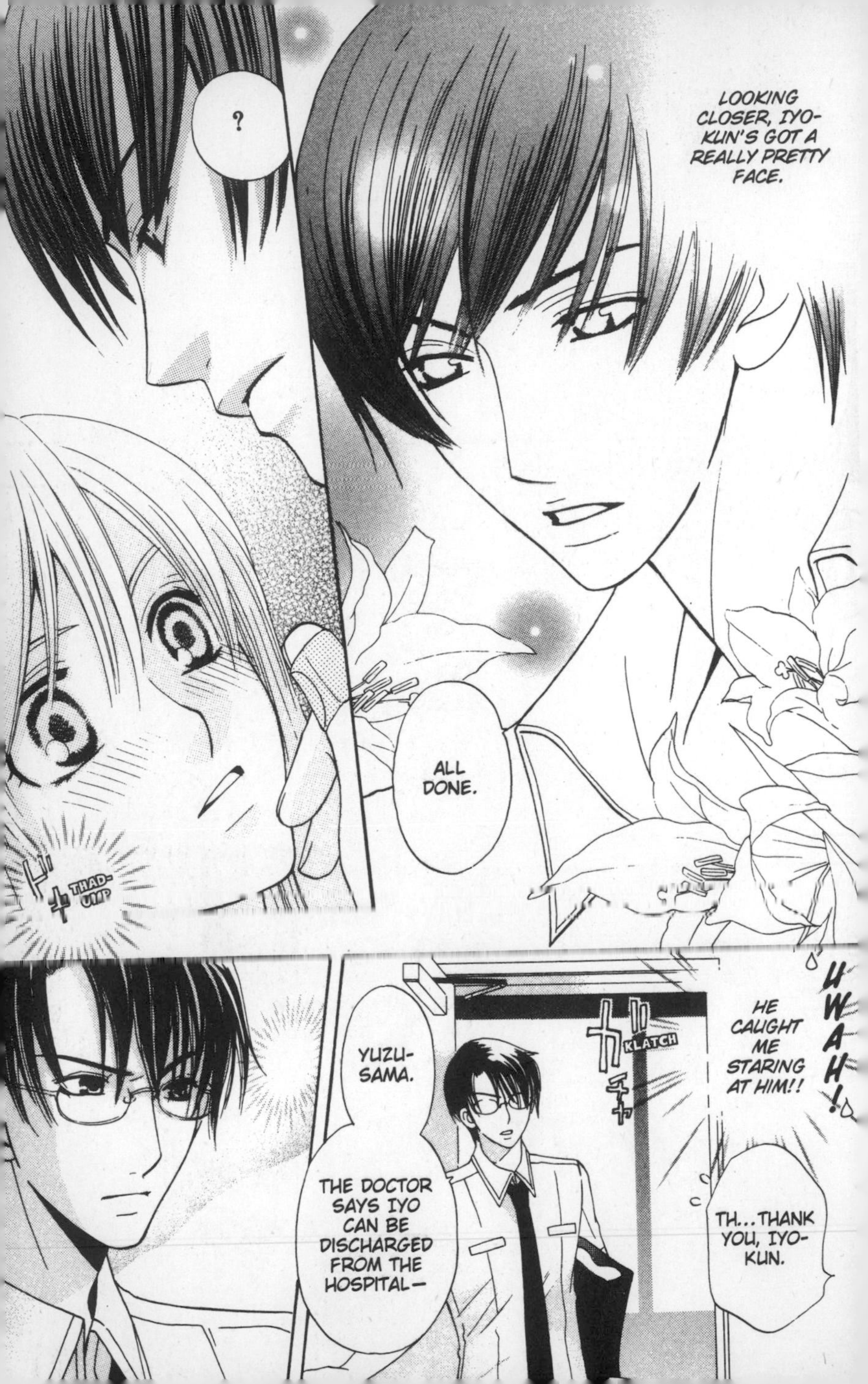
LOOKING CLOSER, IYO-KUN'S GOT A REALLY PRETTY FACE.
?
ALL DONE.
THAD-UMP
UWAH!
HE CAUGHT ME STARING AT HIM!!
TH...THANK YOU, IYO-KUN.
KLATCH
YUZU-SAMA.
THE DOCTOR SAYS IYO CAN BE DISCHARGED FROM THE HOSPITAL—

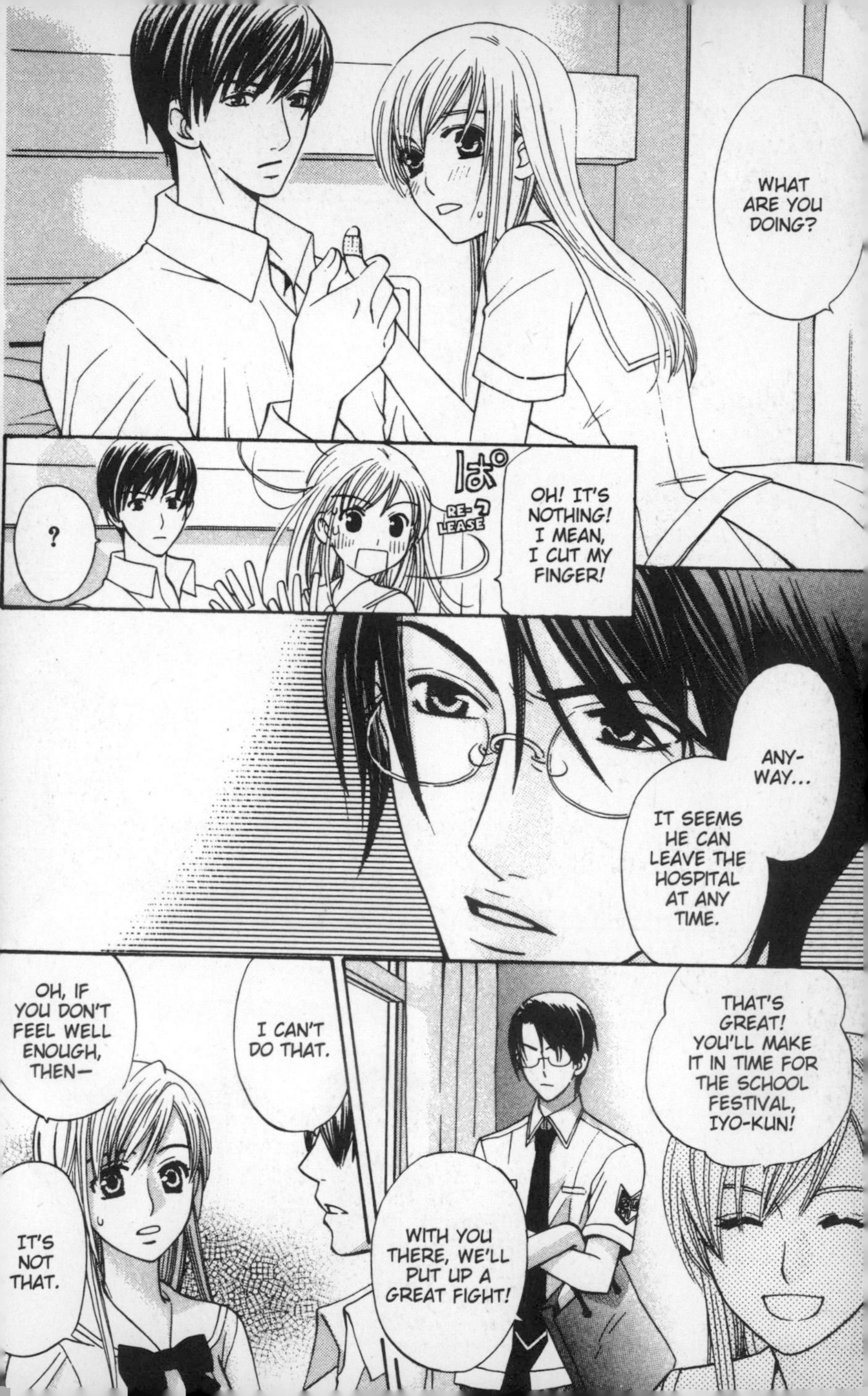
WHAT ARE YOU DOING?
ぱ
RE-LEASE
OH! IT'S NOTHING! I MEAN, I CUT MY FINGER!
?
ANY-WAY...
IT SEEMS HE CAN LEAVE THE HOSPITAL AT ANY TIME.
THAT'S GREAT! YOU'LL MAKE IT IN TIME FOR THE SCHOOL FESTIVAL, IYO-KUN!
WITH YOU THERE, WE'LL PUT UP A GREAT FIGHT!
I CAN'T DO THAT.
OH, IF YOU DON'T FEEL WELL ENOUGH, THEN—
IT'S NOT THAT.

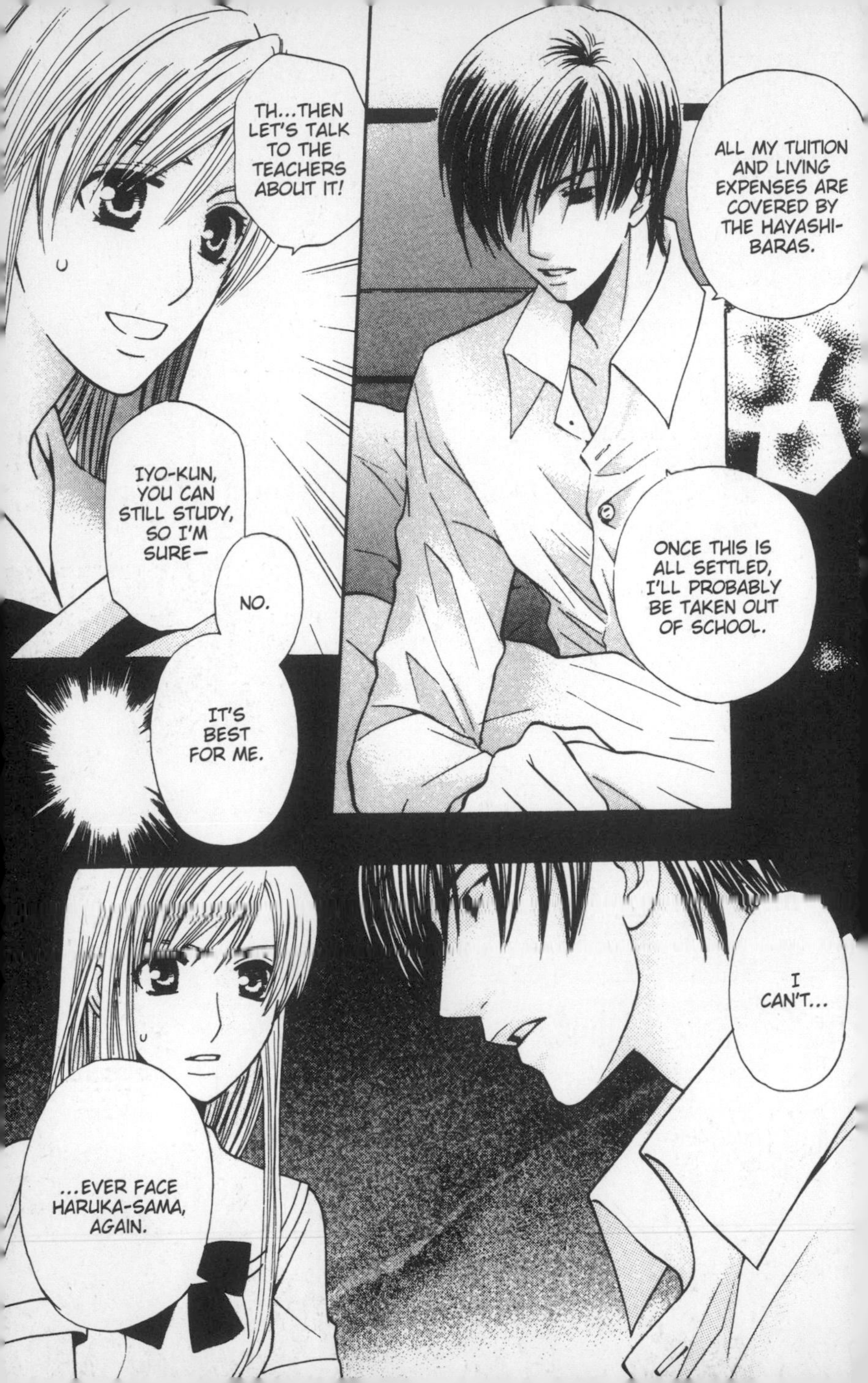
ALL MY TUITION AND LIVING EXPENSES ARE COVERED BY THE HAYASHI-BARAS.
ONCE THIS IS ALL SETTLED, I'LL PROBABLY BE TAKEN OUT OF SCHOOL.
TH...THEN LET'S TALK TO THE TEACHERS ABOUT IT!
IYO-KUN, YOU CAN STILL STUDY, SO I'M SURE—
NO.
IT'S BEST FOR ME.
I CAN'T...
...EVER FACE HARUKA-SAMA, AGAIN.

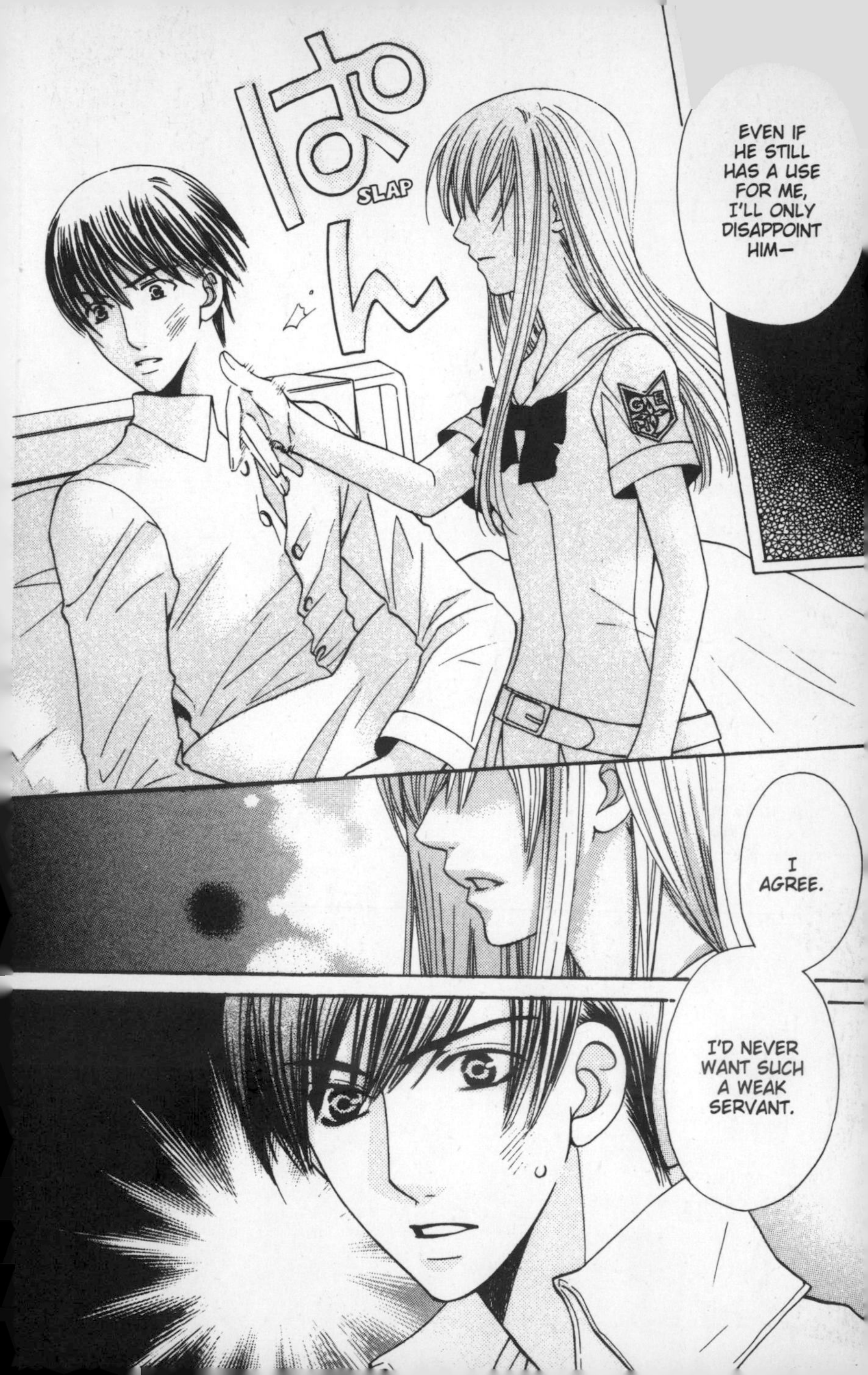
EVEN IF HE STILL HAS A USE FOR ME, I'LL ONLY DISAPPOINT HIM—
ぱぁん
SLAP
I AGREE.
I'D NEVER WANT SUCH A WEAK SERVANT.

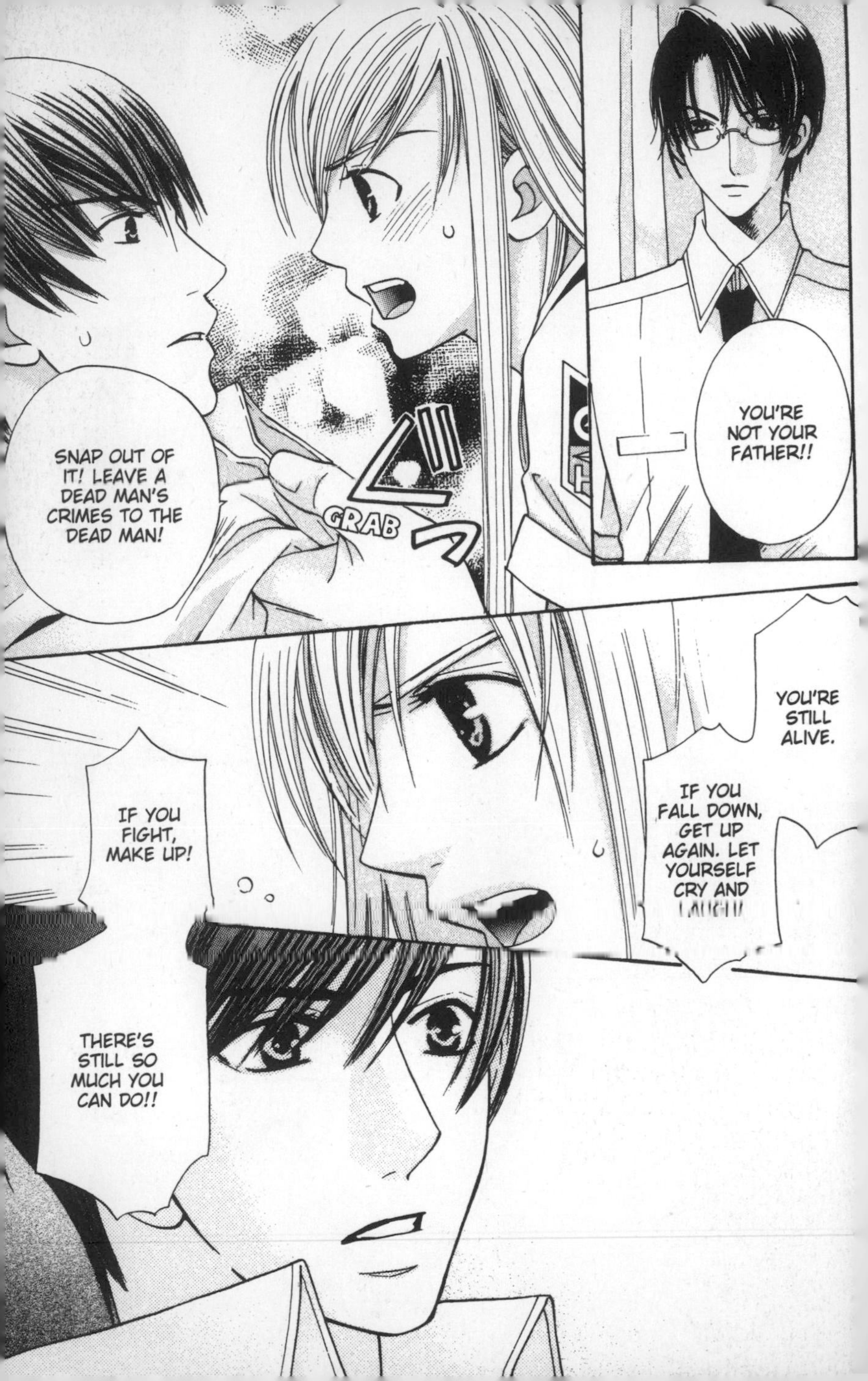
YOU'RE NOT YOUR FATHER!!
SNAP OUT OF IT! LEAVE A DEAD MAN'S CRIMES TO THE DEAD MAN!
GRAB
YOU'RE STILL ALIVE.
IF YOU FALL DOWN, GET UP AGAIN. LET YOURSELF CRY AND
IF YOU FIGHT, MAKE UP!
THERE'S STILL SO MUCH YOU CAN DO!!

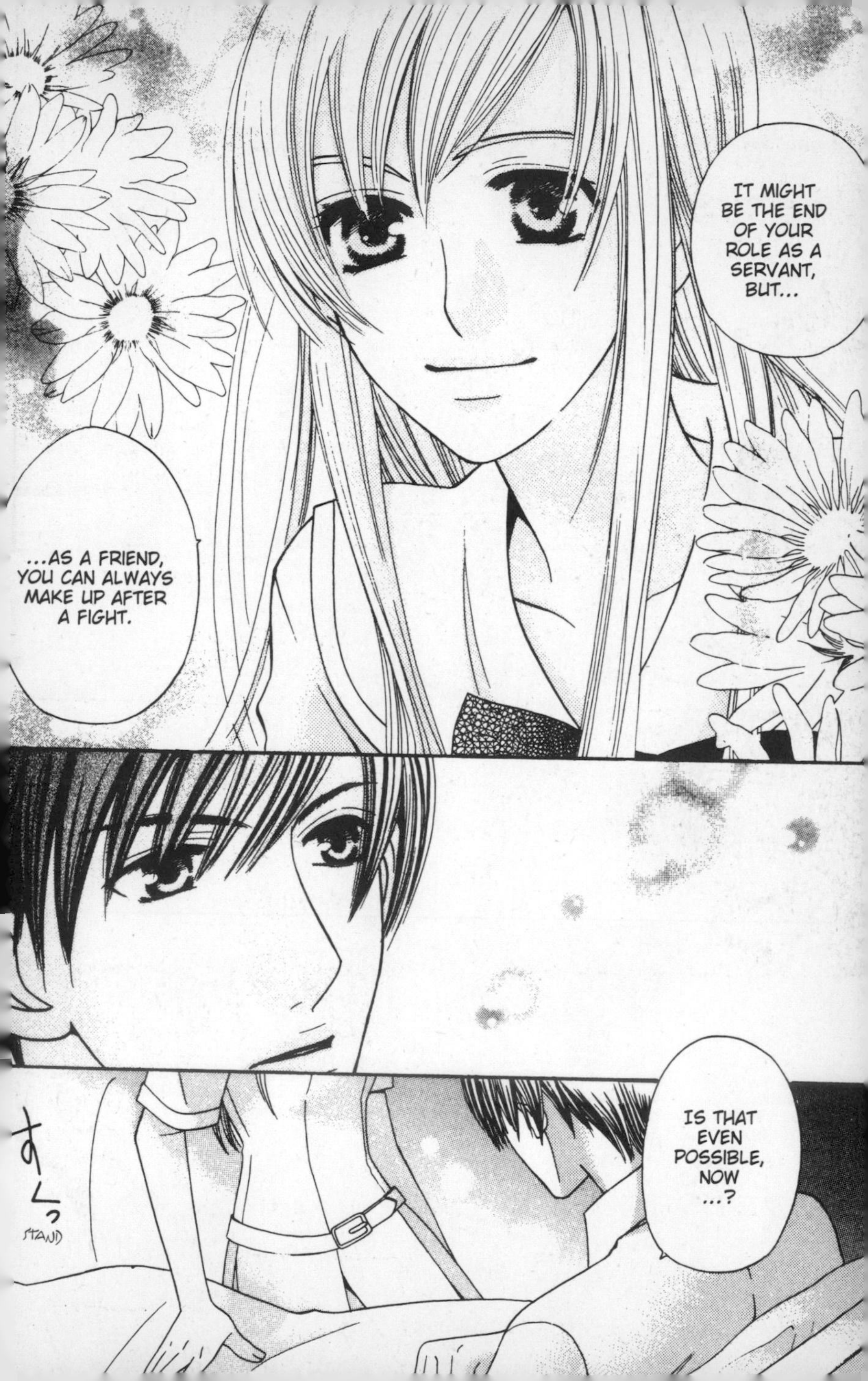
IT MIGHT BE THE END OF YOUR ROLE AS A SERVANT, BUT...
...AS A FRIEND, YOU CAN ALWAYS MAKE UP AFTER A FIGHT.
IS THAT EVEN POSSIBLE, NOW ...?
すくっ
STAND

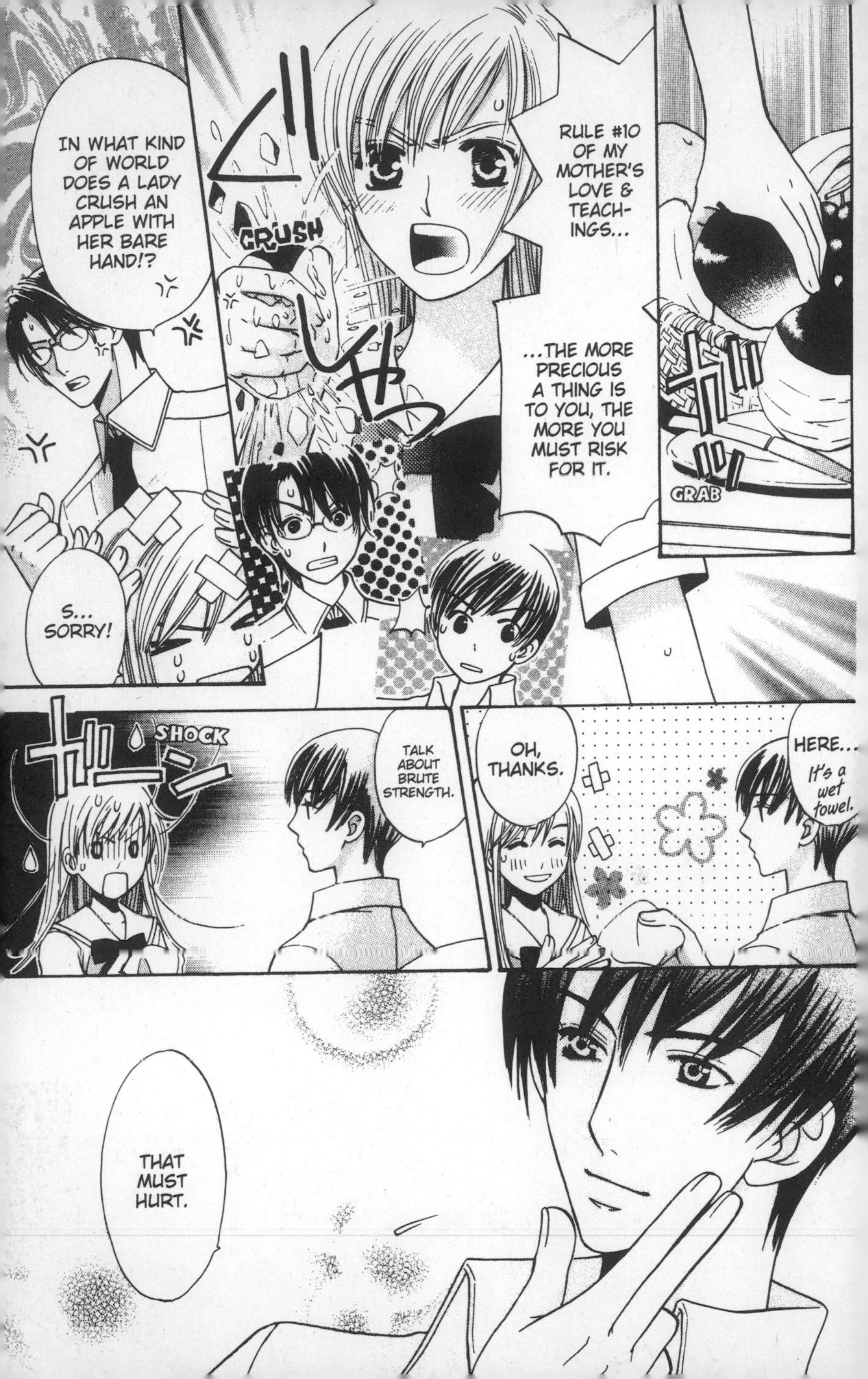
GRAB
RULE #10 OF MY MOTHER'S LOVE & TEACHINGS...
CRUSH
...THE MORE PRECIOUS A THING IS TO YOU, THE MORE YOU MUST RISK FOR IT.
IN WHAT KIND OF WORLD DOES A LADY CRUSH AN APPLE WITH HER BARE HAND!?
S... SORRY!
HERE... It's a wet towel.
OH, THANKS.
TALK ABOUT BRUTE STRENGTH.
SHOCK
THAT MUST HURT.

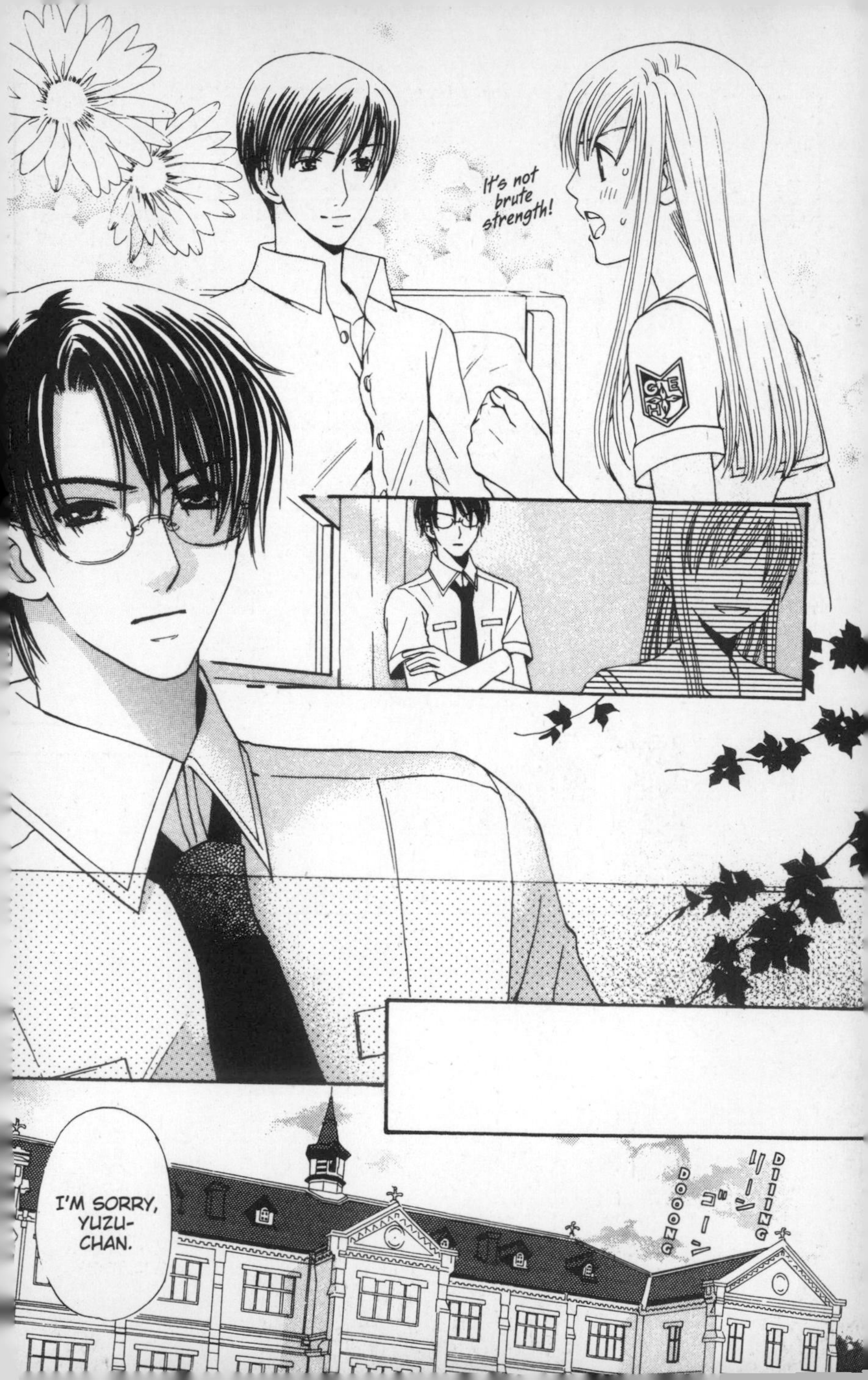
It's not brute strength!
DIIIING
リーン
ゴーン
DOOONG
I'M SORRY, YUZU-CHAN.

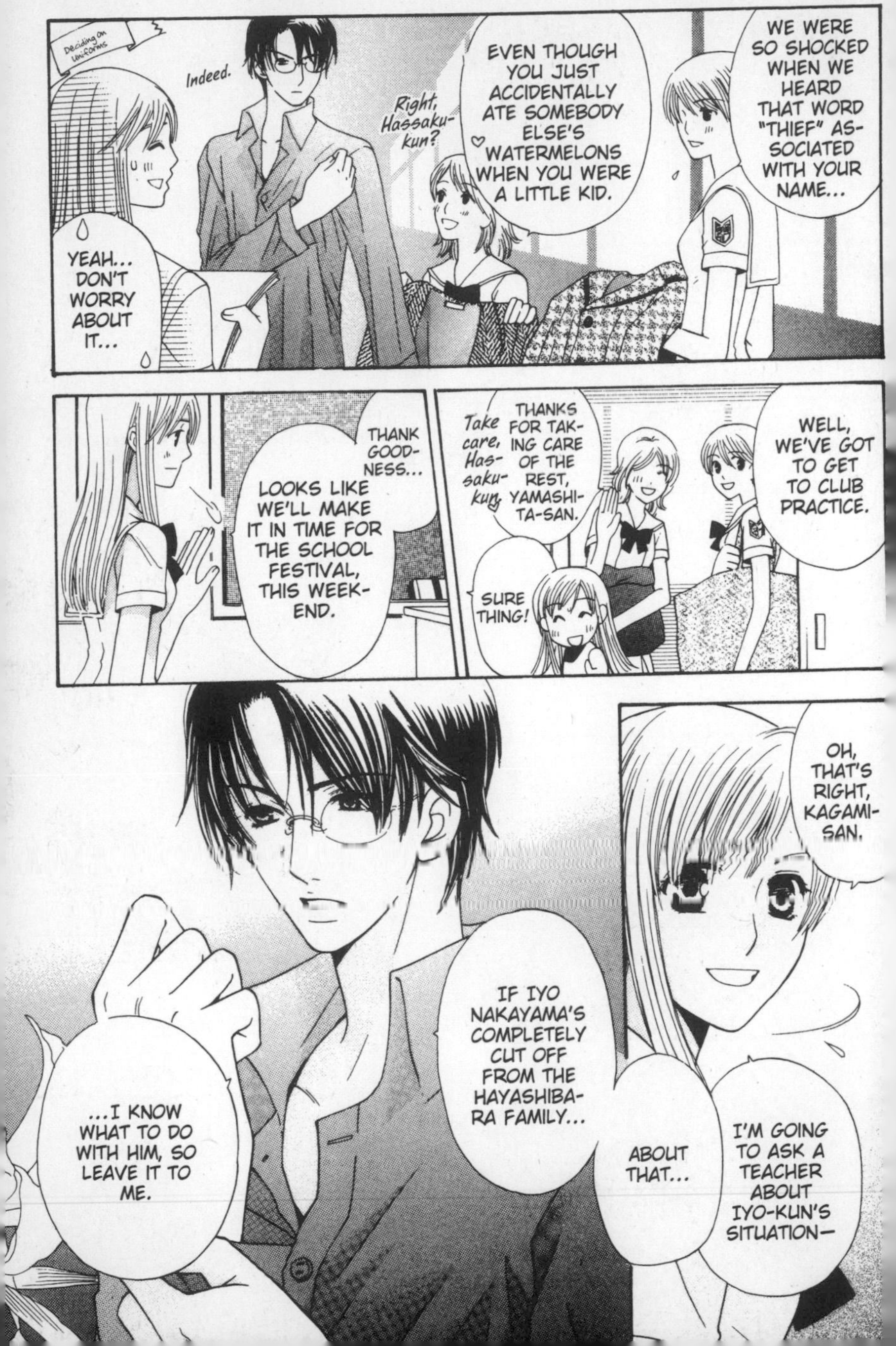
WE WERE SO SHOCKED WHEN WE HEARD THAT WORD "THIEF" ASSOCIATED WITH YOUR NAME...
EVEN THOUGH YOU JUST ACCIDENTALLY ATE SOMEBODY ELSE'S WATERMELONS WHEN YOU WERE A LITTLE KID.
Right, Hassaku-kun?
Indeed.
Deciding on Uniforms
YEAH... DON'T WORRY ABOUT IT...
WELL, WE'VE GOT TO GET TO CLUB PRACTICE.
THANKS FOR TAKING CARE OF THE REST, YAMASHITA-SAN.
Take care, Hassaku-kun
SURE THING!
THANK GOODNESS...
LOOKS LIKE WE'LL MAKE IT IN TIME FOR THE SCHOOL FESTIVAL, THIS WEEKEND.
OH, THAT'S RIGHT, KAGAMI-SAN.
I'M GOING TO ASK A TEACHER ABOUT IYO-KUN'S SITUATION—
ABOUT THAT...
IF IYO NAKAYAMA'S COMPLETELY CUT OFF FROM THE HAYASHIBARA FAMILY...
...I KNOW WHAT TO DO WITH HIM, SO LEAVE IT TO ME.

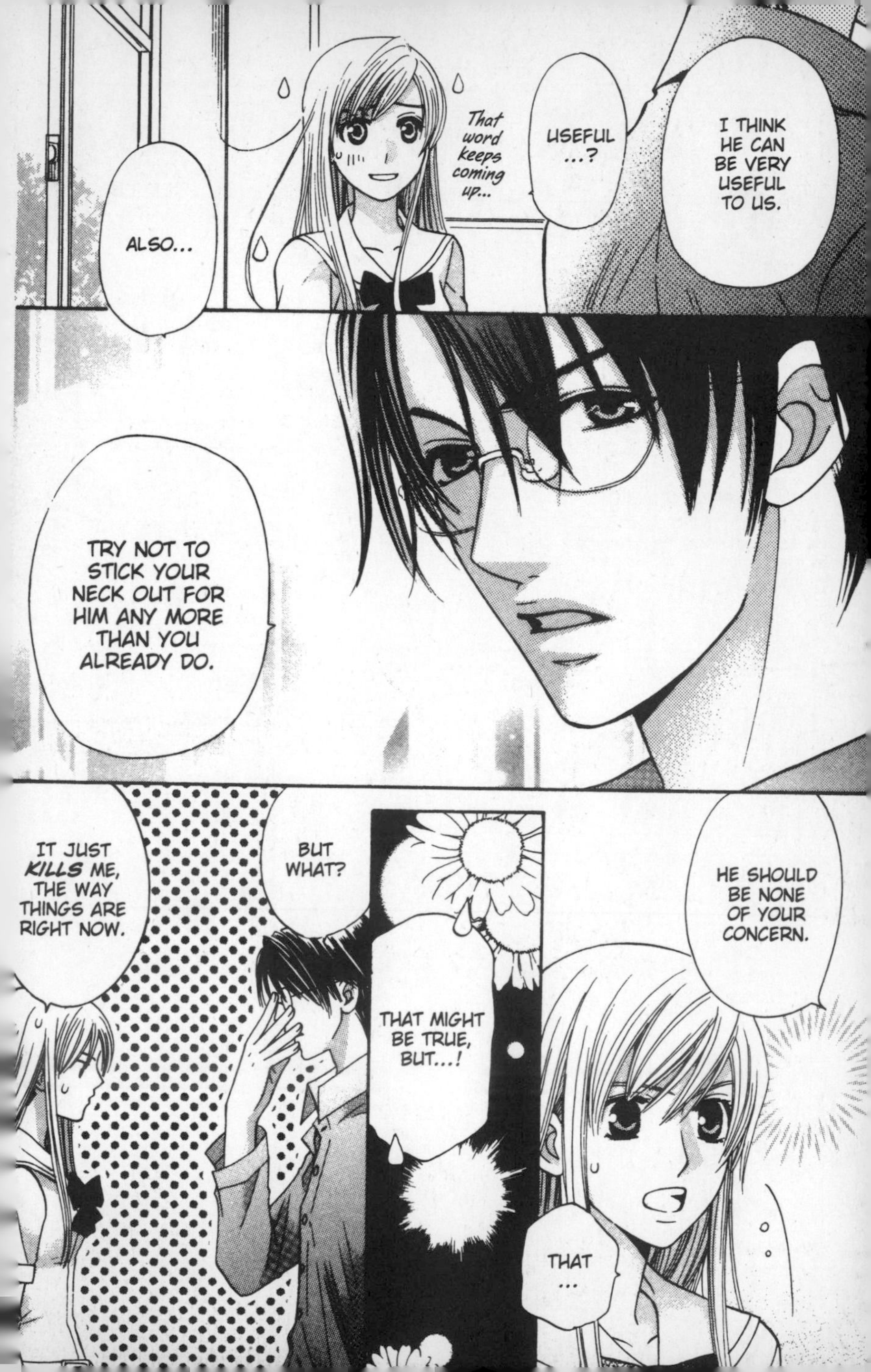
I THINK HE CAN BE VERY USEFUL TO US.
USEFUL ...?
That word keeps coming up...
ALSO...
TRY NOT TO STICK YOUR NECK OUT FOR HIM ANY MORE THAN YOU ALREADY DO.
HE SHOULD BE NONE OF YOUR CONCERN.
THAT ...
THAT MIGHT BE TRUE, BUT...!
BUT WHAT?
IT JUST *KILLS* ME, THE WAY THINGS ARE RIGHT NOW.

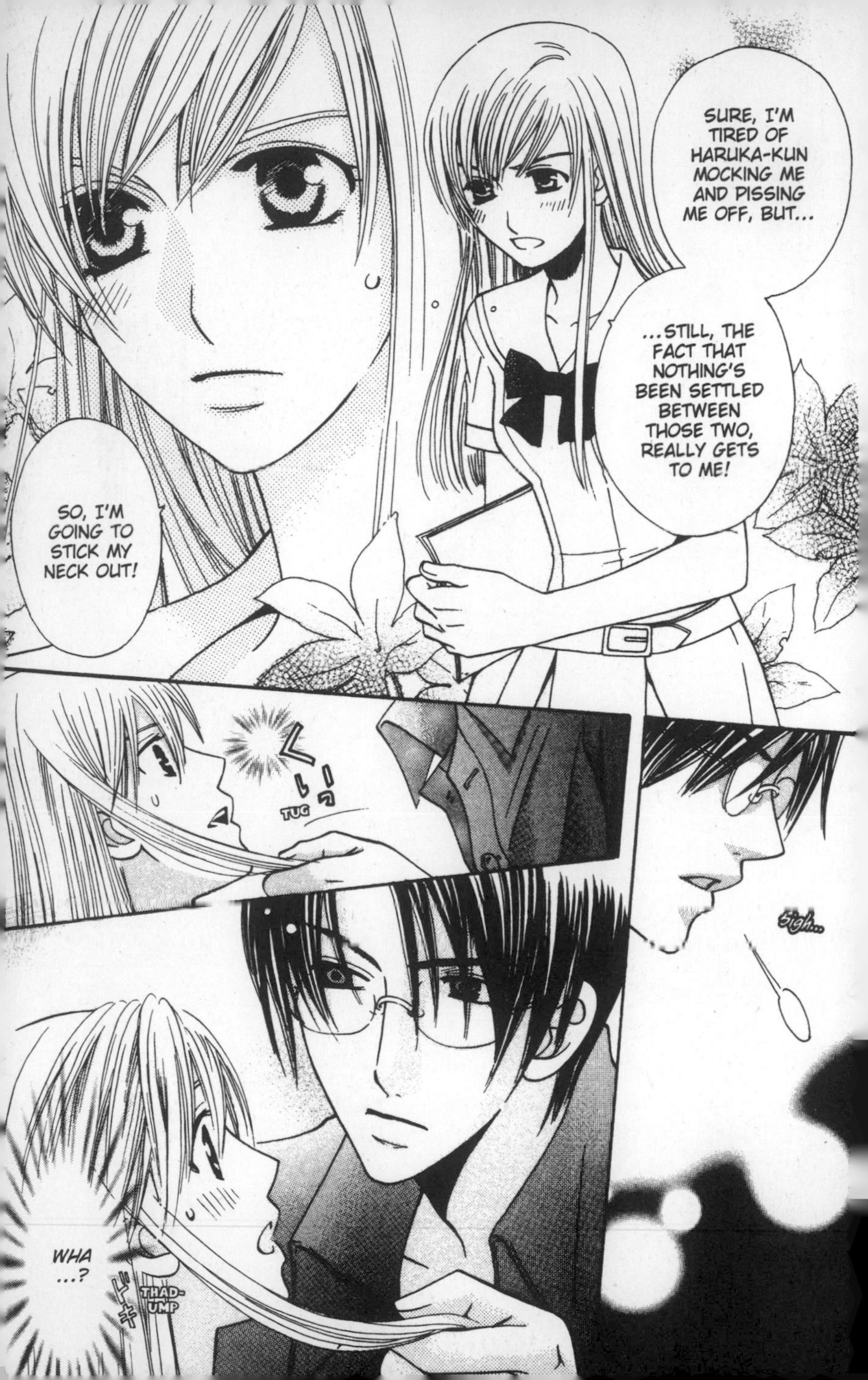
SURE, I'M TIRED OF HARUKA-KUN MOCKING ME AND PISSING ME OFF, BUT...
...STILL, THE FACT THAT NOTHING'S BEEN SETTLED BETWEEN THOSE TWO, REALLY GETS TO ME!
SO, I'M GOING TO STICK MY NECK OUT!
Sigh...
TUG
WHA ...?
THAD-UMP

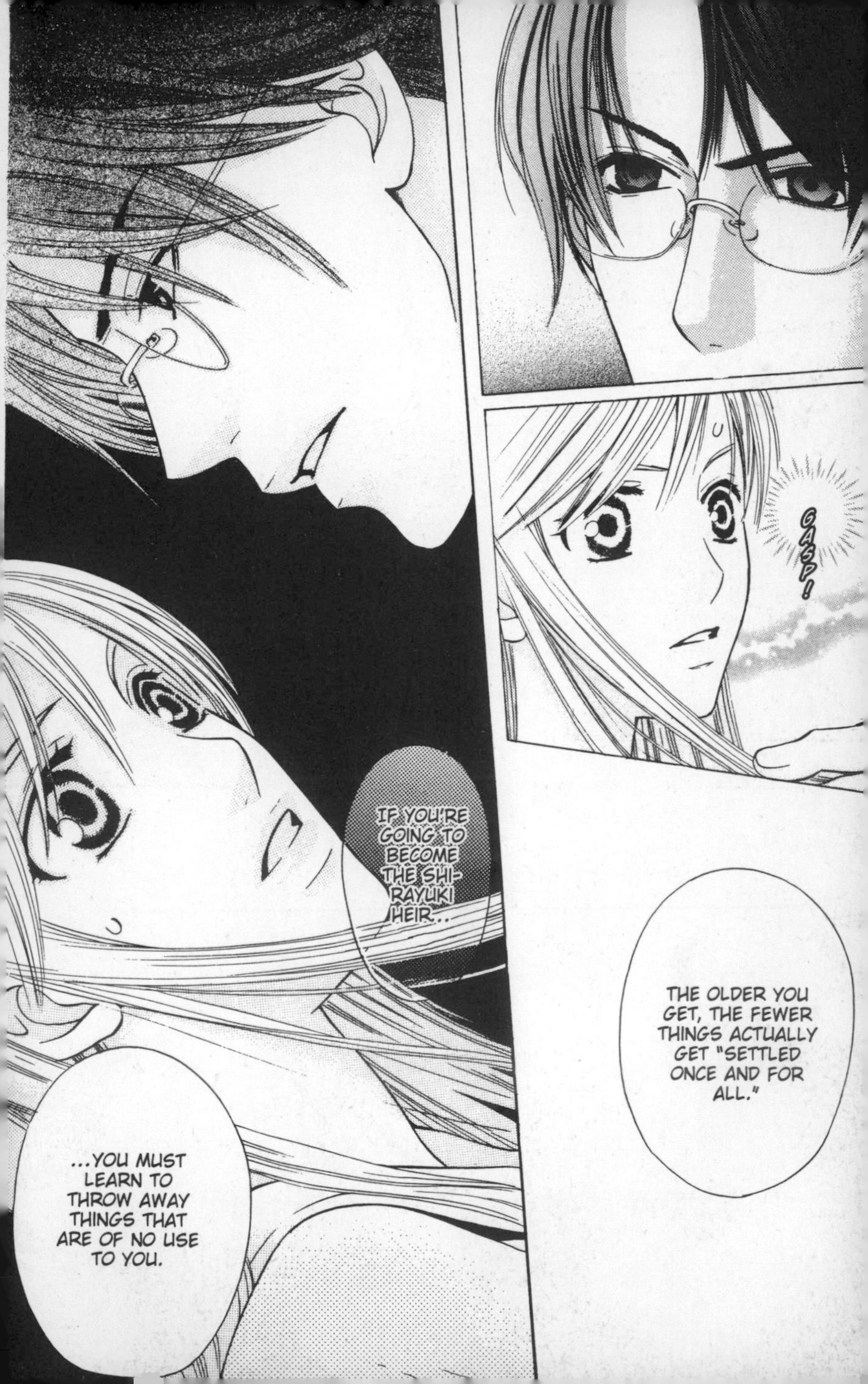
GASP!
THE OLDER YOU GET, THE FEWER THINGS ACTUALLY GET "SETTLED ONCE AND FOR ALL."
IF YOU'RE GOING TO BECOME THE SHI-RAYUKI HEIR...
...YOU MUST LEARN TO THROW AWAY THINGS THAT ARE OF NO USE TO YOU.

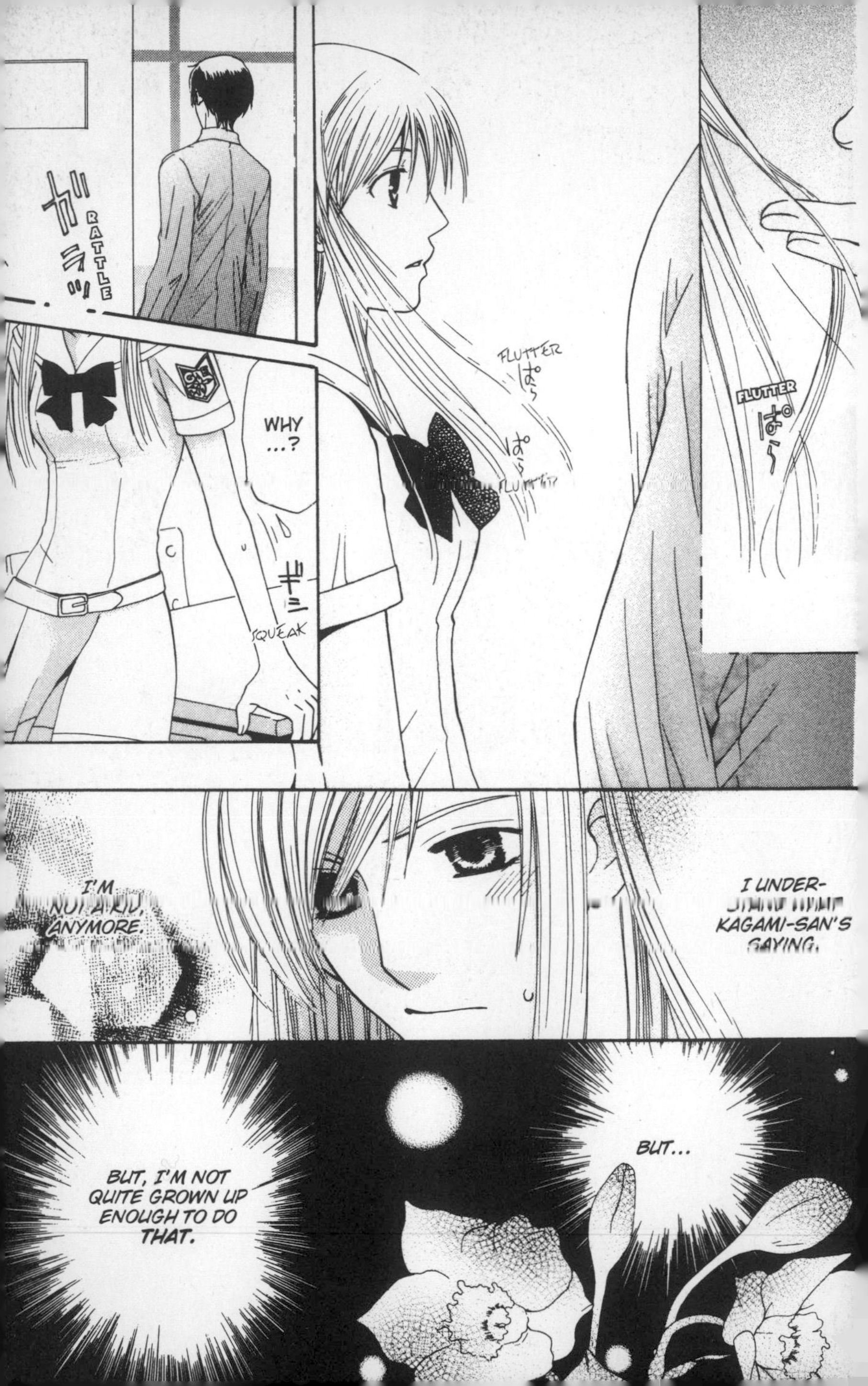
FLUTTER
ぱら
FLUTTER
ぱら
ぱら
FLUTTER
ガラッ
RATTLE
WHY ...?
ギシ
SQUEAK
I UNDER-STAND WHAT KAGAMI-SAN'S SAYING.
I'M NOT A KID, ANYMORE.
BUT...
BUT, I'M NOT QUITE GROWN UP ENOUGH TO DO THAT.

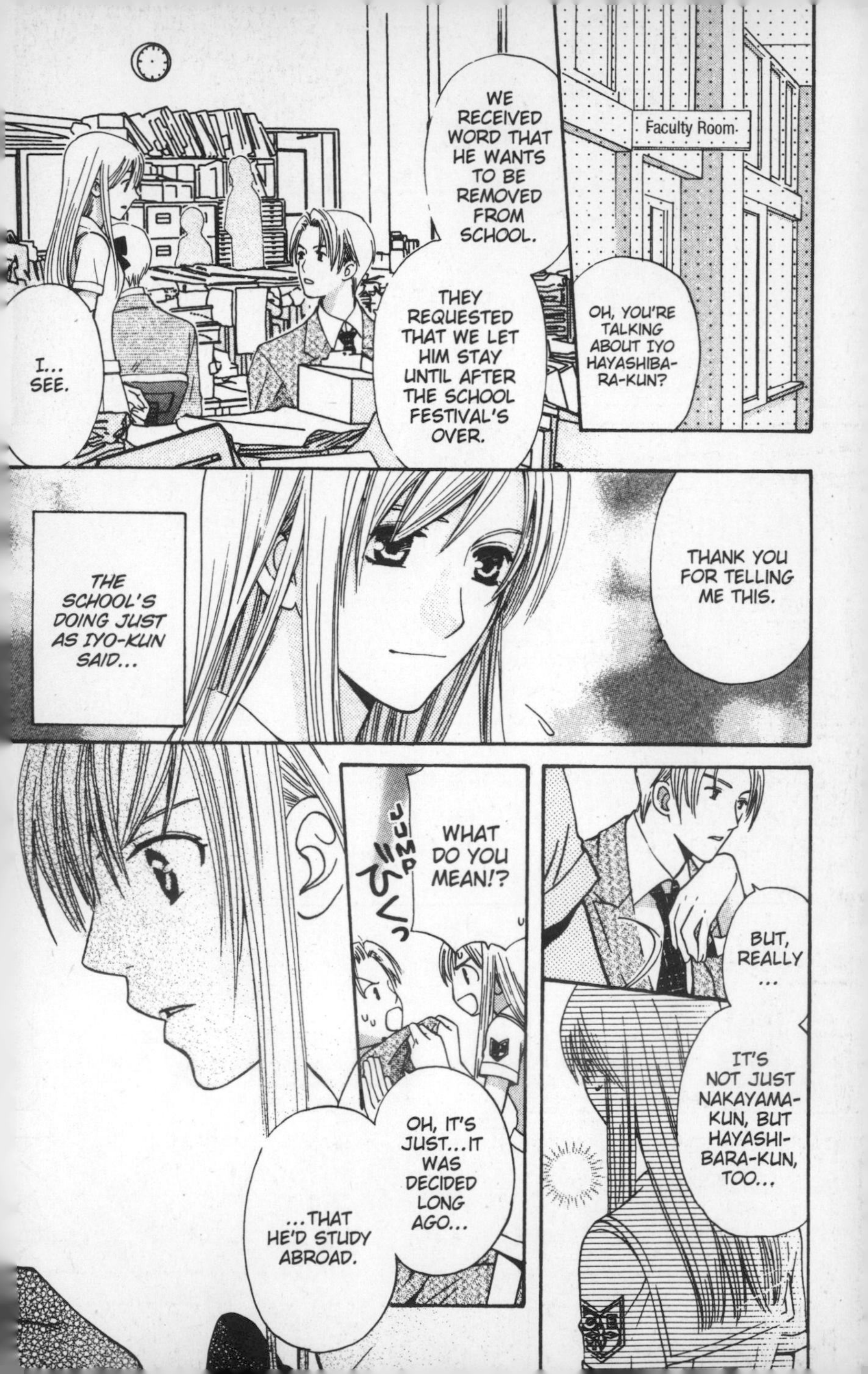
Faculty Room
OH, YOU'RE TALKING ABOUT IYO HAYASHIBARA-KUN?
WE RECEIVED WORD THAT HE WANTS TO BE REMOVED FROM SCHOOL.
THEY REQUESTED THAT WE LET HIM STAY UNTIL AFTER THE SCHOOL FESTIVAL'S OVER.
I... SEE.
THANK YOU FOR TELLING ME THIS.
THE SCHOOL'S DOING JUST AS IYO-KUN SAID...
BUT, REALLY ...
IT'S NOT JUST NAKAYAMA-KUN, BUT HAYASHIBARA-KUN, TOO...
JUMP
ひくっ
WHAT DO YOU MEAN!?
OH, IT'S JUST...IT WAS DECIDED LONG AGO...
...THAT HE'D STUDY ABROAD.

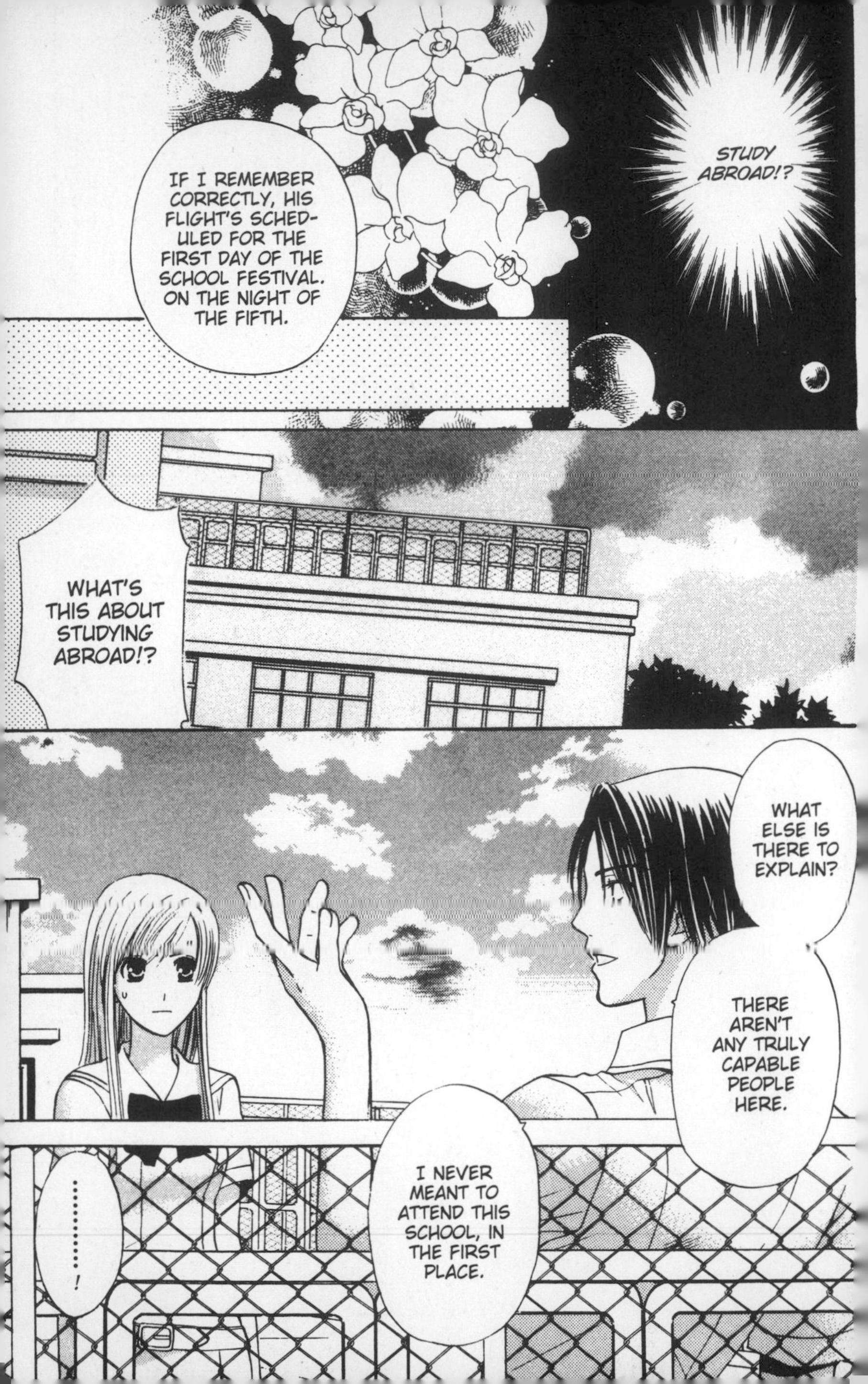
STUDY ABROAD!?
IF I REMEMBER CORRECTLY, HIS FLIGHT'S SCHED-ULED FOR THE FIRST DAY OF THE SCHOOL FESTIVAL. ON THE NIGHT OF THE FIFTH.
WHAT'S THIS ABOUT STUDYING ABROAD!?
WHAT ELSE IS THERE TO EXPLAIN?
THERE AREN'T ANY TRULY CAPABLE PEOPLE HERE.
I NEVER MEANT TO ATTEND THIS SCHOOL, IN THE FIRST PLACE.
.........!

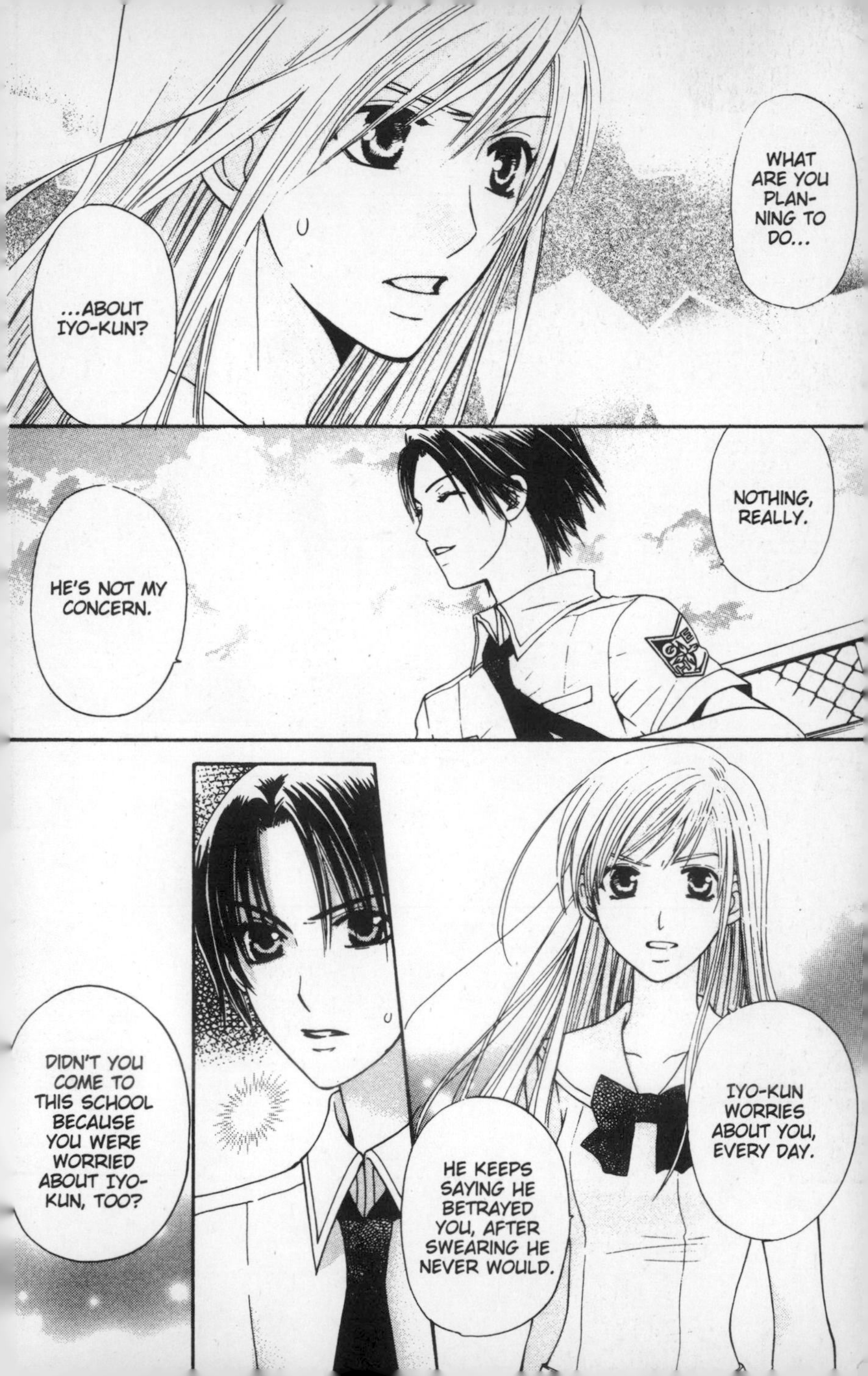
WHAT ARE YOU PLAN-NING TO DO...
...ABOUT IYO-KUN?
NOTHING, REALLY.
HE'S NOT MY CONCERN.
IYO-KUN WORRIES ABOUT YOU, EVERY DAY.
HE KEEPS SAYING HE BETRAYED YOU, AFTER SWEARING HE NEVER WOULD.
DIDN'T YOU COME TO THIS SCHOOL BECAUSE YOU WERE WORRIED ABOUT IYO-KUN, TOO?

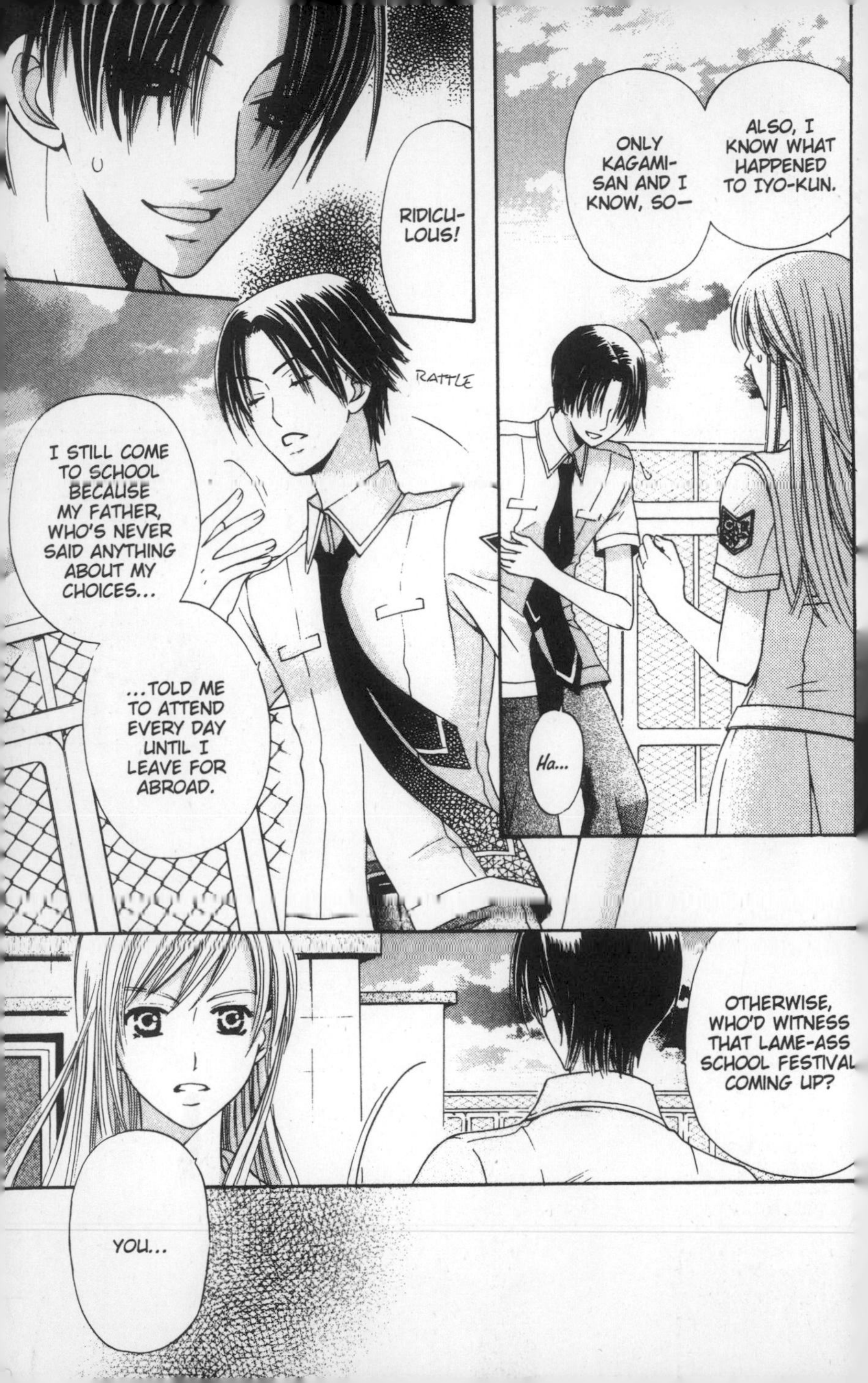
ALSO, I KNOW WHAT HAPPENED TO IYO-KUN.
ONLY KAGAMI-SAN AND I KNOW, SO—
Ha...
RIDICULOUS!
RATTLE
I STILL COME TO SCHOOL BECAUSE MY FATHER, WHO'S NEVER SAID ANYTHING ABOUT MY CHOICES...
...TOLD ME TO ATTEND EVERY DAY UNTIL I LEAVE FOR ABROAD.
OTHERWISE, WHO'D WITNESS THAT LAME-ASS SCHOOL FESTIVAL COMING UP?
YOU...

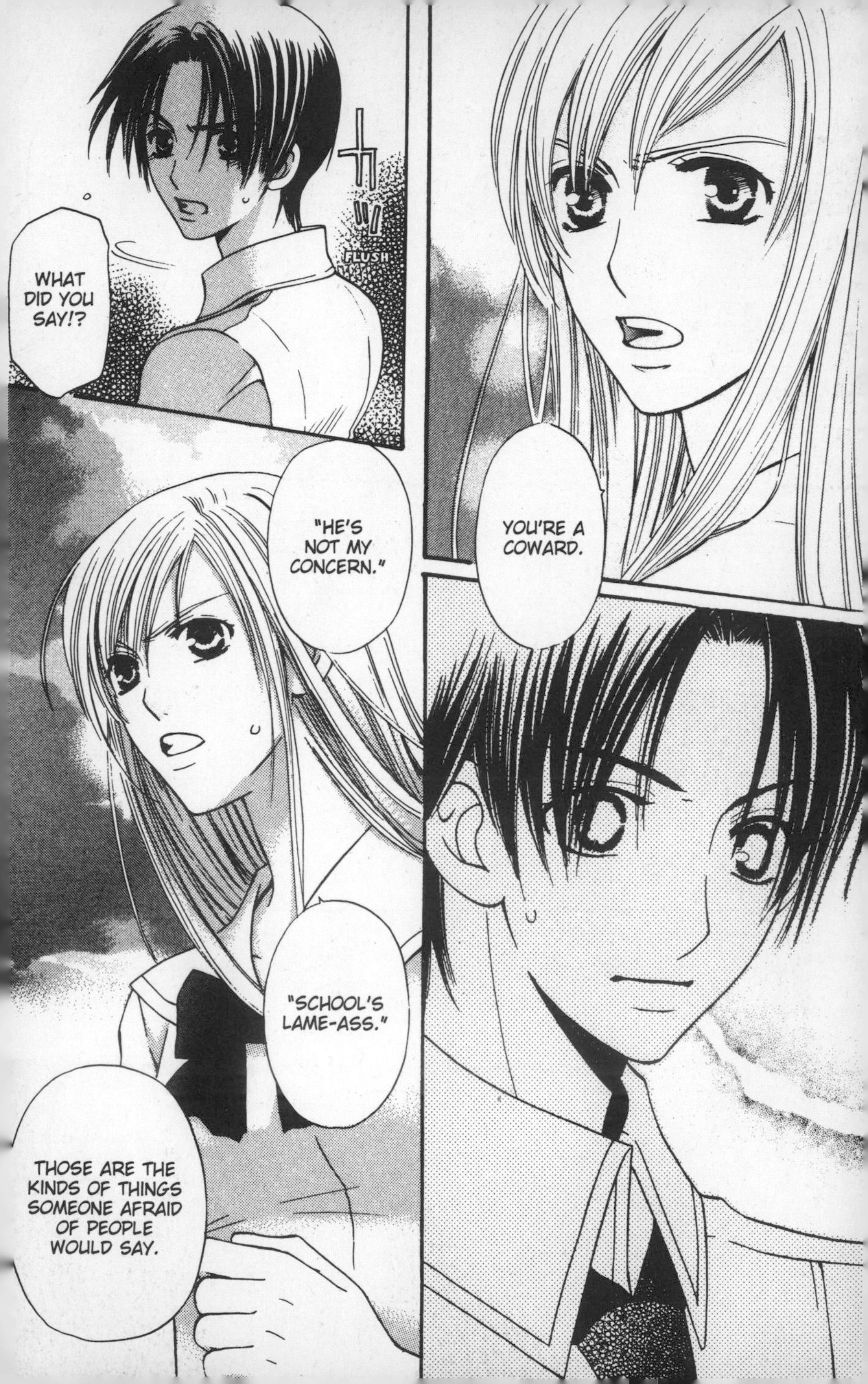
YOU'RE A COWARD.
WHAT DID YOU SAY!?
FLUSH
"HE'S NOT MY CONCERN."
"SCHOOL'S LAME-ASS."
THOSE ARE THE KINDS OF THINGS SOMEONE AFRAID OF PEOPLE WOULD SAY.

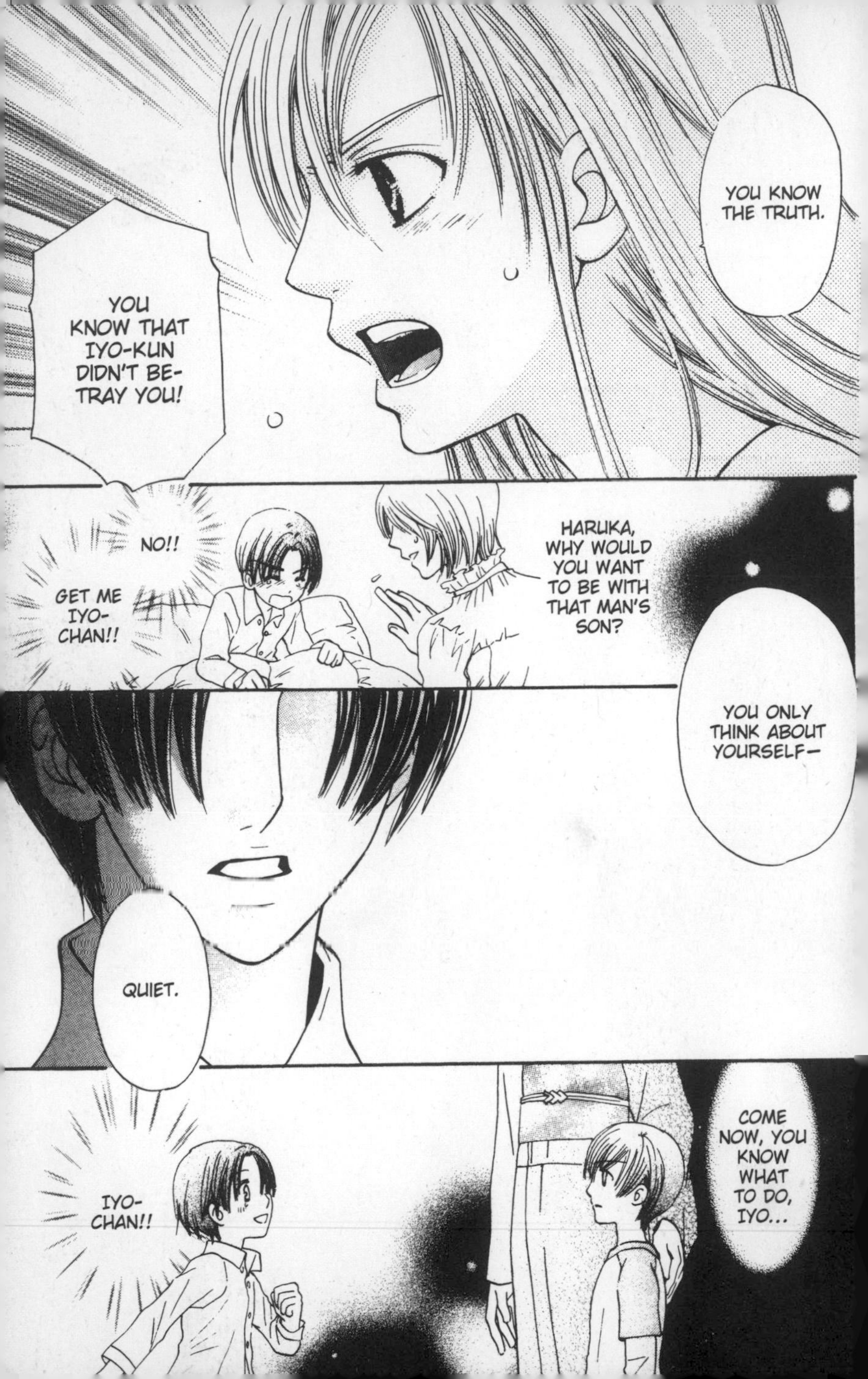

YOU KNOW THE TRUTH.
YOU KNOW THAT IYO-KUN DIDN'T BE-TRAY YOU!
HARUKA, WHY WOULD YOU WANT TO BE WITH THAT MAN'S SON?
NO!!
GET ME IYO-CHAN!!
YOU ONLY THINK ABOUT YOURSELF—
QUIET.
COME NOW, YOU KNOW WHAT TO DO, IYO...
IYO-CHAN!!

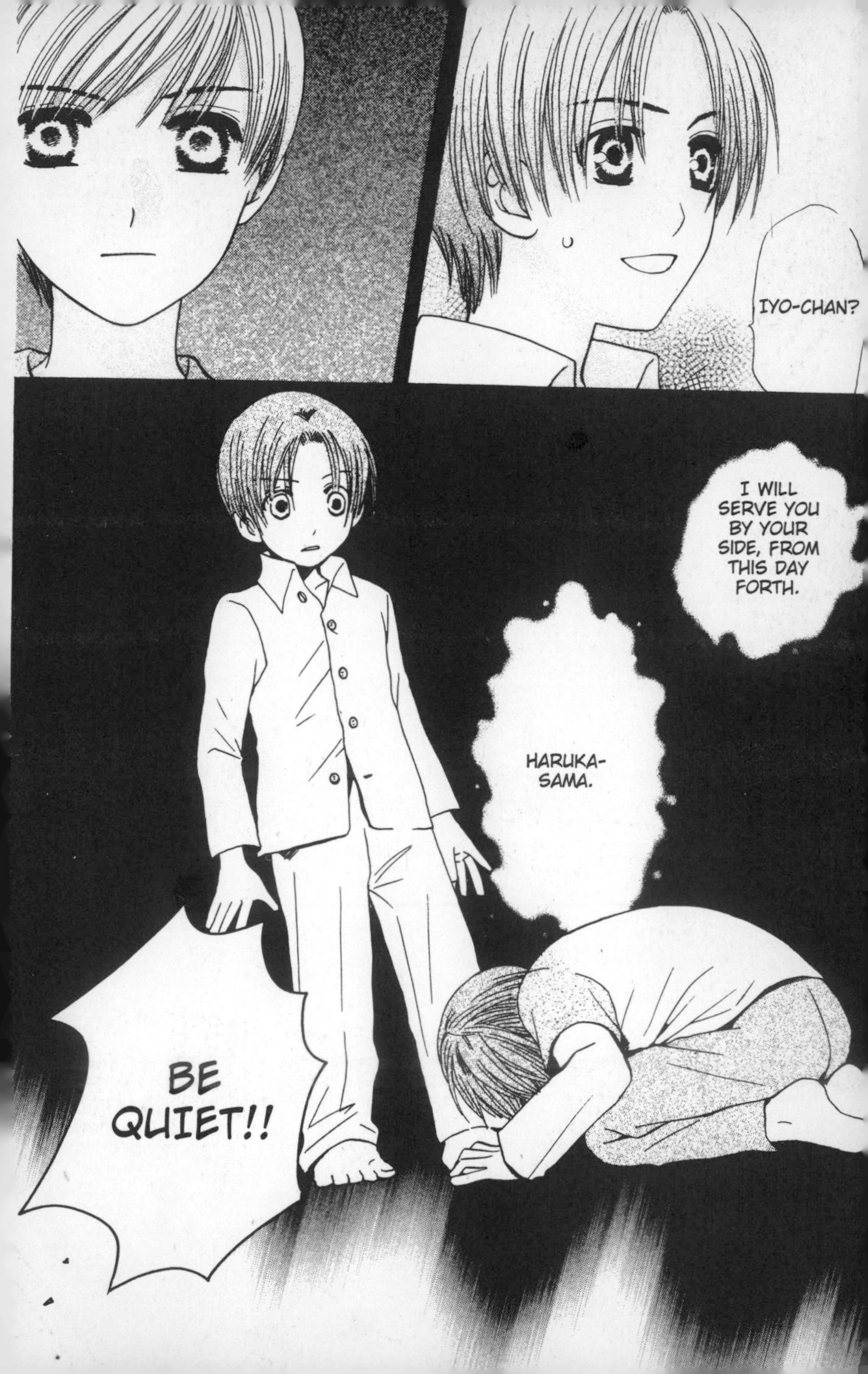
IYO-CHAN?
I WILL SERVE YOU BY YOUR SIDE, FROM THIS DAY FORTH.
HARUKA-SAMA.
BE QUIET!!

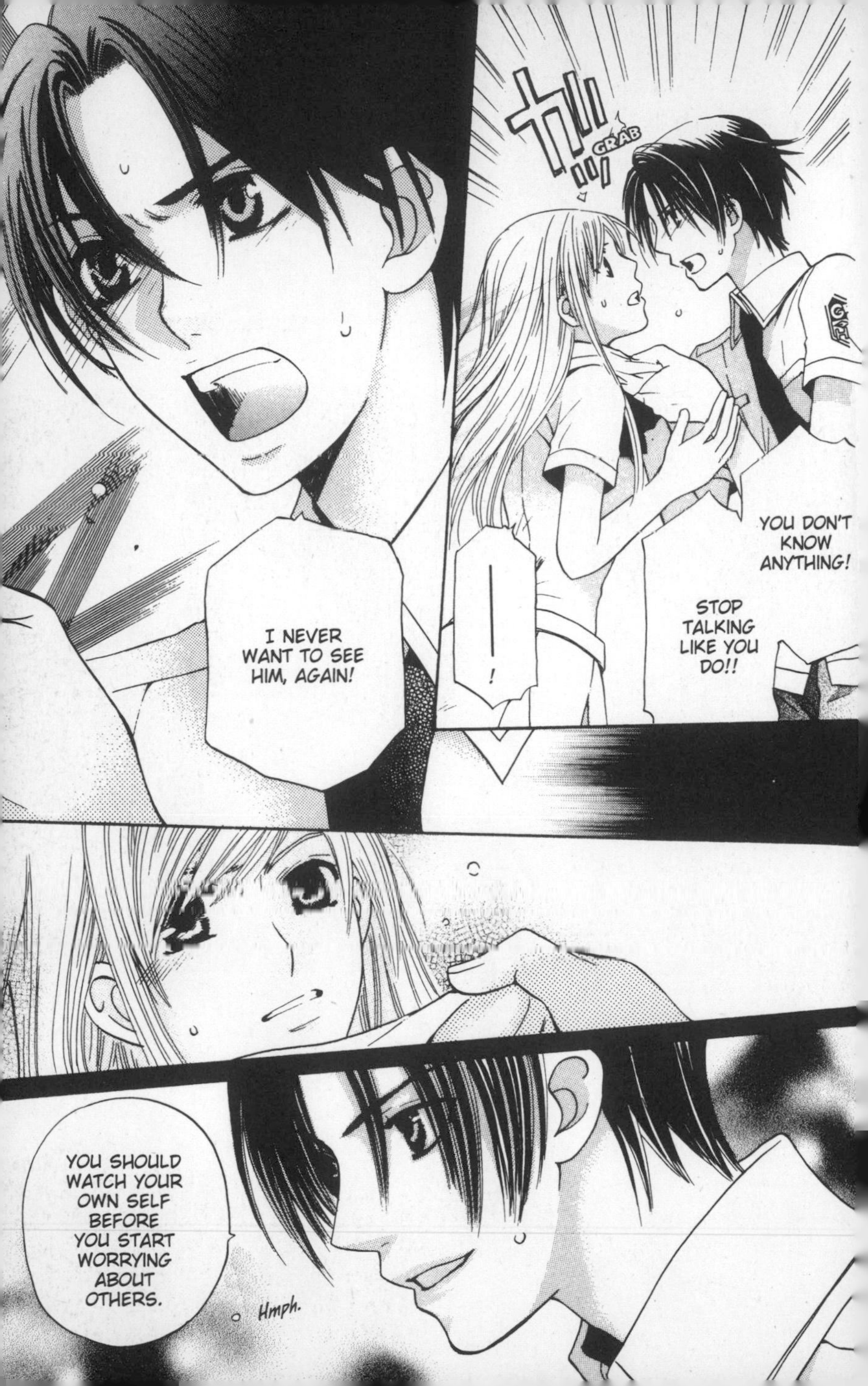
GRAB
YOU DON'T KNOW ANYTHING!
STOP TALKING LIKE YOU DO!!
!
I NEVER WANT TO SEE HIM, AGAIN!
YOU SHOULD WATCH YOUR OWN SELF BEFORE YOU START WORRYING ABOUT OTHERS.
Hmph.

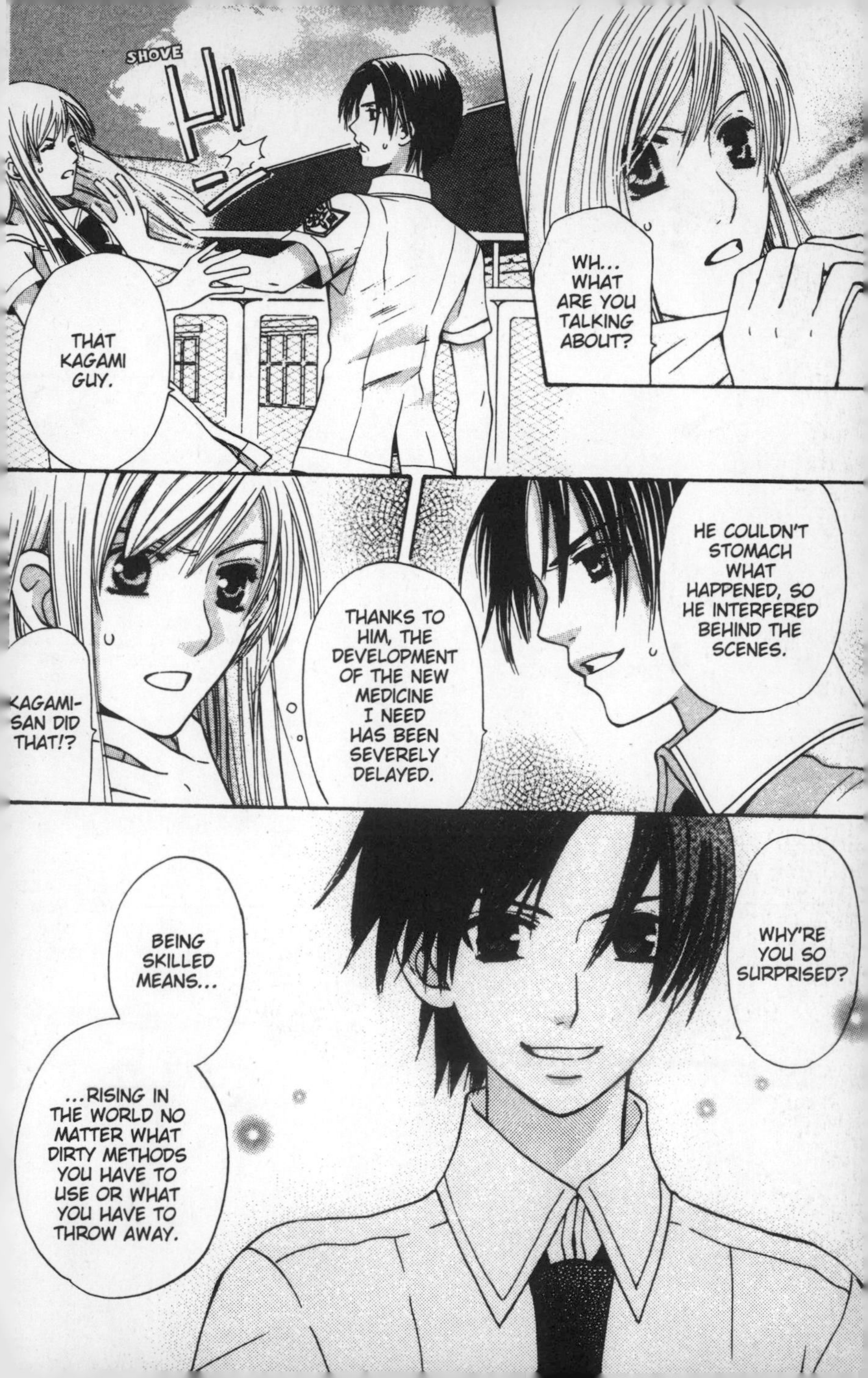
WH... WHAT ARE YOU TALKING ABOUT?
SHOVE
THAT KAGAMI GUY.
HE COULDN'T STOMACH WHAT HAPPENED, SO HE INTERFERED BEHIND THE SCENES.
THANKS TO HIM, THE DEVELOPMENT OF THE NEW MEDICINE I NEED HAS BEEN SEVERELY DELAYED.
KAGAMI-SAN DID THAT!?
WHY'RE YOU SO SURPRISED?
BEING SKILLED MEANS...
...RISING IN THE WORLD NO MATTER WHAT DIRTY METHODS YOU HAVE TO USE OR WHAT YOU HAVE TO THROW AWAY.

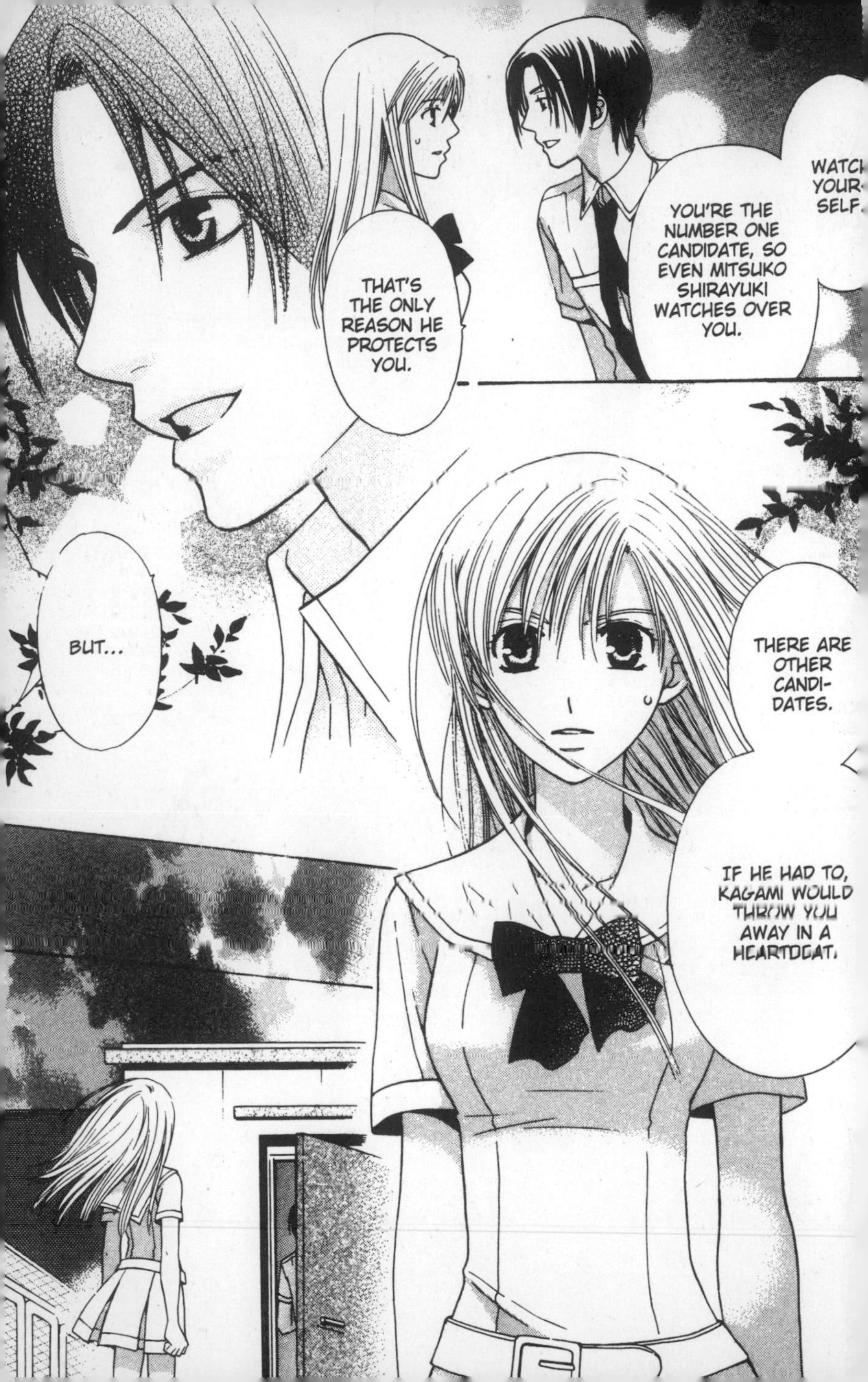

WATC YOUR-SELF.
YOU'RE THE NUMBER ONE CANDIDATE, SO EVEN MITSUKO SHIRAYUKI WATCHES OVER YOU.
THAT'S THE ONLY REASON HE PROTECTS YOU.
THERE ARE OTHER CANDI-DATES.
IF HE HAD TO, KAGAMI WOULD THROW YOU AWAY IN A HEARTBEAT.
BUT...

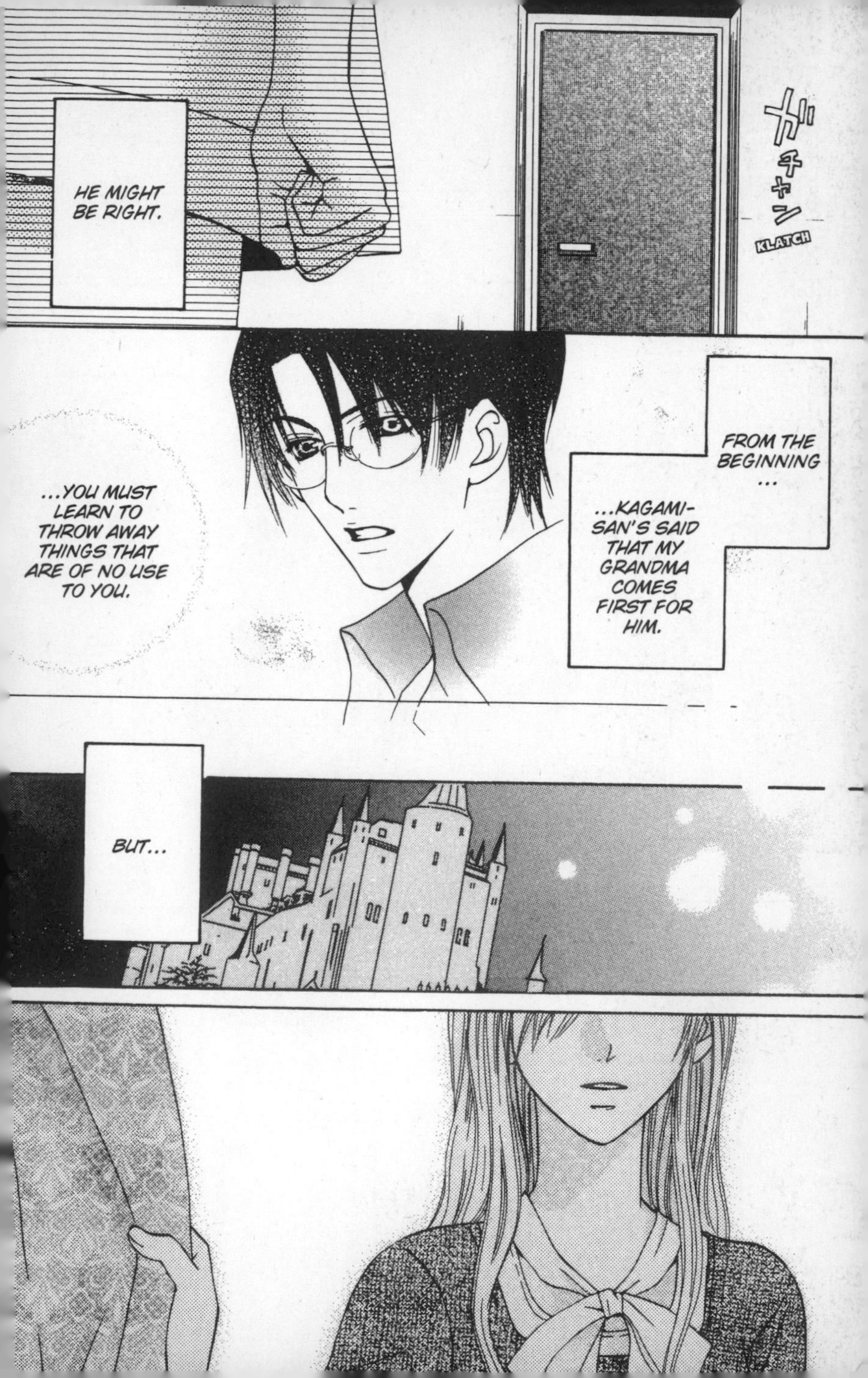
ガチャン
KLATCH
HE MIGHT BE RIGHT.
FROM THE BEGINNING ...
...KAGAMI-SAN'S SAID THAT MY GRANDMA COMES FIRST FOR HIM.
...YOU MUST LEARN TO THROW AWAY THINGS THAT ARE OF NO USE TO YOU.
BUT...

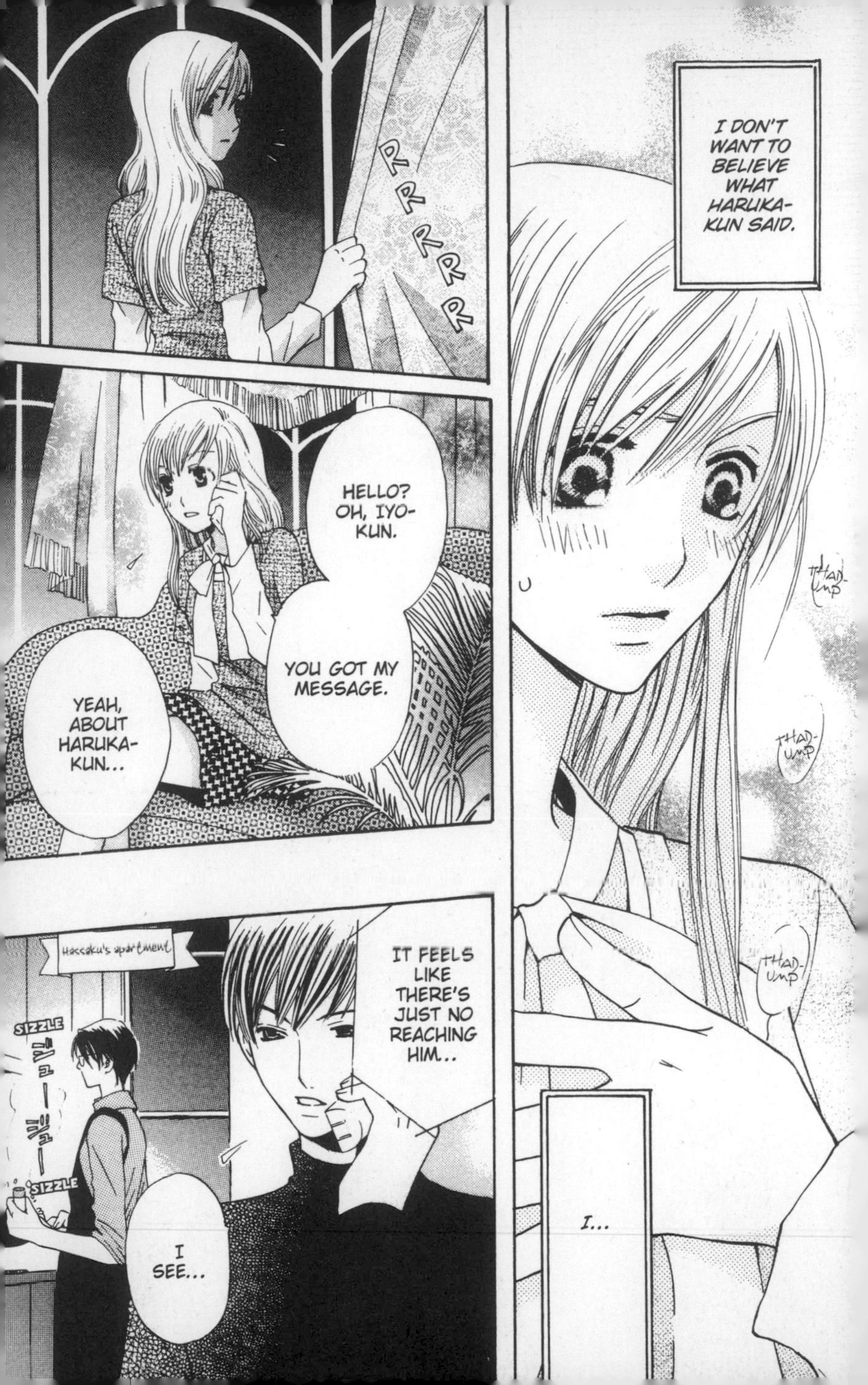
I DON'T WANT TO BELIEVE WHAT HARUKA-KUN SAID.
THAD-UMP
THAD-UMP
THAD-UMP
I...
RRRRRR
HELLO? OH, IYO-KUN.
YOU GOT MY MESSAGE.
YEAH, ABOUT HARUKA-KUN...
Hassaku's apartment
IT FEELS LIKE THERE'S JUST NO REACHING HIM...
SIZZLE
ジュージュー
SIZZLE
I SEE...

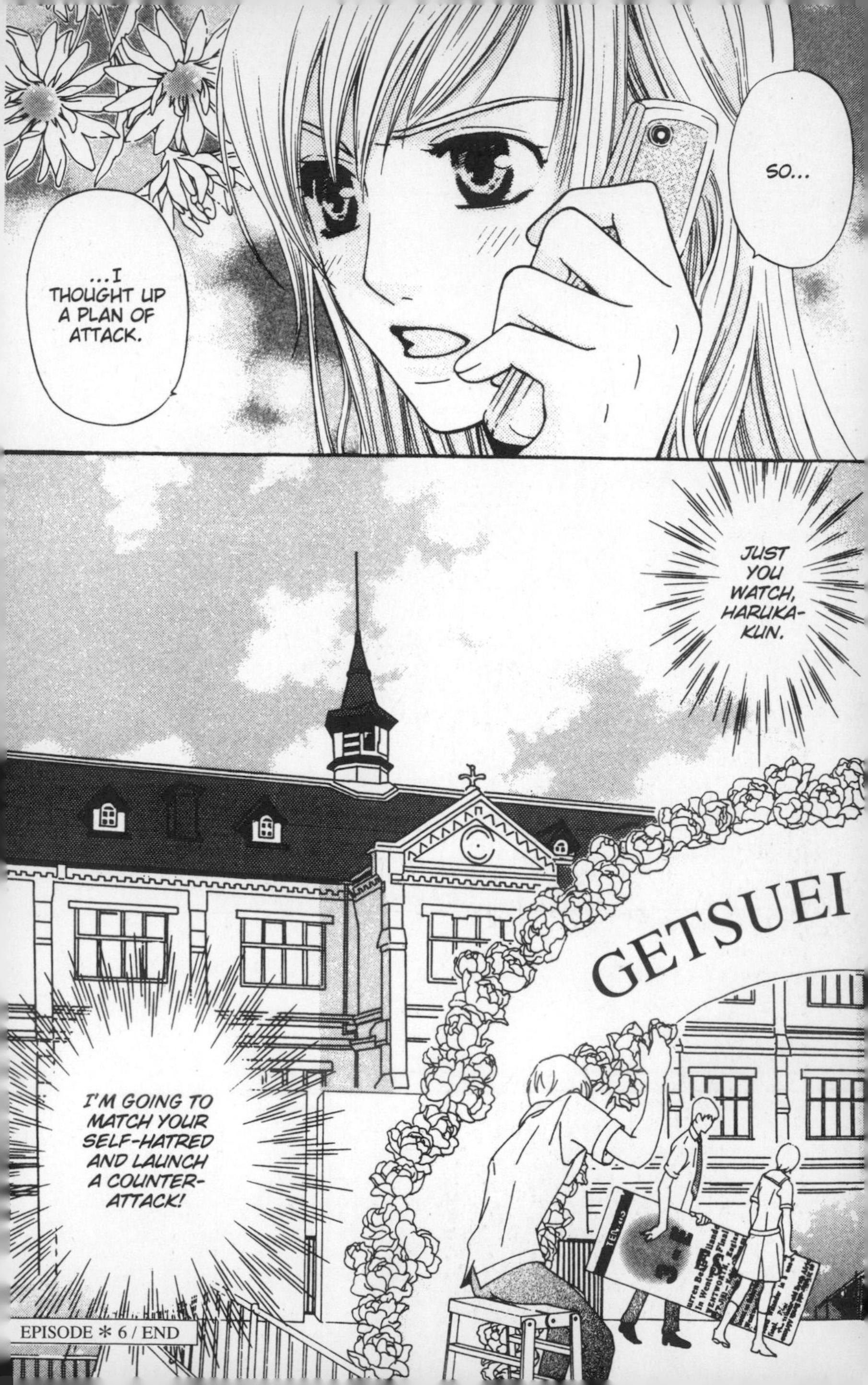
SO...
...I THOUGHT UP A PLAN OF ATTACK.
JUST YOU WATCH, HARUKA-KUN.
GETSUEI
I'M GOING TO MATCH YOUR SELF-HATRED AND LAUNCH A COUNTER-ATTACK!
EPISODE ✻ 6 / END

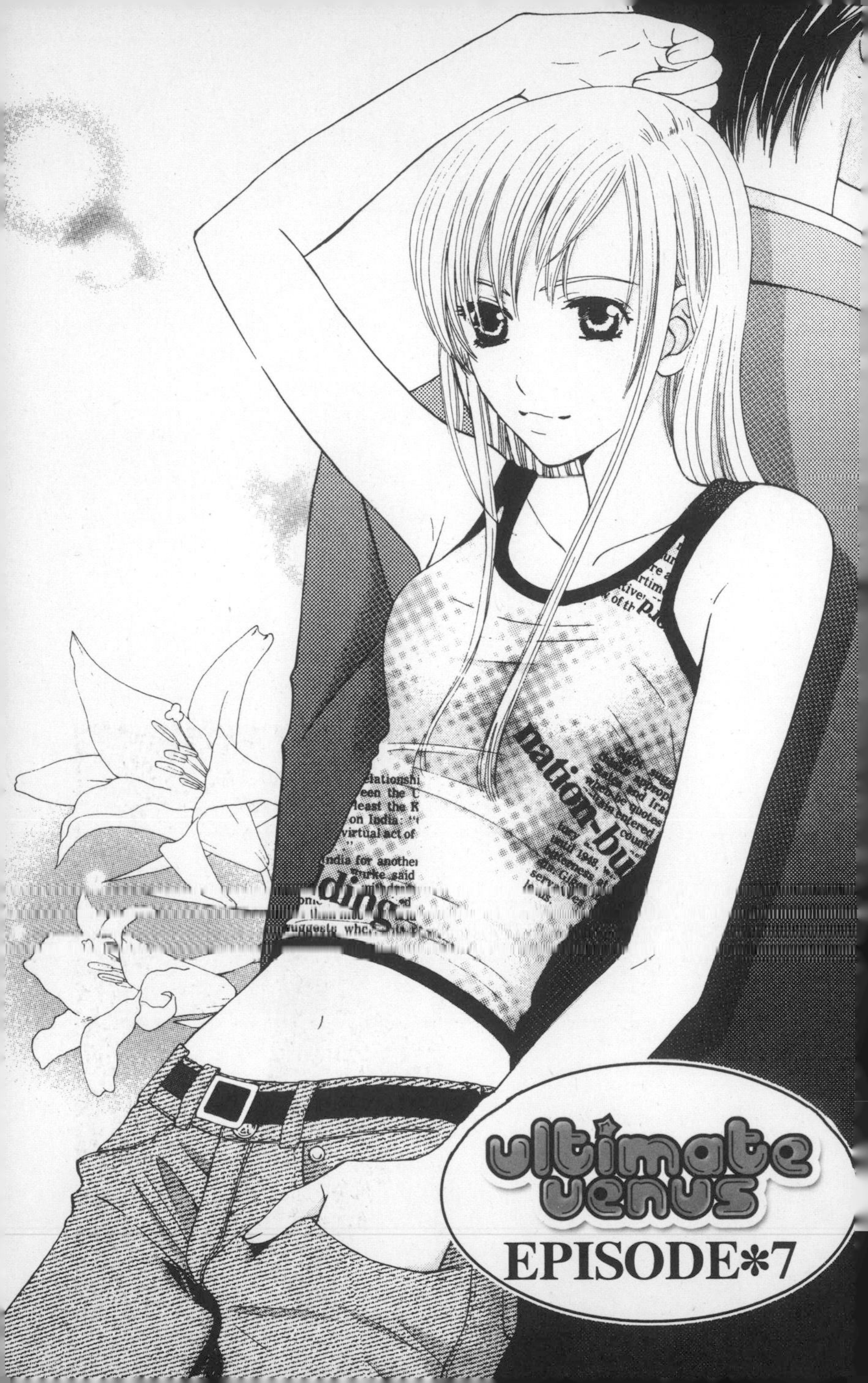
ultimate venus
EPISODE*7

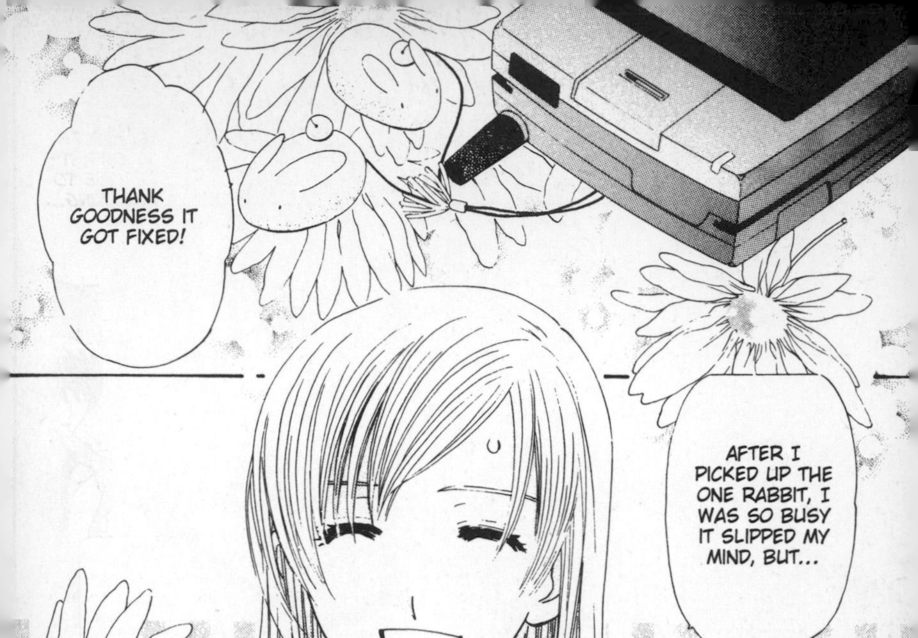
THANK GOODNESS IT GOT FIXED!
AFTER I PICKED UP THE ONE RABBIT, I WAS SO BUSY IT SLIPPED MY MIND, BUT...
WELL, SORRY.

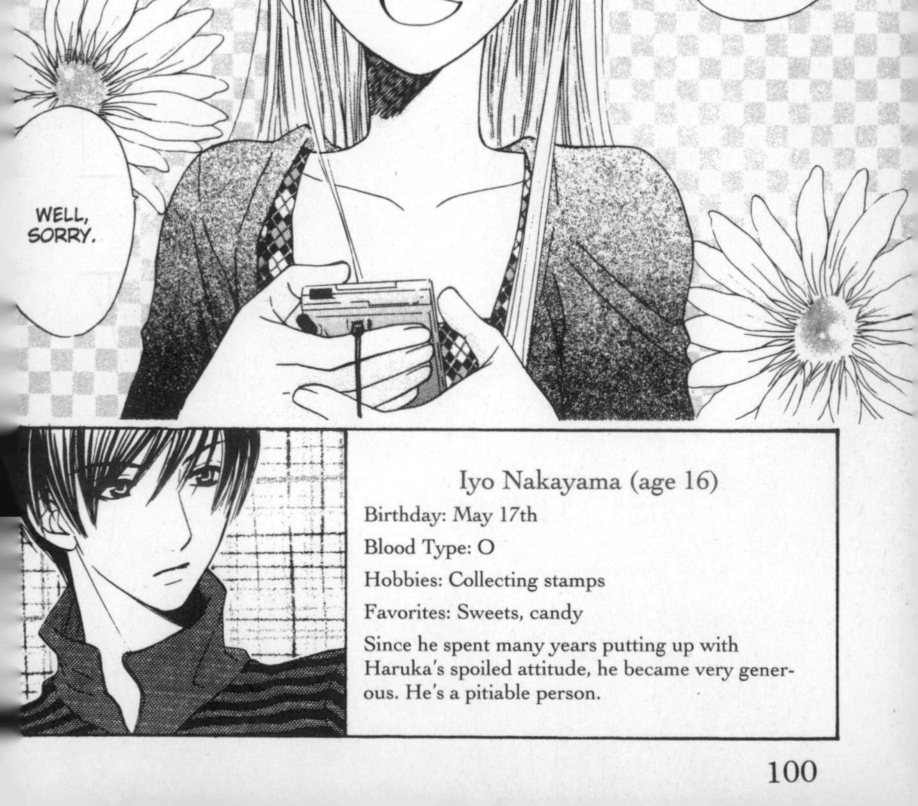

Iyo Nakayama (age 16)

Birthday: May 17th

Blood Type: O

Hobbies: Collecting stamps

Favorites: Sweets, candy

Since he spent many years putting up with Haruka's spoiled attitude, he became very generous. He's a pitiable person.

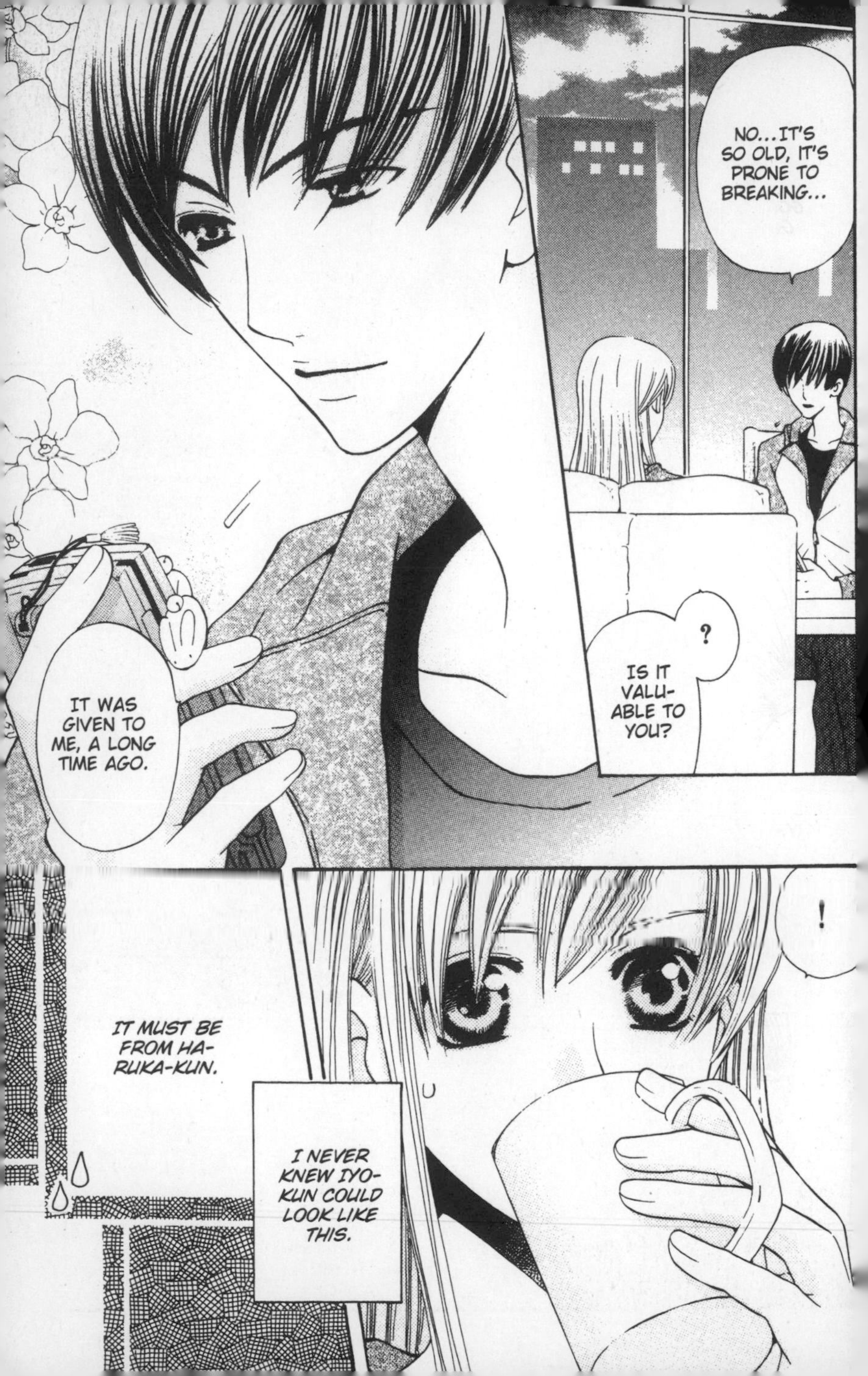
NO...IT'S SO OLD, IT'S PRONE TO BREAKING...
?
IS IT VALU-ABLE TO YOU?
IT WAS GIVEN TO ME, A LONG TIME AGO.
!
I NEVER KNEW IYO-KUN COULD LOOK LIKE THIS.
IT MUST BE FROM HA-RUKA-KUN.

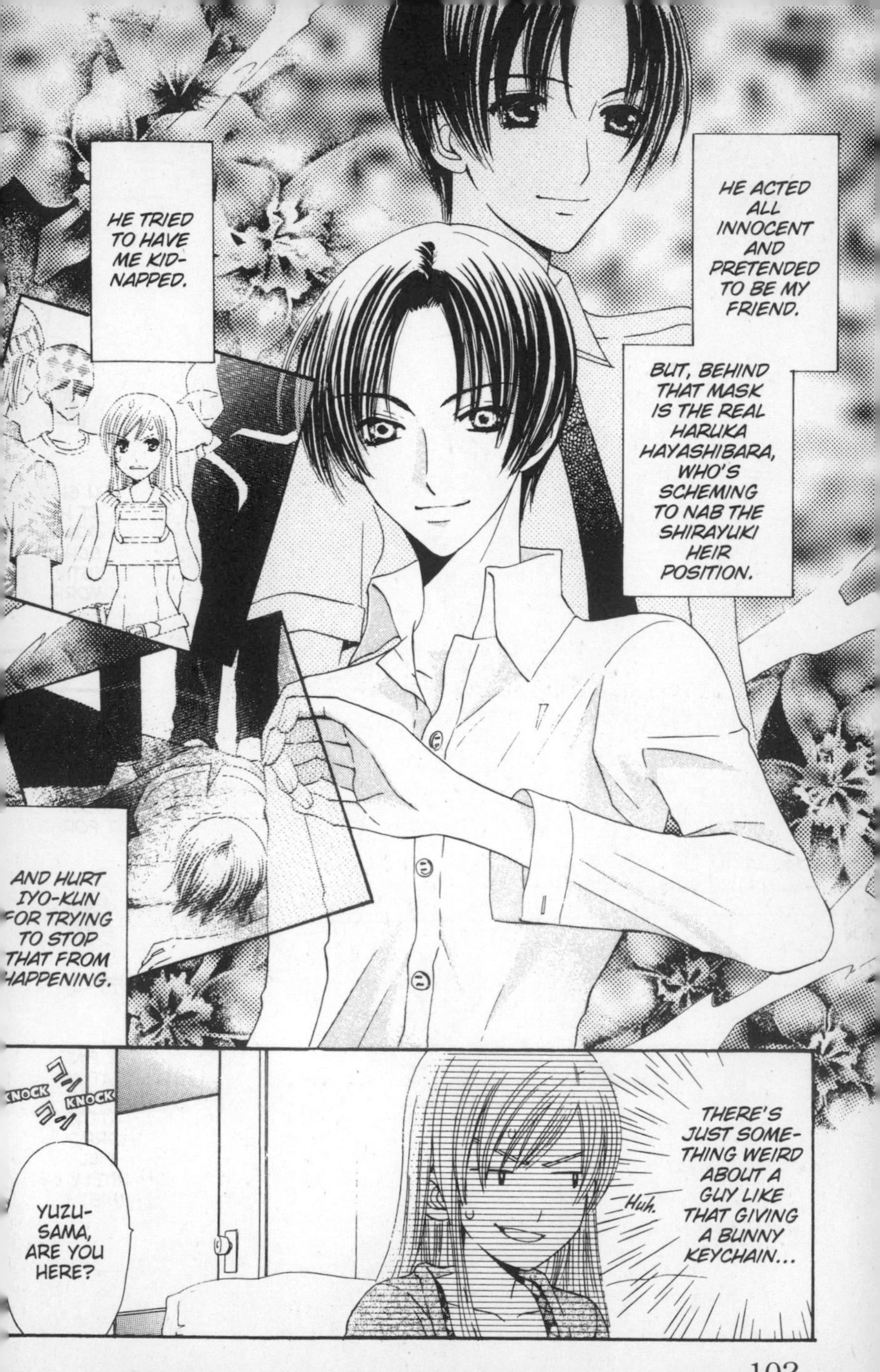
HE ACTED ALL INNOCENT AND PRETENDED TO BE MY FRIEND.
BUT, BEHIND THAT MASK IS THE REAL HARUKA HAYASHIBARA, WHO'S SCHEMING TO NAB THE SHIRAYUKI HEIR POSITION.
HE TRIED TO HAVE ME KIDNAPPED.
AND HURT IYO-KUN FOR TRYING TO STOP THAT FROM HAPPENING.
THERE'S JUST SOMETHING WEIRD ABOUT A GUY LIKE THAT GIVING A BUNNY KEYCHAIN...
Huh.
KNOCK KNOCK
YUZU-SAMA, ARE YOU HERE?

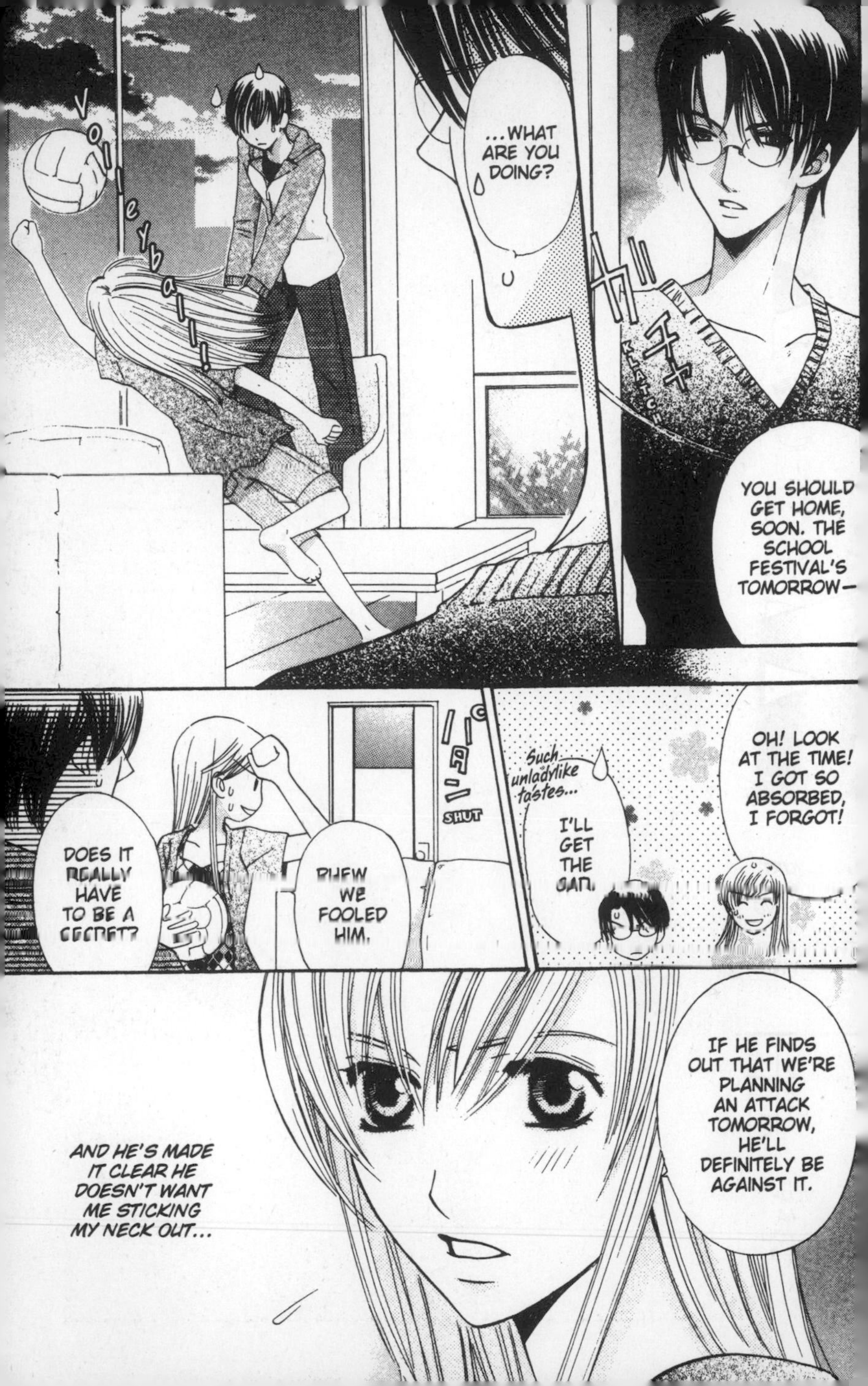

...WHAT ARE YOU DOING?
KLATCH
YOU SHOULD GET HOME, SOON. THE SCHOOL FESTIVAL'S TOMORROW—
Volleyball!!
OH! LOOK AT THE TIME! I GOT SO ABSORBED, I FORGOT!
Such unladylike tastes...
I'LL GET THE CAR.
SHUT
PHEW WE FOOLED HIM.
DOES IT REALLY HAVE TO BE A SECRET?
IF HE FINDS OUT THAT WE'RE PLANNING AN ATTACK TOMORROW, HE'LL DEFINITELY BE AGAINST IT.
AND HE'S MADE IT CLEAR HE DOESN'T WANT ME STICKING MY NECK OUT...

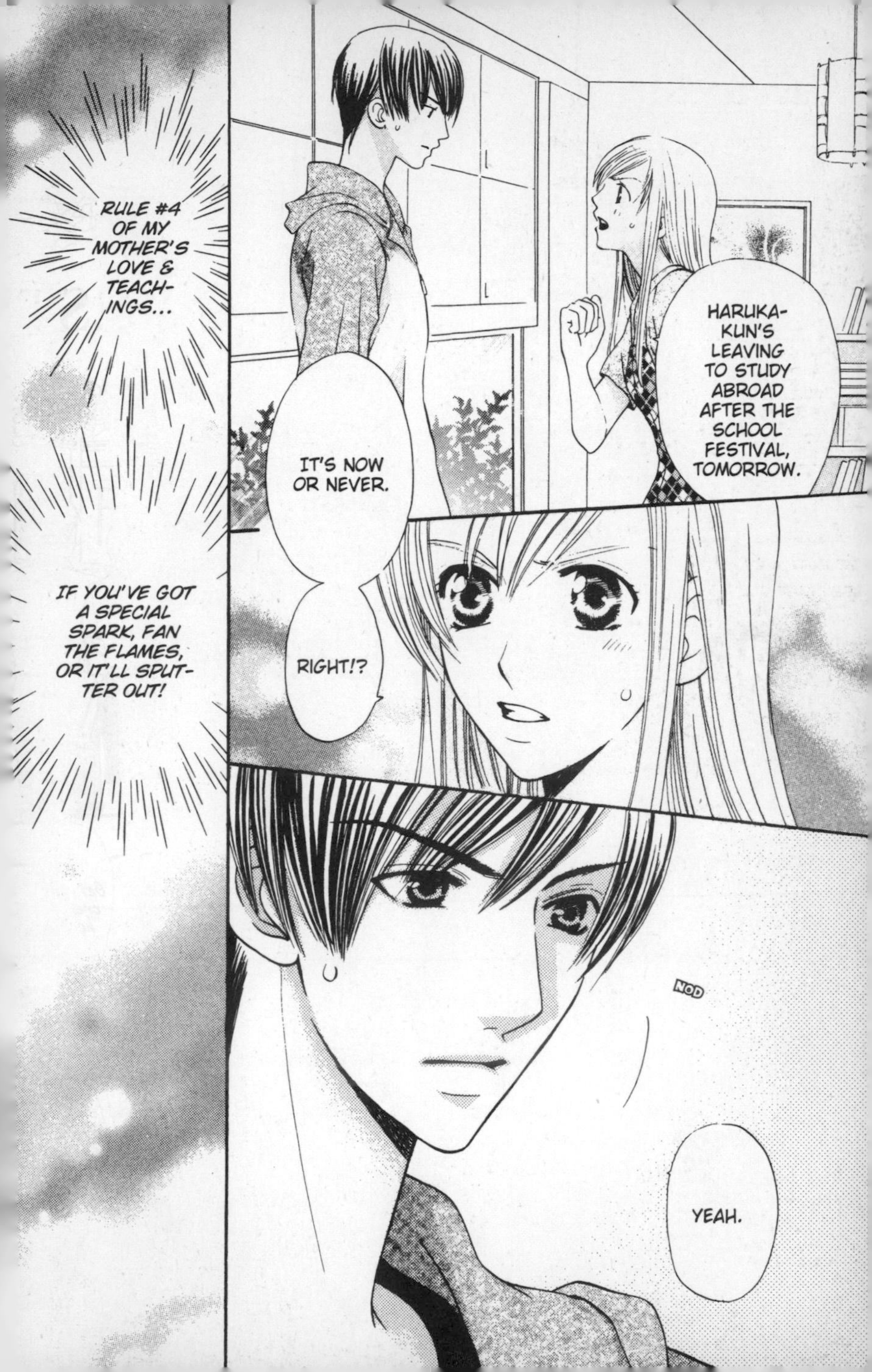
HARUKA-KUN'S LEAVING TO STUDY ABROAD AFTER THE SCHOOL FESTIVAL, TOMORROW.
IT'S NOW OR NEVER.
RIGHT!?
NOD
YEAH.
RULE #4 OF MY MOTHER'S LOVE & TEACHINGS...
IF YOU'VE GOT A SPECIAL SPARK, FAN THE FLAMES, OR IT'LL SPUTTER OUT!

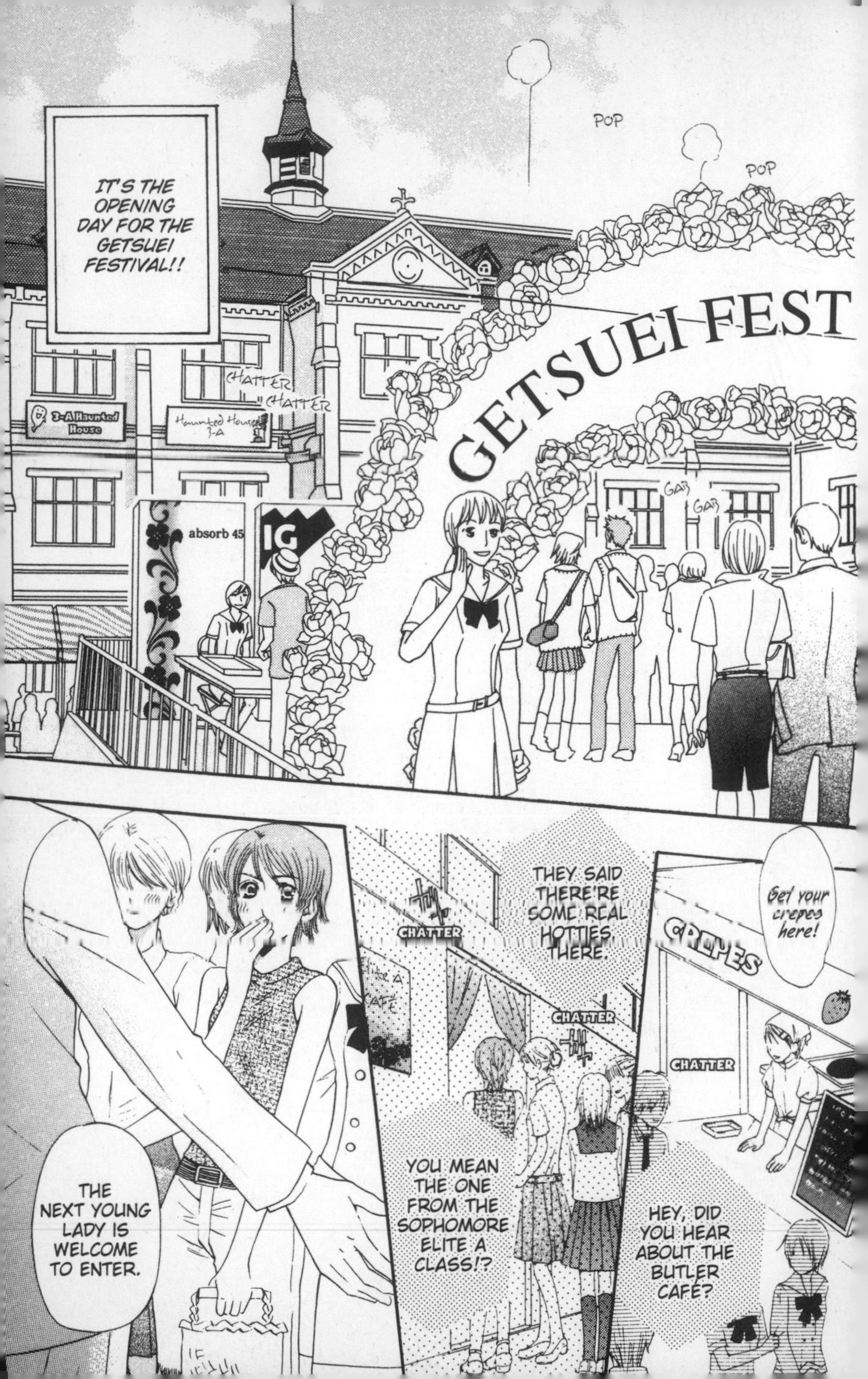
POP
POP
GETSUEI FEST
GAB GAB
IT'S THE OPENING DAY FOR THE GETSUEI FESTIVAL!!
CHATTER CHATTER
3-A Haunted House
Haunted House 3-A
absorb 45
IG
Get your crepes here!
CREPES
CHATTER
HEY, DID YOU HEAR ABOUT THE BUTLER CAFÉ?
THEY SAID THERE'RE SOME REAL HOTTIES THERE.
CHATTER
CHATTER
YOU MEAN THE ONE FROM THE SOPHOMORE ELITE A CLASS!?
Elite A Café
THE NEXT YOUNG LADY IS WELCOME TO ENTER.

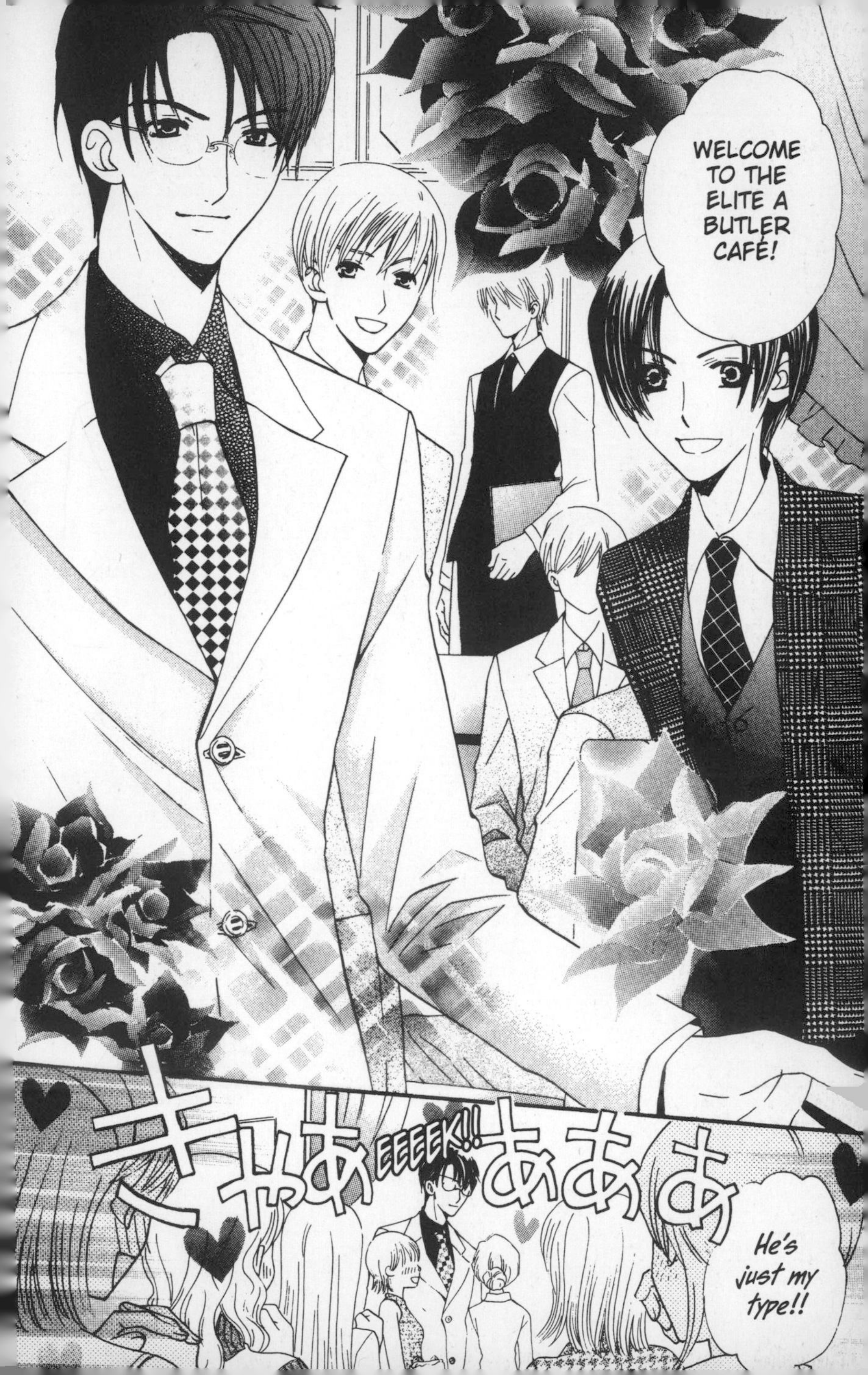
WELCOME TO THE ELITE A BUTLER CAFÉ!
きゃあ EEEEK!! あああ
He's just my type!!

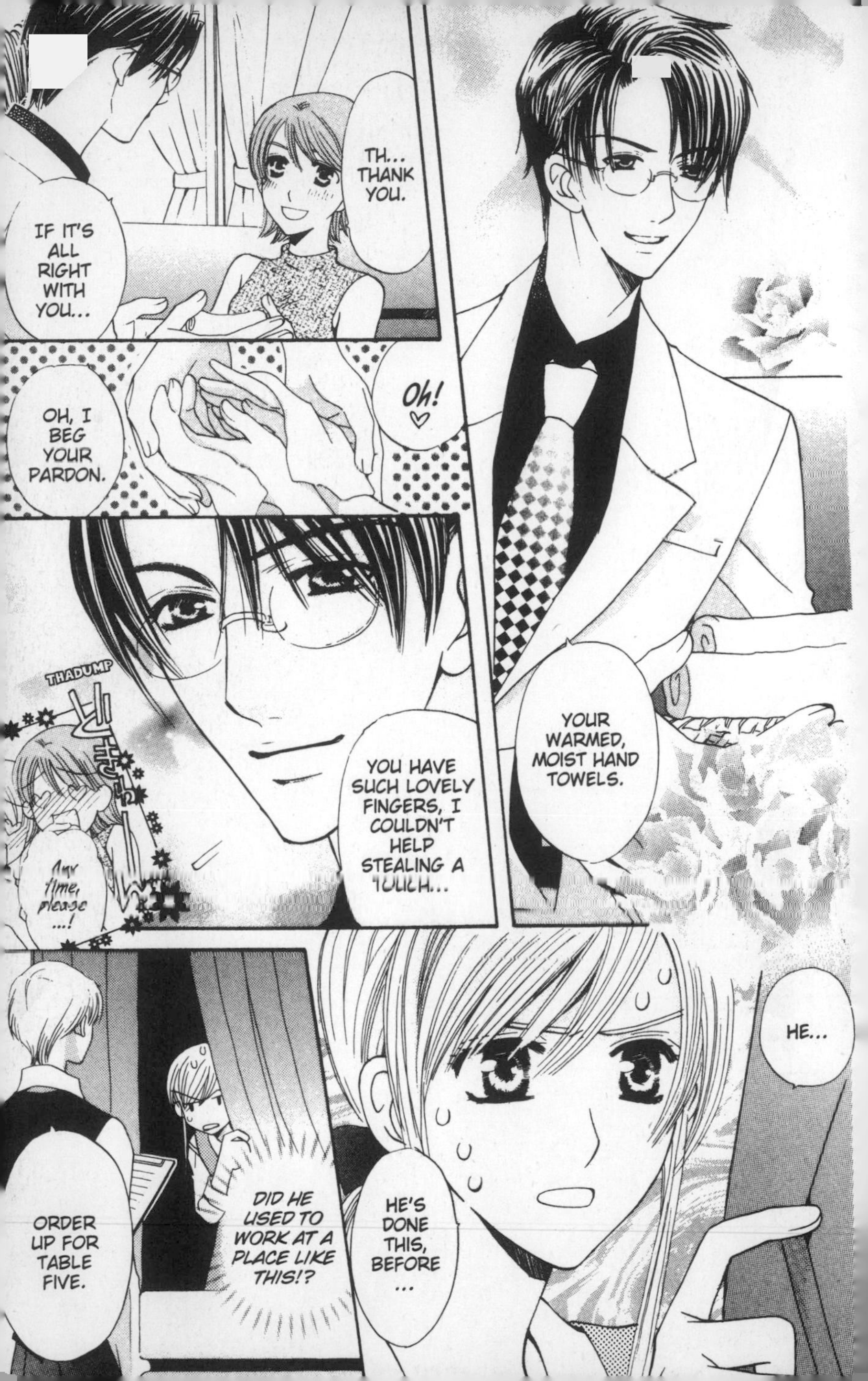
YOUR WARMED, MOIST HAND TOWELS.
TH... THANK YOU.
IF IT'S ALL RIGHT WITH YOU...
Oh! ♡
OH, I BEG YOUR PARDON.
YOU HAVE SUCH LOVELY FINGERS, I COULDN'T HELP STEALING A TOUCH...
THADUMP
Any time, please ...!
HE...
HE'S DONE THIS, BEFORE ...
DID HE USED TO WORK AT A PLACE LIKE THIS!?
ORDER UP FOR TABLE FIVE.

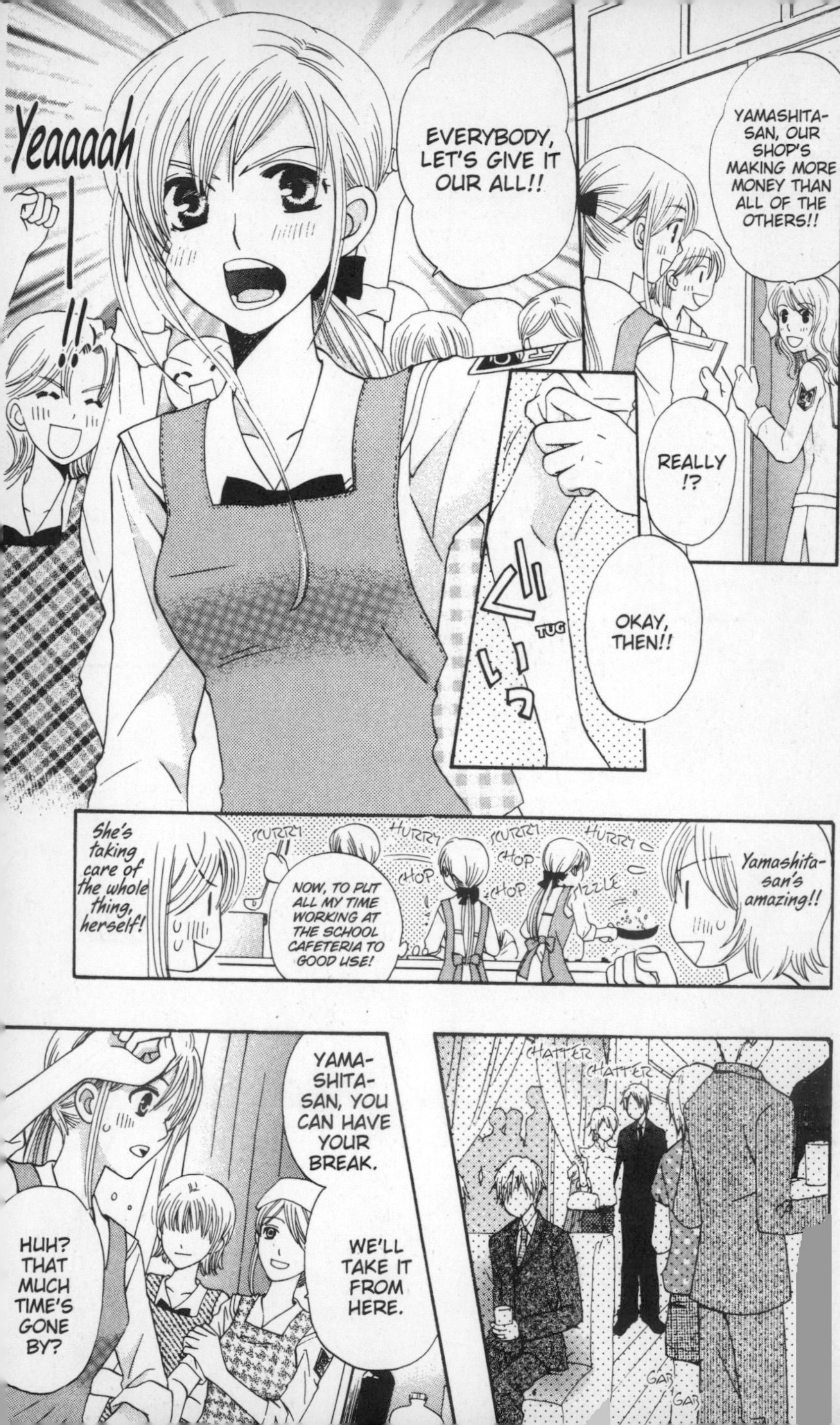
YAMASHITA-SAN, OUR SHOP'S MAKING MORE MONEY THAN ALL OF THE OTHERS!!
REALLY!?
OKAY, THEN!!
TUG
EVERYBODY, LET'S GIVE IT OUR ALL!!
Yeaaaah—!!
Yamashita-san's amazing!!
HURRY
SCURRY
CHOP
CHOP
HURRY
NOW, TO PUT ALL MY TIME WORKING AT THE SCHOOL CAFETERIA TO GOOD USE!
CHOP
SCURRY
She's taking care of the whole thing, herself!
CHATTER
CHATTER
GAB
GAB
YAMA-SHITA-SAN, YOU CAN HAVE YOUR BREAK.
WE'LL TAKE IT FROM HERE.
HUH? THAT MUCH TIME'S GONE BY?

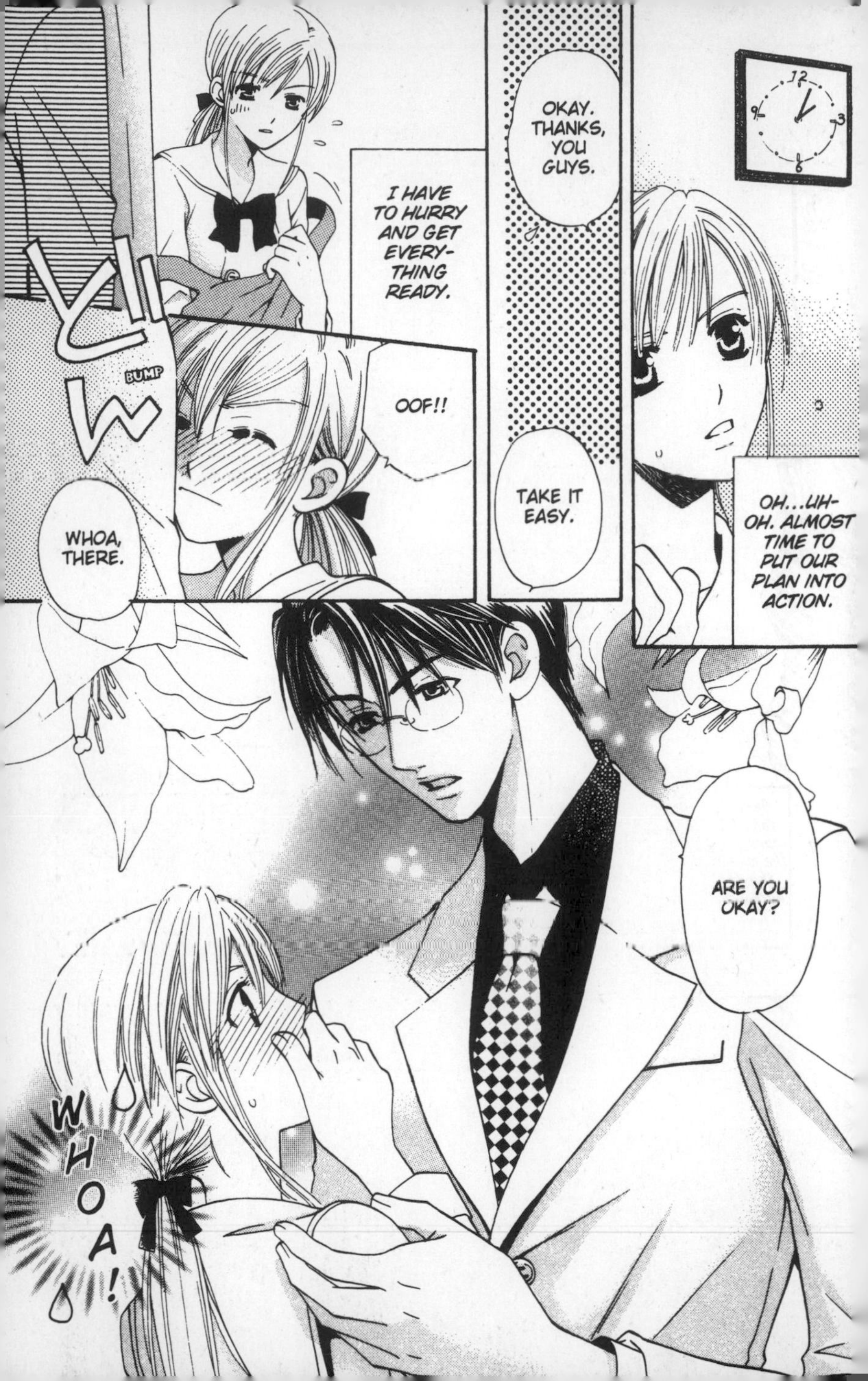
OH...UH-OH. ALMOST TIME TO PUT OUR PLAN INTO ACTION.
OKAY. THANKS, YOU GUYS.
TAKE IT EASY.
I HAVE TO HURRY AND GET EVERY-THING READY.
BUMP
OOF!!
WHOA, THERE.
ARE YOU OKAY?
WHOA!

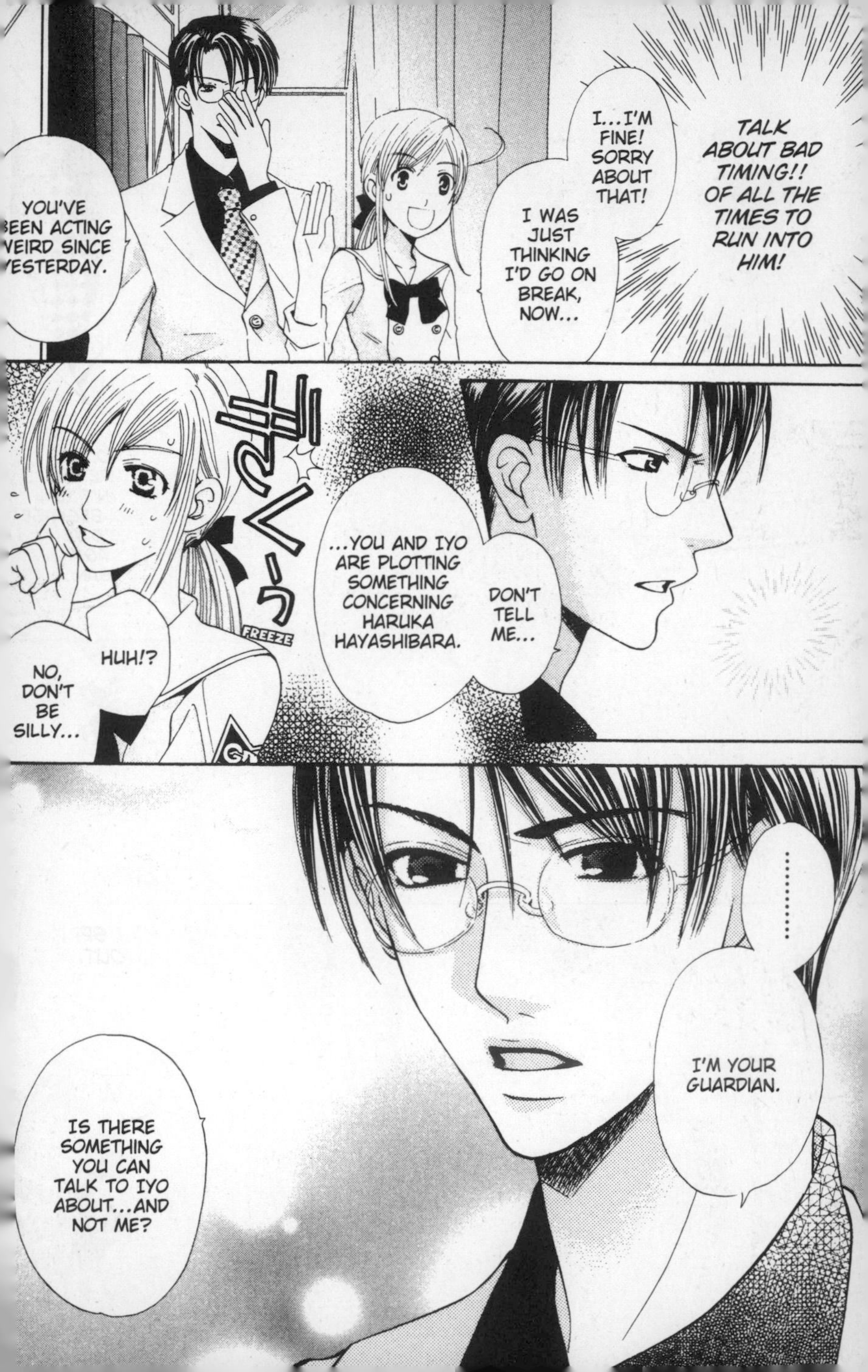
TALK ABOUT BAD TIMING!! OF ALL THE TIMES TO RUN INTO HIM!
I...I'M FINE! SORRY ABOUT THAT!
I WAS JUST THINKING I'D GO ON BREAK, NOW...
YOU'VE BEEN ACTING WEIRD SINCE YESTERDAY.
DON'T TELL ME...
...YOU AND IYO ARE PLOTTING SOMETHING CONCERNING HARUKA HAYASHIBARA.
ぎくぅ
FREEZE
HUH!?
NO, DON'T BE SILLY...
......
I'M YOUR GUARDIAN.
IS THERE SOMETHING YOU CAN TALK TO IYO ABOUT...AND NOT ME?

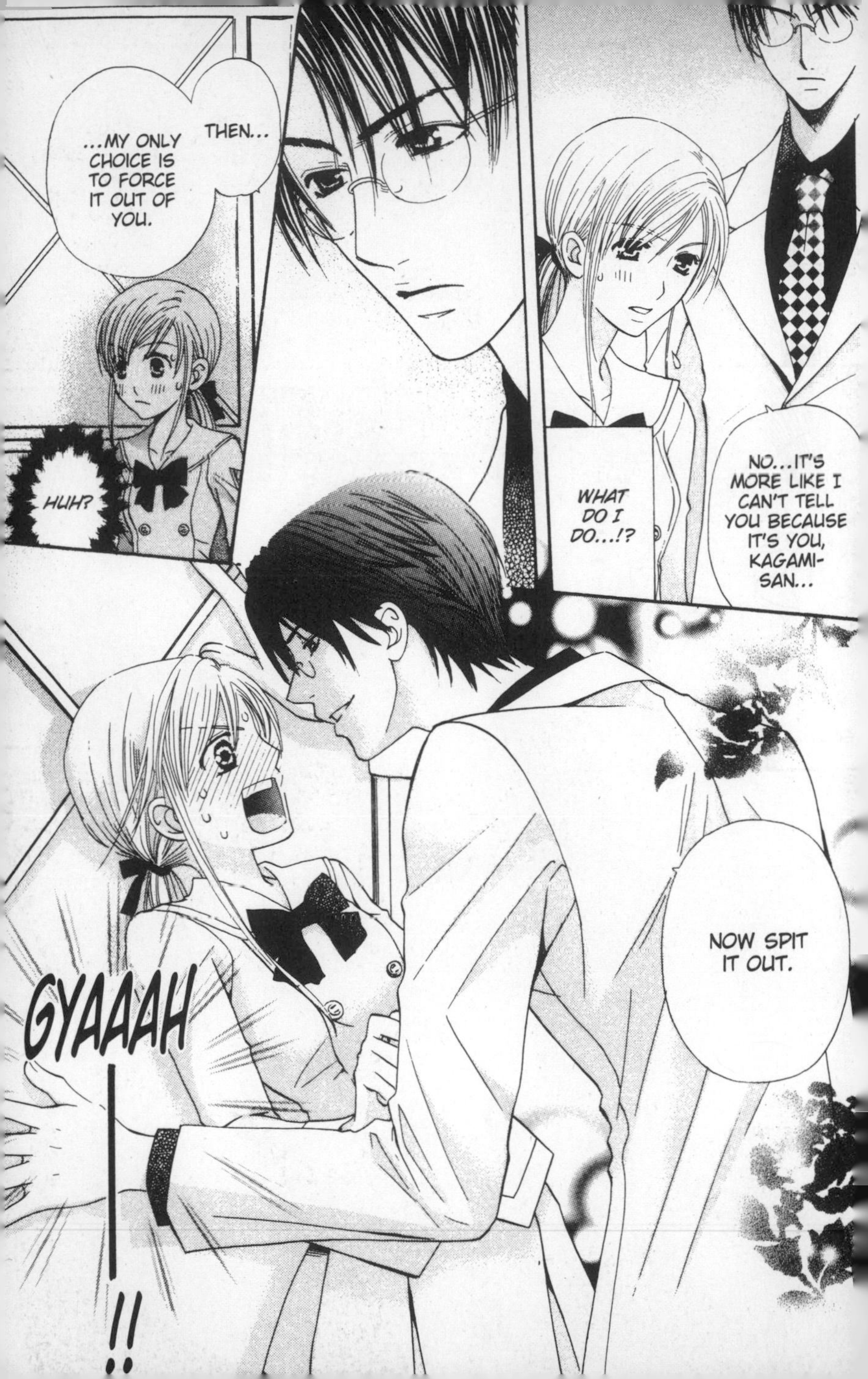
NO...IT'S MORE LIKE I CAN'T TELL YOU BECAUSE IT'S YOU, KAGAMI-SAN...
WHAT DO I DO...!?
THEN...
...MY ONLY CHOICE IS TO FORCE IT OUT OF YOU.
HUH?
NOW SPIT IT OUT.
GYAAAH—!!

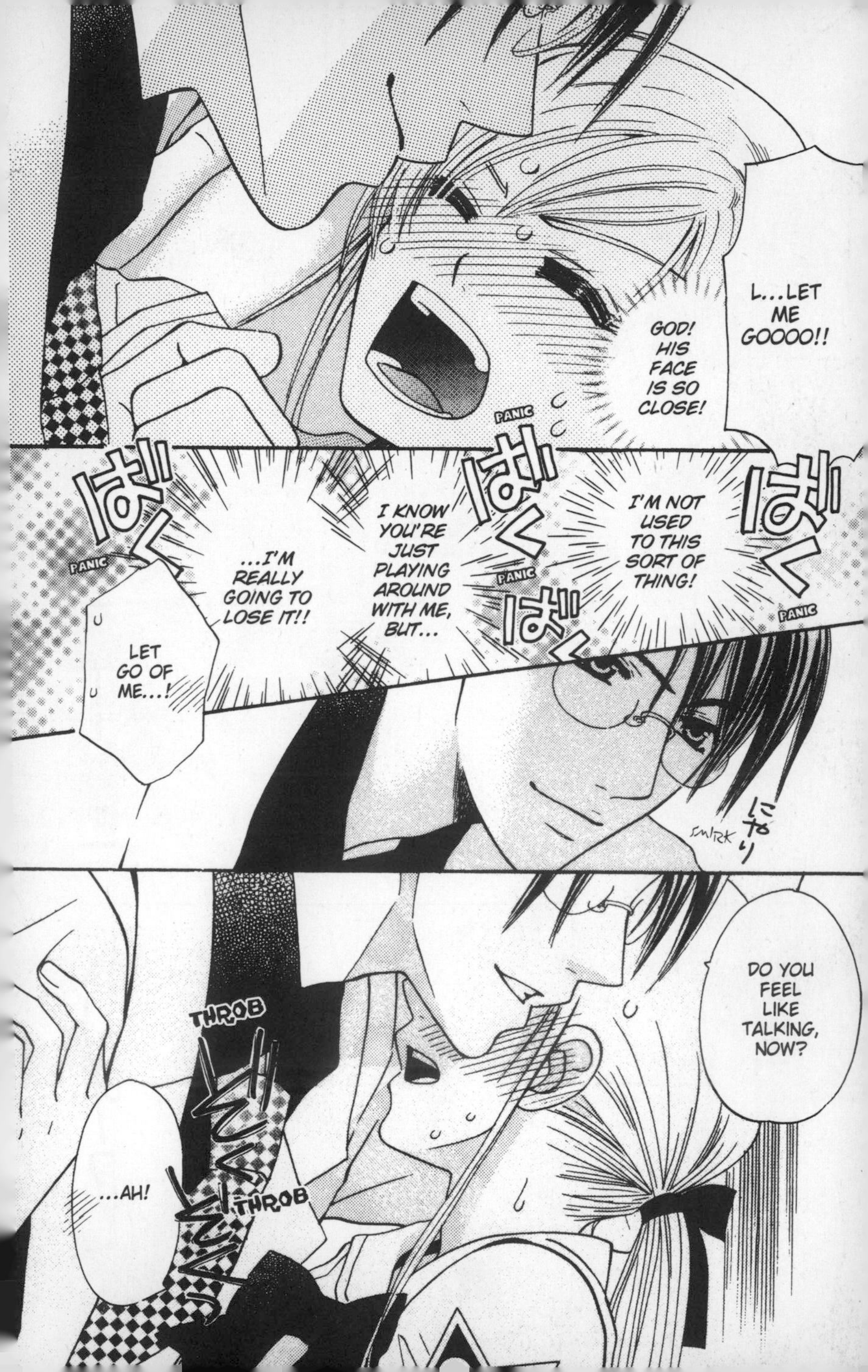
L...LET ME GOOOO!!
GOD! HIS FACE IS SO CLOSE!
PANIC
ばく
PANIC
I'M NOT USED TO THIS SORT OF THING!
ばく
PANIC
ばく
I KNOW YOU'RE JUST PLAYING AROUND WITH ME, BUT...
...I'M REALLY GOING TO LOSE IT!!
ばく
PANIC
LET GO OF ME...!
にやり
SMIRK
DO YOU FEEL LIKE TALKING, NOW?
THROB
...AH!
THROB

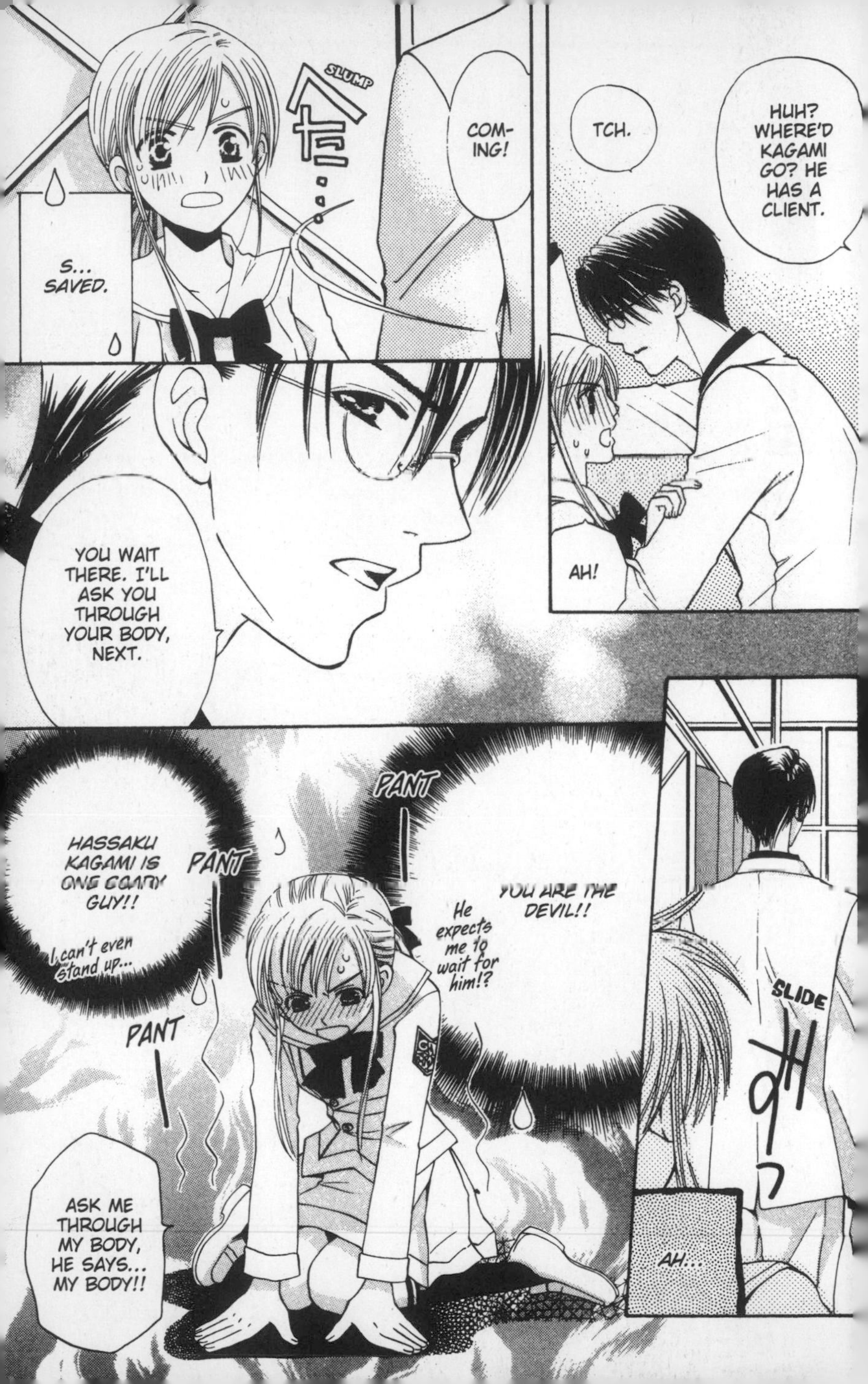

HUH? WHERE'D KAGAMI GO? HE HAS A CLIENT.
TCH.
AH!
COM-ING!
SLUMP
S... SAVED.
YOU WAIT THERE. I'LL ASK YOU THROUGH YOUR BODY, NEXT.
SLIDE
AH...
YOU ARE THE DEVIL!!
He expects me to wait for him!?
PANT
HASSAKU KAGAMI IS ONE SCARY GUY!!
PANT
I can't even stand up...
PANT
ASK ME THROUGH MY BODY, HE SAYS... MY BODY!!

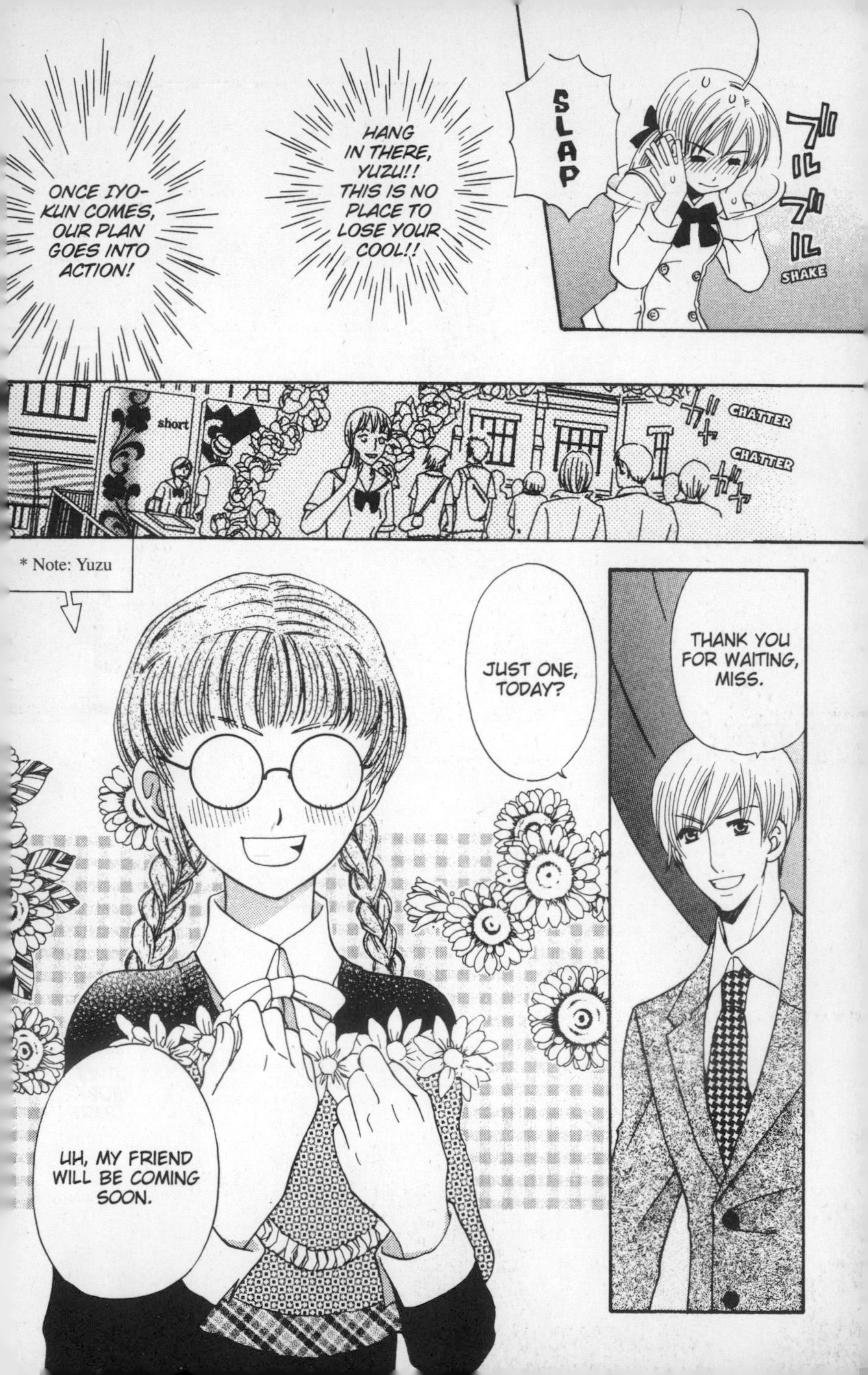
SLAP
ブルブル
SHAKE
HANG IN THERE, YUZU!! THIS IS NO PLACE TO LOSE YOUR COOL!!
ONCE IYO-KUN COMES, OUR PLAN GOES INTO ACTION!
ガヤ
CHATTER
CHATTER
ガヤ
short
THANK YOU FOR WAITING, MISS.
JUST ONE, TODAY?
* Note: Yuzu
UH, MY FRIEND WILL BE COMING SOON.

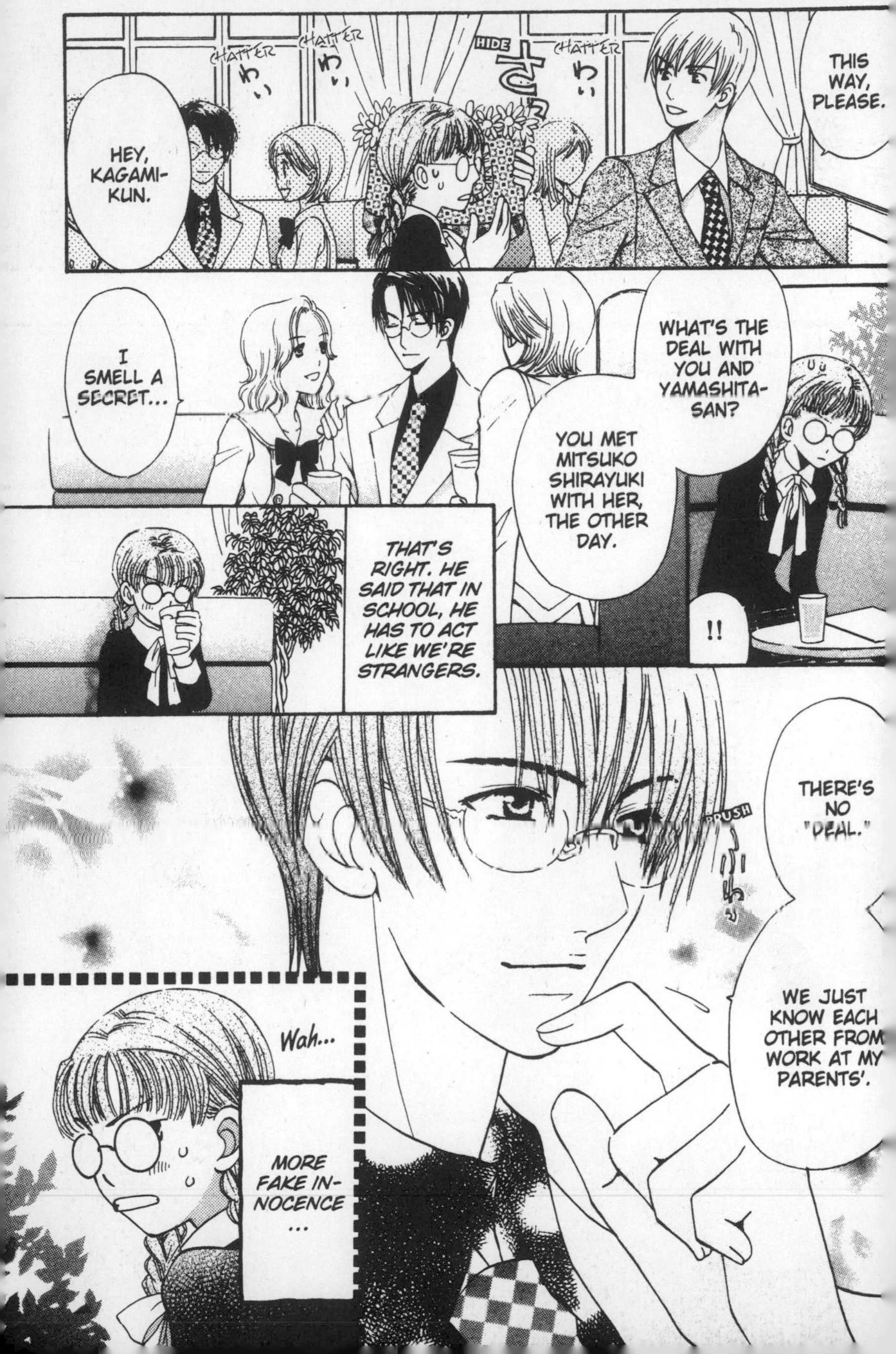
THIS WAY, PLEASE.
CHATTER
HIDE
CHATTER
CHATTER
HEY, KAGAMI-KUN.
WHAT'S THE DEAL WITH YOU AND YAMASHITA-SAN?
YOU MET MITSUKO SHIRAYUKI WITH HER, THE OTHER DAY.
!!
I SMELL A SECRET...
THAT'S RIGHT. HE SAID THAT IN SCHOOL, HE HAS TO ACT LIKE WE'RE STRANGERS.
THERE'S NO "DEAL."
PUSH
WE JUST KNOW EACH OTHER FROM WORK AT MY PARENTS'.
Wah...
MORE FAKE IN-NOCENCE ...

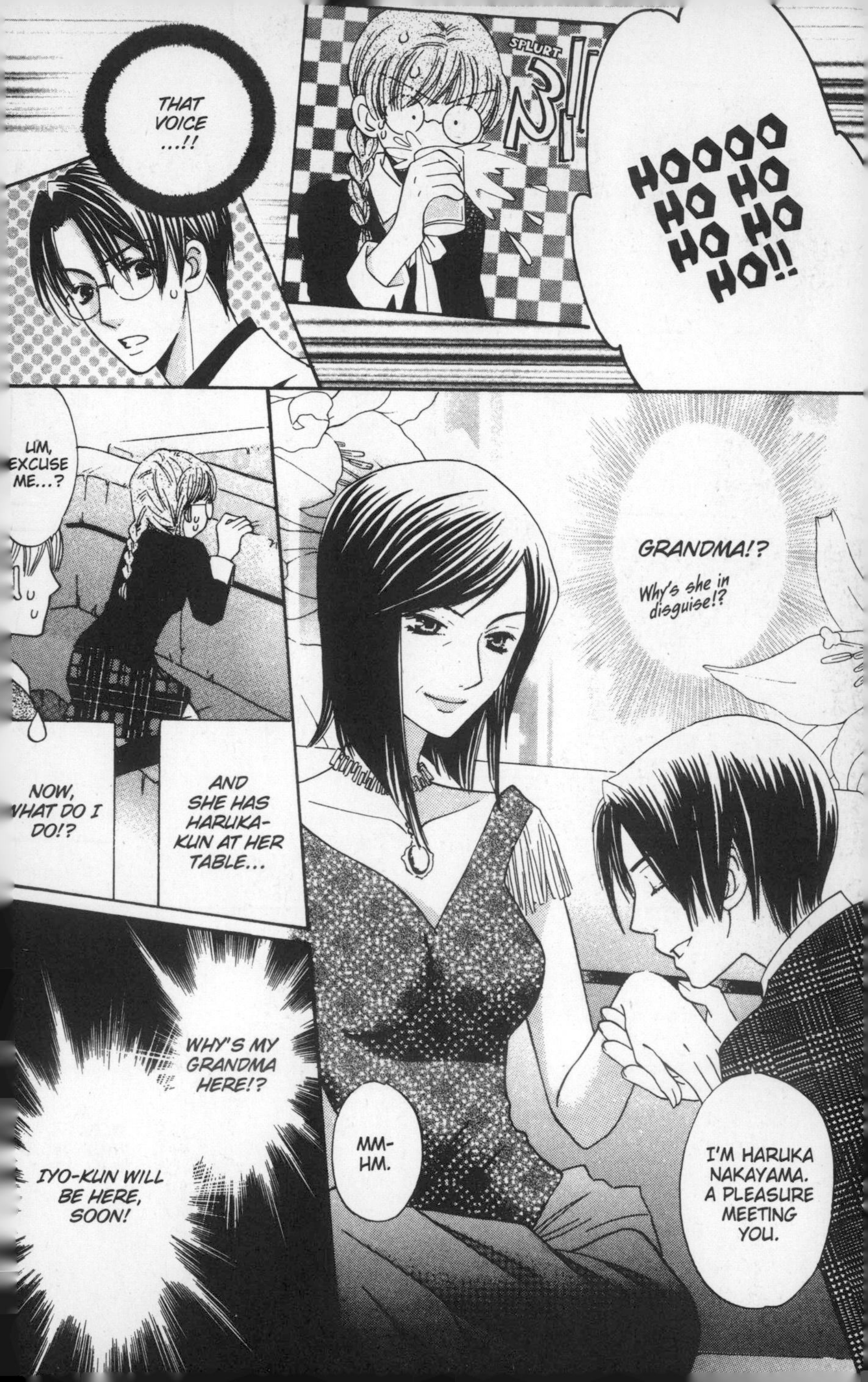
HOOOOO HO HO HO HO HO!!
SPLURT
THAT VOICE ...!!
GRANDMA!?
Why's she in disguise!?
I'M HARUKA NAKAYAMA. A PLEASURE MEETING YOU.
MM-HM.
UM, EXCUSE ME...?
AND SHE HAS HARUKA-KUN AT HER TABLE...
NOW, WHAT DO I DO!?
WHY'S MY GRANDMA HERE!?
IYO-KUN WILL BE HERE, SOON!

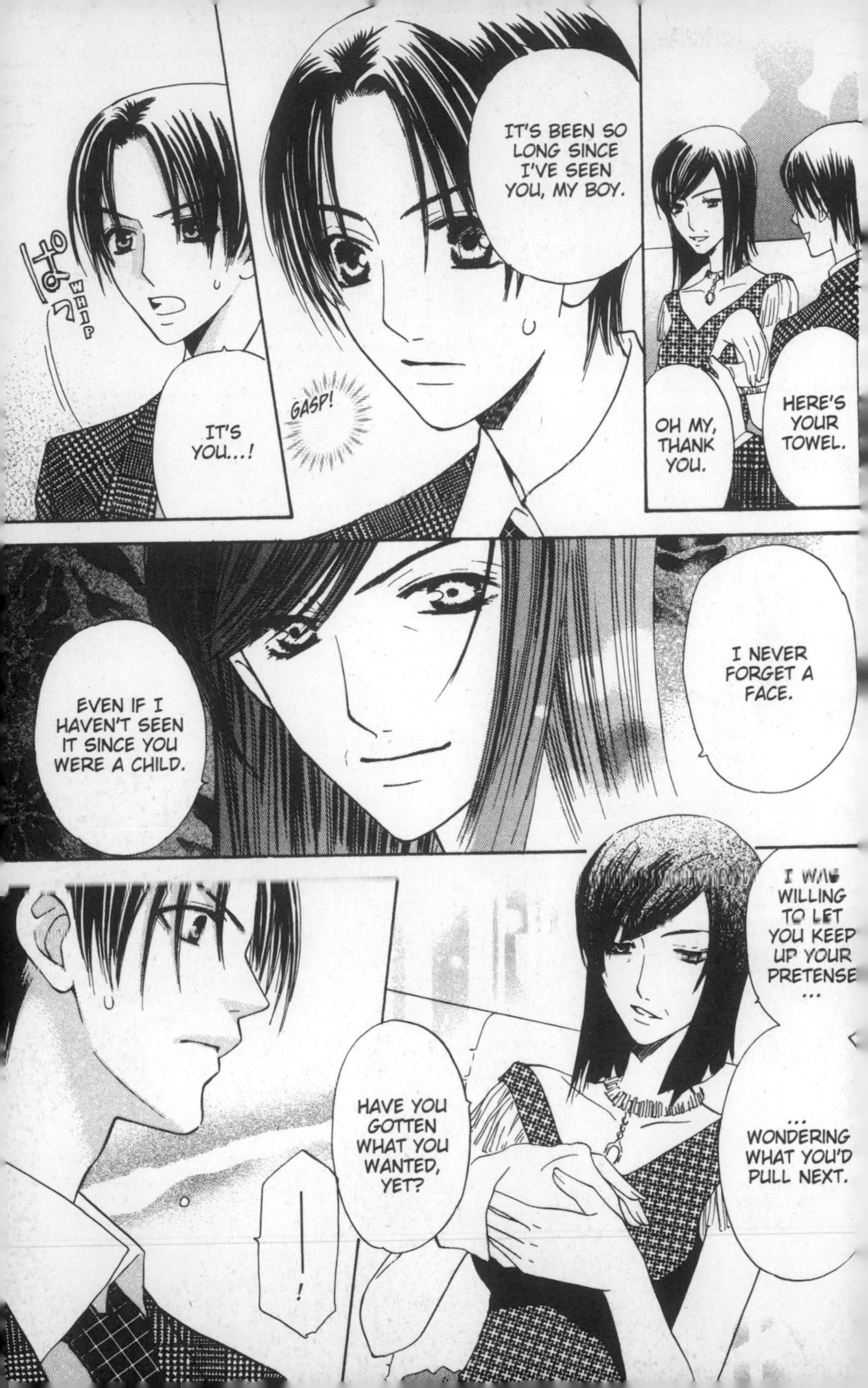
HERE'S YOUR TOWEL.
OH MY, THANK YOU.
IT'S BEEN SO LONG SINCE I'VE SEEN YOU, MY BOY.
GASP!
WHIP
IT'S YOU...!
I NEVER FORGET A FACE.
EVEN IF I HAVEN'T SEEN IT SINCE YOU WERE A CHILD.
I WAS WILLING TO LET YOU KEEP UP YOUR PRETENSE...
...WONDERING WHAT YOU'D PULL NEXT.
HAVE YOU GOTTEN WHAT YOU WANTED, YET?
!

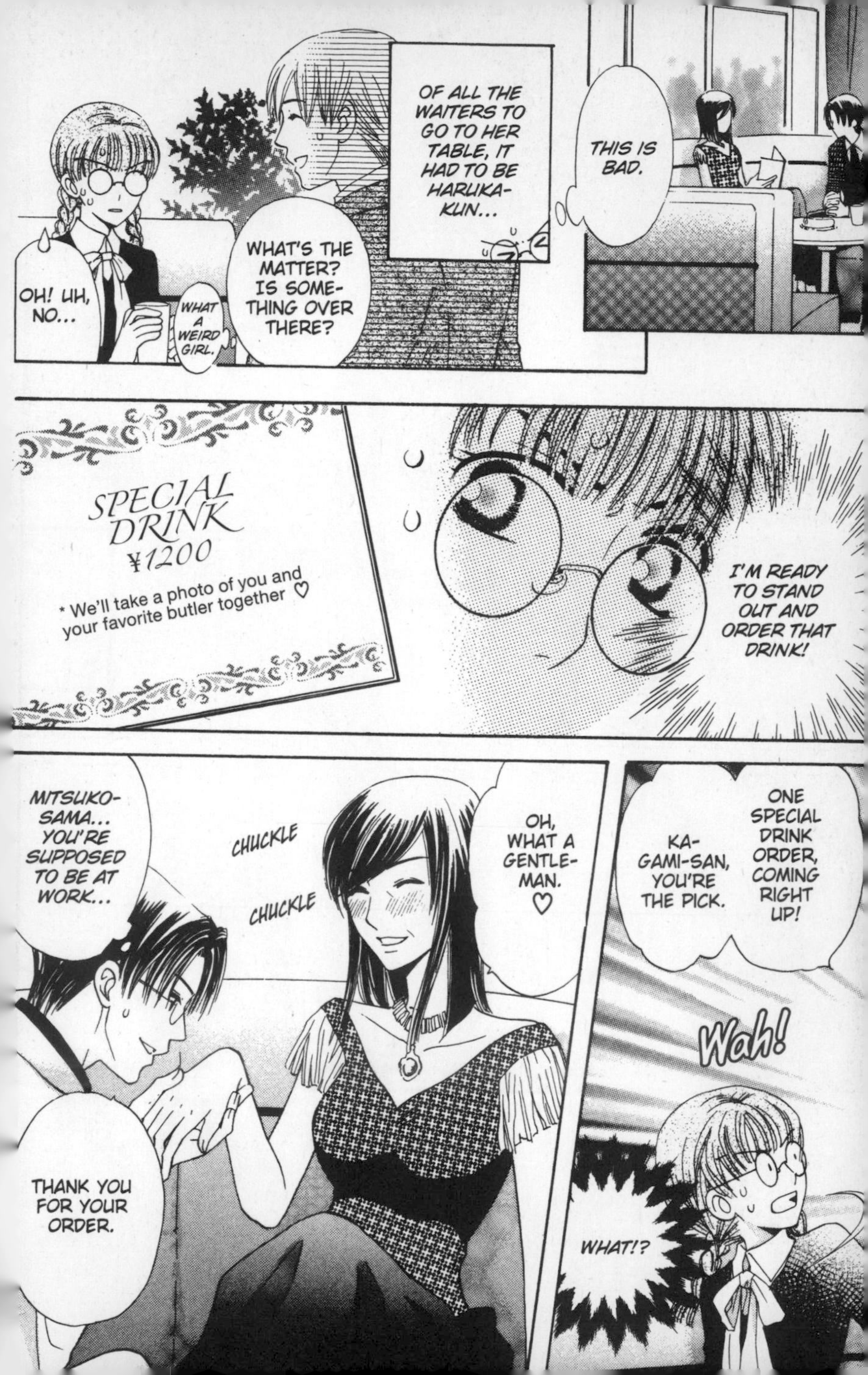
THIS IS BAD.
OF ALL THE WAITERS TO GO TO HER TABLE, IT HAD TO BE HARUKA-KUN...
WHAT'S THE MATTER? IS SOME-THING OVER THERE?
WHAT A WEIRD GIRL.
OH! UH, NO...
I'M READY TO STAND OUT AND ORDER THAT DRINK!
SPECIAL DRINK ¥1200
* We'll take a photo of you and your favorite butler together ♡
ONE SPECIAL DRINK ORDER, COMING RIGHT UP!
KA-GAMI-SAN, YOU'RE THE PICK.
Wah!
WHAT!?
OH, WHAT A GENTLE-MAN. ♡
CHUCKLE
CHUCKLE
MITSUKO-SAMA... YOU'RE SUPPOSED TO BE AT WORK...
THANK YOU FOR YOUR ORDER.

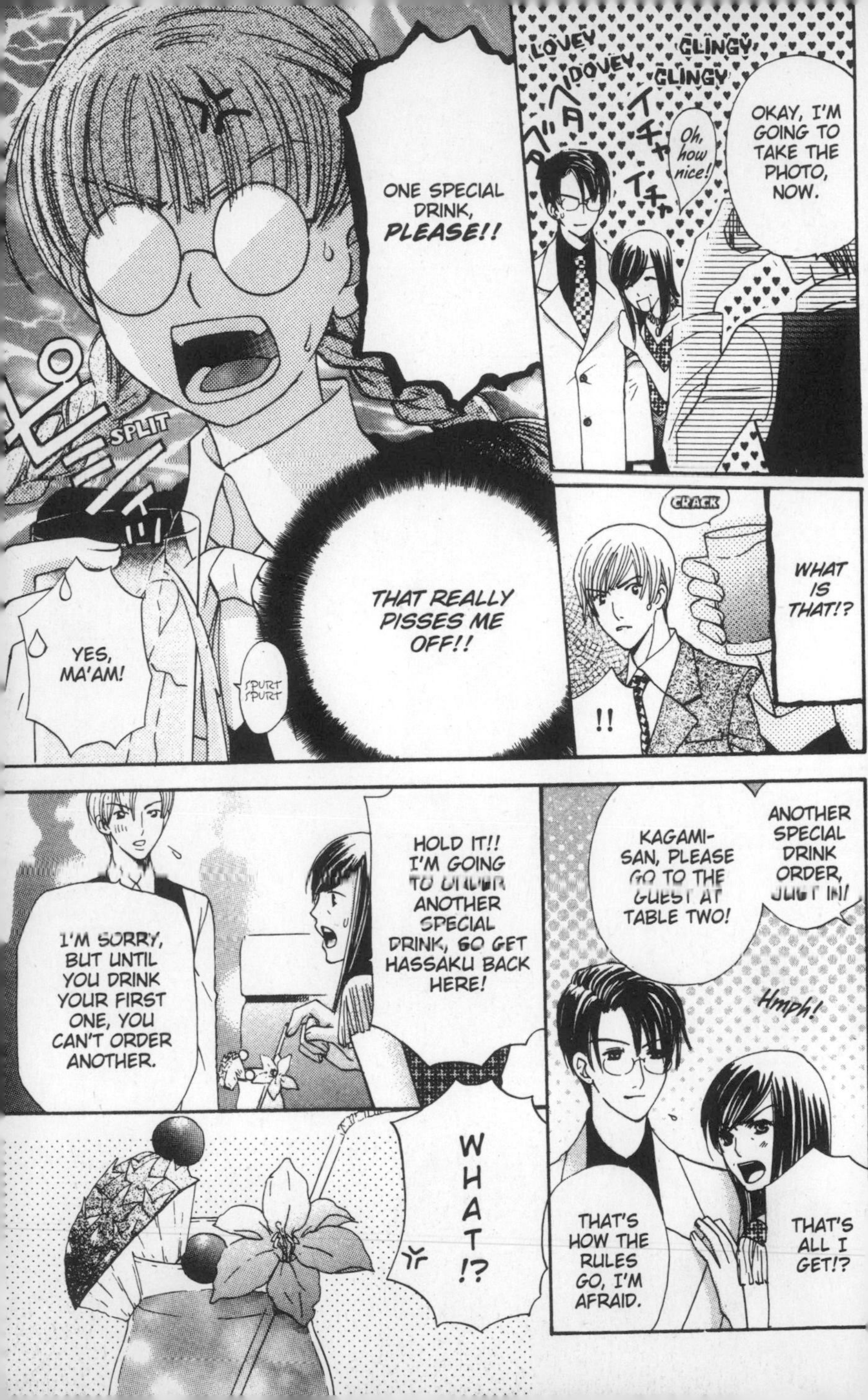

OKAY, I'M GOING TO TAKE THE PHOTO, NOW.
Oh, how nice!
LOVEY DOVEY
CLINGY CLINGY
CRACK
WHAT IS THAT!?
!!
ONE SPECIAL DRINK, PLEASE!!
THAT REALLY PISSES ME OFF!!
SPLIT
YES, MA'AM!
SPURT SPURT
ANOTHER SPECIAL DRINK ORDER, JUST IN!
KAGAMI-SAN, PLEASE GO TO THE GUEST AT TABLE TWO!
Hmph!
THAT'S ALL I GET!?
THAT'S HOW THE RULES GO, I'M AFRAID.
HOLD IT!! I'M GOING TO ORDER ANOTHER SPECIAL DRINK, GO GET HASSAKU BACK HERE!
I'M SORRY, BUT UNTIL YOU DRINK YOUR FIRST ONE, YOU CAN'T ORDER ANOTHER.
WHAT!?

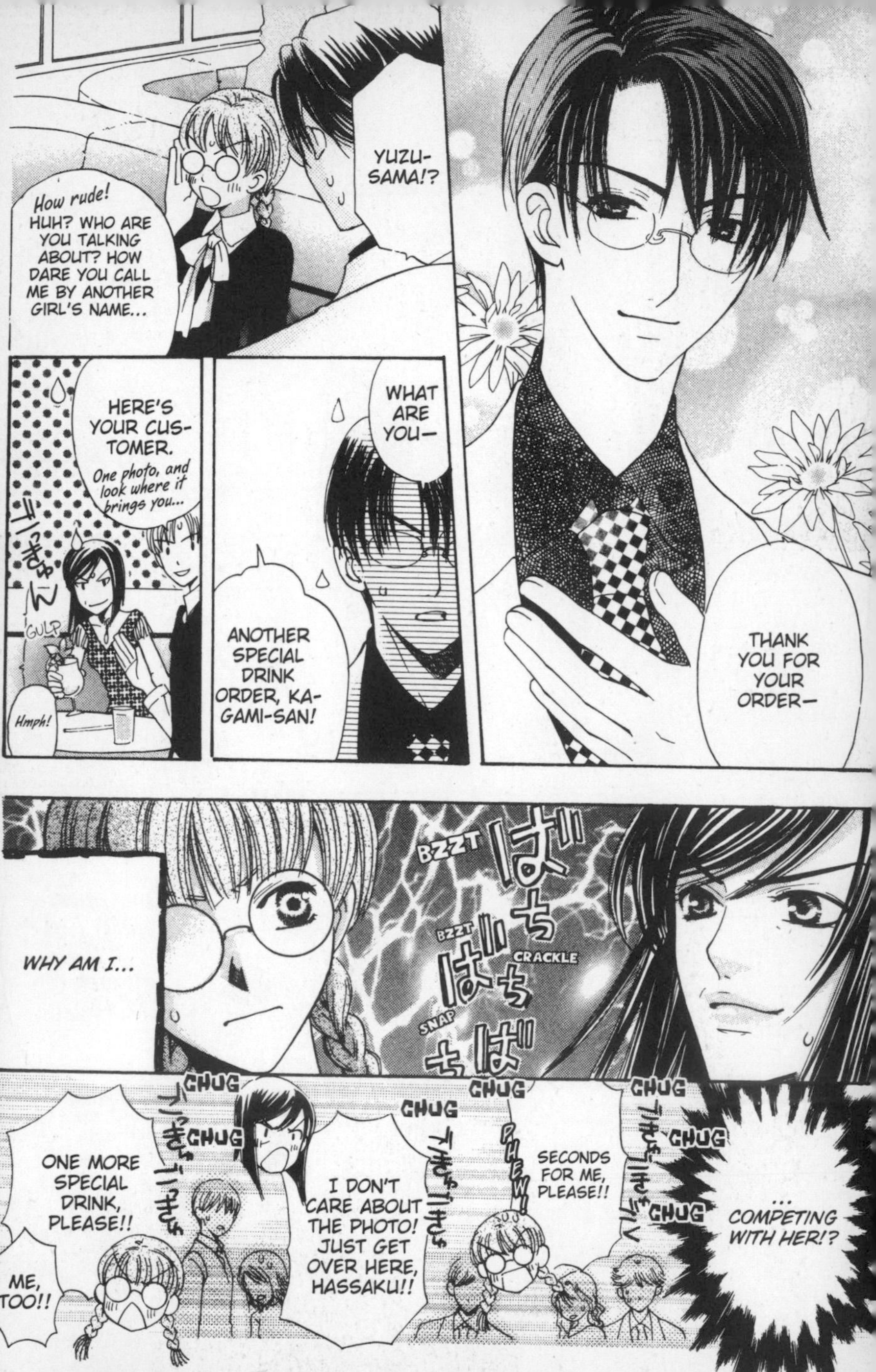
THANK YOU FOR YOUR ORDER—
YUZU-SAMA!?
How rude!
HUH? WHO ARE YOU TALKING ABOUT? HOW DARE YOU CALL ME BY ANOTHER GIRL'S NAME...
WHAT ARE YOU—
ANOTHER SPECIAL DRINK ORDER, KA-GAMI-SAN!
HERE'S YOUR CUS-TOMER.
One photo, and look where it brings you...
GULP
Hmph!
BZZT
BZZT
CRACKLE
SNAP
WHY AM I...
... COMPETING WITH HER!?
CHUG
CHUG
CHUG
SECONDS FOR ME, PLEASE!!
PHEW!
CHUG
CHUG
I DON'T CARE ABOUT THE PHOTO! JUST GET OVER HERE, HASSAKU!!
CHUG
CHUG
ONE MORE SPECIAL DRINK, PLEASE!!
ME, TOO!!

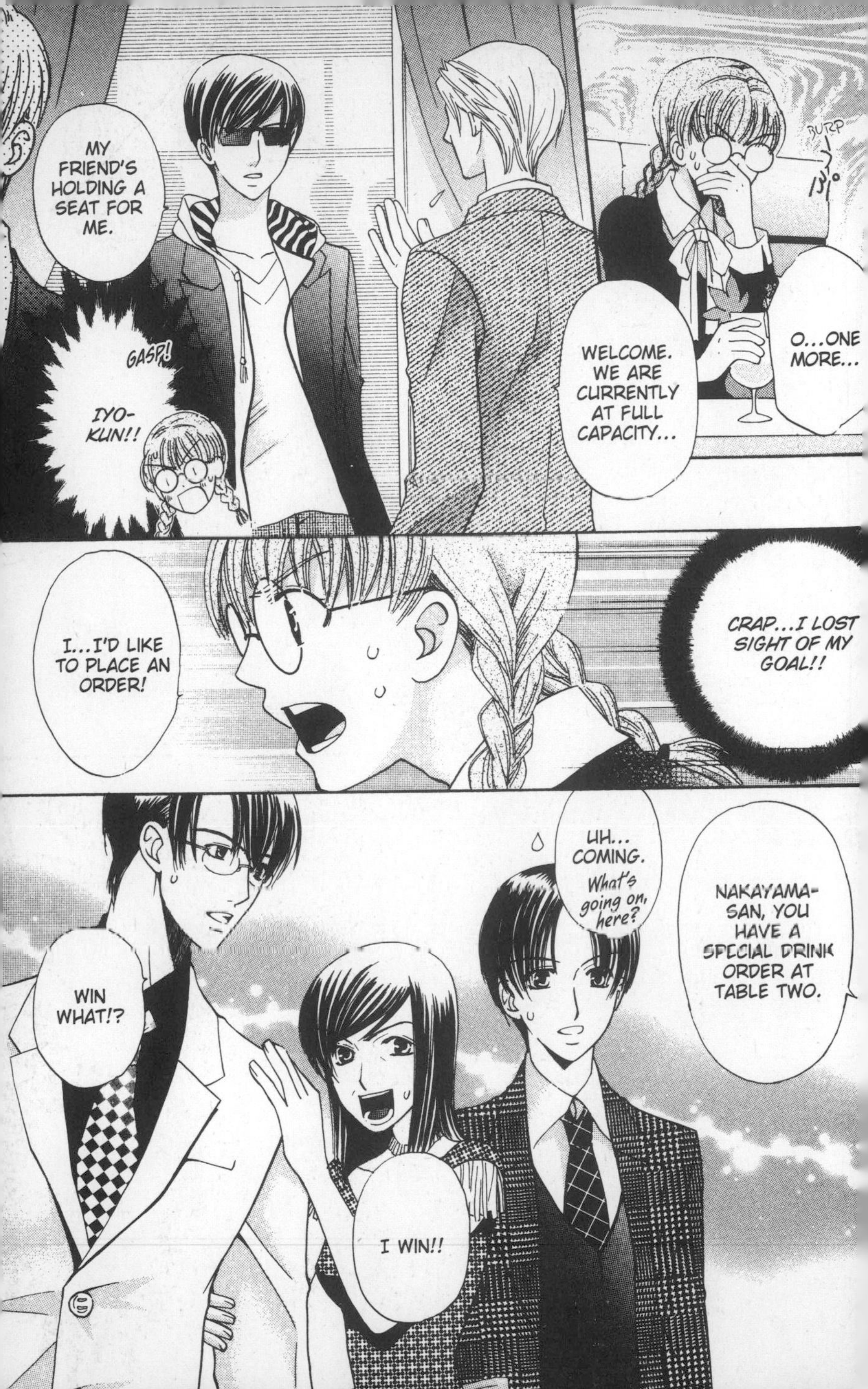
BURP
O...ONE MORE...
WELCOME. WE ARE CURRENTLY AT FULL CAPACITY...
MY FRIEND'S HOLDING A SEAT FOR ME.
GASP!
IYO-KUN!!
CRAP...I LOST SIGHT OF MY GOAL!!
I...I'D LIKE TO PLACE AN ORDER!
NAKAYAMA-SAN, YOU HAVE A SPECIAL DRINK ORDER AT TABLE TWO.
UH... COMING. What's going on, here?
I WIN!!
WIN WHAT!?

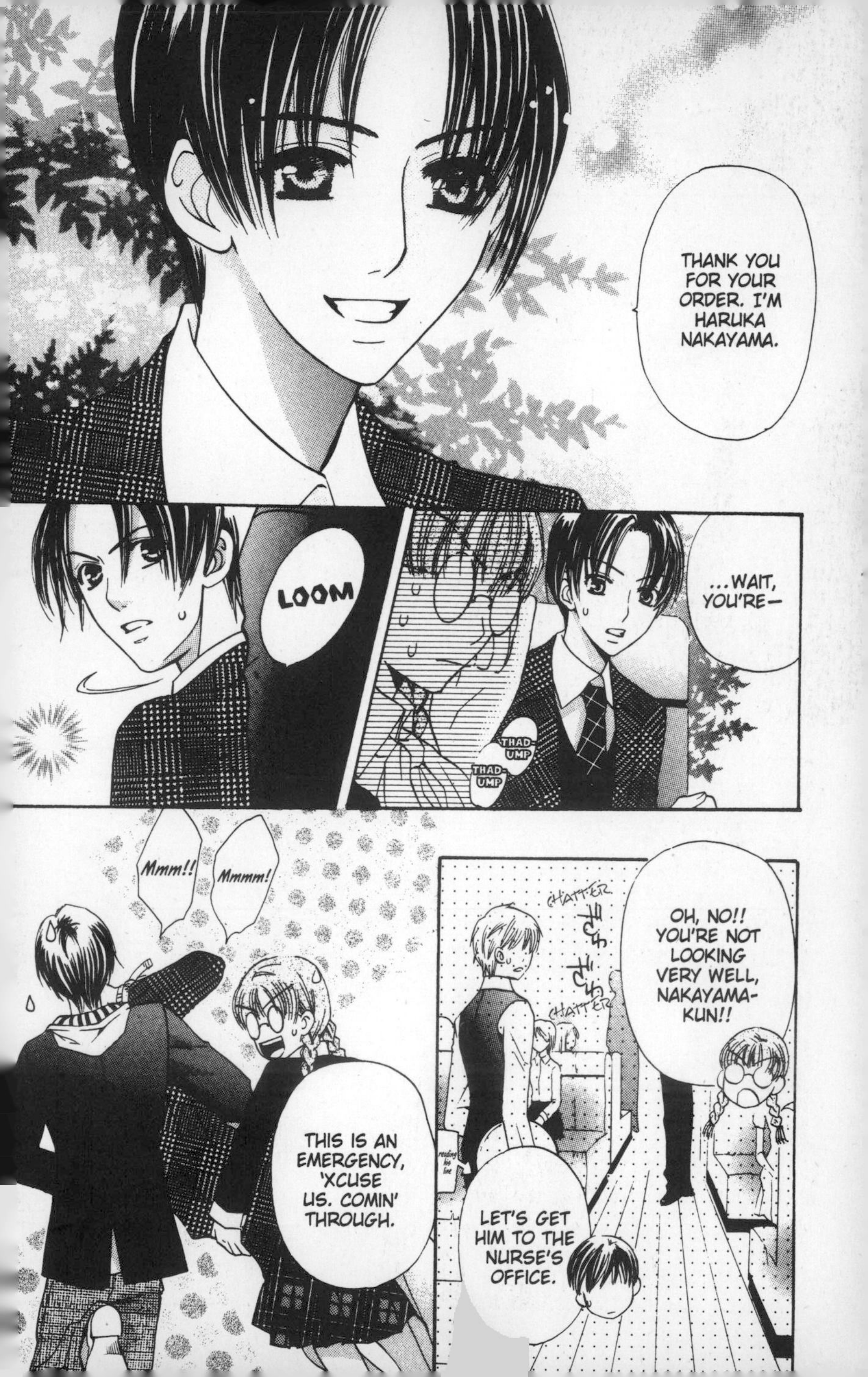
THANK YOU FOR YOUR ORDER. I'M HARUKA NAKAYAMA.
...WAIT, YOU'RE—
THAD-UMP
THAD-UMP
LOOM
OH, NO!! YOU'RE NOT LOOKING VERY WELL, NAKAYAMA-KUN!!
CHATTER
CHATTER
reading his line
LET'S GET HIM TO THE NURSE'S OFFICE.
Mmmm!
Mmm!!
THIS IS AN EMERGENCY, 'XCUSE US. COMIN' THROUGH.

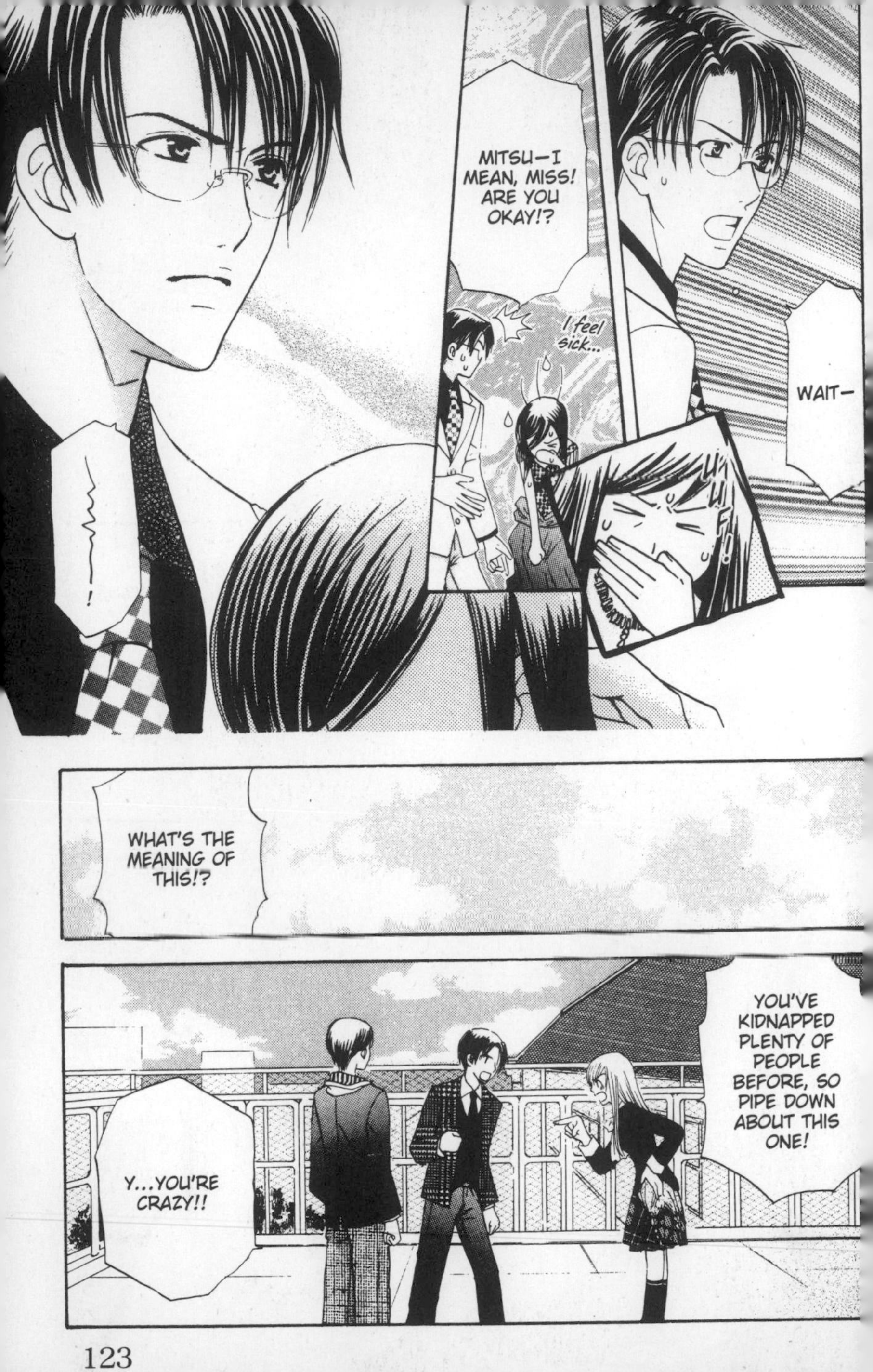

WAIT—
MITSU—I MEAN, MISS! ARE YOU OKAY!?
I feel sick...
UUF!!
...!
WHAT'S THE MEANING OF THIS!?
YOU'VE KIDNAPPED PLENTY OF PEOPLE BEFORE, SO PIPE DOWN ABOUT THIS ONE!
Y...YOU'RE CRAZY!!

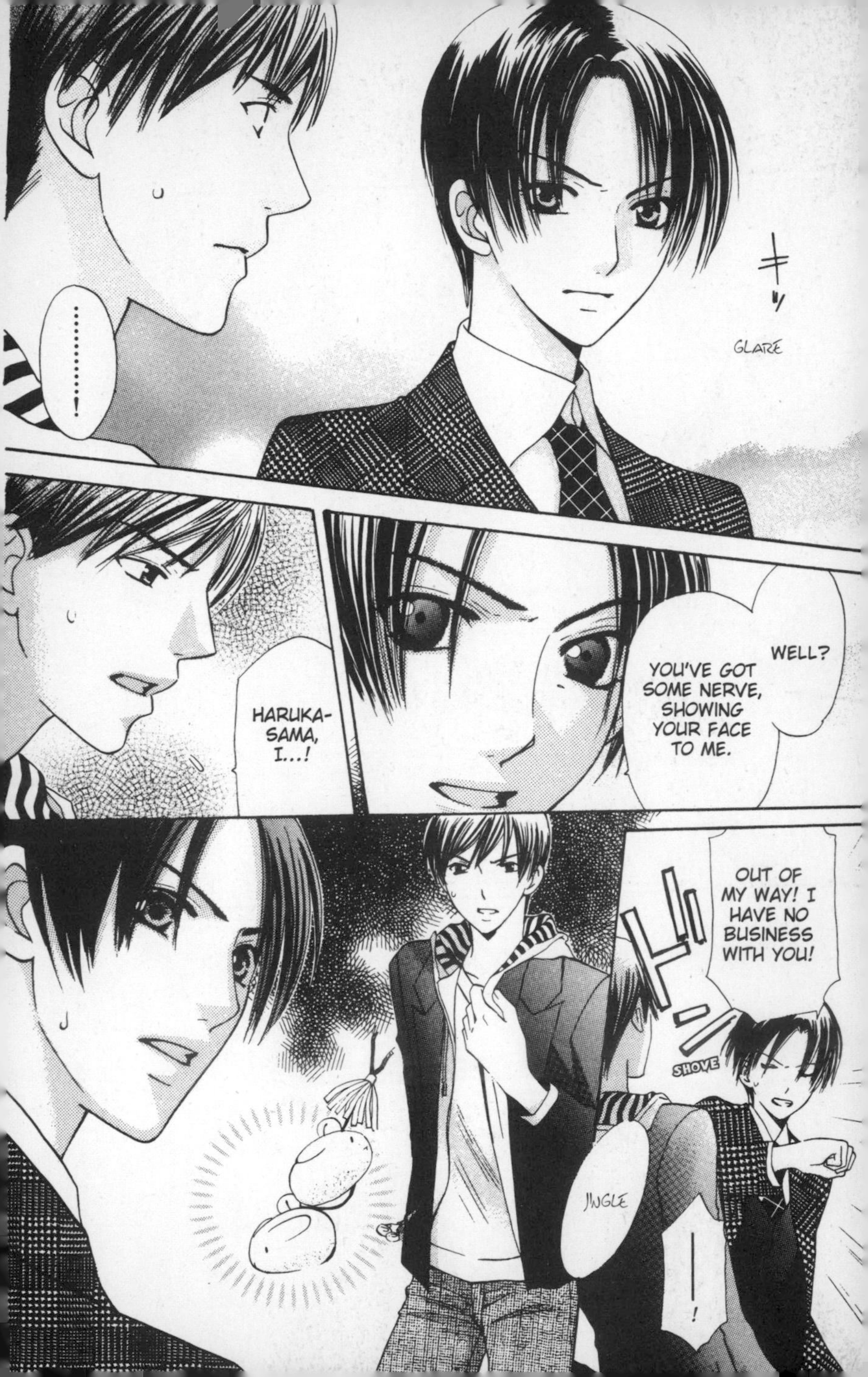
キッ
GLARE
.........!
WELL?
YOU'VE GOT SOME NERVE, SHOWING YOUR FACE TO ME.
HARUKA-SAMA, I...!
OUT OF MY WAY! I HAVE NO BUSINESS WITH YOU!
SHOVE
—!
JINGLE

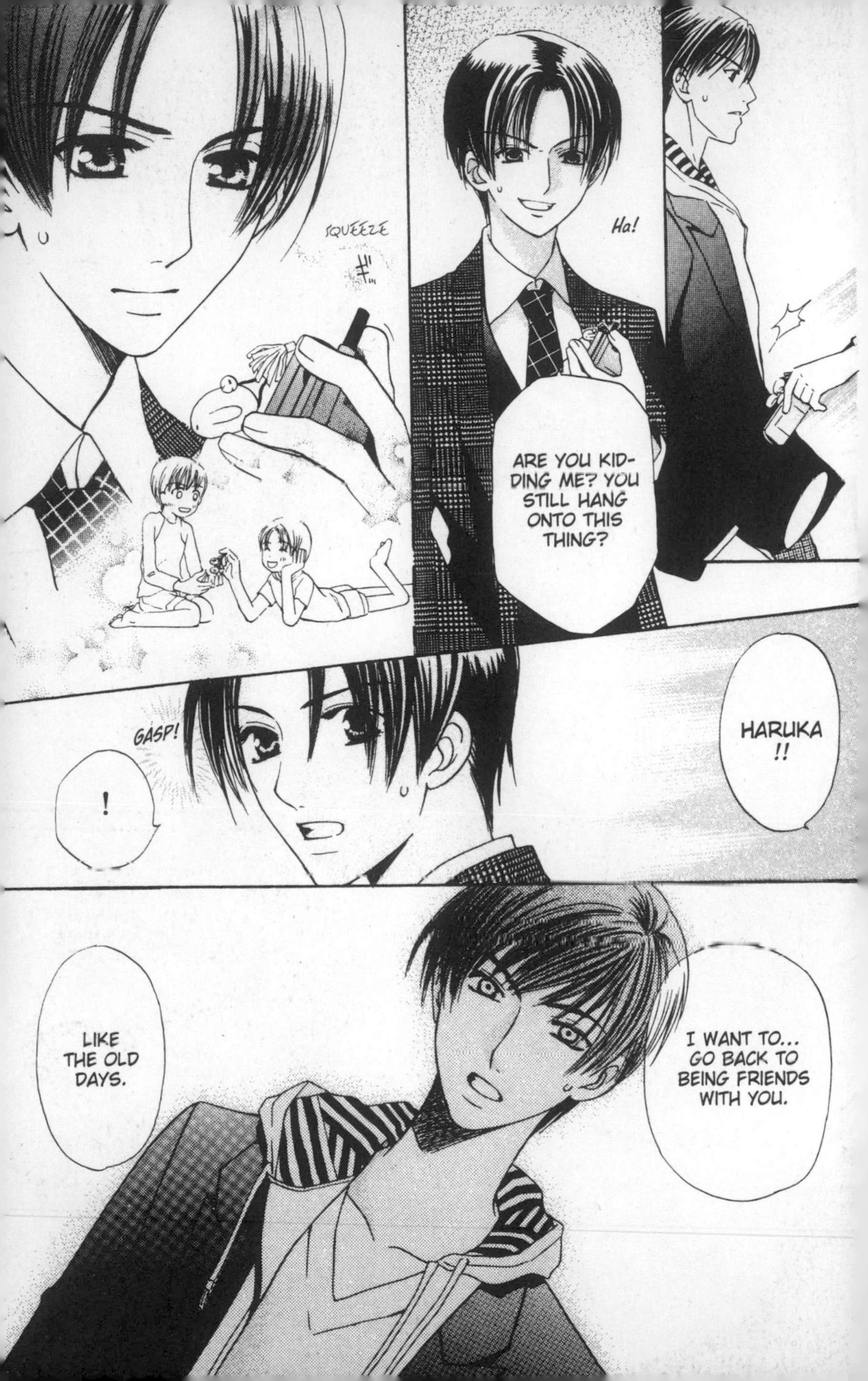
Ha!
ARE YOU KID-DING ME? YOU STILL HANG ONTO THIS THING?
SQUEEZE
HARUKA !!
GASP!
!
I WANT TO... GO BACK TO BEING FRIENDS WITH YOU.
LIKE THE OLD DAYS.

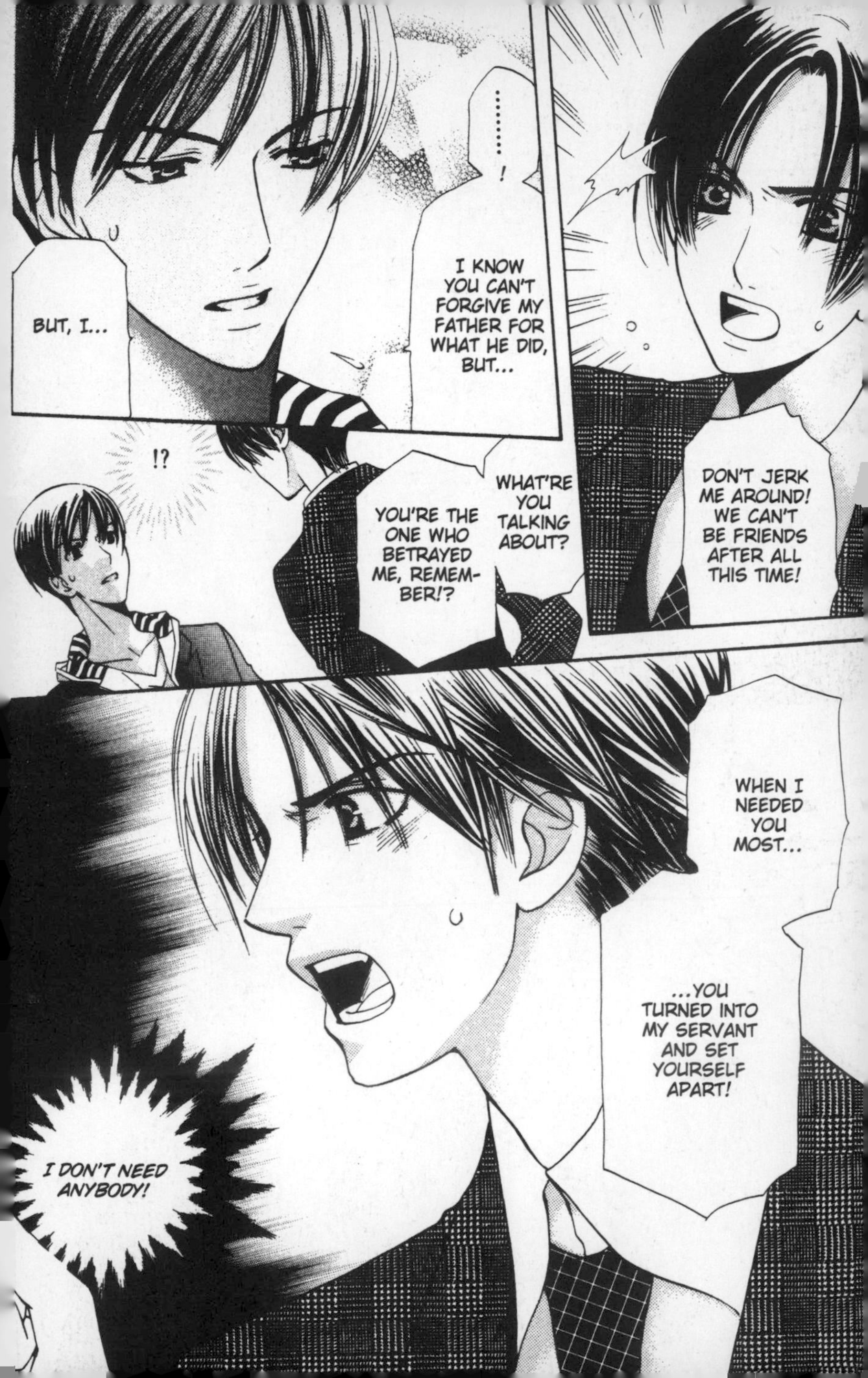
DON'T JERK ME AROUND! WE CAN'T BE FRIENDS AFTER ALL THIS TIME!
......!
I KNOW YOU CAN'T FORGIVE MY FATHER FOR WHAT HE DID, BUT...
BUT, I...
WHAT'RE YOU TALKING ABOUT?
YOU'RE THE ONE WHO BETRAYED ME, REMEMBER!?
!?
WHEN I NEEDED YOU MOST...
...YOU TURNED INTO MY SERVANT AND SET YOURSELF APART!
I DON'T NEED ANYBODY!

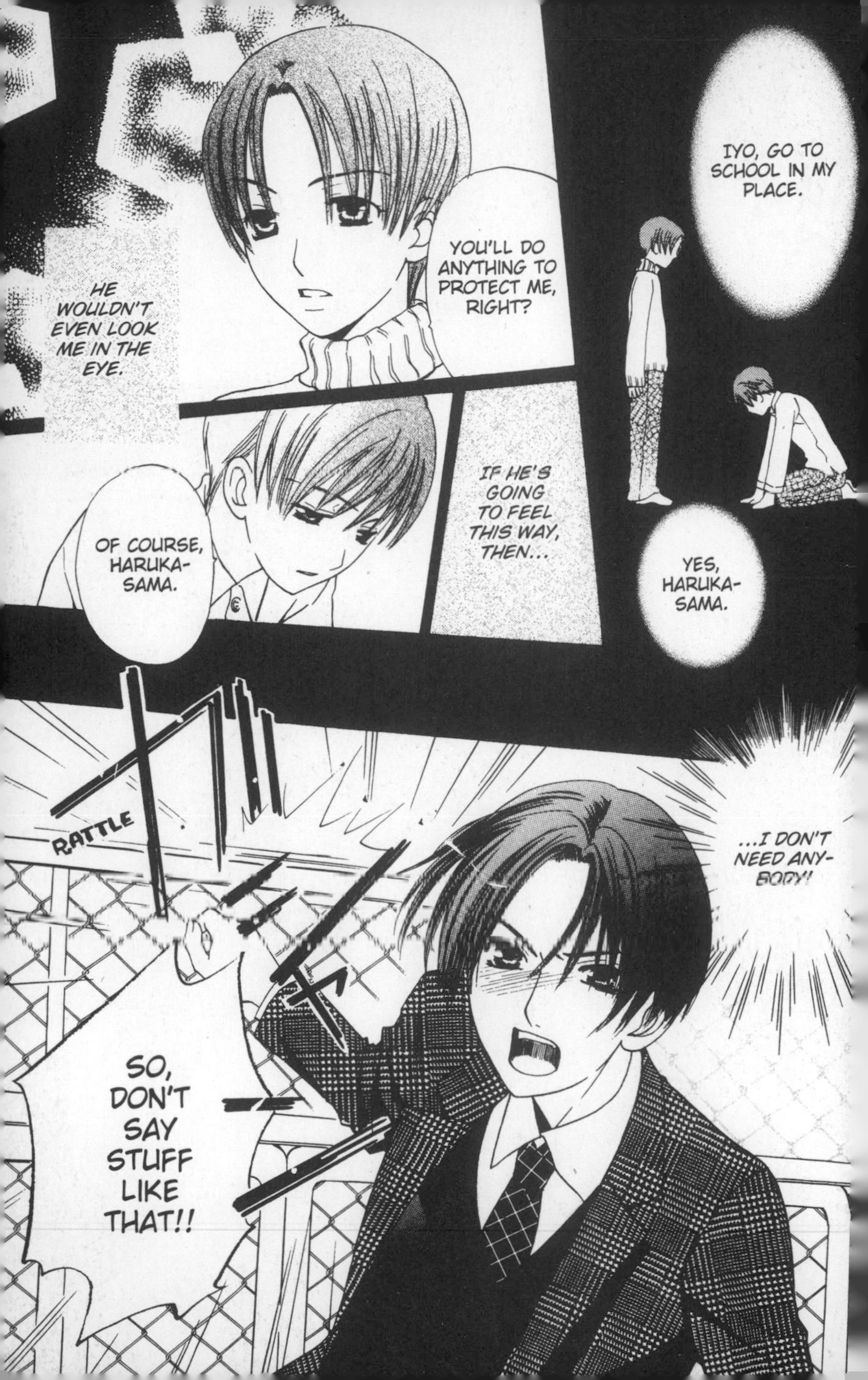
IYO, GO TO SCHOOL IN MY PLACE.
YES, HARUKA-SAMA.
YOU'LL DO ANYTHING TO PROTECT ME, RIGHT?
HE WOULDN'T EVEN LOOK ME IN THE EYE.
IF HE'S GOING TO FEEL THIS WAY, THEN...
OF COURSE, HARUKA-SAMA.
...I DON'T NEED ANY-BODY!!
RATTLE
SO, DON'T SAY STUFF LIKE THAT!!

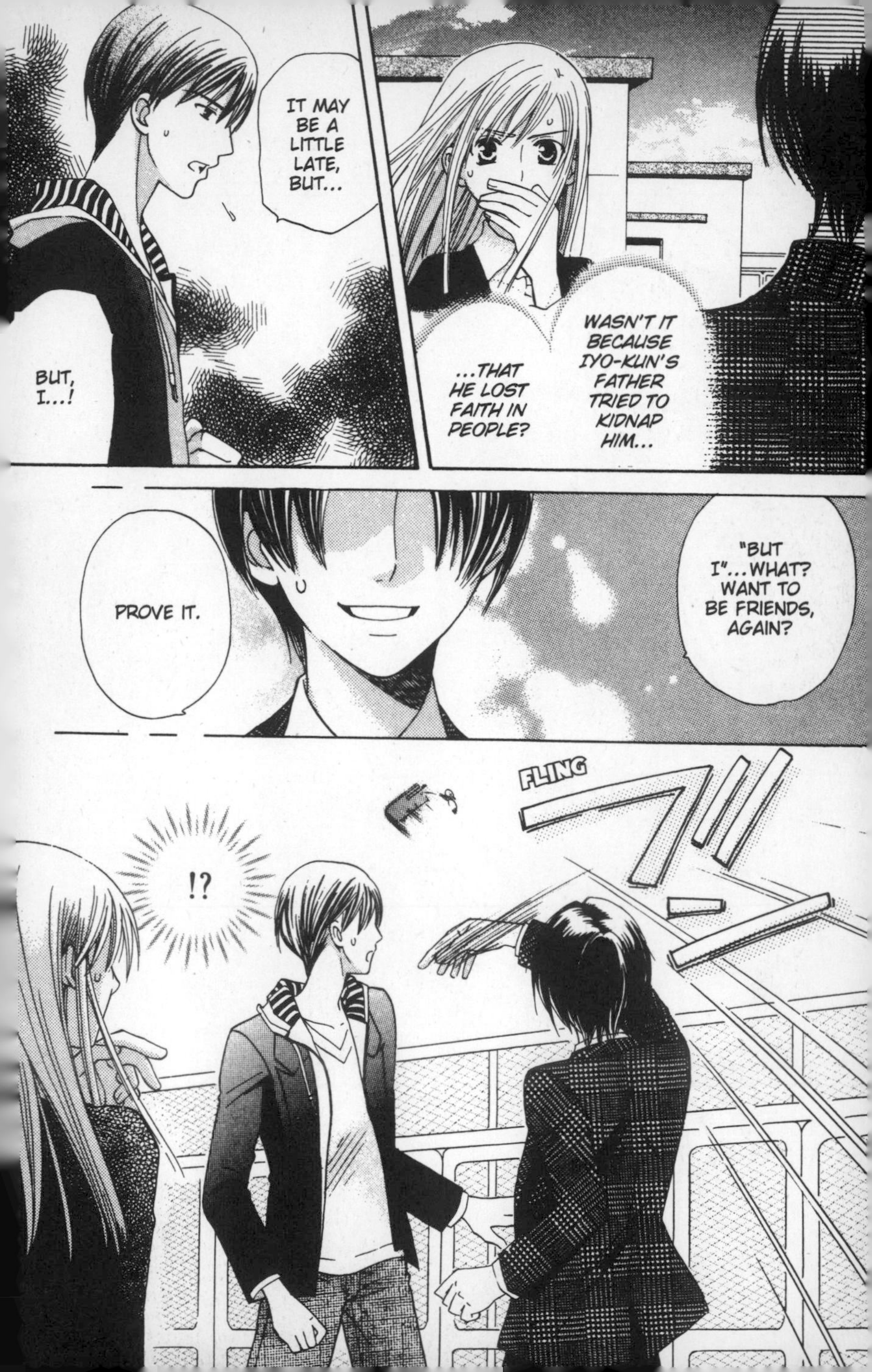
WASN'T IT BECAUSE IYO-KUN'S FATHER TRIED TO KIDNAP HIM...
...THAT HE LOST FAITH IN PEOPLE?
IT MAY BE A LITTLE LATE, BUT...
BUT, I...!
"BUT I"...WHAT? WANT TO BE FRIENDS, AGAIN?
PROVE IT.
FLING
!?

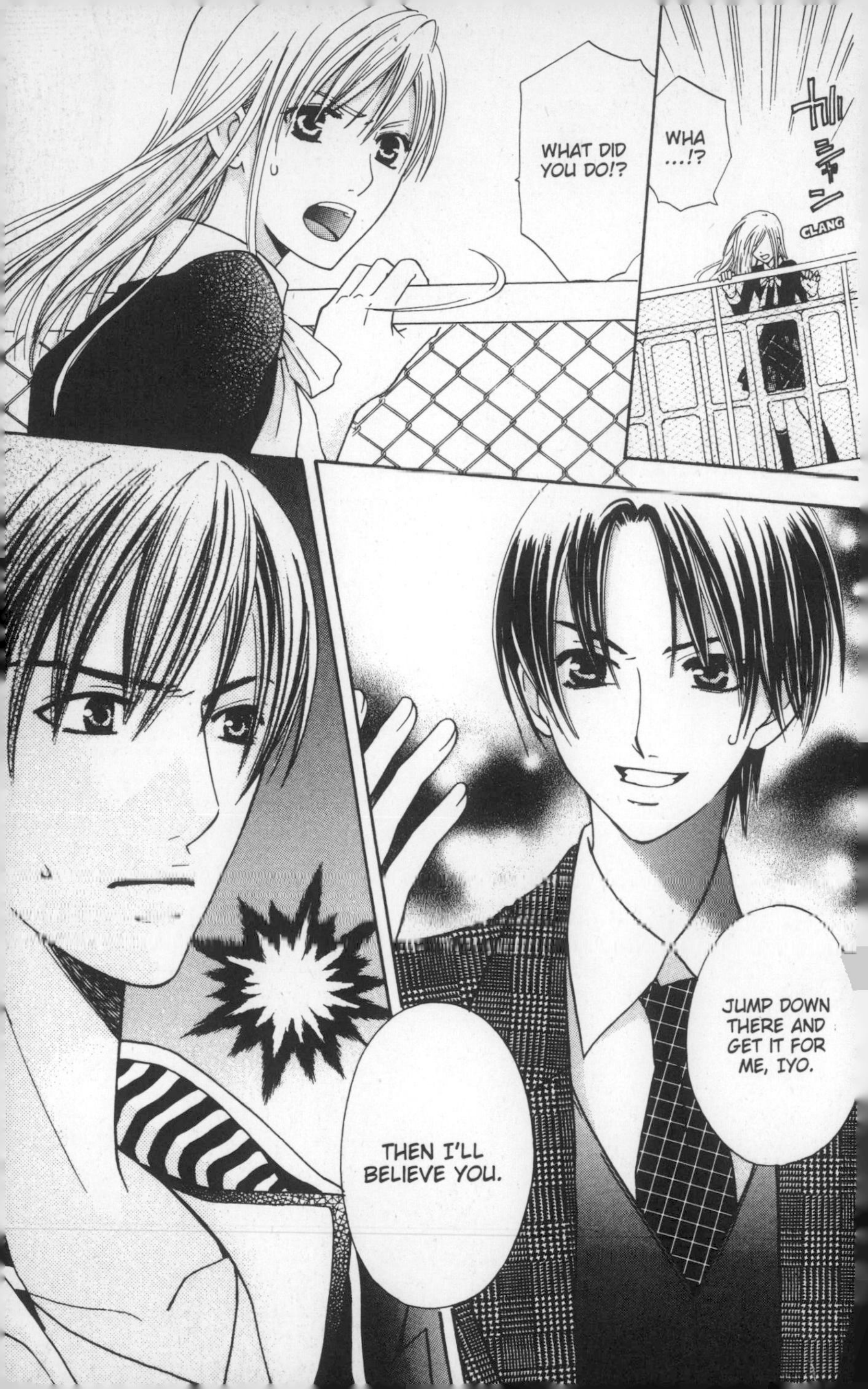
ガシャン
CLANG
WHA ...!?
WHAT DID YOU DO!?
JUMP DOWN THERE AND GET IT FOR ME, IYO.
THEN I'LL BELIEVE YOU.

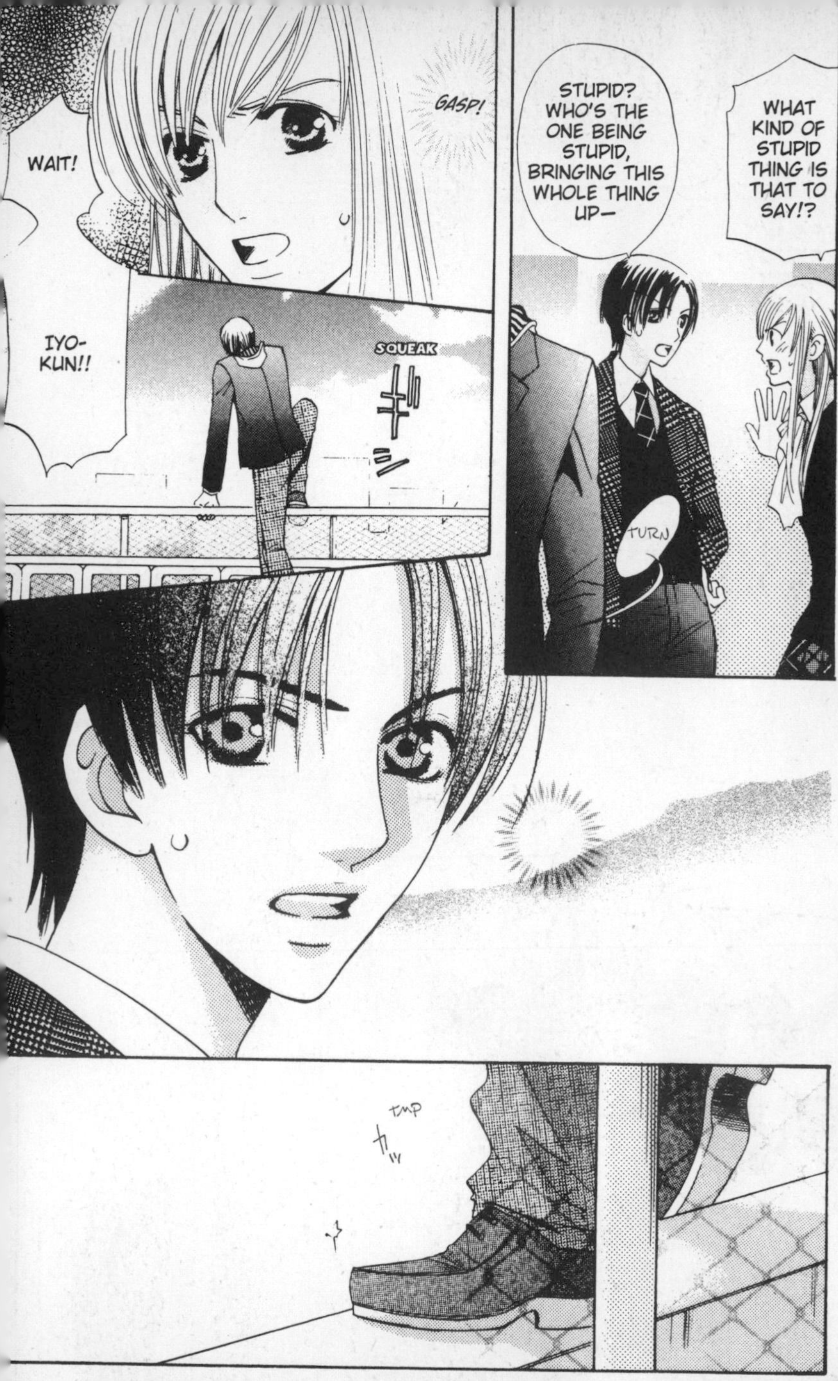
WHAT KIND OF STUPID THING IS THAT TO SAY!?
STUPID? WHO'S THE ONE BEING STUPID, BRINGING THIS WHOLE THING UP—
TURN
GASP!
WAIT!
SQUEAK
IYO-KUN!!
TMP

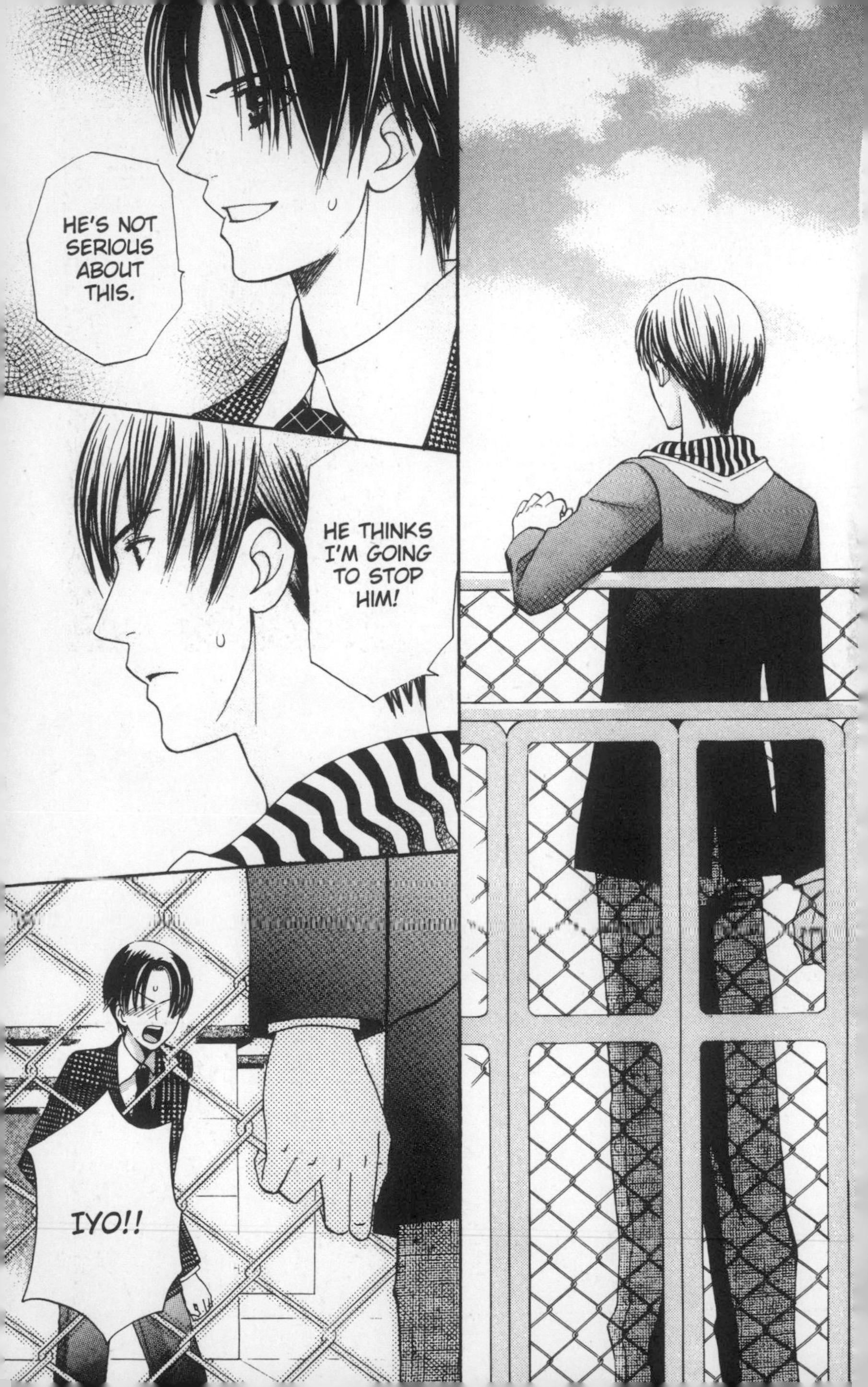
HE'S NOT SERIOUS ABOUT THIS.
HE THINKS I'M GOING TO STOP HIM!
IYO!!

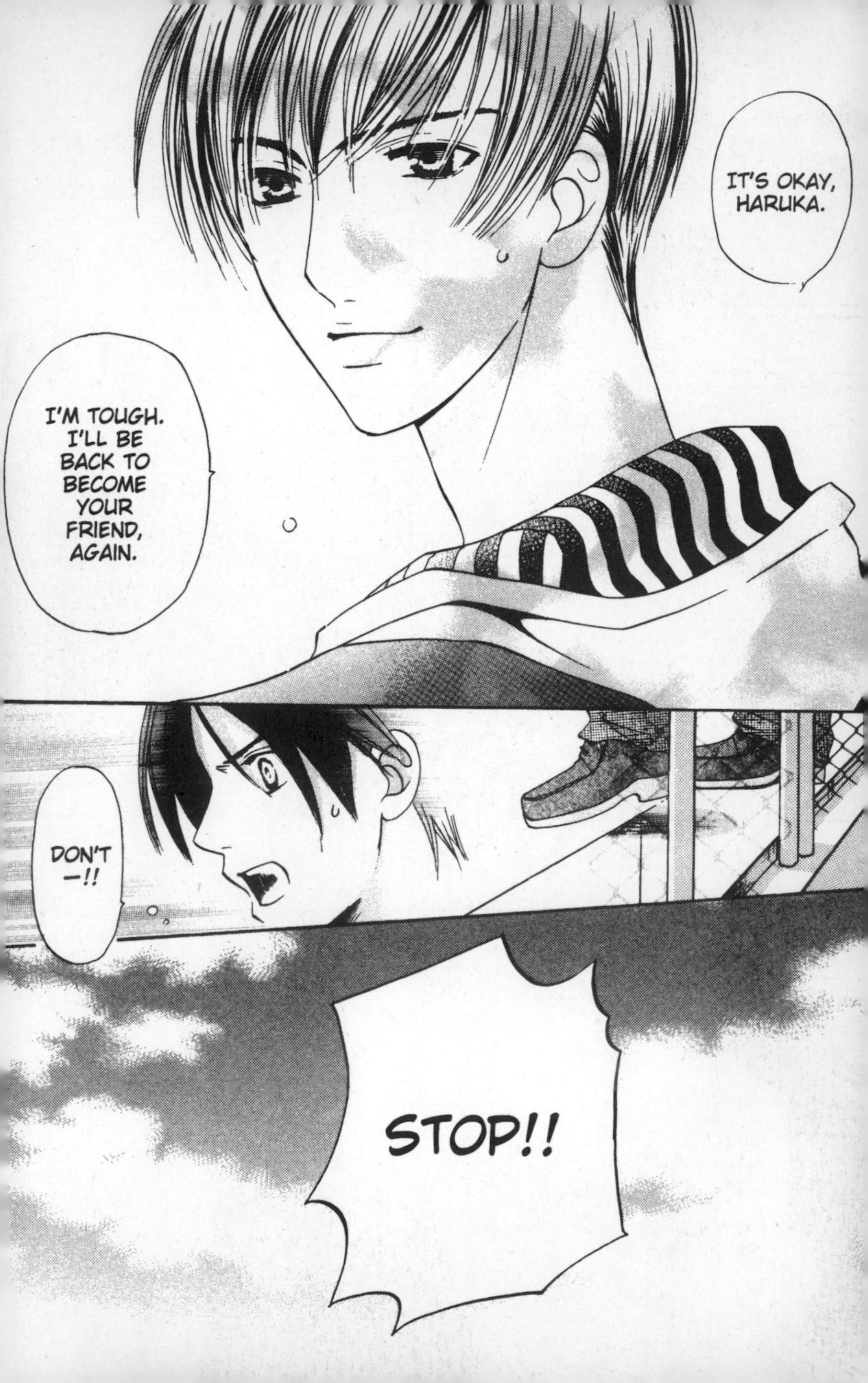
IT'S OKAY, HARUKA.
I'M TOUGH. I'LL BE BACK TO BECOME YOUR FRIEND, AGAIN.
DON'T —!!
STOP!!

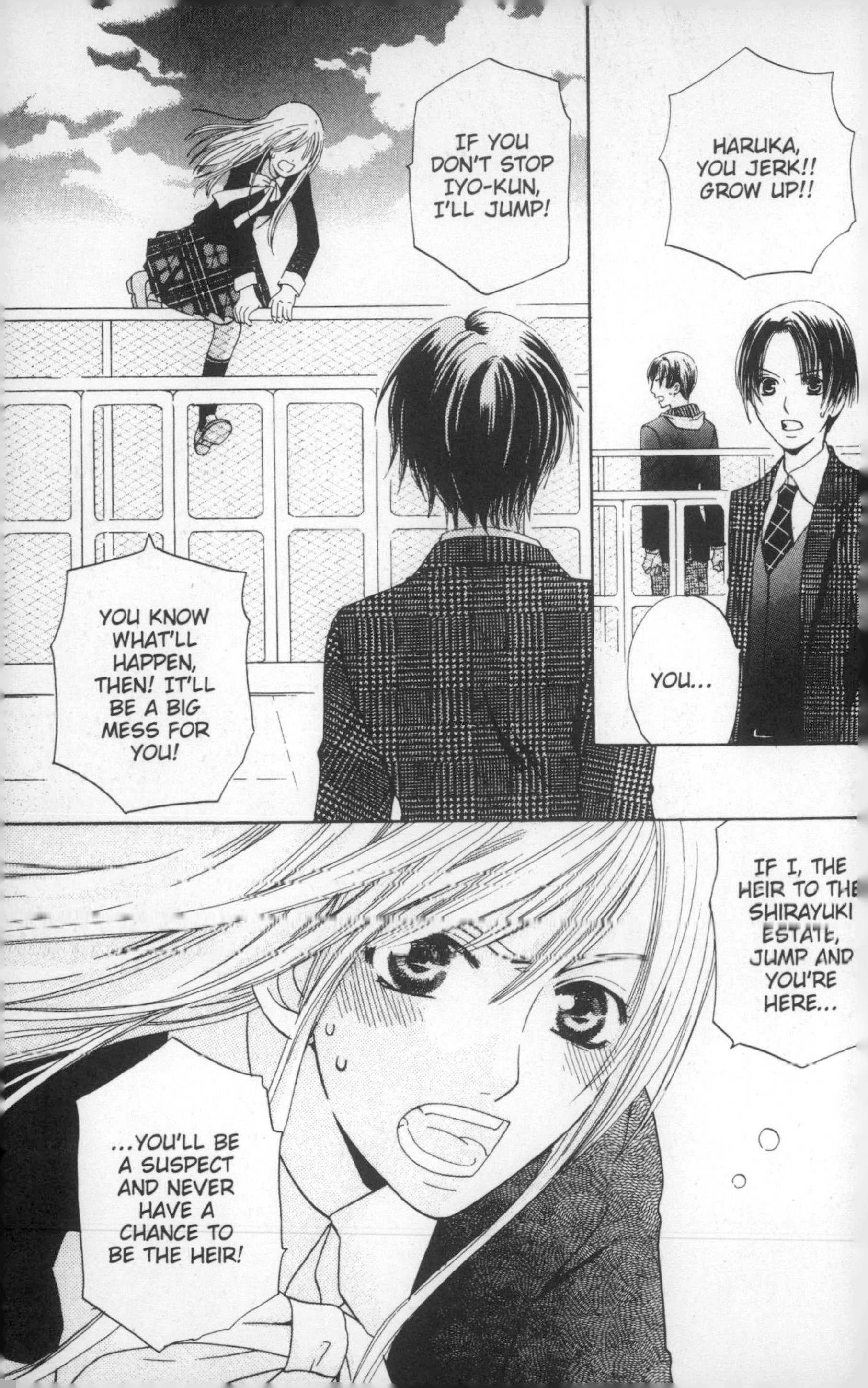
HARUKA, YOU JERK!! GROW UP!!
YOU...
IF YOU DON'T STOP IYO-KUN, I'LL JUMP!
YOU KNOW WHAT'LL HAPPEN, THEN! IT'LL BE A BIG MESS FOR YOU!
IF I, THE HEIR TO THE SHIRAYUKI ESTATE, JUMP AND YOU'RE HERE...
...YOU'LL BE A SUSPECT AND NEVER HAVE A CHANCE TO BE THE HEIR!

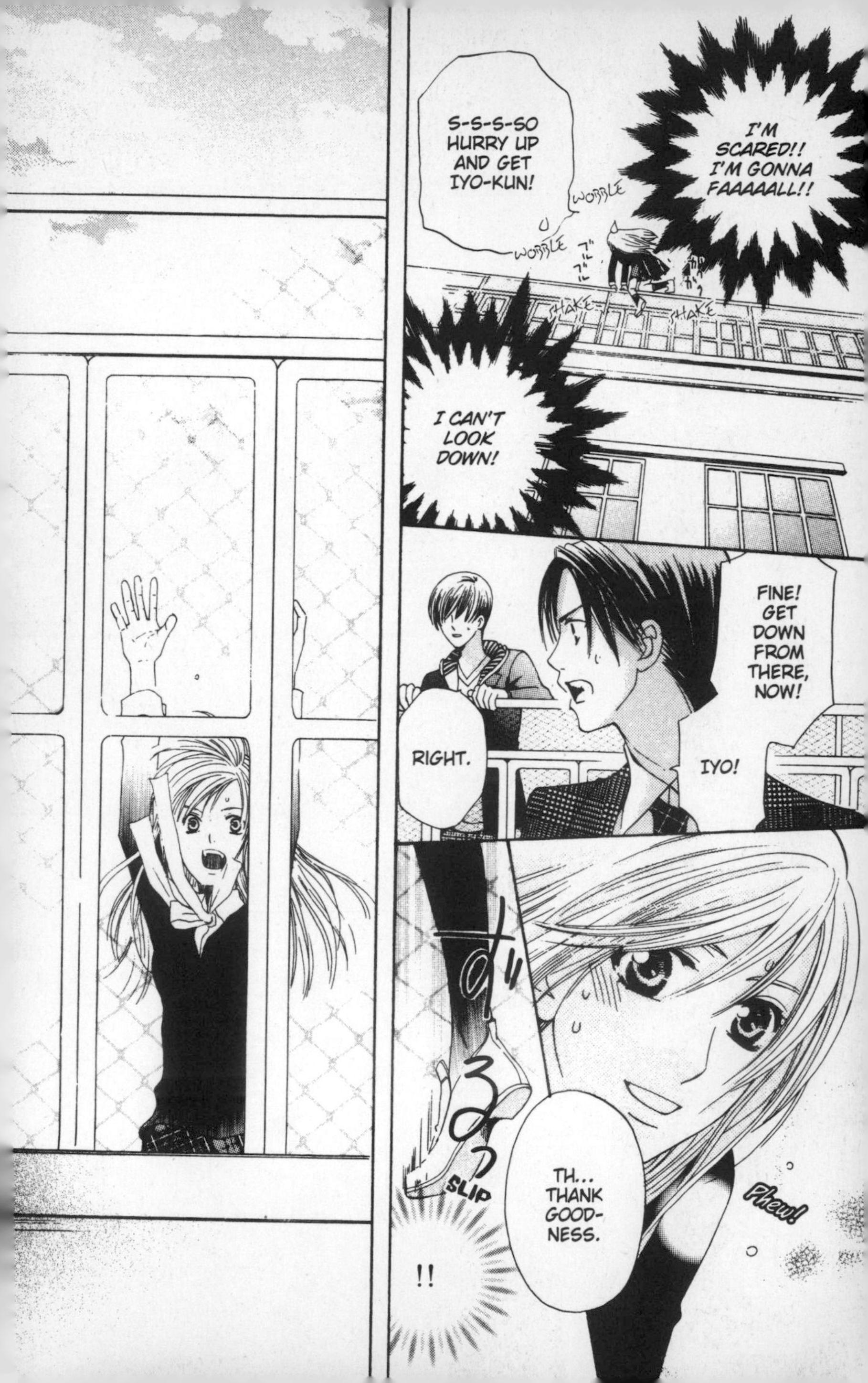
I'M SCARED!! I'M GONNA FAAAAALL!!
S-S-S-SO HURRY UP AND GET IYO-KUN!
WOBBLE
WOBBLE
SHAKE
SHAKE
I CAN'T LOOK DOWN!
FINE! GET DOWN FROM THERE, NOW!
IYO!
RIGHT.
Phew!
TH... THANK GOODNESS.
SLIP
!!

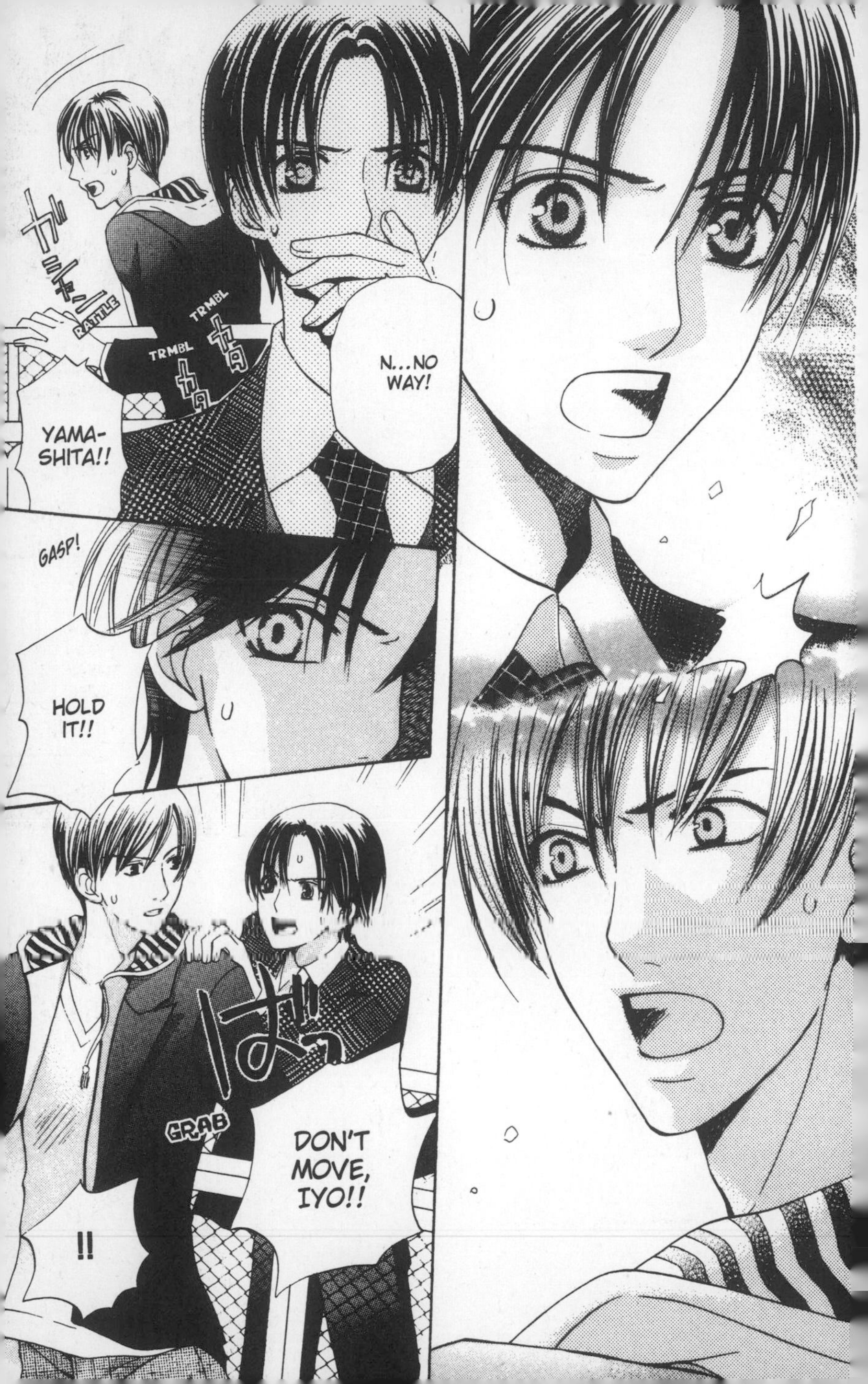
N...NO WAY!
RATTLE
TRMBL
TRMBL
YAMA-SHITA!!
GASP!
HOLD IT!!
GRAB
DON'T MOVE, IYO!!
!!

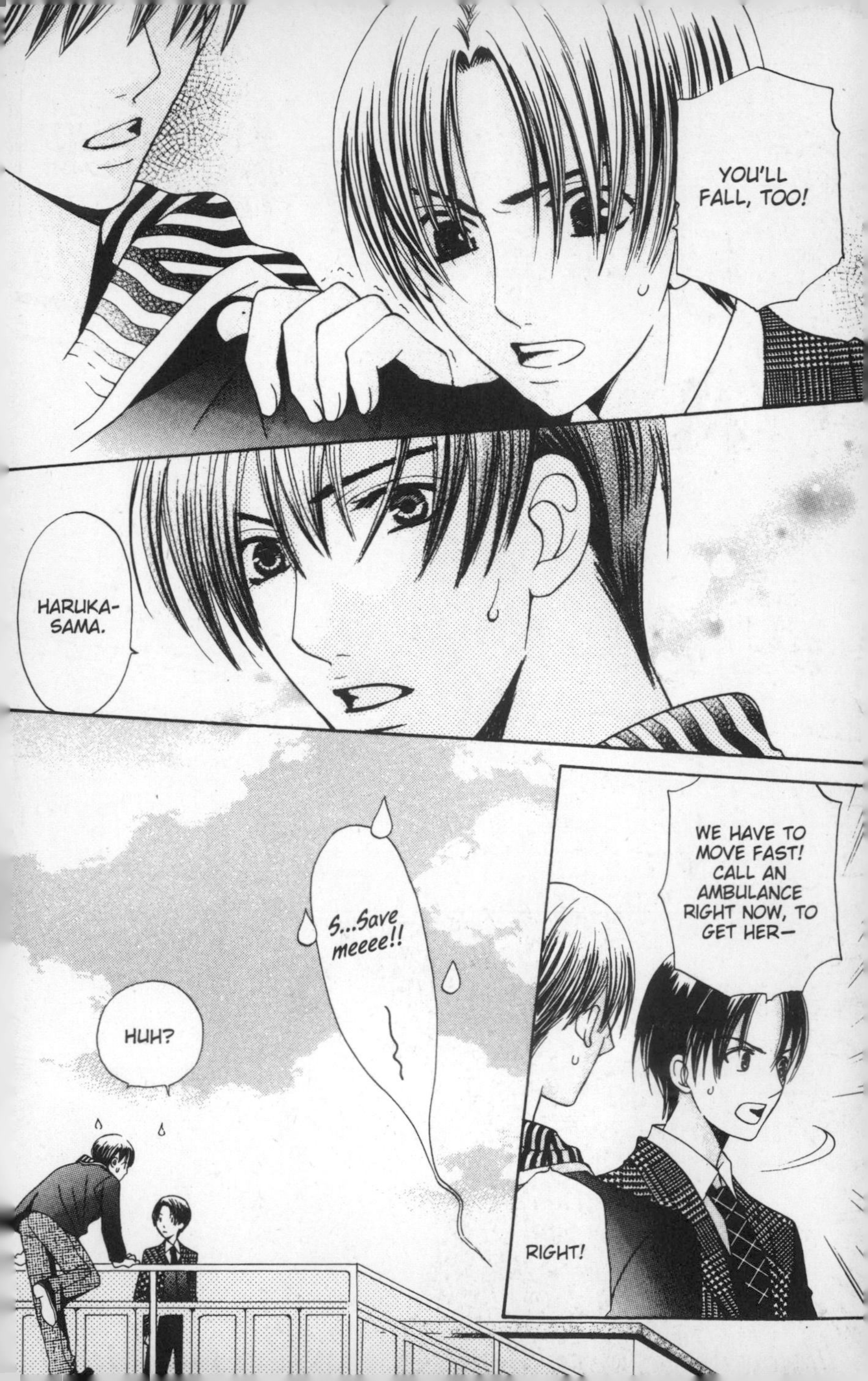
YOU'LL FALL, TOO!
HARUKA-SAMA.
WE HAVE TO MOVE FAST! CALL AN AMBULANCE RIGHT NOW, TO GET HER—
RIGHT!
S...Save meeee!!
HUH?

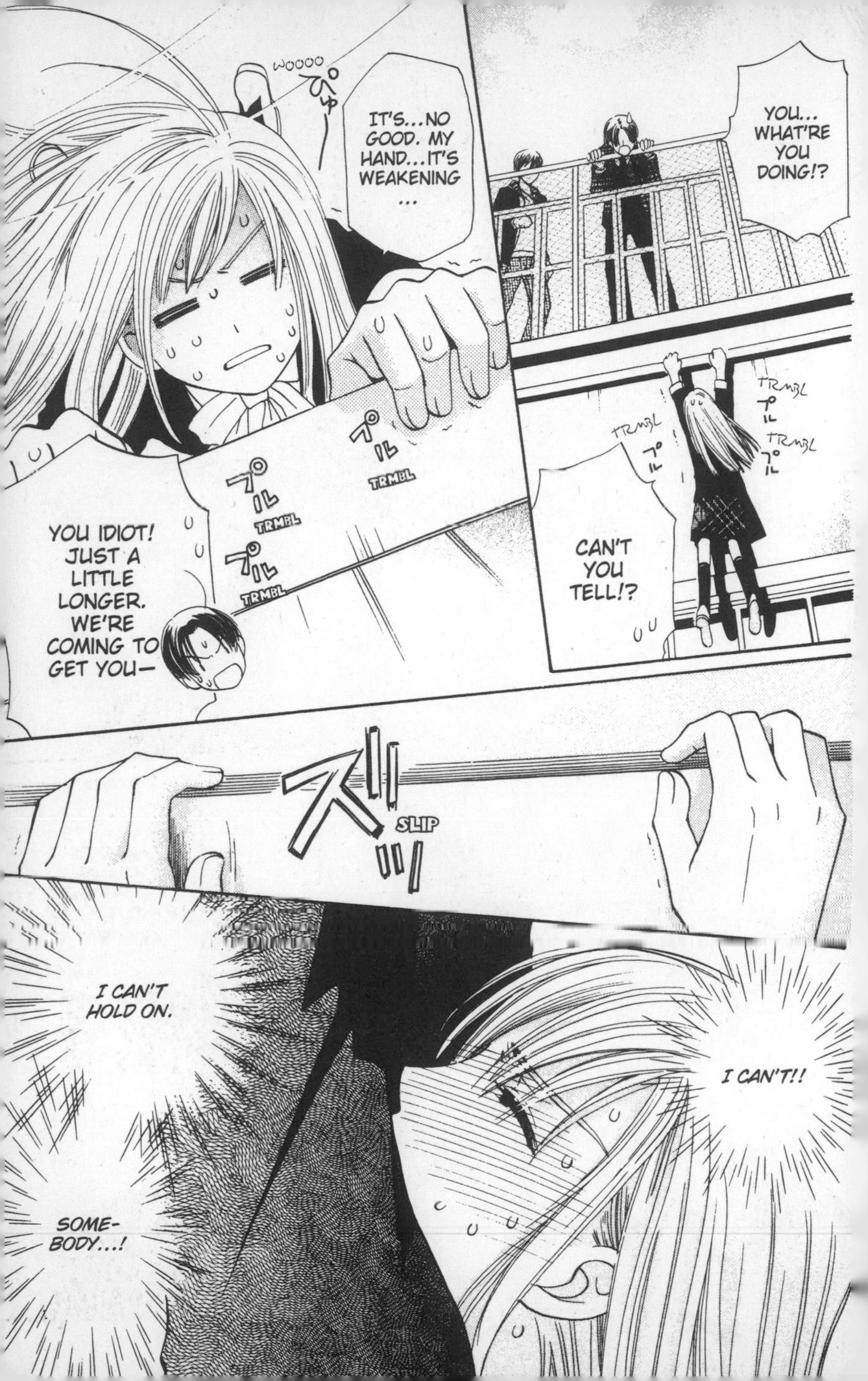
YOU... WHAT'RE YOU DOING!?
CAN'T YOU TELL!?
TRMBL
TRMBL
TRMBL
WOOOO
IT'S...NO GOOD. MY HAND...IT'S WEAKENING ...
TRMBL
TRMBL
TRMBL
YOU IDIOT! JUST A LITTLE LONGER. WE'RE COMING TO GET YOU—
SLIP
I CAN'T HOLD ON.
I CAN'T!!
SOME-BODY...!

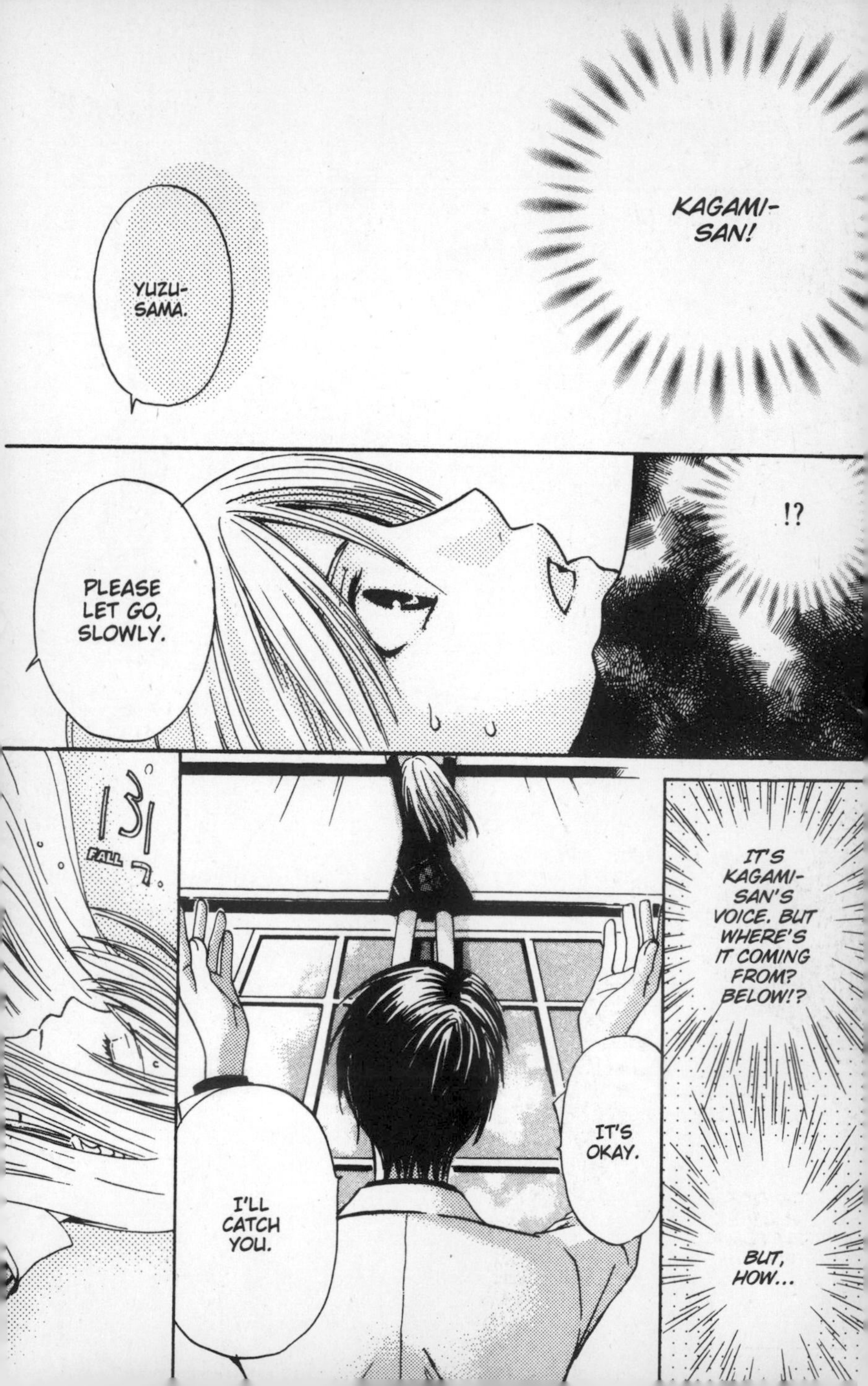
KAGAMI-SAN!
YUZU-SAMA.
!?
PLEASE LET GO, SLOWLY.
IT'S KAGAMI-SAN'S VOICE. BUT WHERE'S IT COMING FROM? BELOW!?
BUT, HOW...
IT'S OKAY.
I'LL CATCH YOU.
FALL

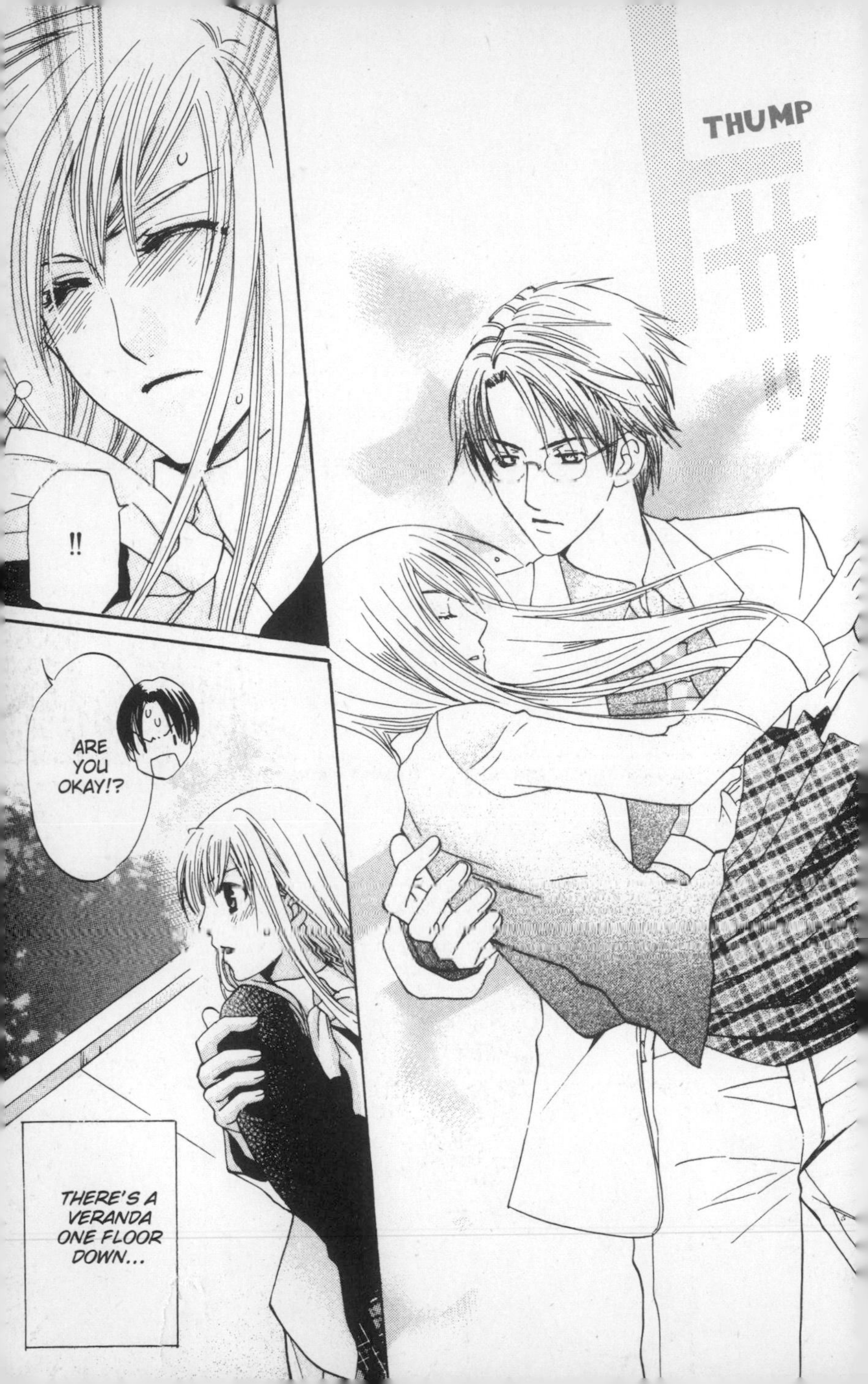
THUMP
!!
ARE YOU OKAY!?
THERE'S A VERANDA ONE FLOOR DOWN...

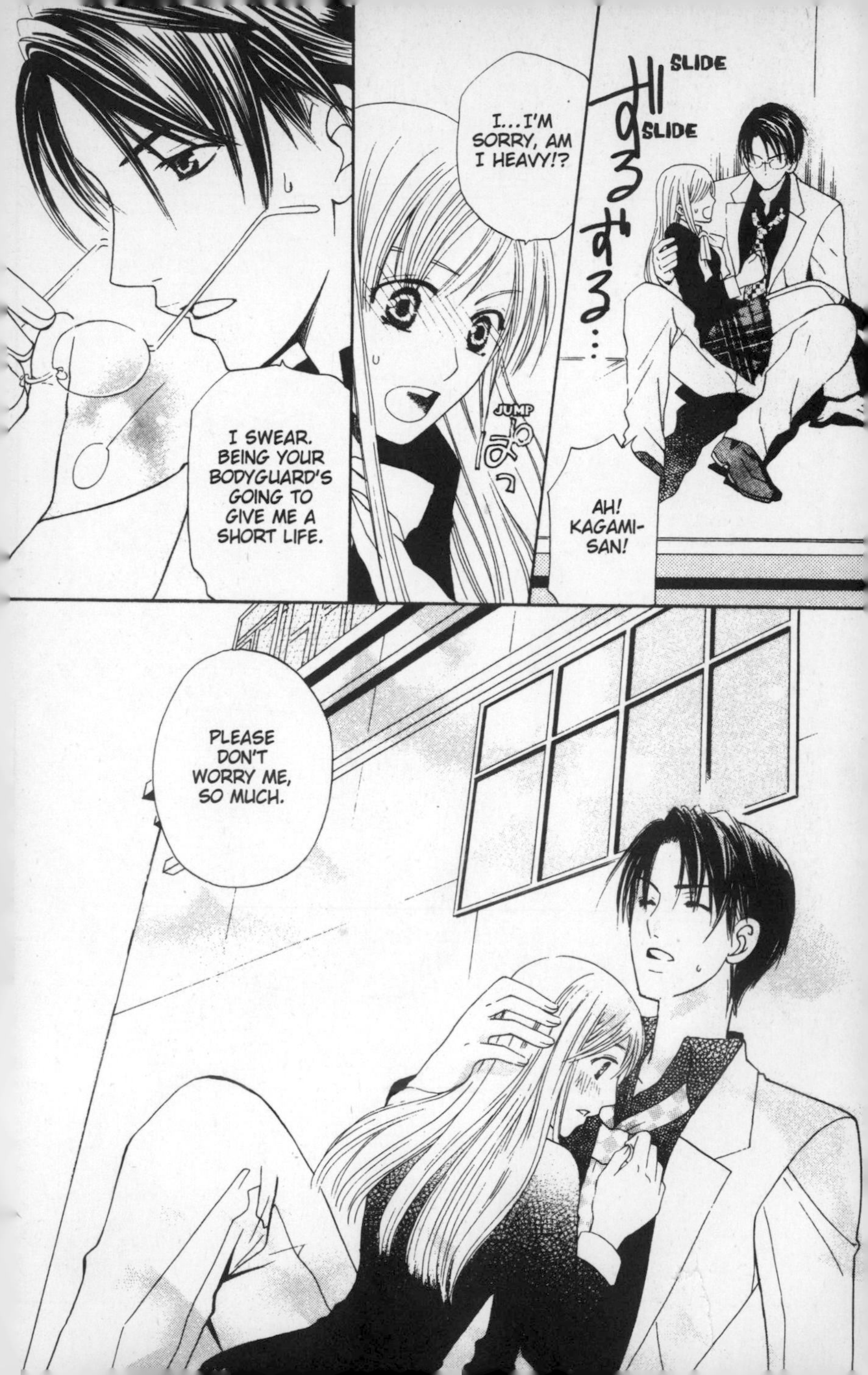
SLIDE
SLIDE
ずるずる…
AH! KAGAMI-SAN!
I…I'M SORRY, AM I HEAVY!?
JUMP
ぱっ
I SWEAR. BEING YOUR BODYGUARD'S GOING TO GIVE ME A SHORT LIFE.
PLEASE DON'T WORRY ME, SO MUCH.

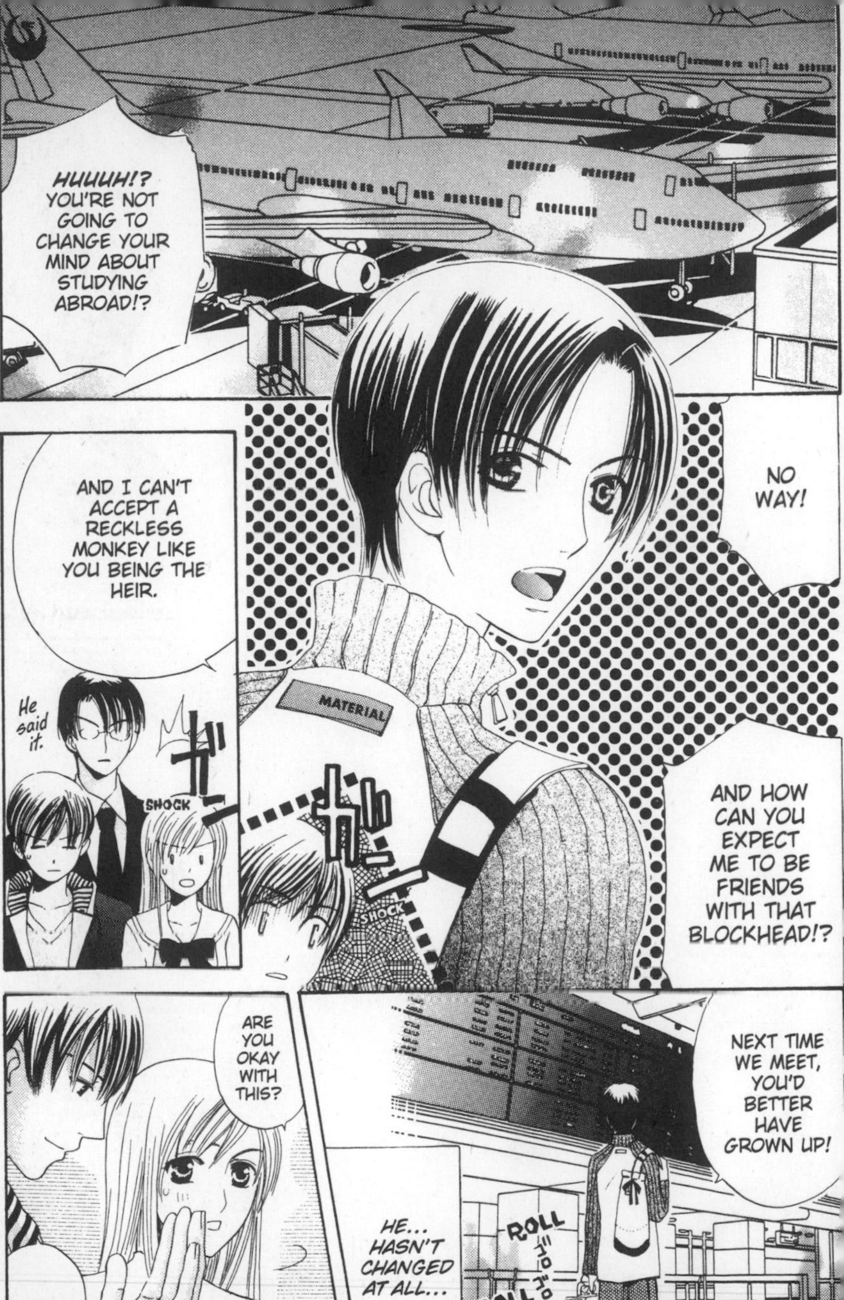
HUUUH!? YOU'RE NOT GOING TO CHANGE YOUR MIND ABOUT STUDYING ABROAD!?
NO WAY!
AND HOW CAN YOU EXPECT ME TO BE FRIENDS WITH THAT BLOCKHEAD!?
SHOCK
MATERIAL
AND I CAN'T ACCEPT A RECKLESS MONKEY LIKE YOU BEING THE HEIR.
He said it.
SHOCK
NEXT TIME WE MEET, YOU'D BETTER HAVE GROWN UP!
ROLL
ROLL
HE... HASN'T CHANGED AT ALL...
ARE YOU OKAY WITH THIS?
... YEAH.

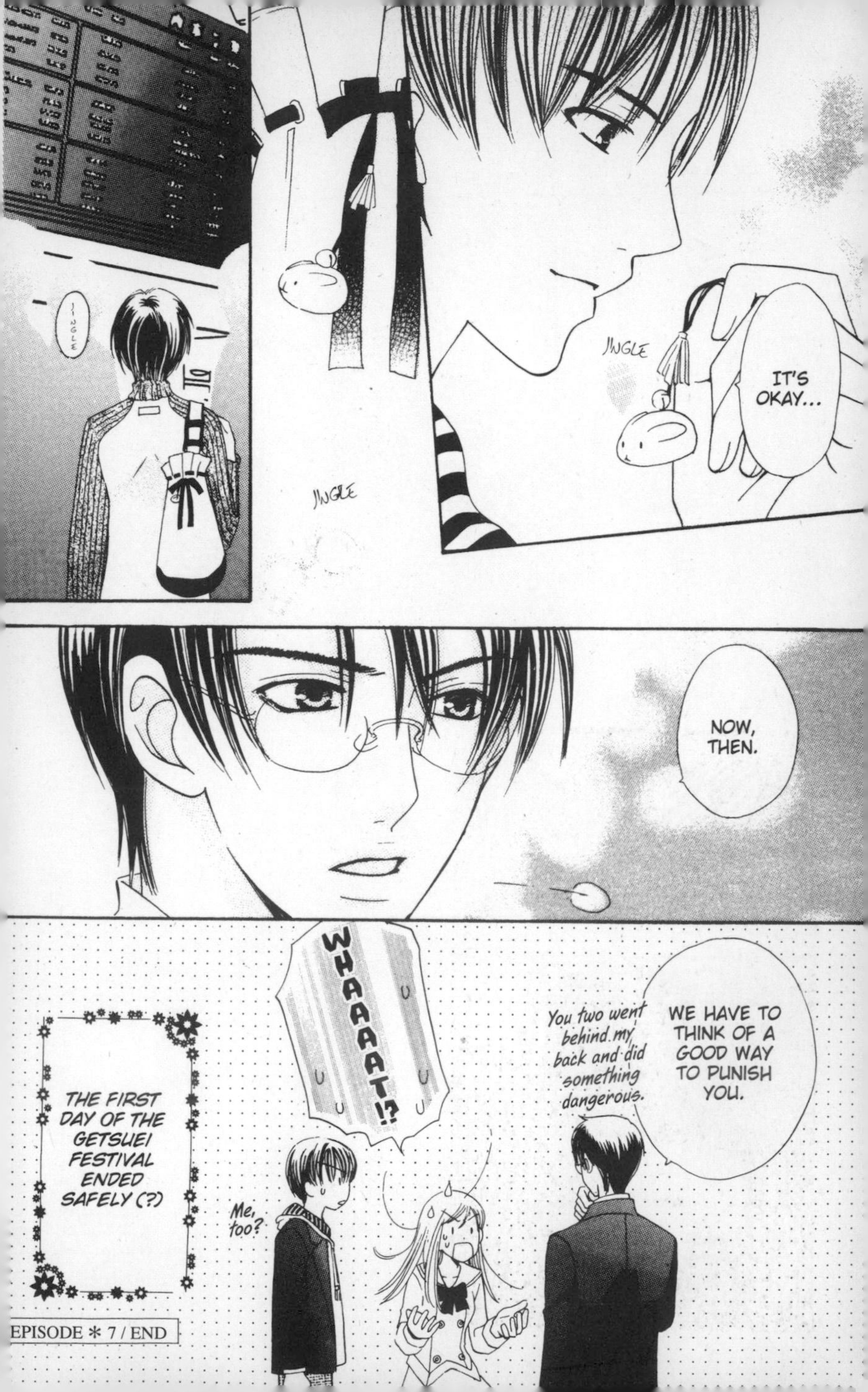
JINGLE
IT'S OKAY...
JINGLE
JINGLE
NOW, THEN.
WE HAVE TO THINK OF A GOOD WAY TO PUNISH YOU.
You two went behind my back and did something dangerous.
WHAAAAT!?
Me, too?
THE FIRST DAY OF THE GETSUEI FESTIVAL ENDED SAFELY (?)
EPISODE * 7 / END

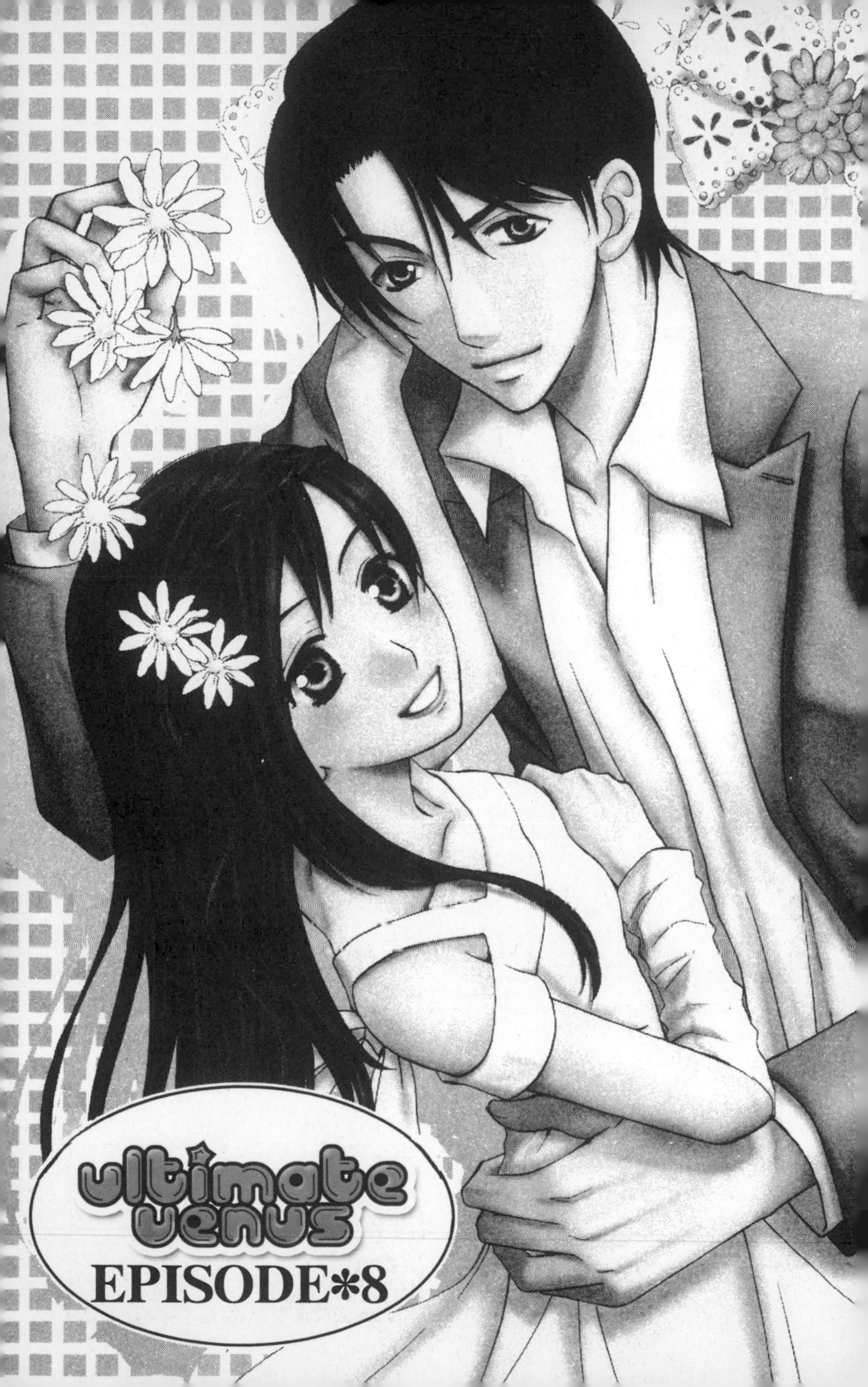
ultimate venus
EPISODE*8

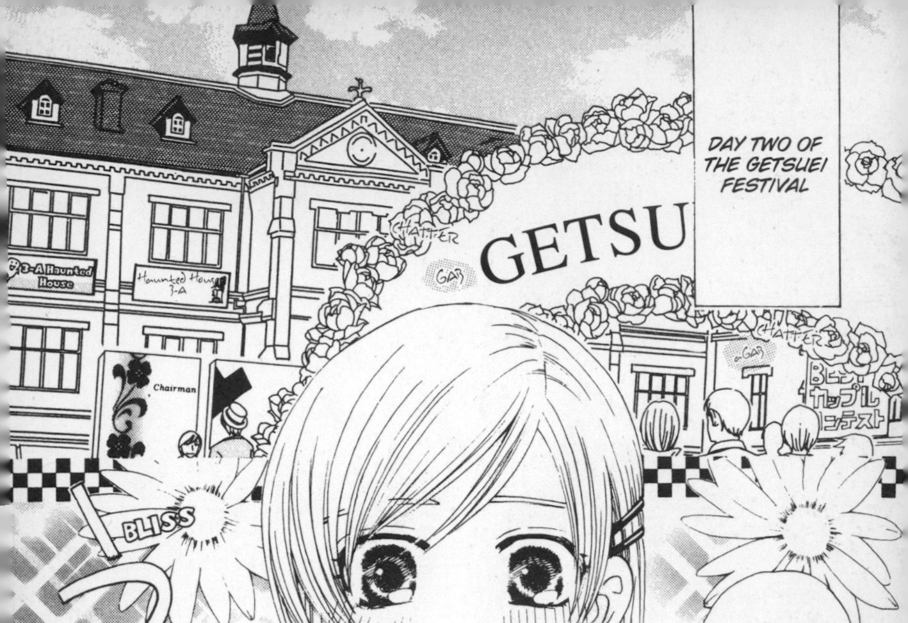
DAY TWO OF THE GETSUEI FESTIVAL
GETSU
CHATTER
GAB
CHATTER
GAB
3-A Haunted House
Haunted House 3-A
Chairman
BLISS
I HAVE ¥5000 IN SPENDING MONEY...

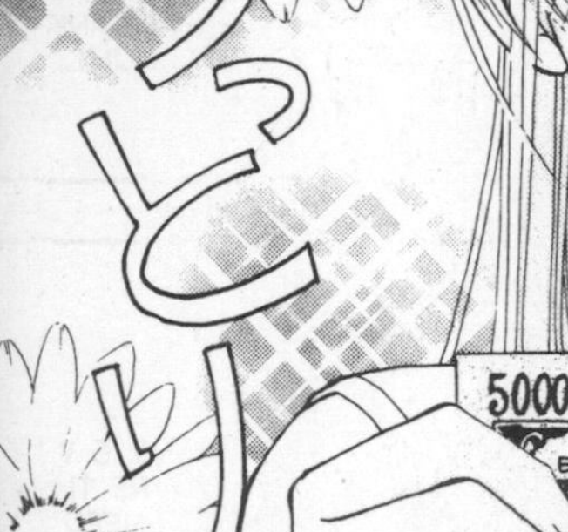

Setoka Kamizuki (age 16)

Birthday: August 5th

Blood Type: B

Hobbies: Making candy

Recent purchases: Diet foods

Hates her plain and slightly plump body type. Serves as a gentle comfort to Yuzu.

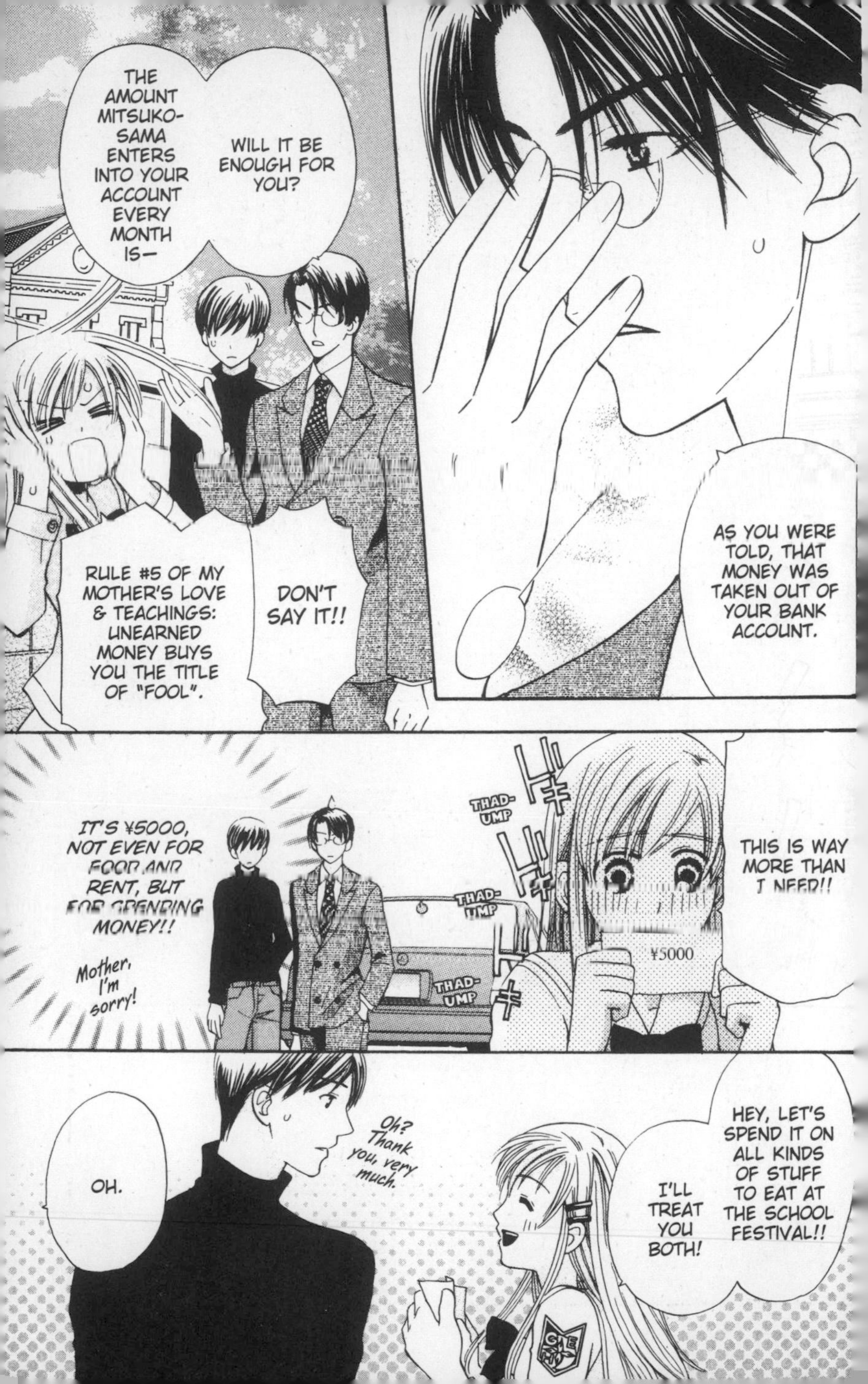
AS YOU WERE TOLD, THAT MONEY WAS TAKEN OUT OF YOUR BANK ACCOUNT.
THE AMOUNT MITSUKO-SAMA ENTERS INTO YOUR ACCOUNT EVERY MONTH IS—
WILL IT BE ENOUGH FOR YOU?
DON'T SAY IT!!
RULE #5 OF MY MOTHER'S LOVE & TEACHINGS: UNEARNED MONEY BUYS YOU THE TITLE OF "FOOL".
THAD-UMP
THAD-UMP
THAD-UMP
THIS IS WAY MORE THAN I NEED!!
¥5000
IT'S ¥5000, NOT EVEN FOR FOOD AND RENT, BUT FOR SPENDING MONEY!!
Mother, I'm sorry!
HEY, LET'S SPEND IT ON ALL KINDS OF STUFF TO EAT AT THE SCHOOL FESTIVAL!!
I'LL TREAT YOU BOTH!
Oh? Thank you, very much.
OH.

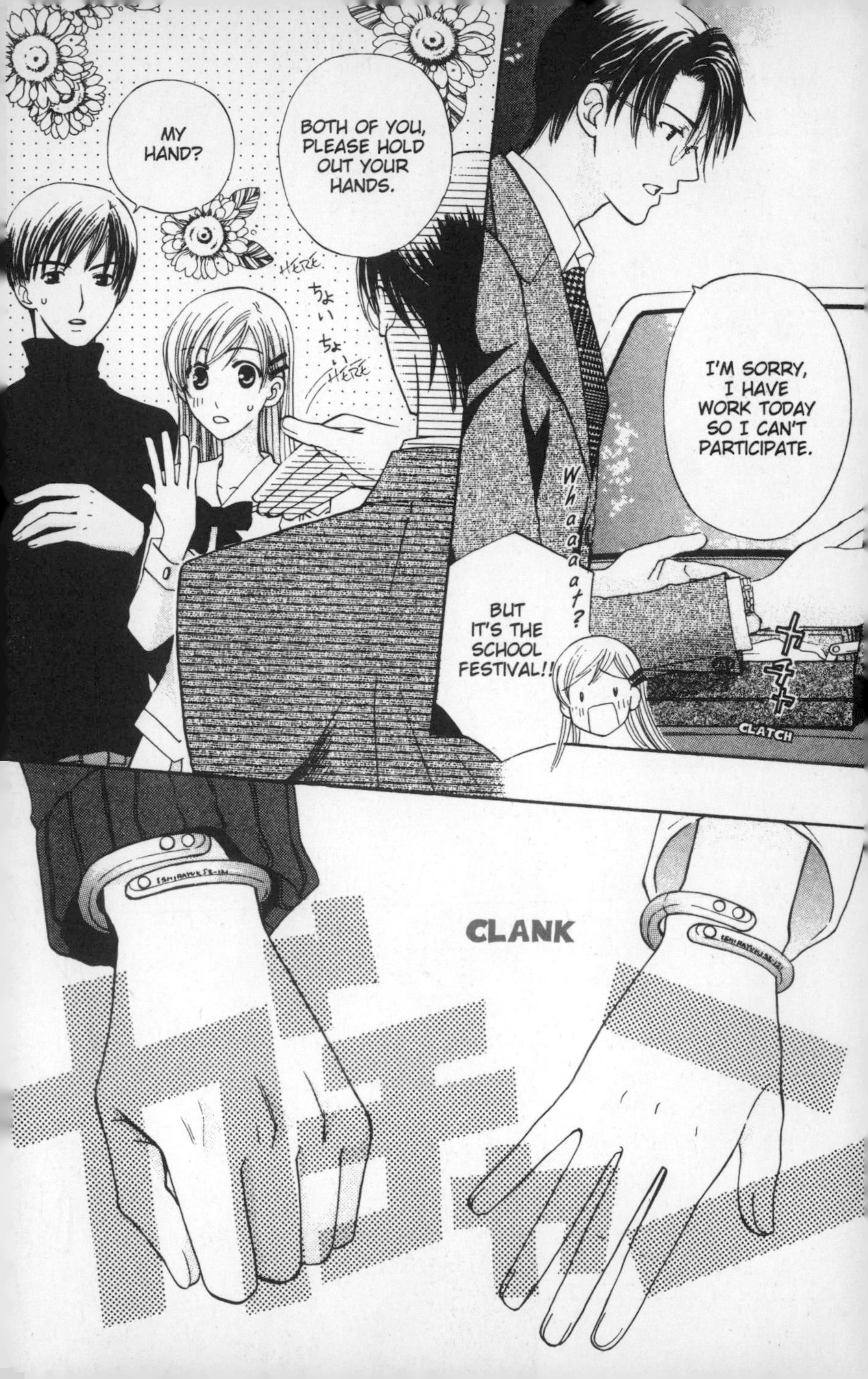
I'M SORRY, I HAVE WORK TODAY SO I CAN'T PARTICIPATE.
Whaaaat?
BUT IT'S THE SCHOOL FESTIVAL!!
CLATCH
BOTH OF YOU, PLEASE HOLD OUT YOUR HANDS.
MY HAND?
HERE
ちょい ちょい
HERE
CLANK

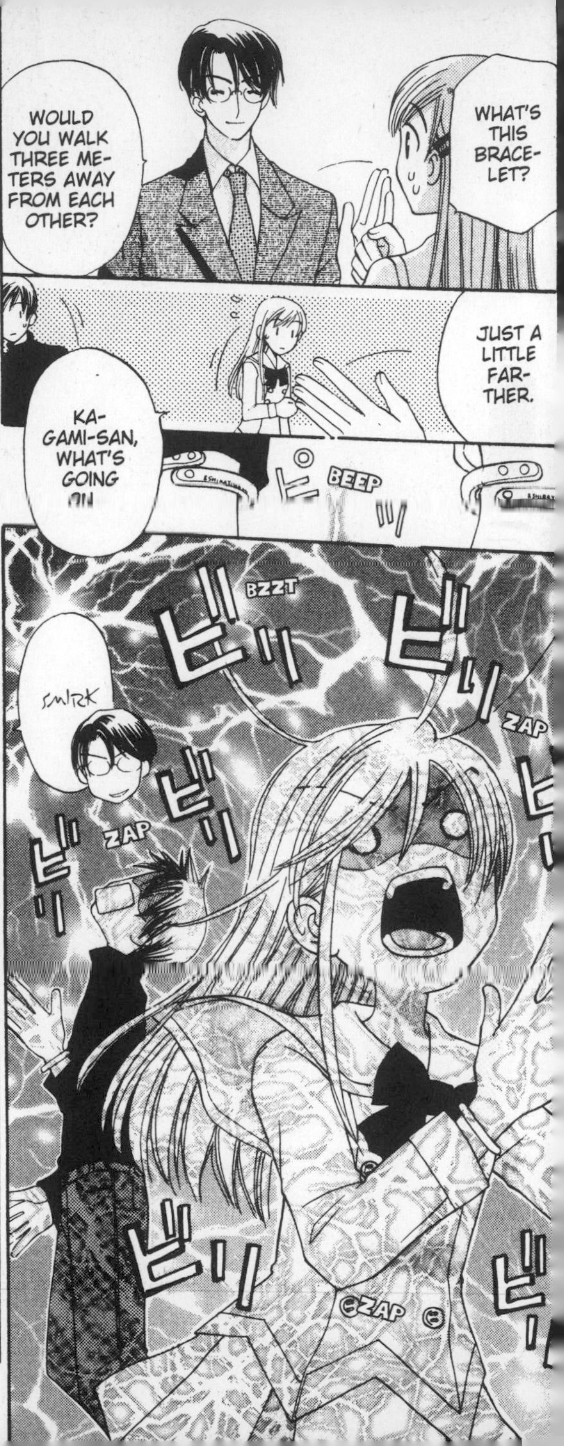
WHAT'S THIS BRACE-LET?
WOULD YOU WALK THREE ME-TERS AWAY FROM EACH OTHER?
JUST A LITTLE FAR-THER.
KA-GAMI-SAN, WHAT'S GOING
BEEP
BZZT
SMIRK
ZAP
ZAP
ZAP

GAME DAYS ②

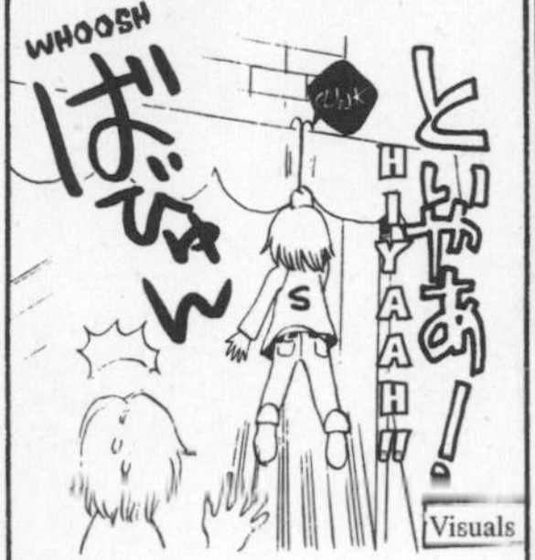
とりゃあ！
HIYAAAH!!
ぱびゅん
WHOOSH
Visuals

I have to put up with it. Also, I've been having a lot of dreams of shooting my rocket launcher. I'm also really into horror adventures. Recently, I've been playing Hayarigami on my PSP. It's so fun, but it's scary! Even the pictures [illegible] It's actually so scary that I forced H-san and T-san to come and help me. I should be more careful. I keep getting nightmares because I play the game at night.

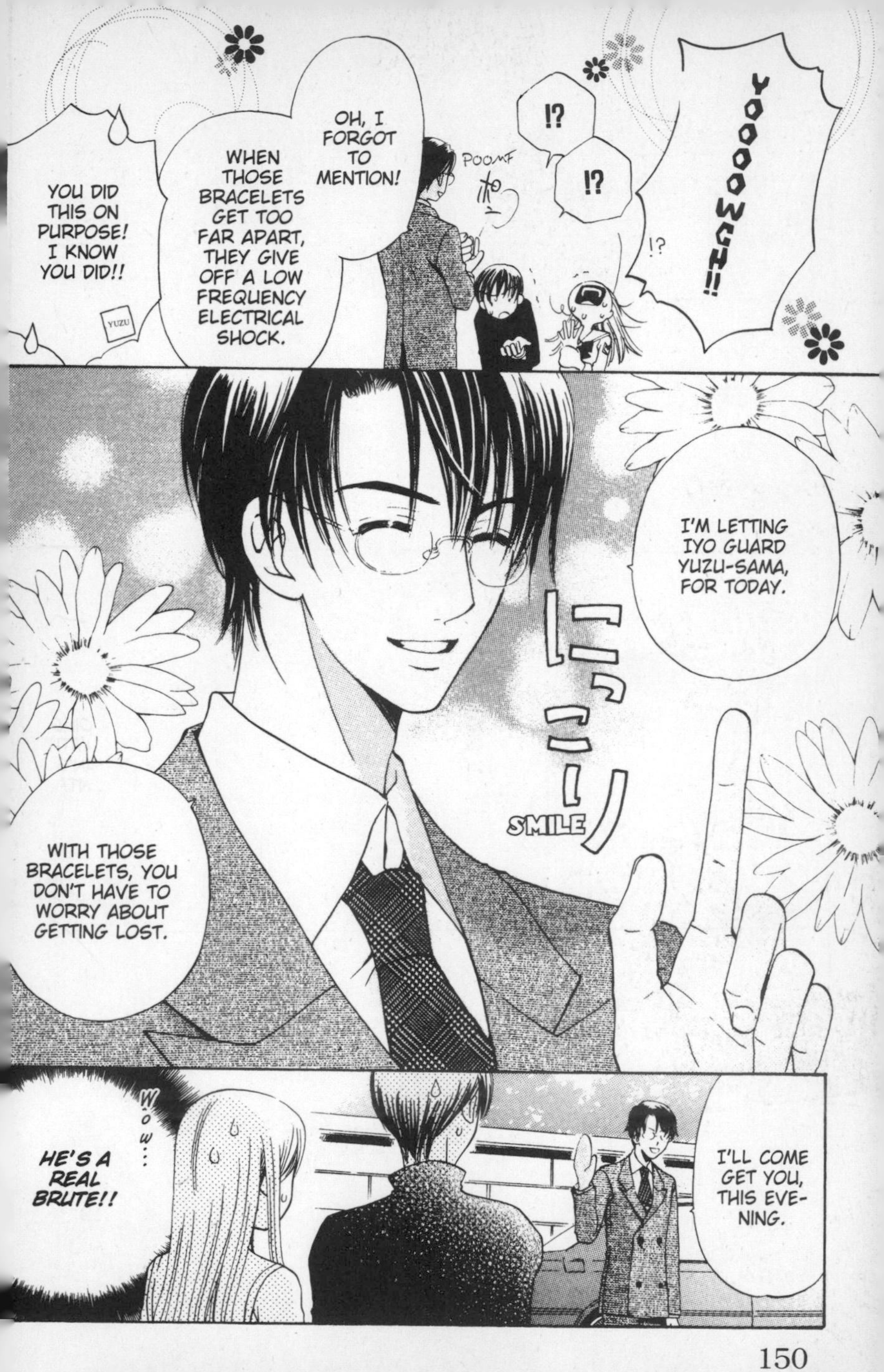
YOOOOOWGH!!
!?
!?
!?
POOMF
OH, I FORGOT TO MENTION!
WHEN THOSE BRACELETS GET TOO FAR APART, THEY GIVE OFF A LOW FREQUENCY ELECTRICAL SHOCK.
YOU DID THIS ON PURPOSE! I KNOW YOU DID!!
YUZU
I'M LETTING IYO GUARD YUZU-SAMA, FOR TODAY.
SMILE
WITH THOSE BRACELETS, YOU DON'T HAVE TO WORRY ABOUT GETTING LOST.
I'LL COME GET YOU, THIS EVENING.
WOW...
HE'S A REAL BRUTE!!

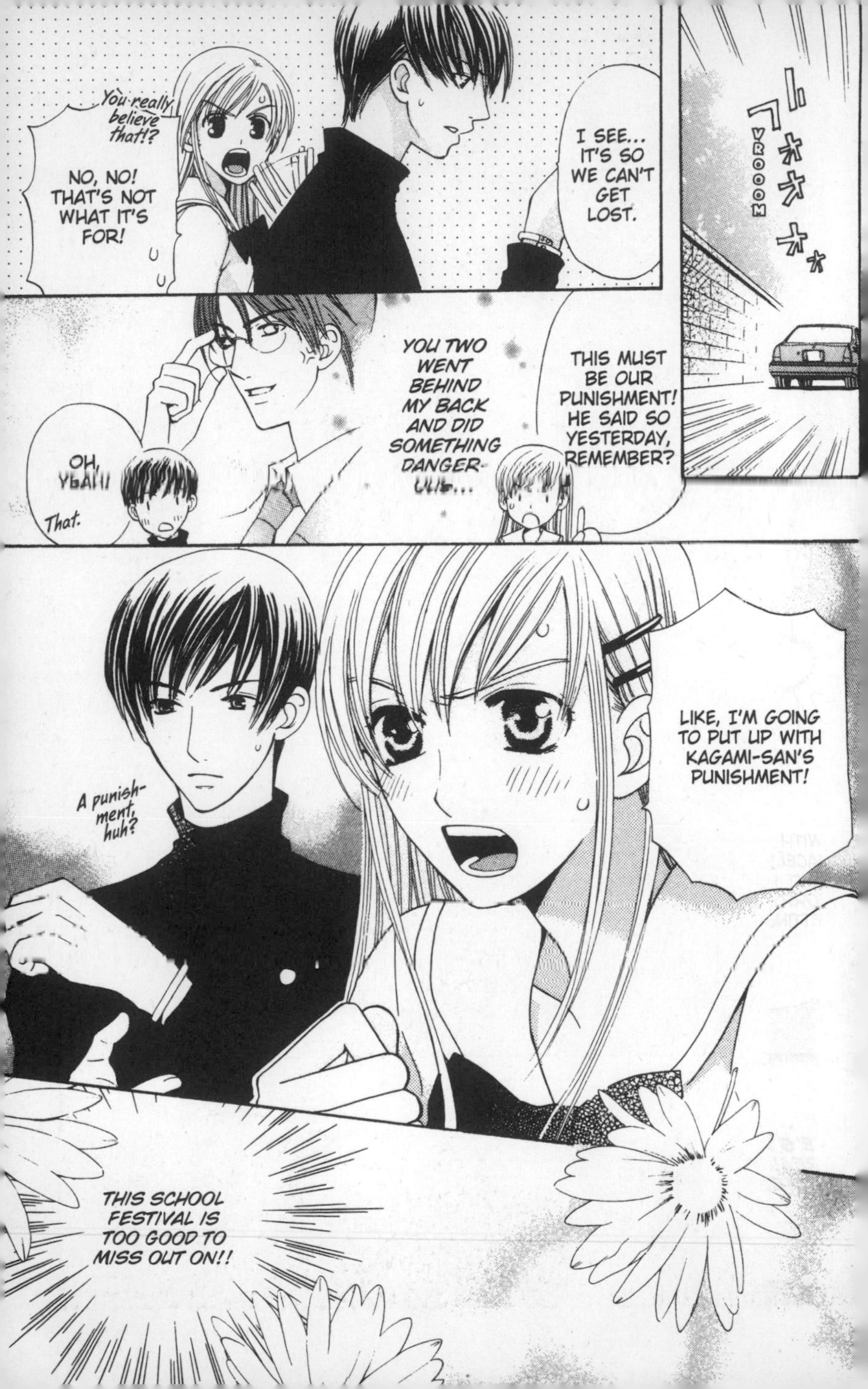
VROOOM
I SEE... IT'S SO WE CAN'T GET LOST.
You really believe that!?
NO, NO! THAT'S NOT WHAT IT'S FOR!
THIS MUST BE OUR PUNISHMENT! HE SAID SO YESTERDAY, REMEMBER?
YOU TWO WENT BEHIND MY BACK AND DID SOMETHING DANGER-OUS...
OH, YEAH!!
That.
LIKE, I'M GOING TO PUT UP WITH KAGAMI-SAN'S PUNISHMENT!
A punish-ment, huh?
THIS SCHOOL FESTIVAL IS TOO GOOD TO MISS OUT ON!!

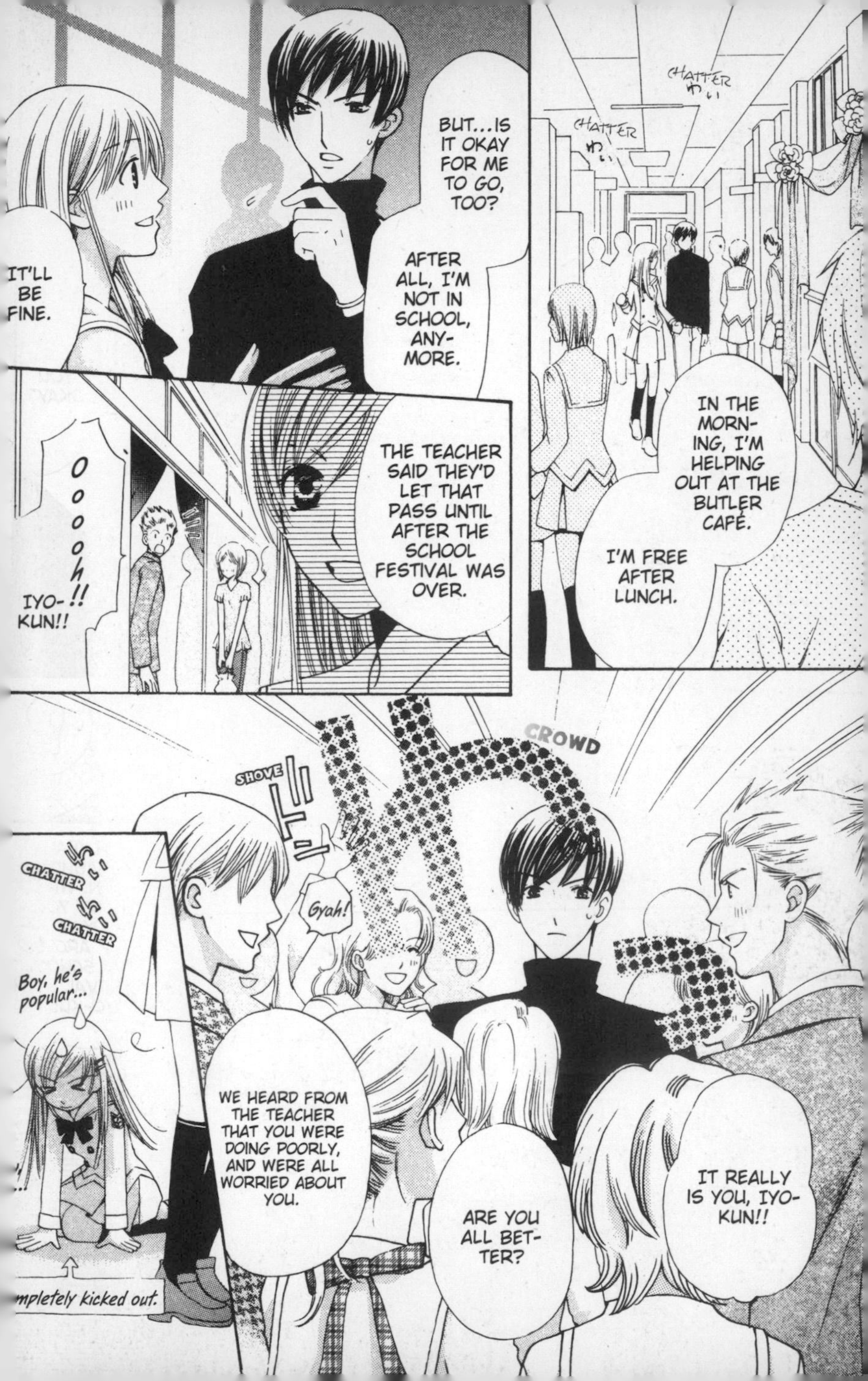
CHATTER
CHATTER
IN THE MORNING, I'M HELPING OUT AT THE BUTLER CAFÉ.
I'M FREE AFTER LUNCH.
BUT...IS IT OKAY FOR ME TO GO, TOO?
AFTER ALL, I'M NOT IN SCHOOL, ANYMORE.
IT'LL BE FINE.
THE TEACHER SAID THEY'D LET THAT PASS UNTIL AFTER THE SCHOOL FESTIVAL WAS OVER.
Ooooh!!
IYO-KUN!!
CROWD
SHOVE
Gyah!
IT REALLY IS YOU, IYO-KUN!!
ARE YOU ALL BETTER?
WE HEARD FROM THE TEACHER THAT YOU WERE DOING POORLY, AND WERE ALL WORRIED ABOUT YOU.
CHATTER
CHATTER
Boy, he's popular...
mpletely kicked out.

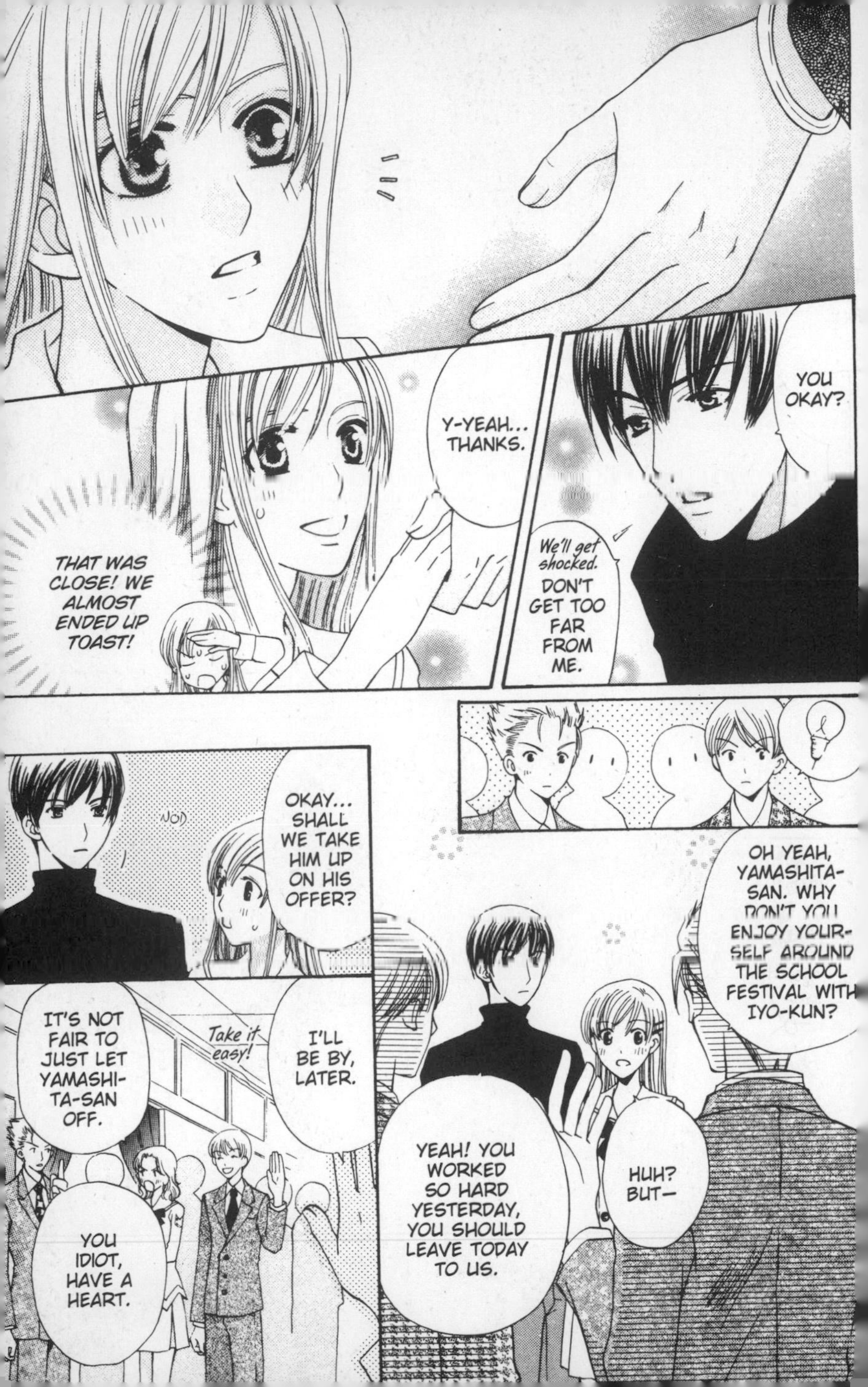
YOU OKAY?
We'll get shocked. DON'T GET TOO FAR FROM ME.
Y-YEAH... THANKS.
THAT WAS CLOSE! WE ALMOST ENDED UP TOAST!
OH YEAH, YAMASHITA-SAN. WHY DON'T YOU ENJOY YOURSELF AROUND THE SCHOOL FESTIVAL WITH IYO-KUN?
HUH? BUT—
YEAH! YOU WORKED SO HARD YESTERDAY, YOU SHOULD LEAVE TODAY TO US.
OKAY... SHALL WE TAKE HIM UP ON HIS OFFER?
NOD
I'LL BE BY, LATER.
Take it easy!
IT'S NOT FAIR TO JUST LET YAMASHITA-SAN OFF.
YOU IDIOT, HAVE A HEART.

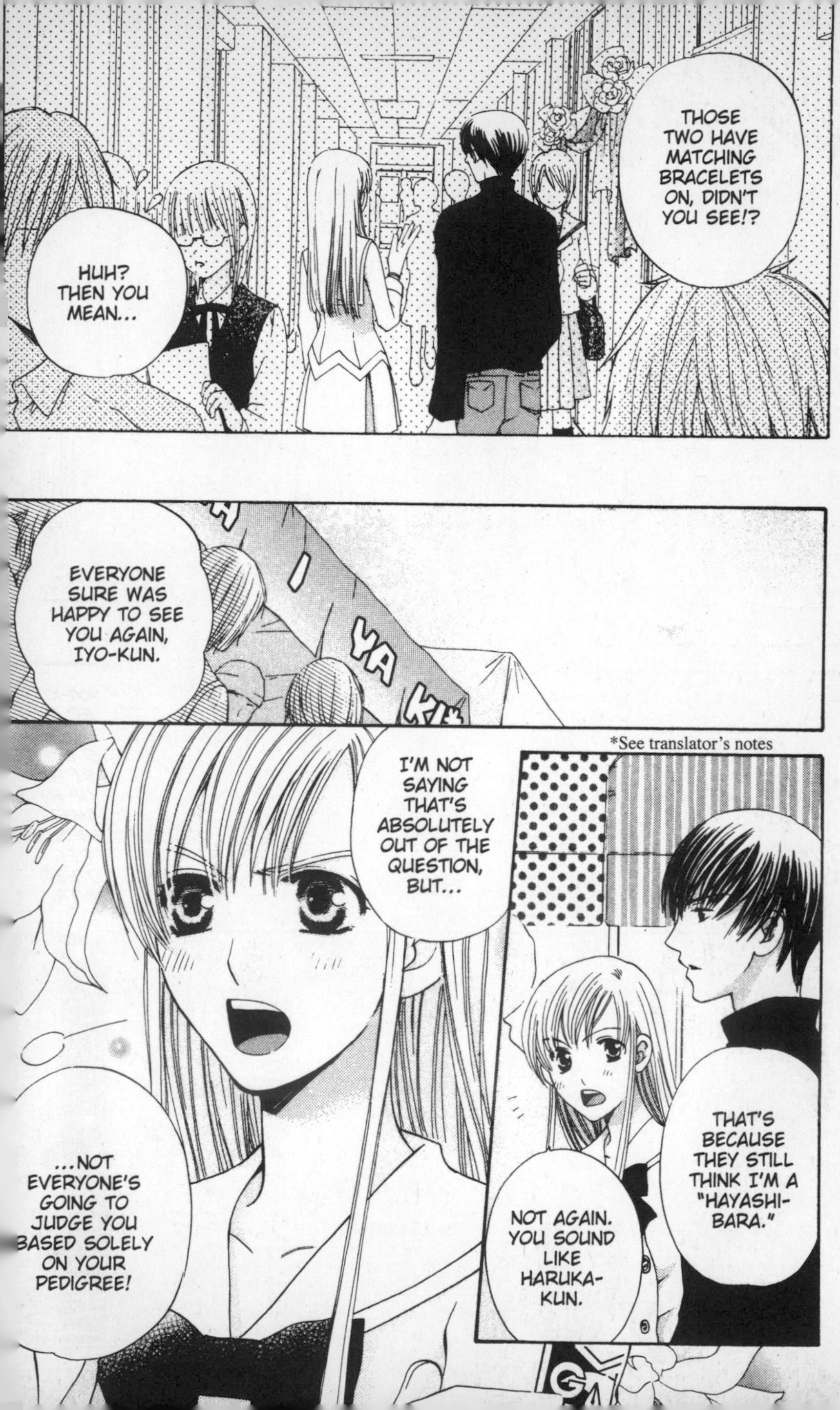
THOSE TWO HAVE MATCHING BRACELETS ON, DIDN'T YOU SEE!?
HUH? THEN YOU MEAN...
EVERYONE SURE WAS HAPPY TO SEE YOU AGAIN, IYO-KUN.
THAT'S BECAUSE THEY STILL THINK I'M A "HAYASHI-BARA."
NOT AGAIN. YOU SOUND LIKE HARUKA-KUN.
I'M NOT SAYING THAT'S ABSOLUTELY OUT OF THE QUESTION, BUT...
...NOT EVERYONE'S GOING TO JUDGE YOU BASED SOLELY ON YOUR PEDIGREE!
*See translator's notes

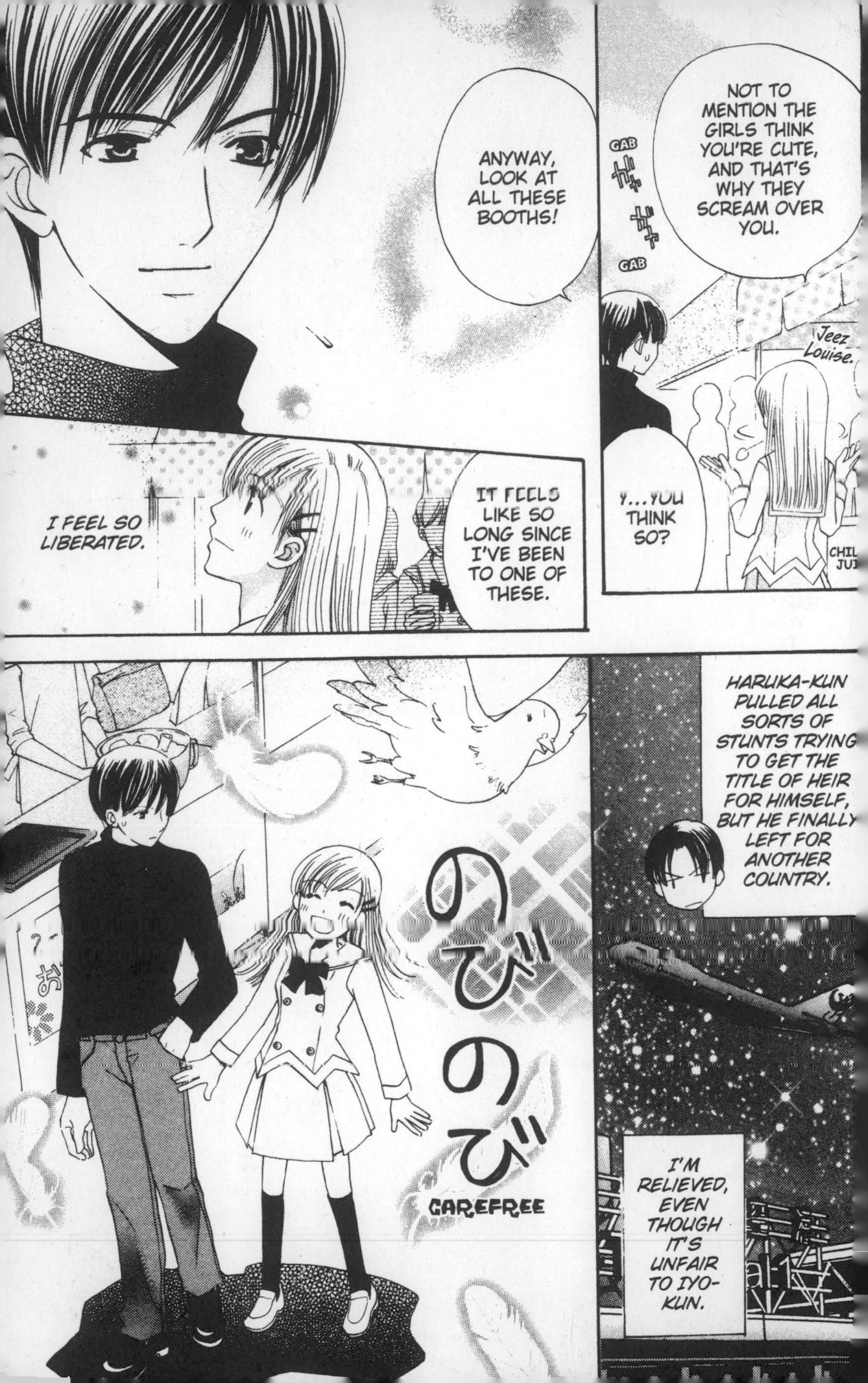
NOT TO MENTION THE GIRLS THINK YOU'RE CUTE, AND THAT'S WHY THEY SCREAM OVER YOU.
GAB
GAB
Jeez Louise.
Y...YOU THINK SO?
ANYWAY, LOOK AT ALL THESE BOOTHS!
IT FEELS LIKE SO LONG SINCE I'VE BEEN TO ONE OF THESE.
I FEEL SO LIBERATED.
HARUKA-KUN PULLED ALL SORTS OF STUNTS TRYING TO GET THE TITLE OF HEIR FOR HIMSELF, BUT HE FINALLY LEFT FOR ANOTHER COUNTRY.
I'M RELIEVED, EVEN THOUGH IT'S UNFAIR TO IYO-KUN.
のびのび
CAREFREE

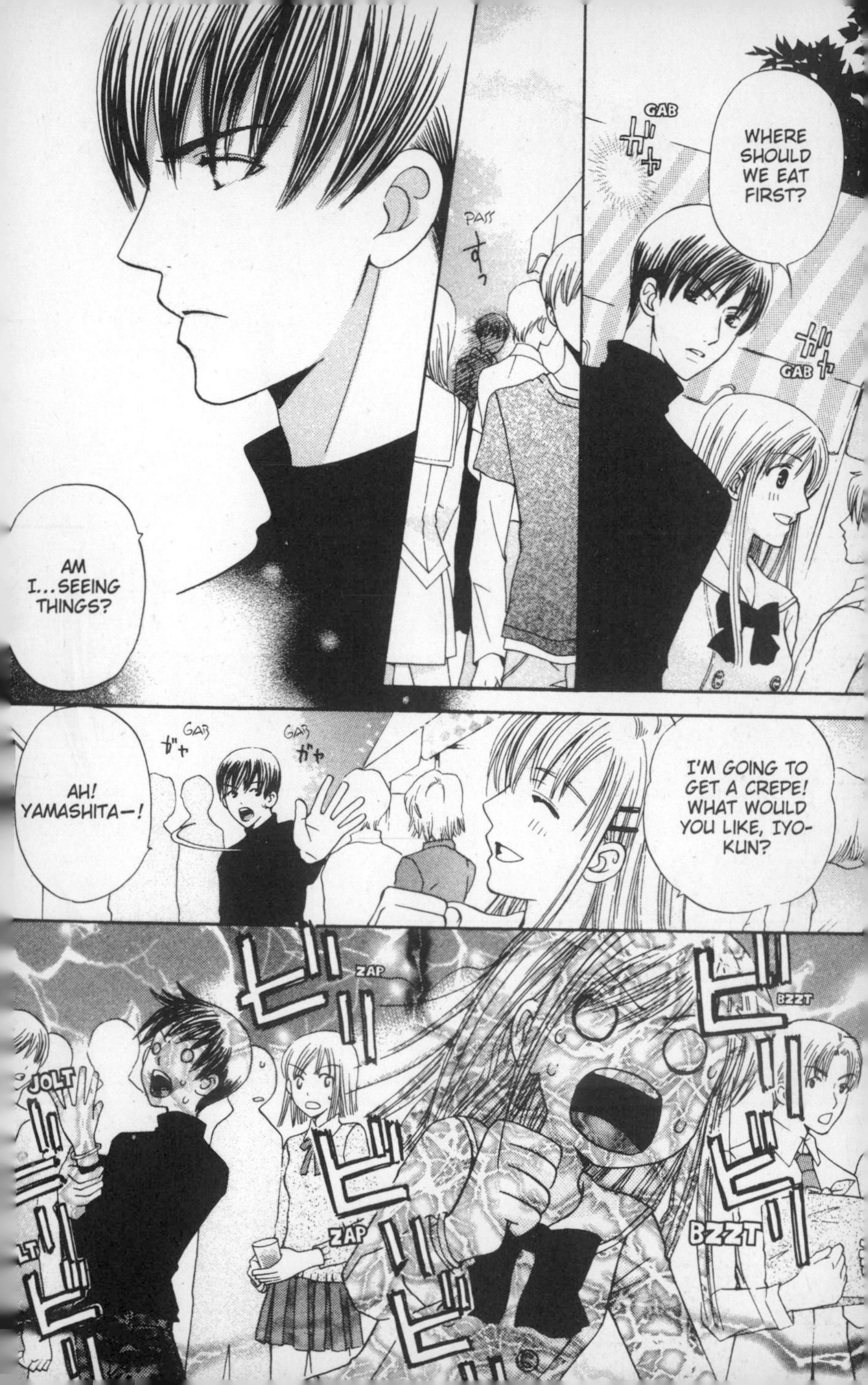
WHERE SHOULD WE EAT FIRST?
GAB
GAB
PASS
AM I...SEEING THINGS?
I'M GOING TO GET A CREPE! WHAT WOULD YOU LIKE, IYO-KUN?
GAB
GAB
AH! YAMASHITA—!
BZZT
ZAP
BZZT
ZAP
JOLT

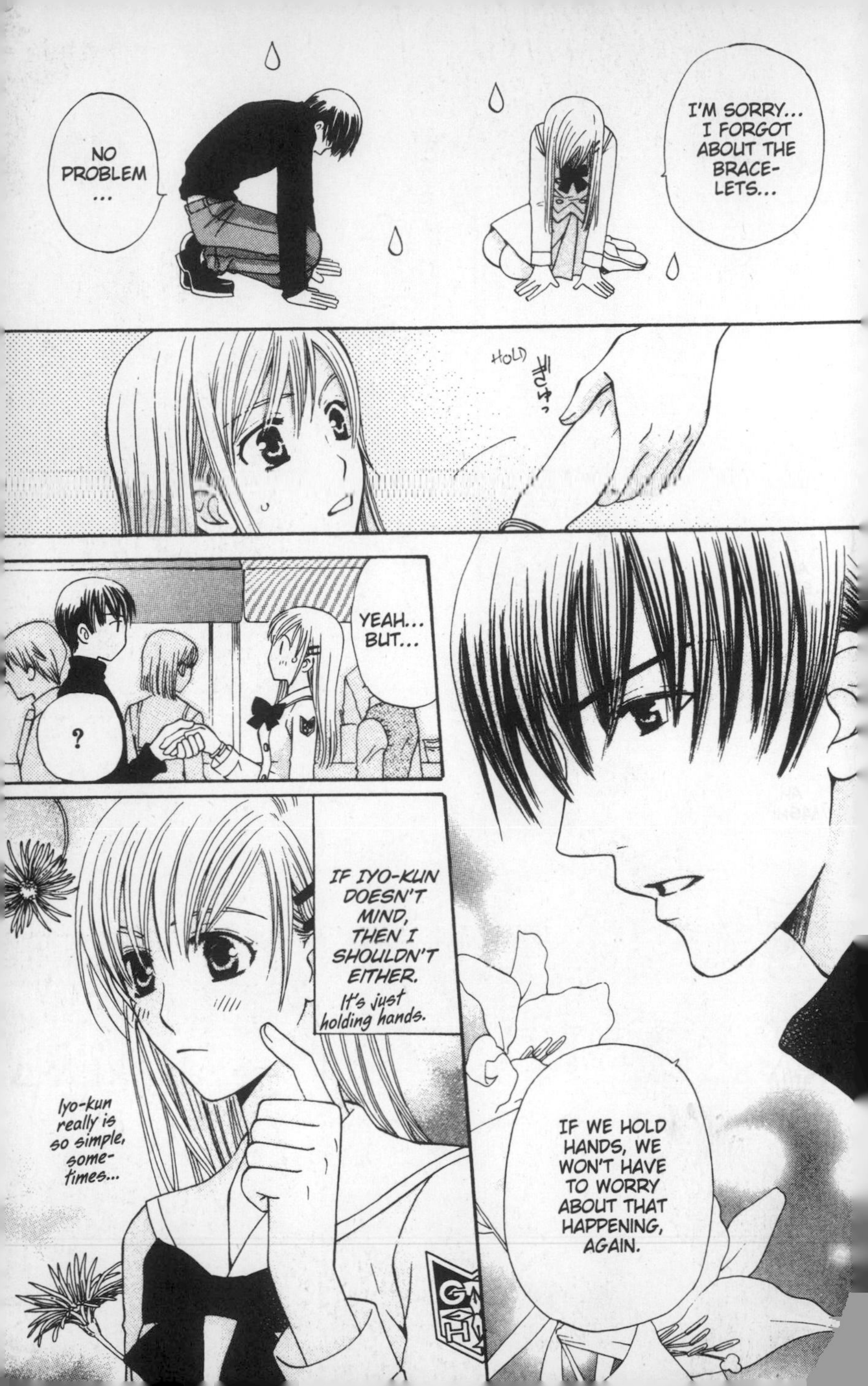
I'M SORRY... I FORGOT ABOUT THE BRACE-LETS...
NO PROBLEM ...
HOLD
ぎゅっ
IF WE HOLD HANDS, WE WON'T HAVE TO WORRY ABOUT THAT HAPPENING, AGAIN.
YEAH... BUT...
?
IF IYO-KUN DOESN'T MIND, THEN I SHOULDN'T EITHER.
It's just holding hands.
Iyo-kun really is so simple, some-times...

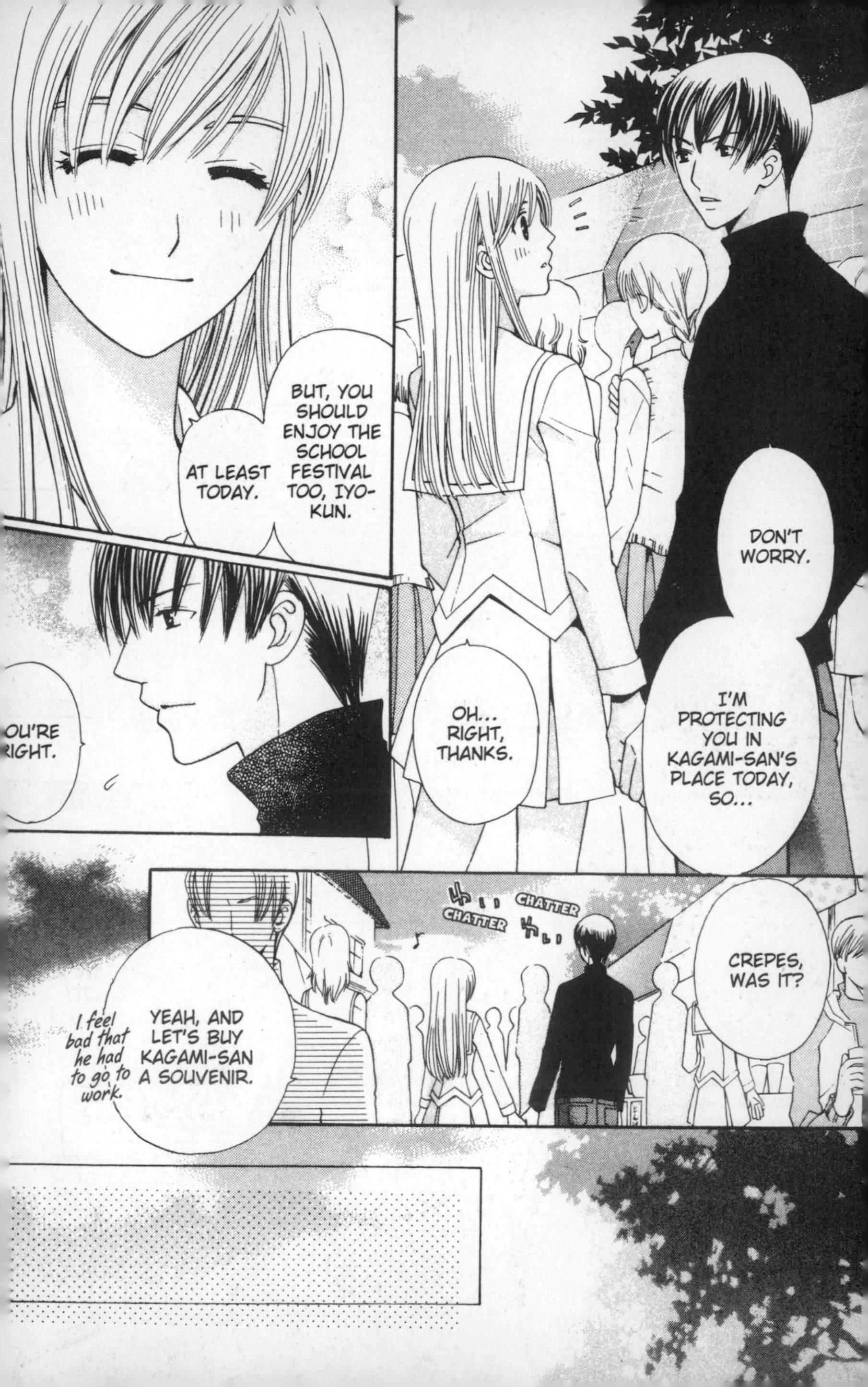
DON'T WORRY.
I'M PROTECTING YOU IN KAGAMI-SAN'S PLACE TODAY, SO...
OH... RIGHT, THANKS.
BUT, YOU SHOULD ENJOY THE SCHOOL FESTIVAL TOO, IYO-KUN.
AT LEAST TODAY.
OU'RE IGHT.
CREPES, WAS IT?
CHATTER
CHATTER
YEAH, AND LET'S BUY KAGAMI-SAN A SOUVENIR.
I feel bad that he had to go to work.

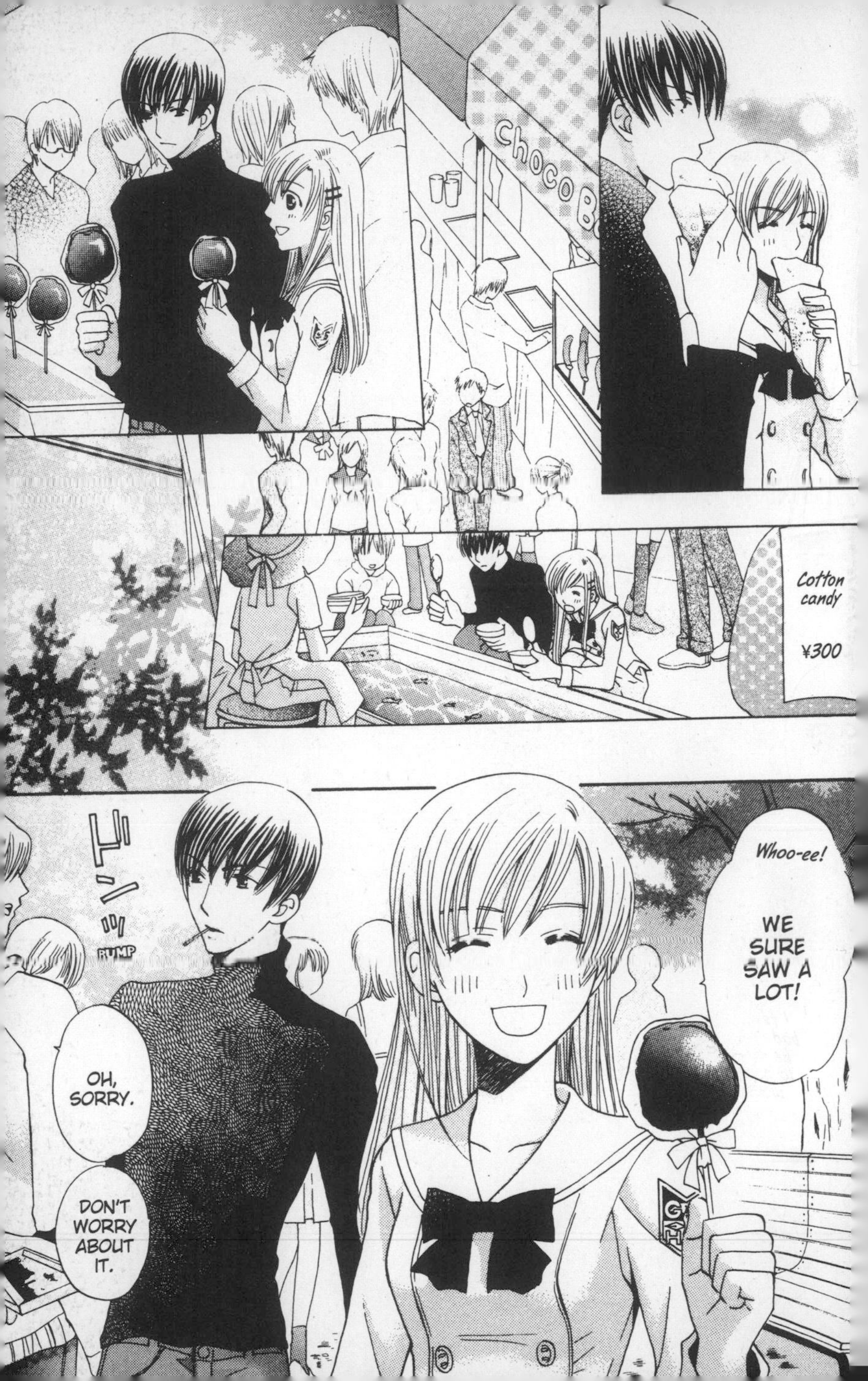
Choco B
Cotton candy
¥300
Whoo-ee!
WE SURE SAW A LOT!
RUMP
OH, SORRY.
DON'T WORRY ABOUT IT.

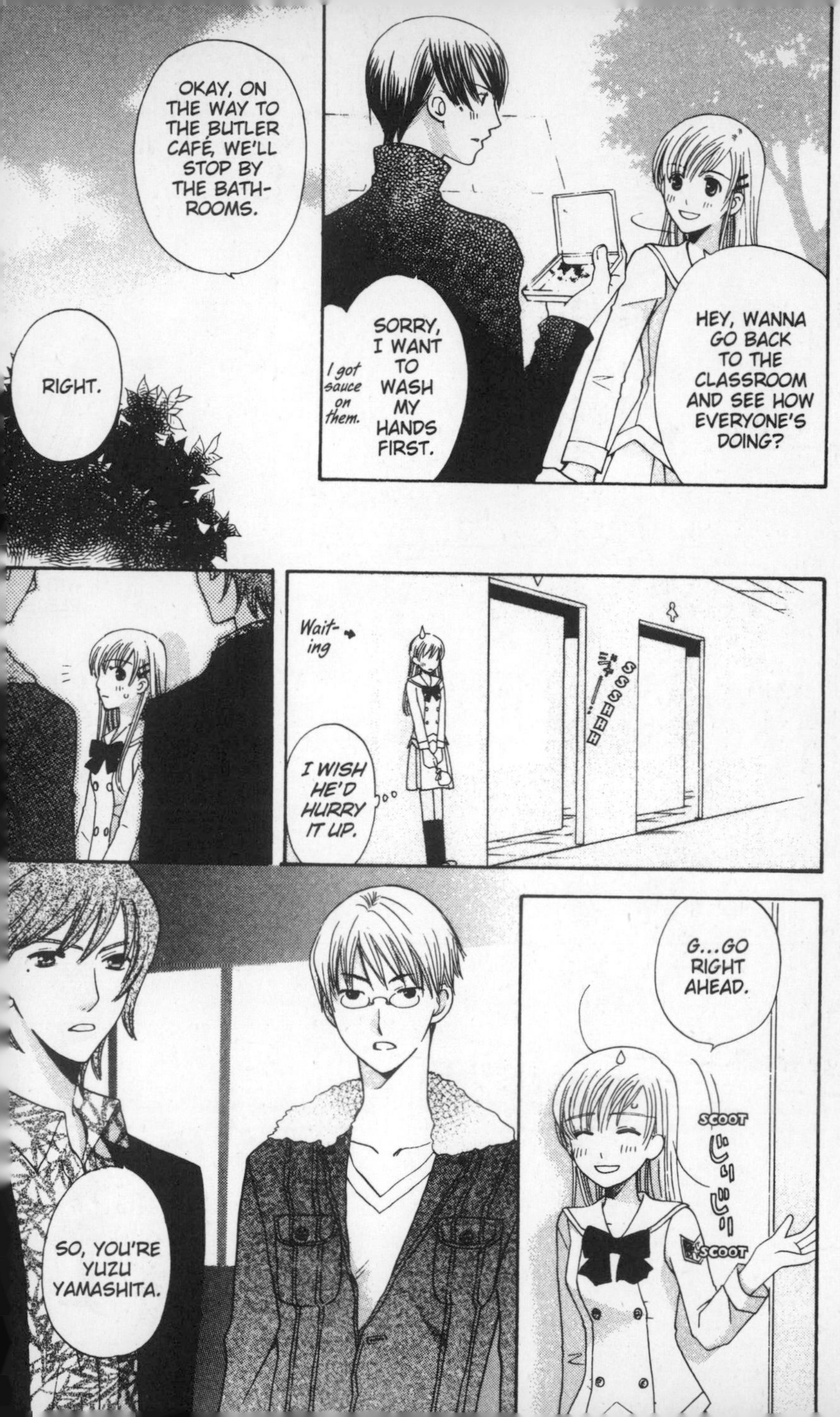
HEY, WANNA GO BACK TO THE CLASSROOM AND SEE HOW EVERYONE'S DOING?
SORRY, I WANT TO WASH MY HANDS FIRST.
I got sauce on them.
OKAY, ON THE WAY TO THE BUTLER CAFÉ, WE'LL STOP BY THE BATH-ROOMS.
RIGHT.
SSSHHH
Wait-ing
I WISH HE'D HURRY IT UP.
G...GO RIGHT AHEAD.
SCOOT
SCOOT
SO, YOU'RE YUZU YAMASHITA.

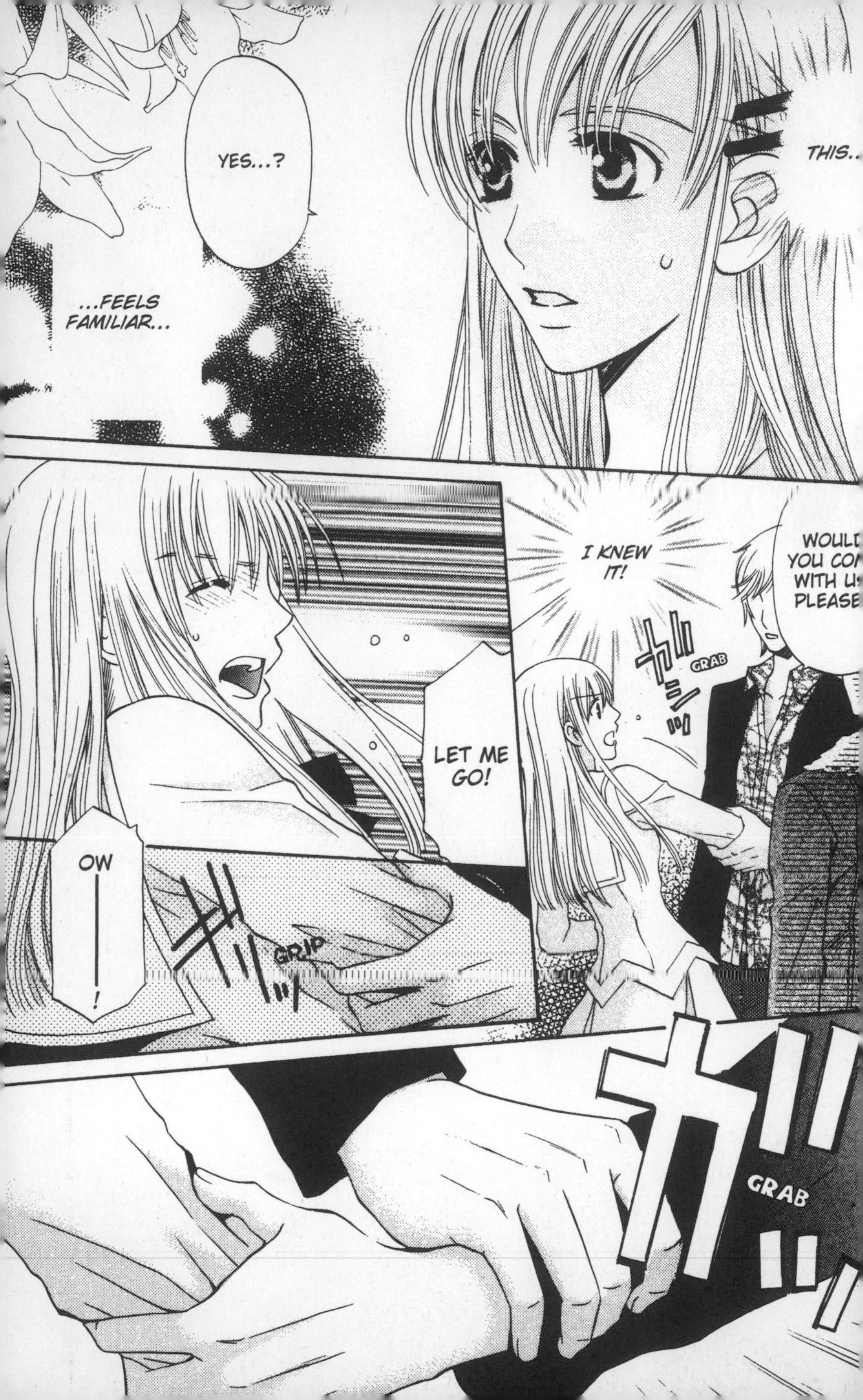
THIS...
YES...?
...FEELS FAMILIAR...
WOULD YOU CO WITH U PLEASE
I KNEW IT!
GRAB
LET ME GO!
OW—!
GRIP
GRAB

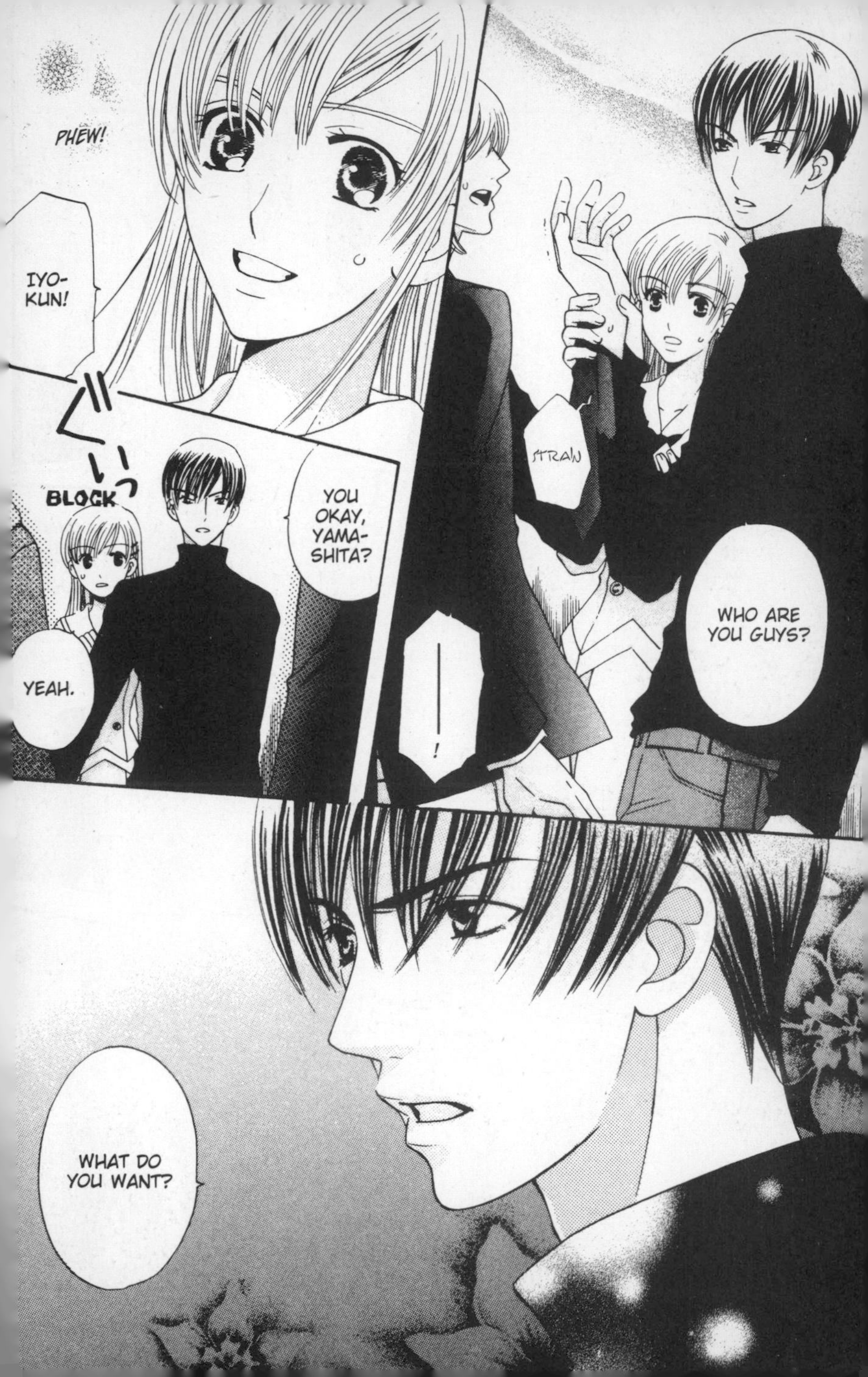
STRAIN
WHO ARE YOU GUYS?
!
PHEW!
IYO-KUN!
ぐいっ
BLOCK
YOU OKAY, YAMA-SHITA?
YEAH.
WHAT DO YOU WANT?

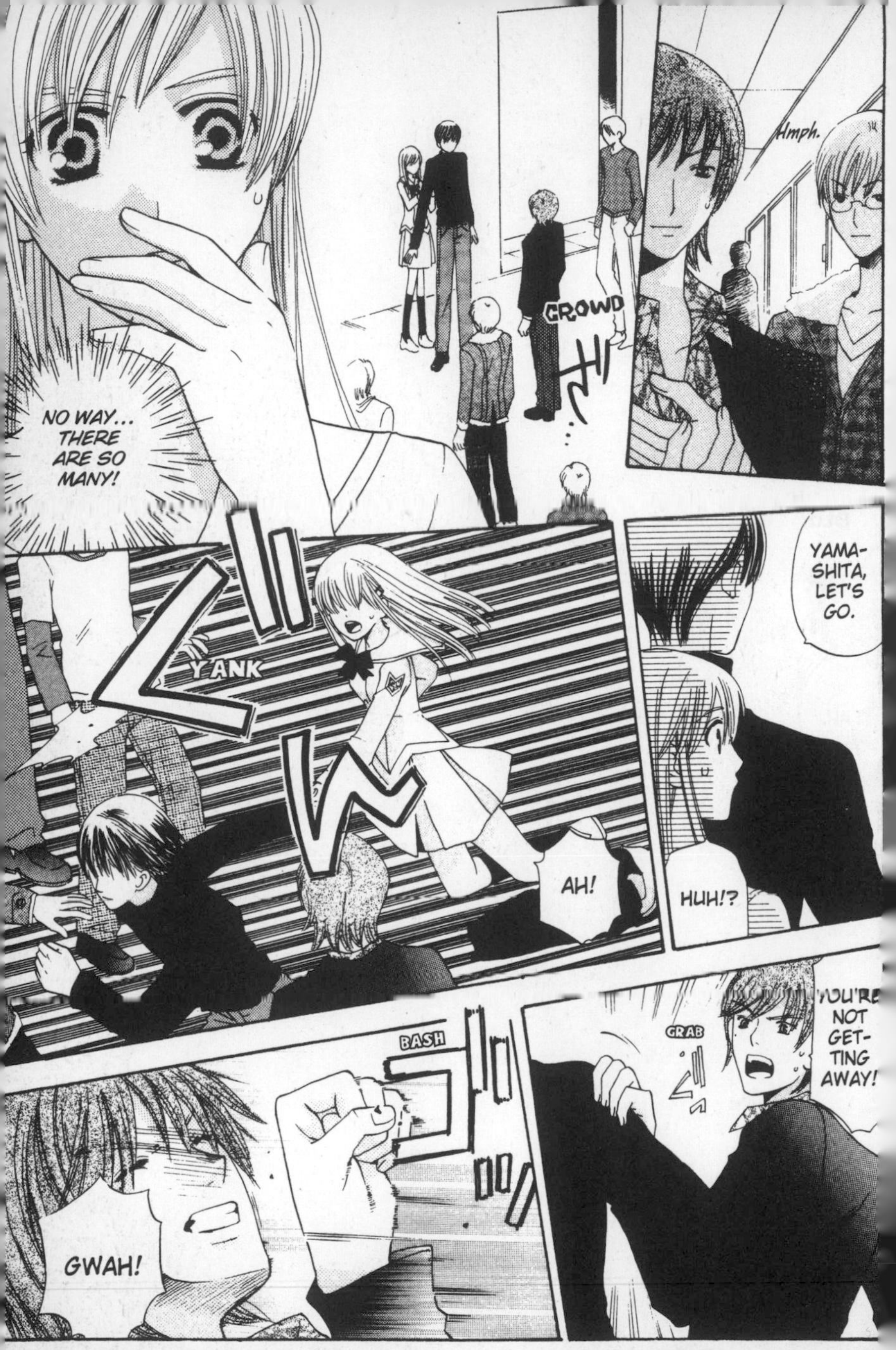
Hmph.
CROWD
NO WAY... THERE ARE SO MANY!
YAMA-SHITA, LET'S GO.
HUH!?
YANK
AH!
YOU'RE NOT GET-TING AWAY!
GRAB
BASH
GWAH!

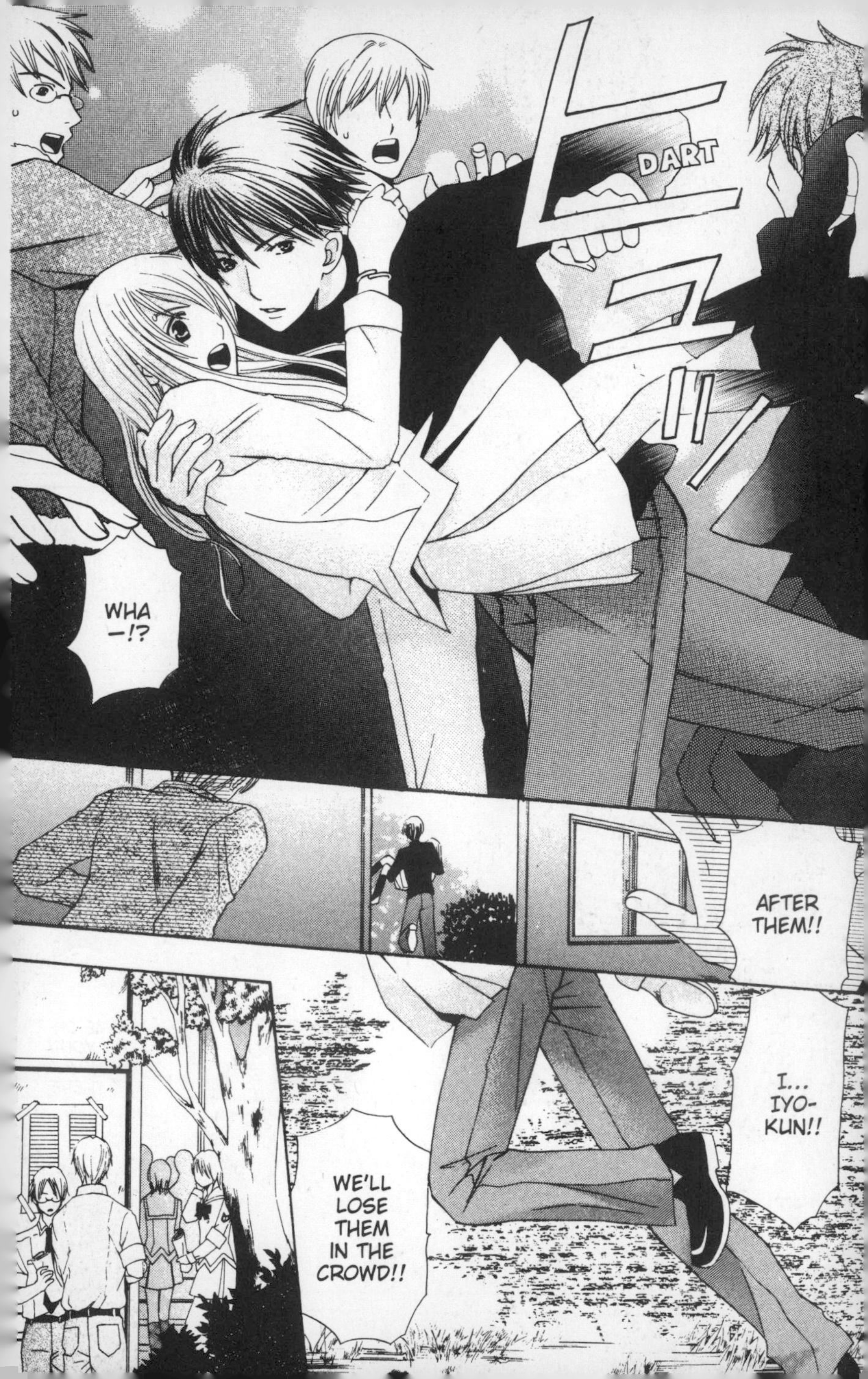
DART
WHA—!?
AFTER THEM!!
I... IYO-KUN!!
WE'LL LOSE THEM IN THE CROWD!!

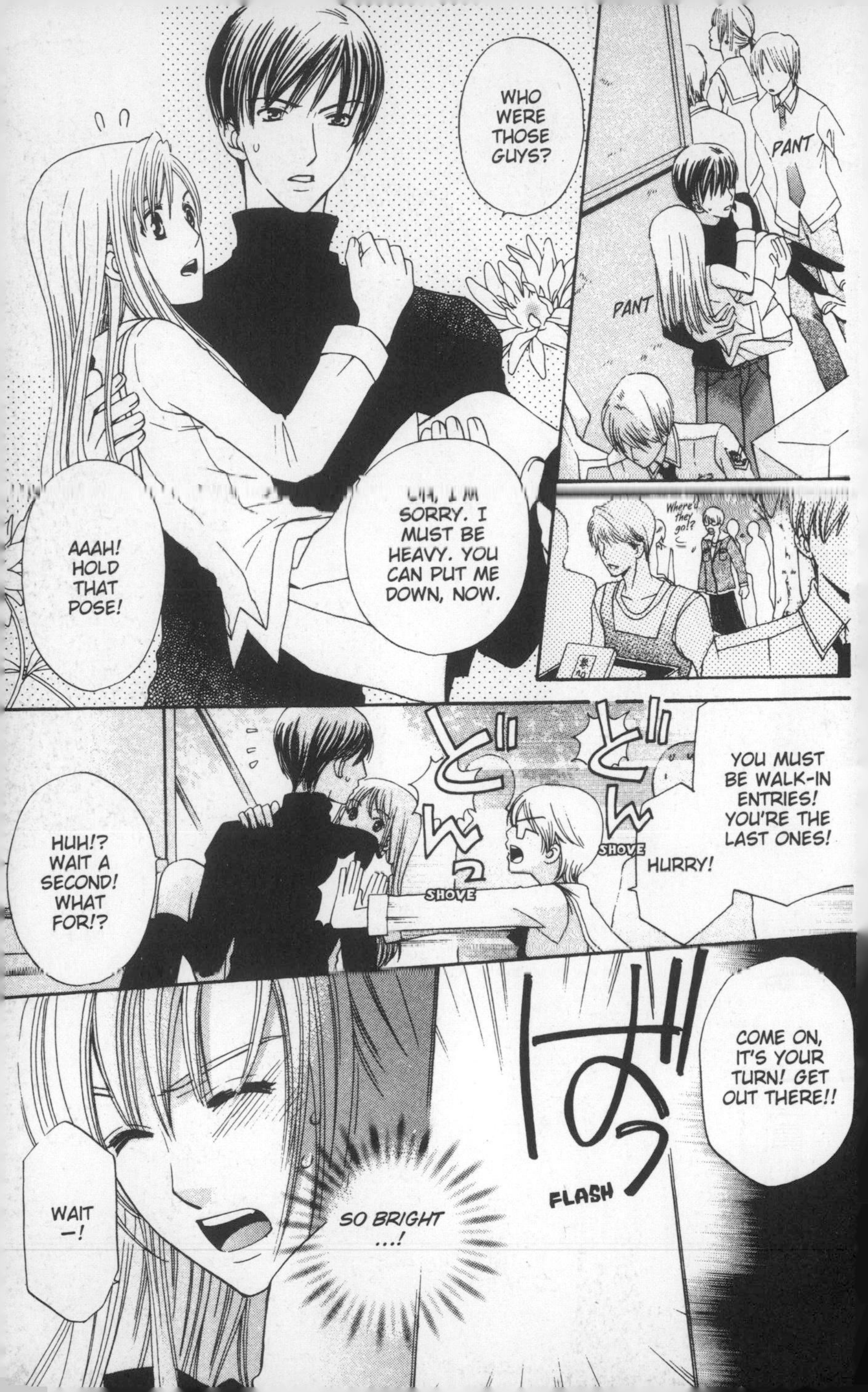
PANT
PANT
Where'd they go!?
WHO WERE THOSE GUYS?
UH, I'M SORRY. I MUST BE HEAVY. YOU CAN PUT ME DOWN, NOW.
AAAH! HOLD THAT POSE!
YOU MUST BE WALK-IN ENTRIES! YOU'RE THE LAST ONES!
HURRY!
どん
SHOVE
どんっ
SHOVE
HUH!? WAIT A SECOND! WHAT FOR!?
COME ON, IT'S YOUR TURN! GET OUT THERE!!
ぱっ
FLASH
SO BRIGHT ...!
WAIT —!

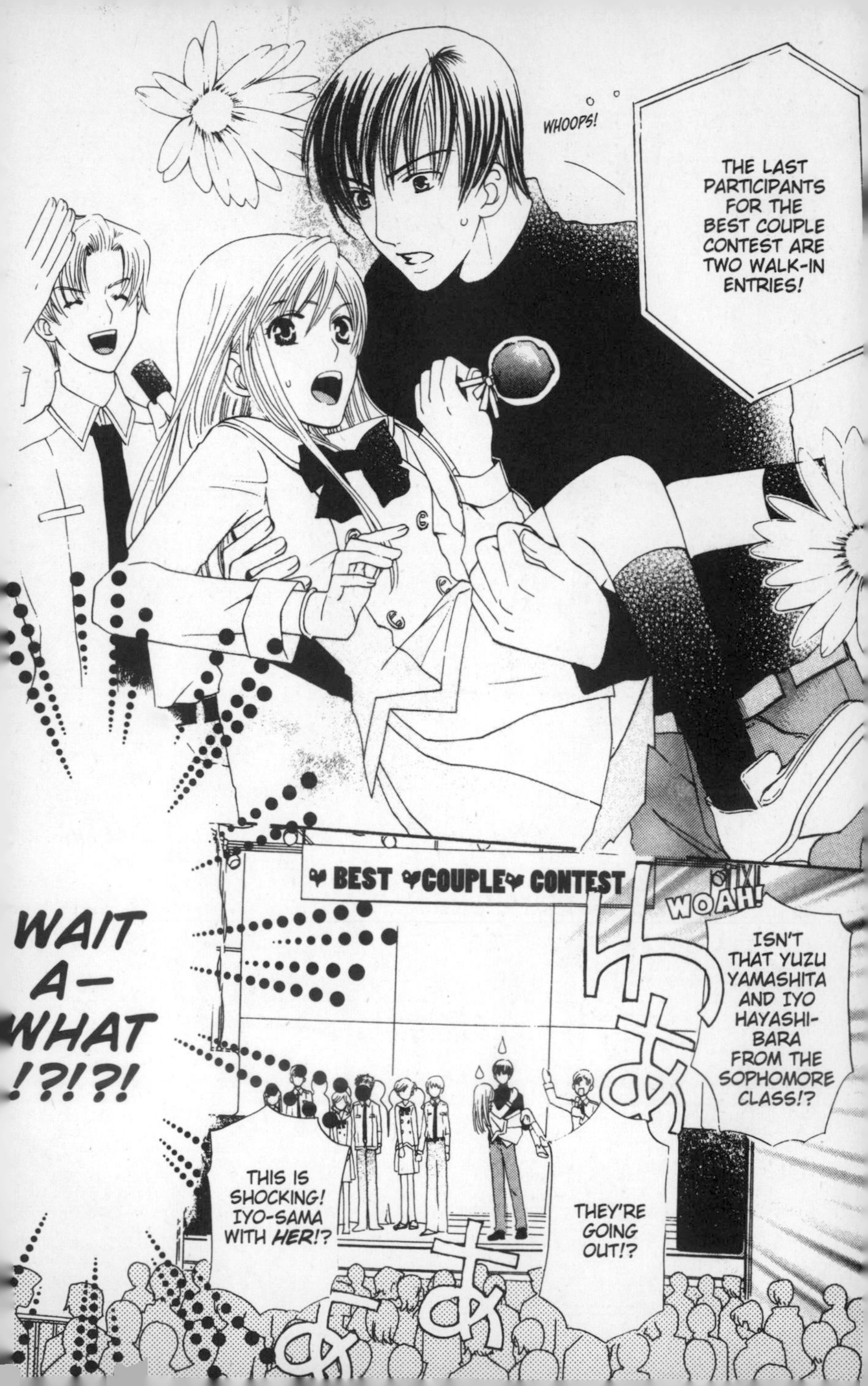
THE LAST PARTICIPANTS FOR THE BEST COUPLE CONTEST ARE TWO WALK-IN ENTRIES!
WHOOPS!
BEST COUPLE CONTEST
WOAH!
ISN'T THAT YUZU YAMASHITA AND IYO HAYASHI-BARA FROM THE SOPHOMORE CLASS!?
WAIT A—WHAT!?!?!
THEY'RE GOING OUT!?
THIS IS SHOCKING! IYO-SAMA WITH HER!?

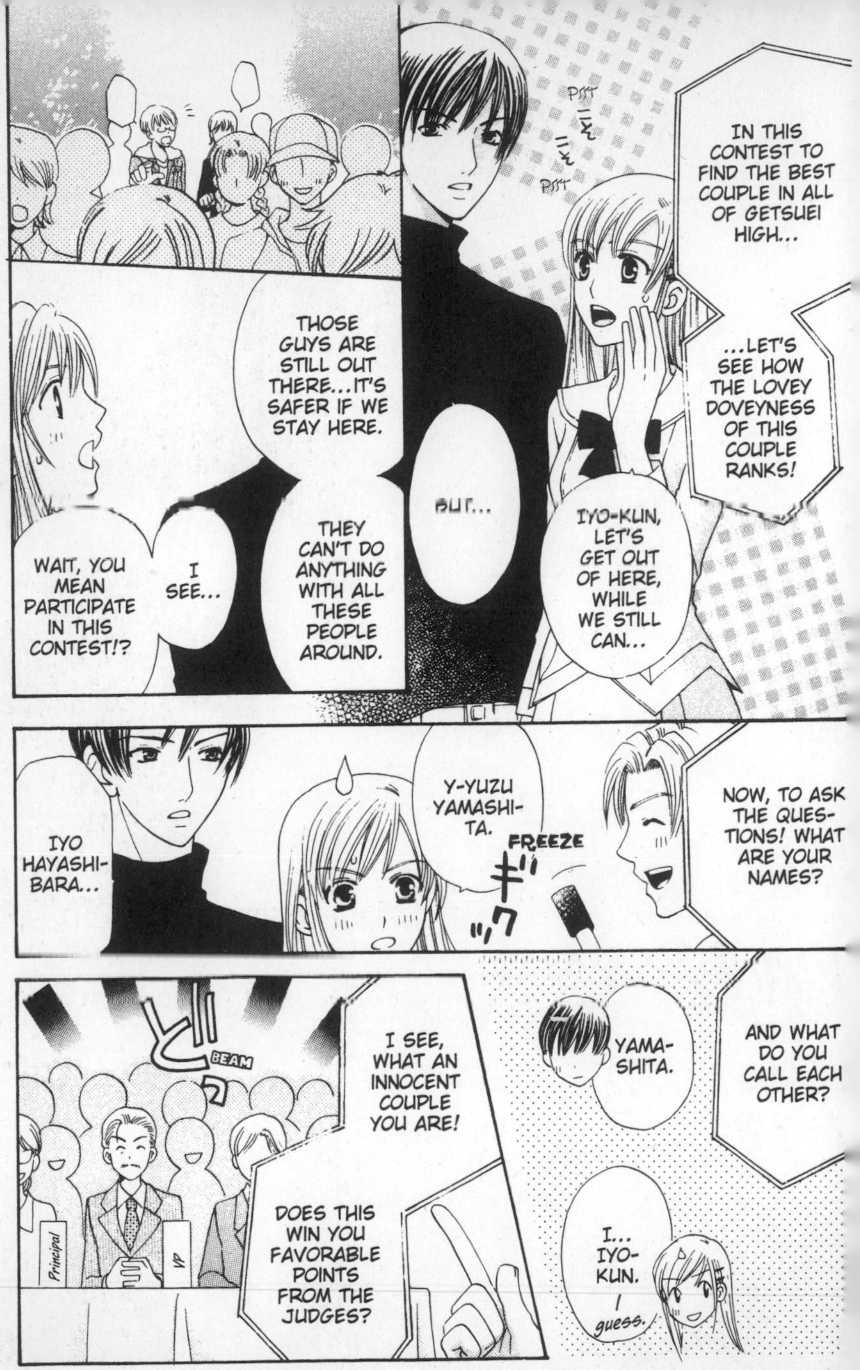
IN THIS CONTEST TO FIND THE BEST COUPLE IN ALL OF GETSUEI HIGH...
PSST
PSST
...LET'S SEE HOW THE LOVEY DOVEYNESS OF THIS COUPLE RANKS!
IYO-KUN, LET'S GET OUT OF HERE, WHILE WE STILL CAN...
BUT...
THOSE GUYS ARE STILL OUT THERE...IT'S SAFER IF WE STAY HERE.
THEY CAN'T DO ANYTHING WITH ALL THESE PEOPLE AROUND.
I SEE...
WAIT, YOU MEAN PARTICIPATE IN THIS CONTEST!?
NOW, TO ASK THE QUES-TIONS! WHAT ARE YOUR NAMES?
FREEZE
Y-YUZU YAMASHI-TA.
IYO HAYASHI-BARA...
AND WHAT DO YOU CALL EACH OTHER?
YAMA-SHITA.
I... IYO-KUN.
I guess.
I SEE, WHAT AN INNOCENT COUPLE YOU ARE!
DOES THIS WIN YOU FAVORABLE POINTS FROM THE JUDGES?
BEAM
Principal
VP

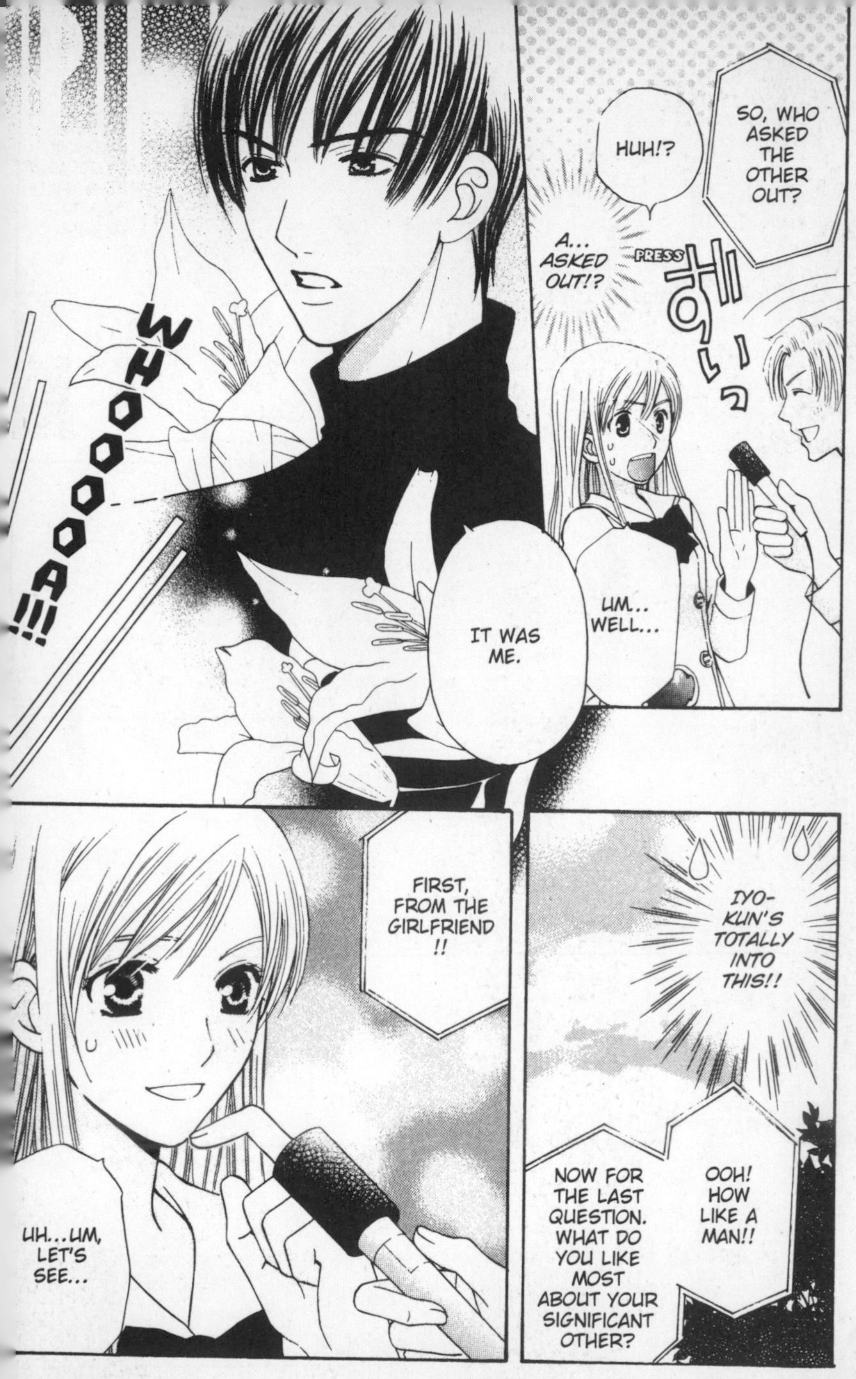

SO, WHO ASKED THE OTHER OUT?
HUH!?
A... ASKED OUT!?
PRESS
すいっ
UM.. WELL...
IT WAS ME.
WHOOOOOOA!!!
IYO-KUN'S TOTALLY INTO THIS!!
OOH! HOW LIKE A MAN!!
NOW FOR THE LAST QUESTION. WHAT DO YOU LIKE MOST ABOUT YOUR SIGNIFICANT OTHER?
FIRST, FROM THE GIRLFRIEND!!
UH...UM, LET'S SEE...

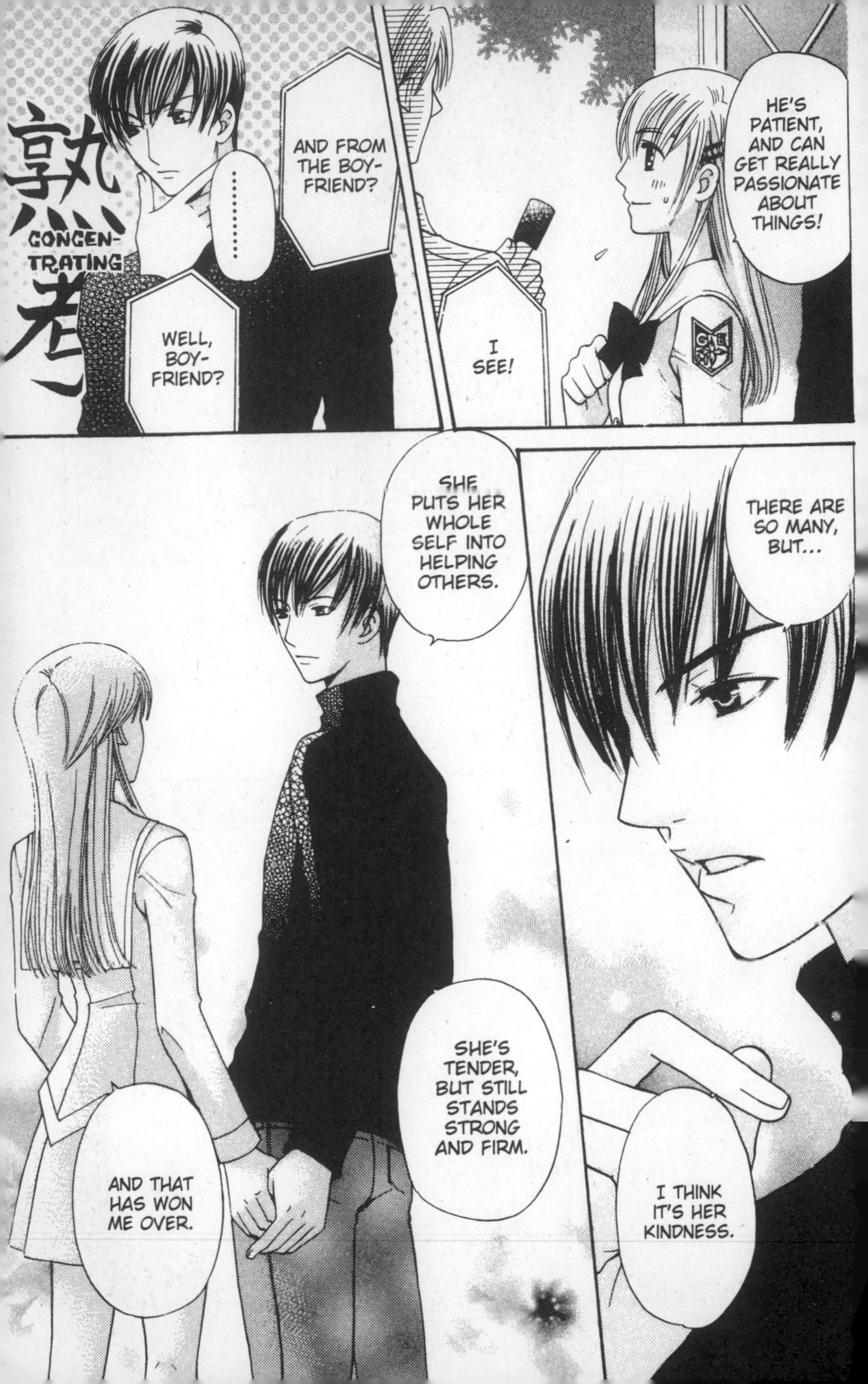
HE'S PATIENT, AND CAN GET REALLY PASSIONATE ABOUT THINGS!
I SEE!
AND FROM THE BOY-FRIEND?
......
熟考
CONCEN-TRATING
WELL, BOY-FRIEND?
THERE ARE SO MANY, BUT...
I THINK IT'S HER KINDNESS.
SHE PUTS HER WHOLE SELF INTO HELPING OTHERS.
SHE'S TENDER, BUT STILL STANDS STRONG AND FIRM.
AND THAT HAS WON ME OVER.

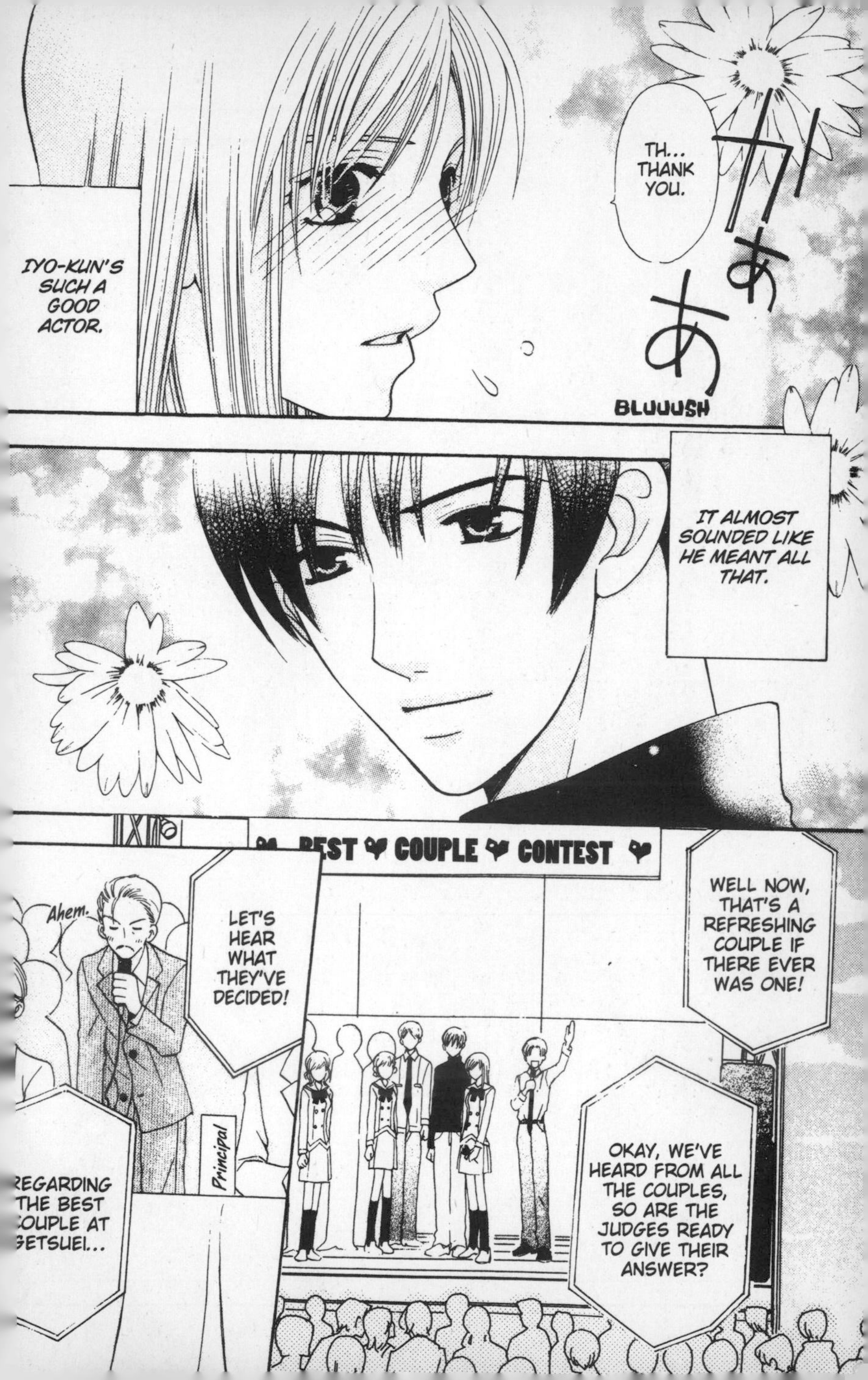
TH... THANK YOU.
かぁあ
BLUUUSH
IYO-KUN'S SUCH A GOOD ACTOR.
IT ALMOST SOUNDED LIKE HE MEANT ALL THAT.
BEST COUPLE CONTEST
WELL NOW, THAT'S A REFRESHING COUPLE IF THERE EVER WAS ONE!
OKAY, WE'VE HEARD FROM ALL THE COUPLES, SO ARE THE JUDGES READY TO GIVE THEIR ANSWER?
LET'S HEAR WHAT THEY'VE DECIDED!
Ahem.
Principal
REGARDING THE BEST COUPLE AT GETSUEI...

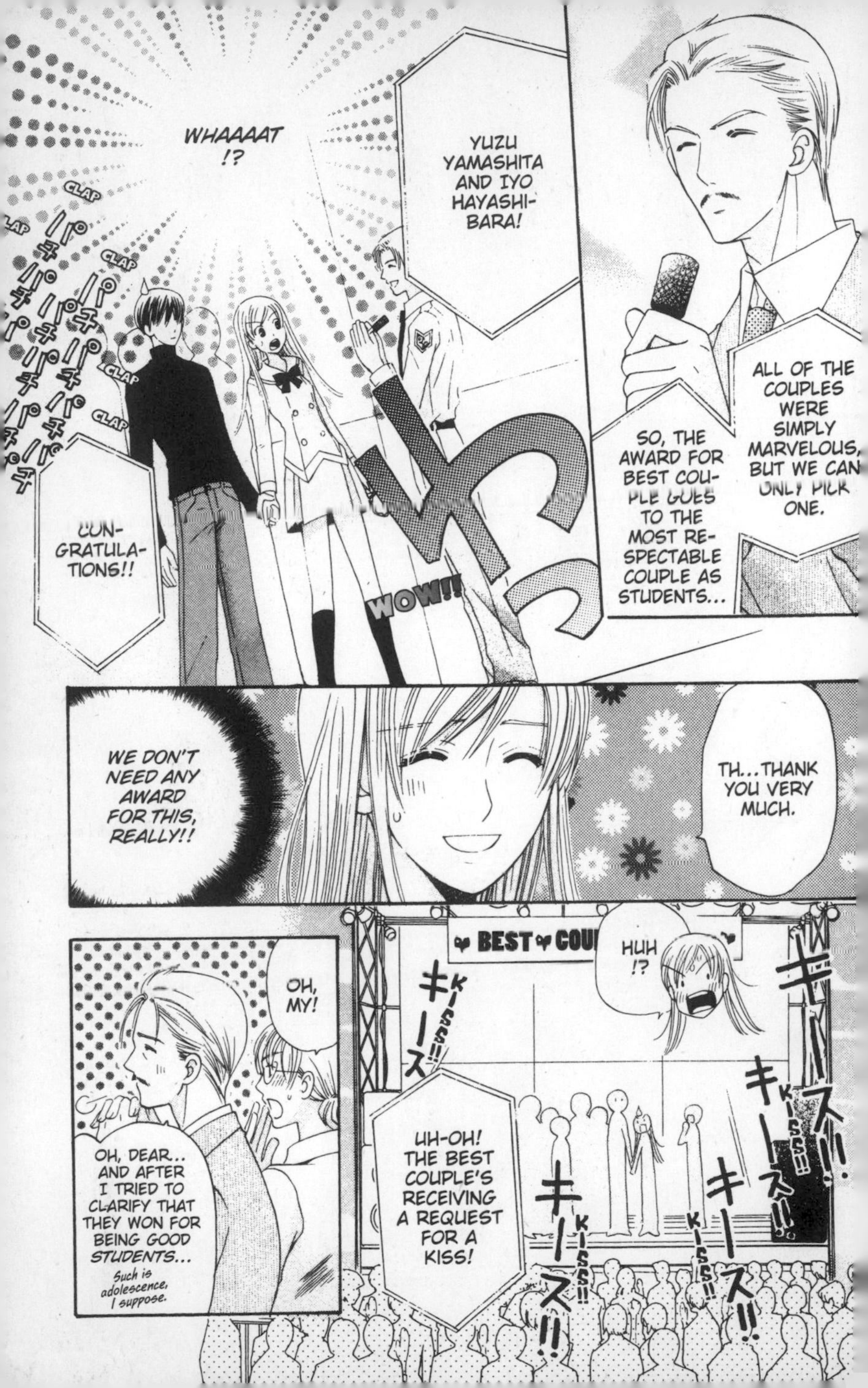
ALL OF THE COUPLES WERE SIMPLY MARVELOUS, BUT WE CAN ONLY PICK ONE.
SO, THE AWARD FOR BEST COUPLE GOES TO THE MOST RESPECTABLE COUPLE AS STUDENTS...
YUZU YAMASHITA AND IYO HAYASHIBARA!
WHAAAAT !?
CLAP
CLAP
CLAP
CLAP
CLAP
パチパチパチパチ
パチパチパチパチ
WOW!!
CONGRATULATIONS!!
TH...THANK YOU VERY MUCH.
WE DON'T NEED ANY AWARD FOR THIS, REALLY!!
BEST COU
HUH !?
キース KISS!!
キース KISS!!
キース KISS!!
キース KISS!!
UH-OH! THE BEST COUPLE'S RECEIVING A REQUEST FOR A KISS!
OH, MY!
OH, DEAR... AND AFTER I TRIED TO CLARIFY THAT THEY WON FOR BEING GOOD STUDENTS...
Such is adolescence, I suppose.

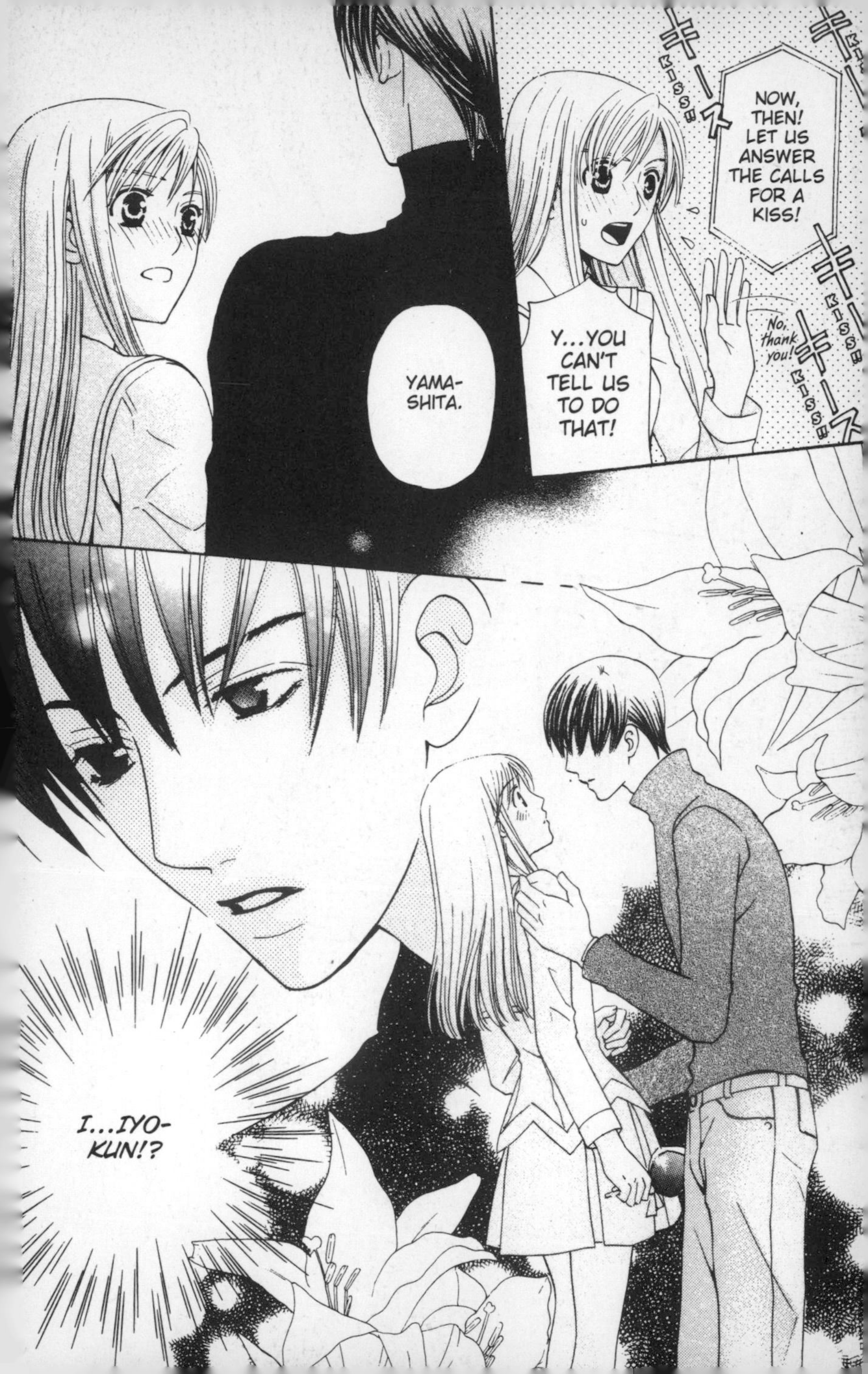
NOW, THEN! LET US ANSWER THE CALLS FOR A KISS!
キース
KISS!!
キース
KISS!!
キース
KISS!!
No, thank you!
Y...YOU CAN'T TELL US TO DO THAT!
YAMA-SHITA.
I...IYO-KUN!?

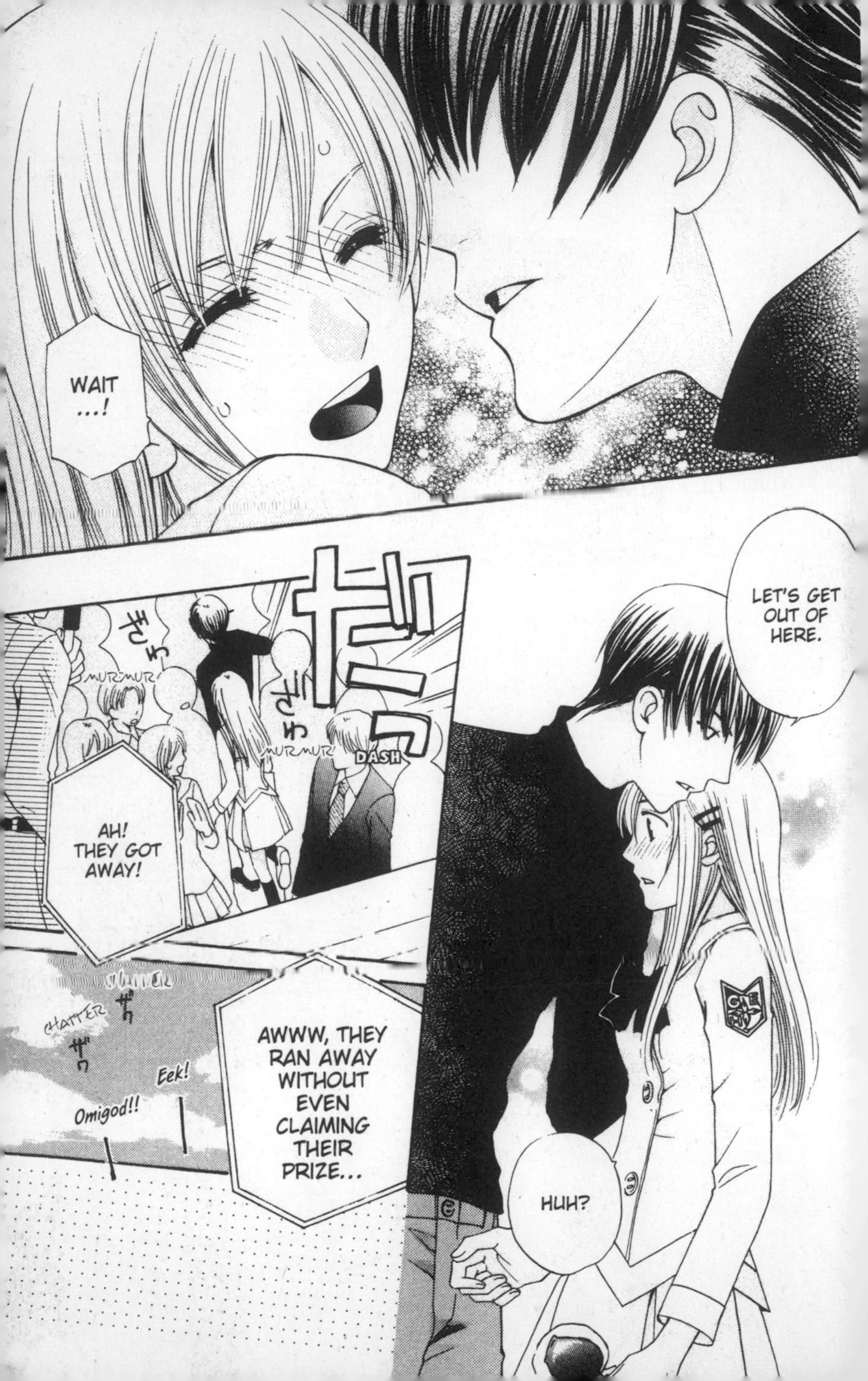
WAIT ...!
LET'S GET OUT OF HERE.
HUH?
MURMUR
MURMUR
DASH
AH! THEY GOT AWAY!
AWWW, THEY RAN AWAY WITHOUT EVEN CLAIMING THEIR PRIZE...
CHATTER
Eek!
Omigod!!

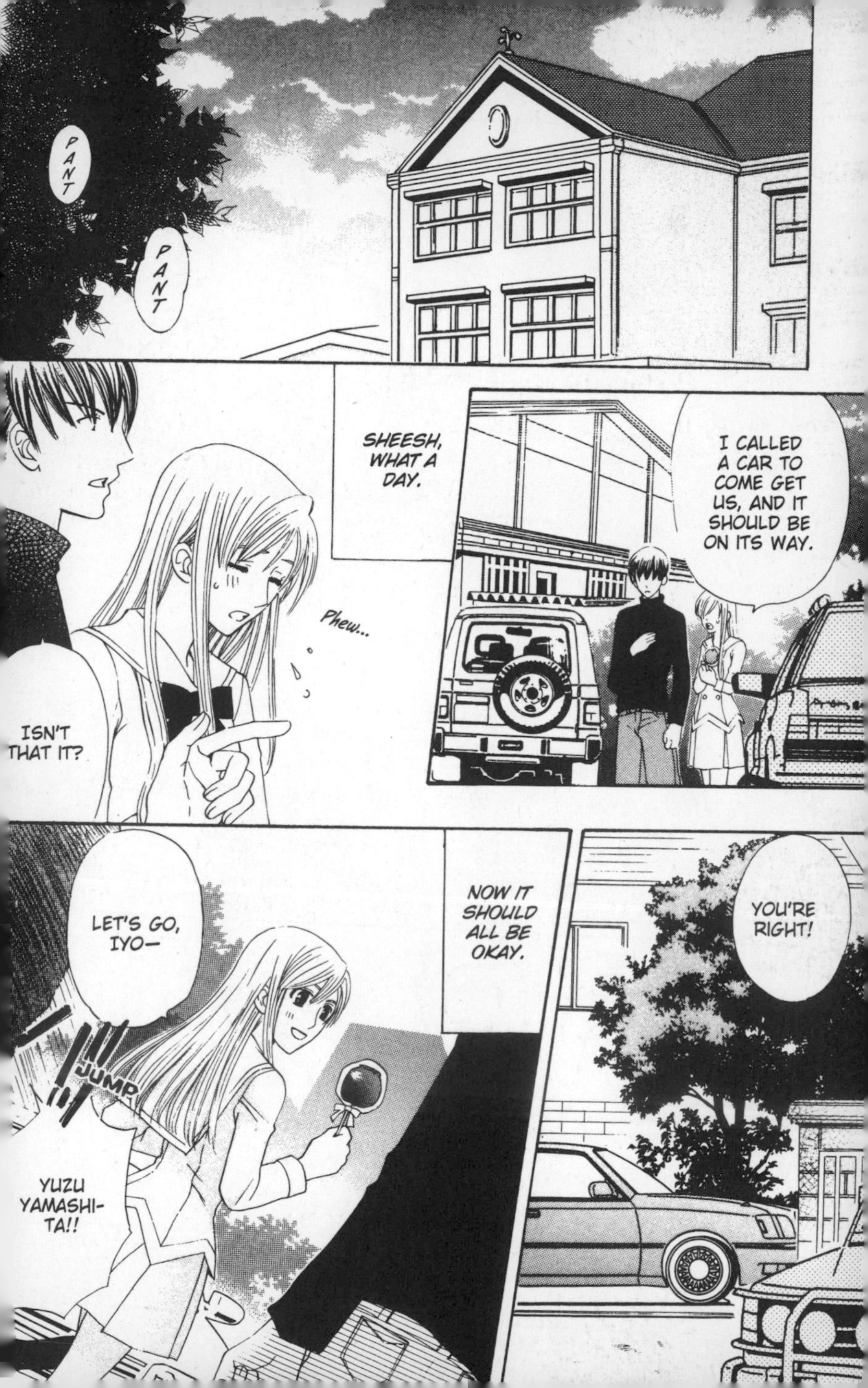
PANT
PANT
I CALLED A CAR TO COME GET US, AND IT SHOULD BE ON ITS WAY.
SHEESH, WHAT A DAY.
Phew...
ISN'T THAT IT?
YOU'RE RIGHT!
NOW IT SHOULD ALL BE OKAY.
LET'S GO, IYO—
JUMP
YUZU YAMASHITA!!

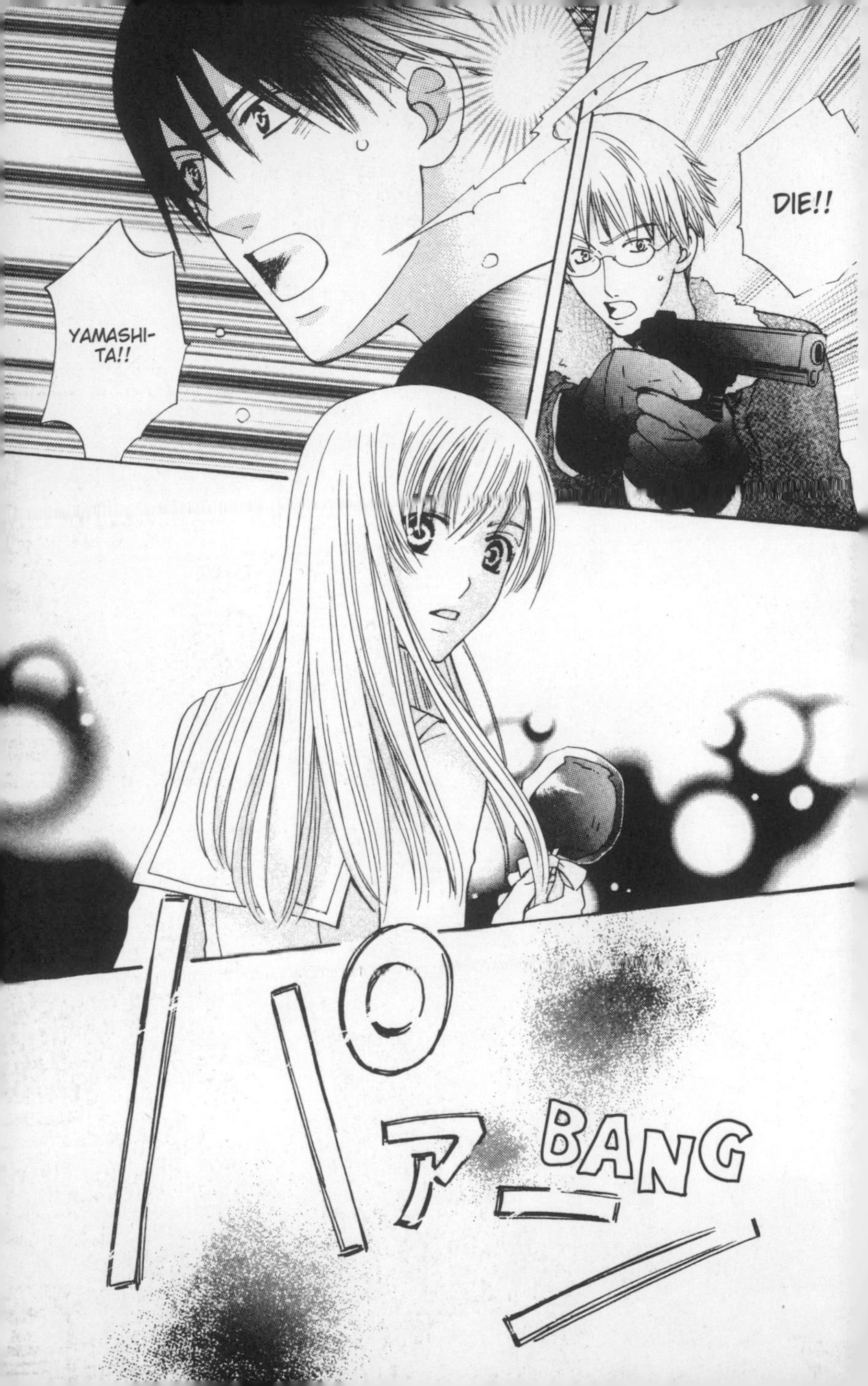
DIE!!
YAMASHITA!!
パアー
BANG

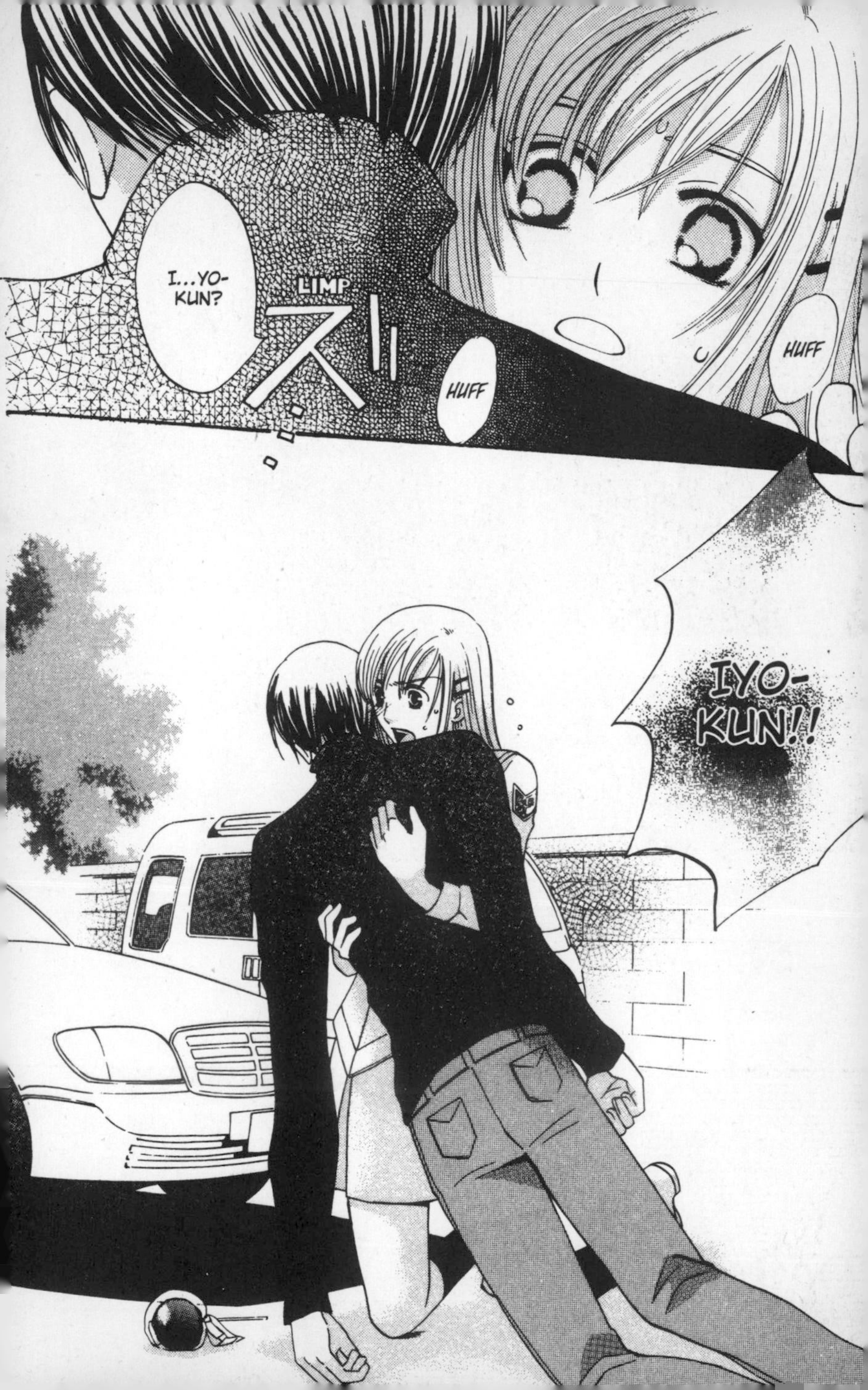
HUFF
HUFF
LIMP
I...YO-KUN?
IYO-KUN!!

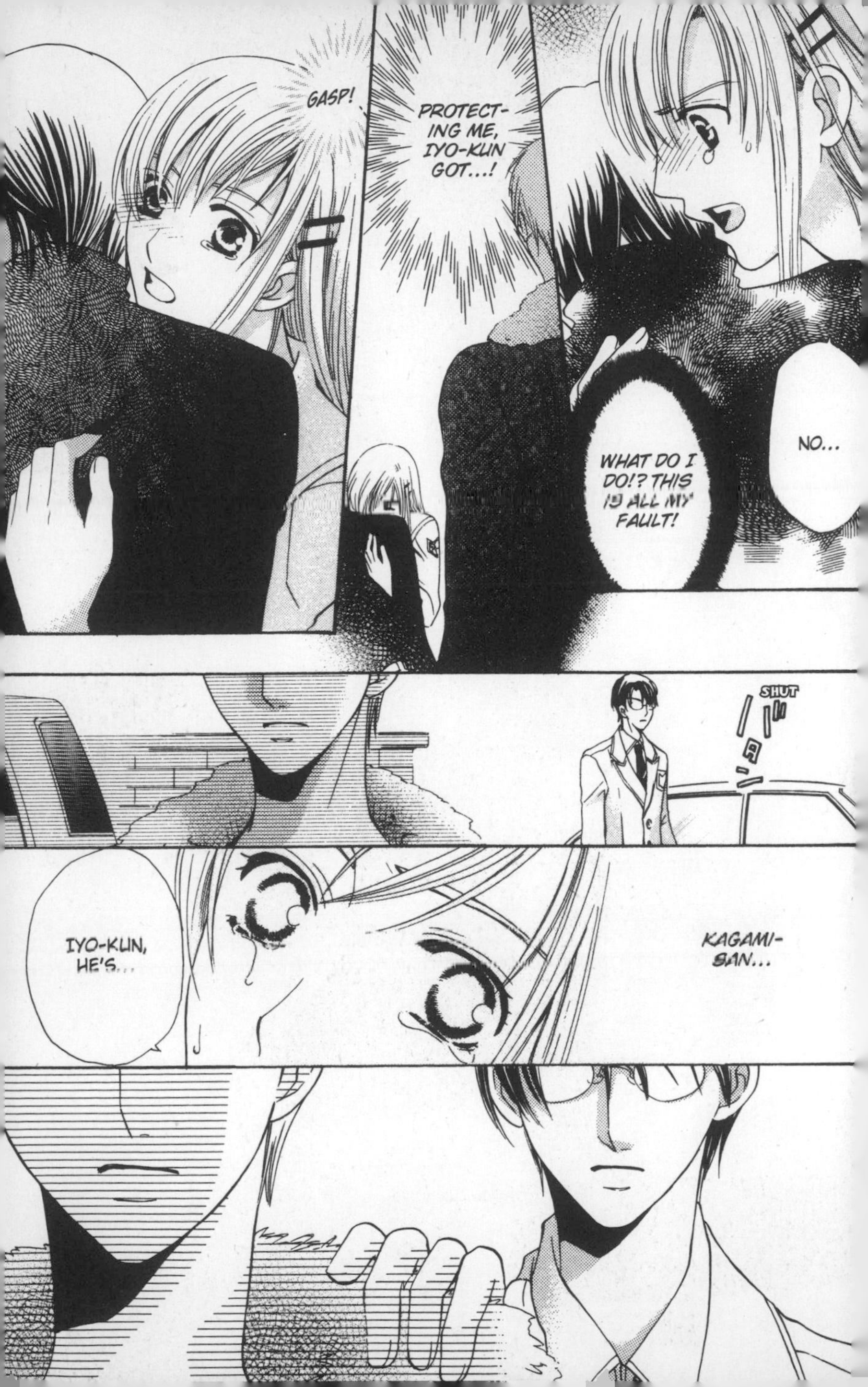
NO...
WHAT DO I DO!? THIS IS ALL MY FAULT!
PROTECTING ME, IYO-KUN GOT...!
GASP!
SHUT
KAGAMI-SAN...
IYO-KUN, HE'S...

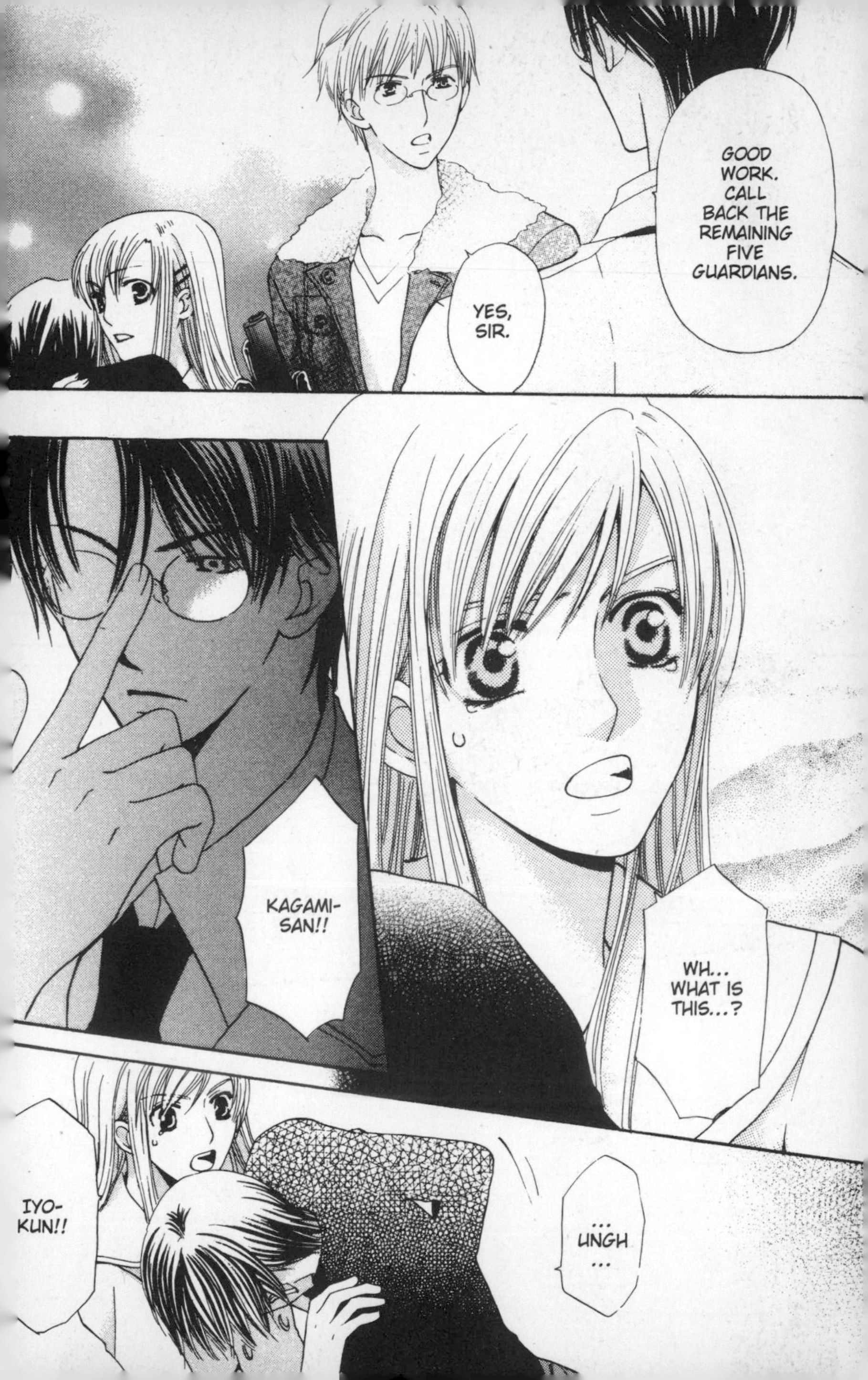
GOOD WORK. CALL BACK THE REMAINING FIVE GUARDIANS.
YES, SIR.
WH... WHAT IS THIS...?
KAGAMI-SAN!!
... UNGH ...
IYO-KUN!!

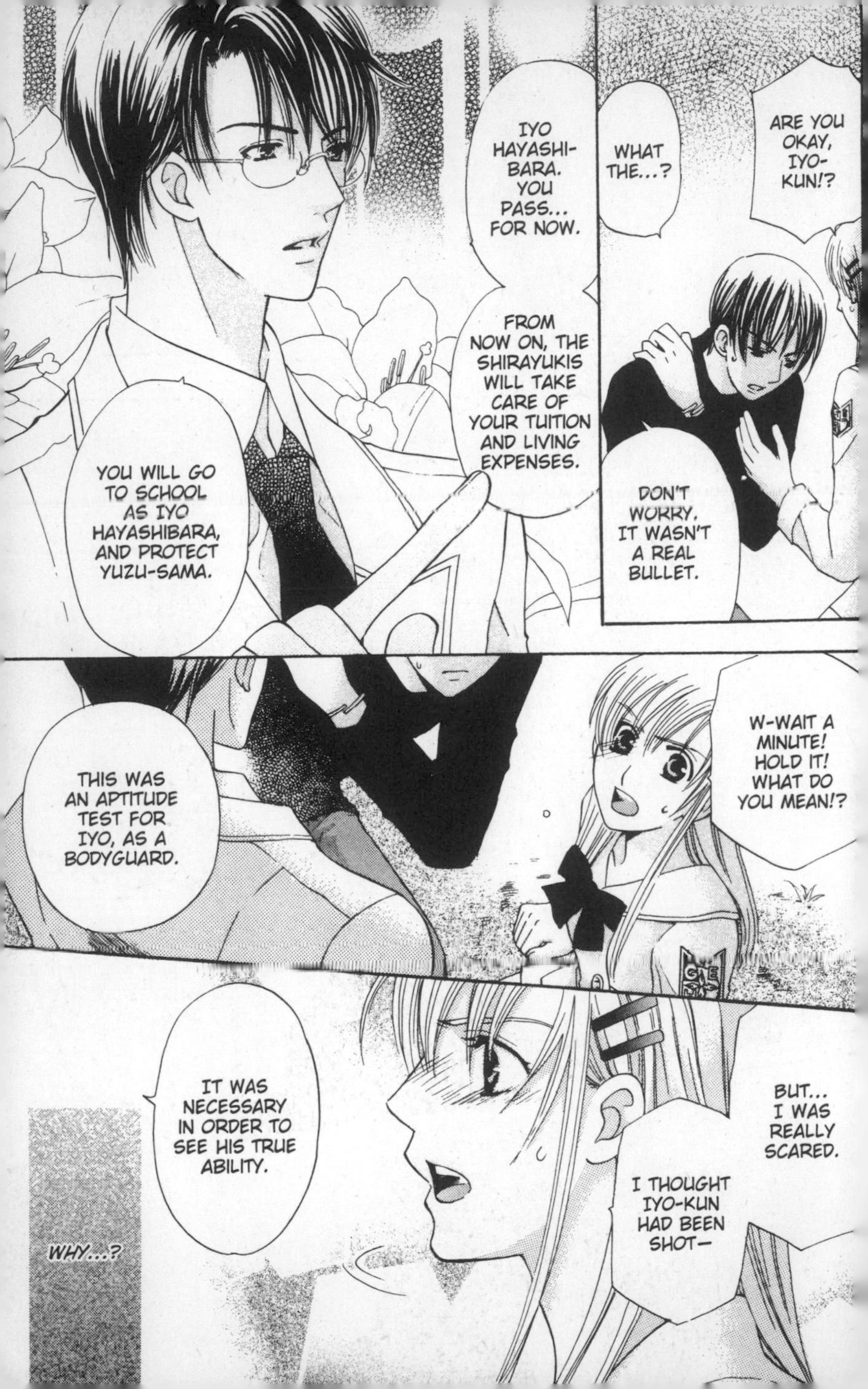
ARE YOU OKAY, IYO-KUN!?
WHAT THE...?
DON'T WORRY. IT WASN'T A REAL BULLET.
IYO HAYASHIBARA. YOU PASS... FOR NOW.
FROM NOW ON, THE SHIRAYUKIS WILL TAKE CARE OF YOUR TUITION AND LIVING EXPENSES.
YOU WILL GO TO SCHOOL AS IYO HAYASHIBARA, AND PROTECT YUZU-SAMA.
W-WAIT A MINUTE! HOLD IT! WHAT DO YOU MEAN!?
THIS WAS AN APTITUDE TEST FOR IYO, AS A BODYGUARD.
BUT... I WAS REALLY SCARED.
I THOUGHT IYO-KUN HAD BEEN SHOT—
IT WAS NECESSARY IN ORDER TO SEE HIS TRUE ABILITY.
WHY...?

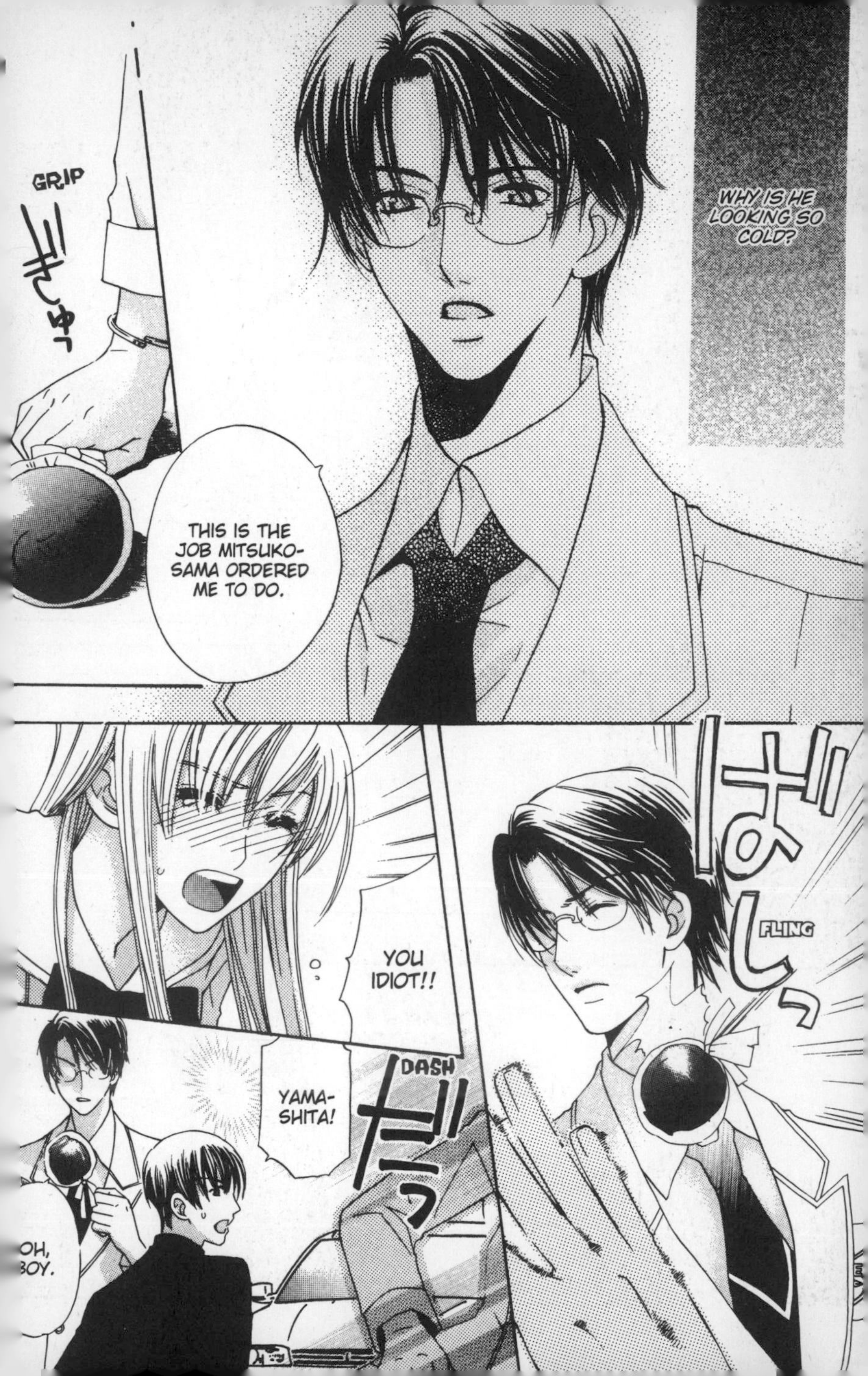
WHY IS HE LOOKING SO COLD?
THIS IS THE JOB MITSUKO-SAMA ORDERED ME TO DO.
GRIP
ぎゅっ
ばしっ
FLING
YOU IDIOT!!
DASH
ダーっ
YAMA-SHITA!
OH, BOY.

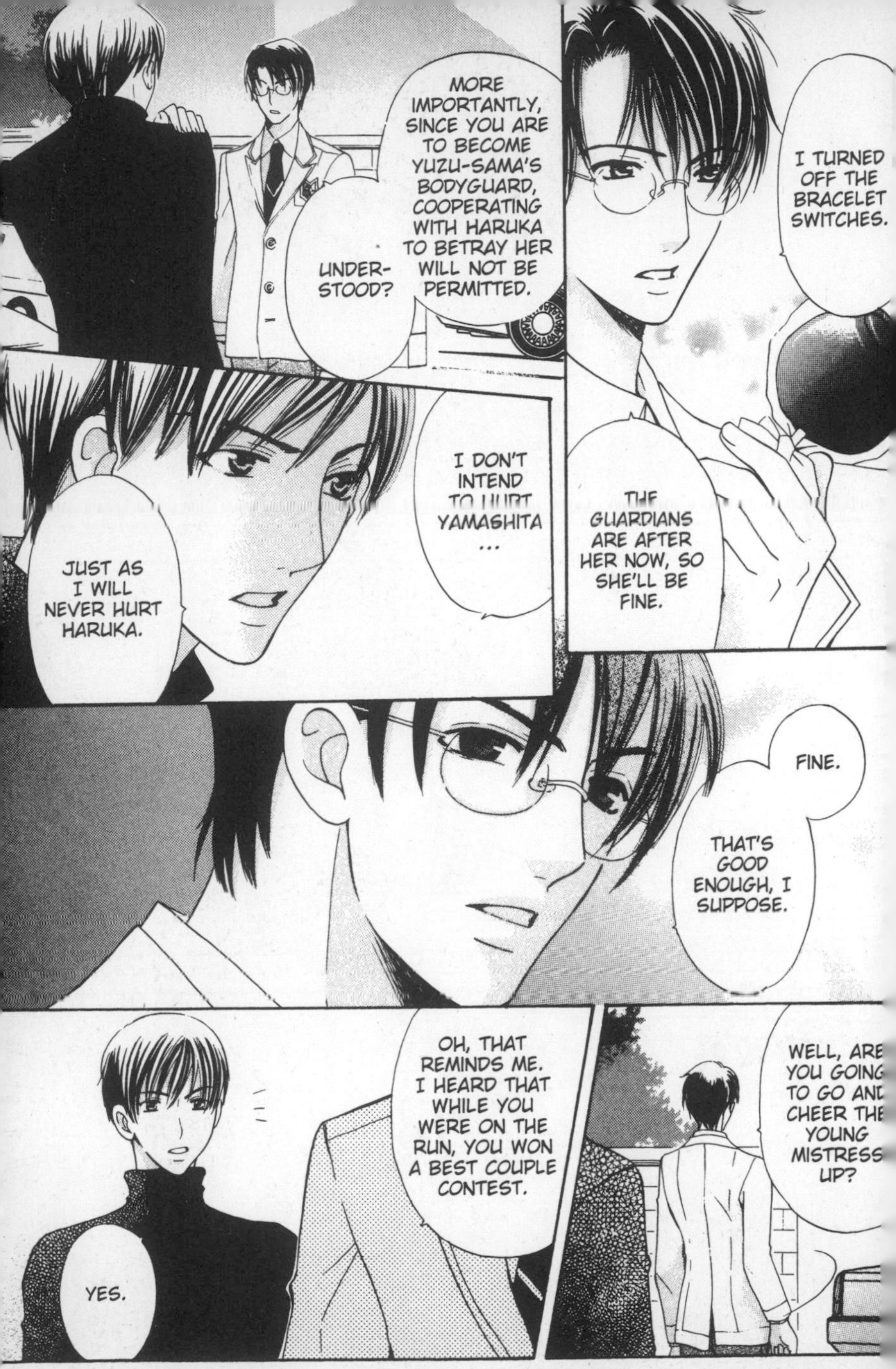
I TURNED OFF THE BRACELET SWITCHES.
THE GUARDIANS ARE AFTER HER NOW, SO SHE'LL BE FINE.
MORE IMPORTANTLY, SINCE YOU ARE TO BECOME YUZU-SAMA'S BODYGUARD, COOPERATING WITH HARUKA TO BETRAY HER WILL NOT BE PERMITTED.
UNDER-STOOD?
I DON'T INTEND TO HURT YAMASHITA ...
JUST AS I WILL NEVER HURT HARUKA.
FINE.
THAT'S GOOD ENOUGH, I SUPPOSE.
WELL, ARE YOU GOING TO GO AND CHEER THE YOUNG MISTRESS UP?
OH, THAT REMINDS ME. I HEARD THAT WHILE YOU WERE ON THE RUN, YOU WON A BEST COUPLE CONTEST.
YES.

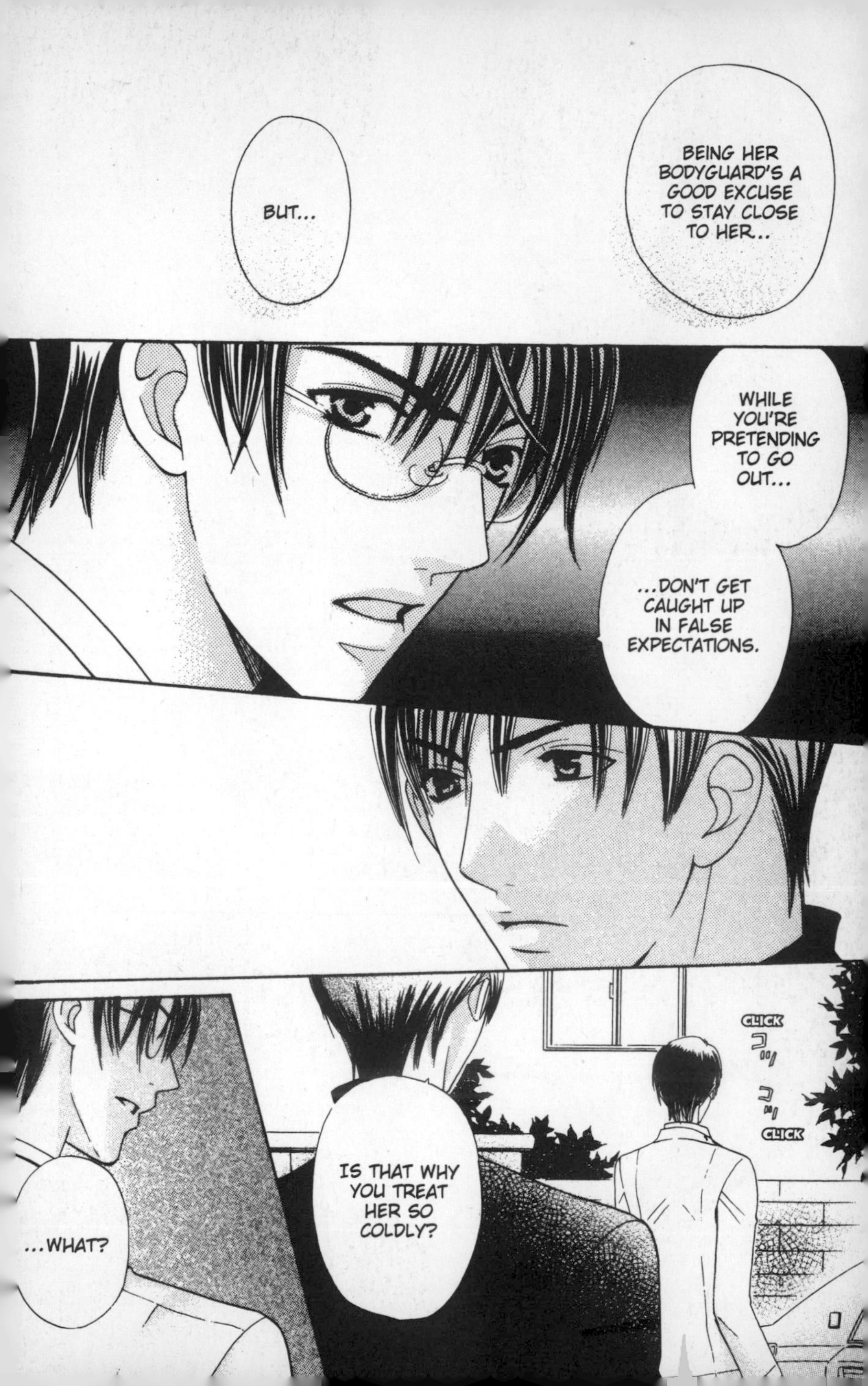
BEING HER BODYGUARD'S A GOOD EXCUSE TO STAY CLOSE TO HER...
BUT...
WHILE YOU'RE PRETENDING TO GO OUT...
...DON'T GET CAUGHT UP IN FALSE EXPECTATIONS.
CLICK
コッ
コッ
CLICK
IS THAT WHY YOU TREAT HER SO COLDLY?
...WHAT?

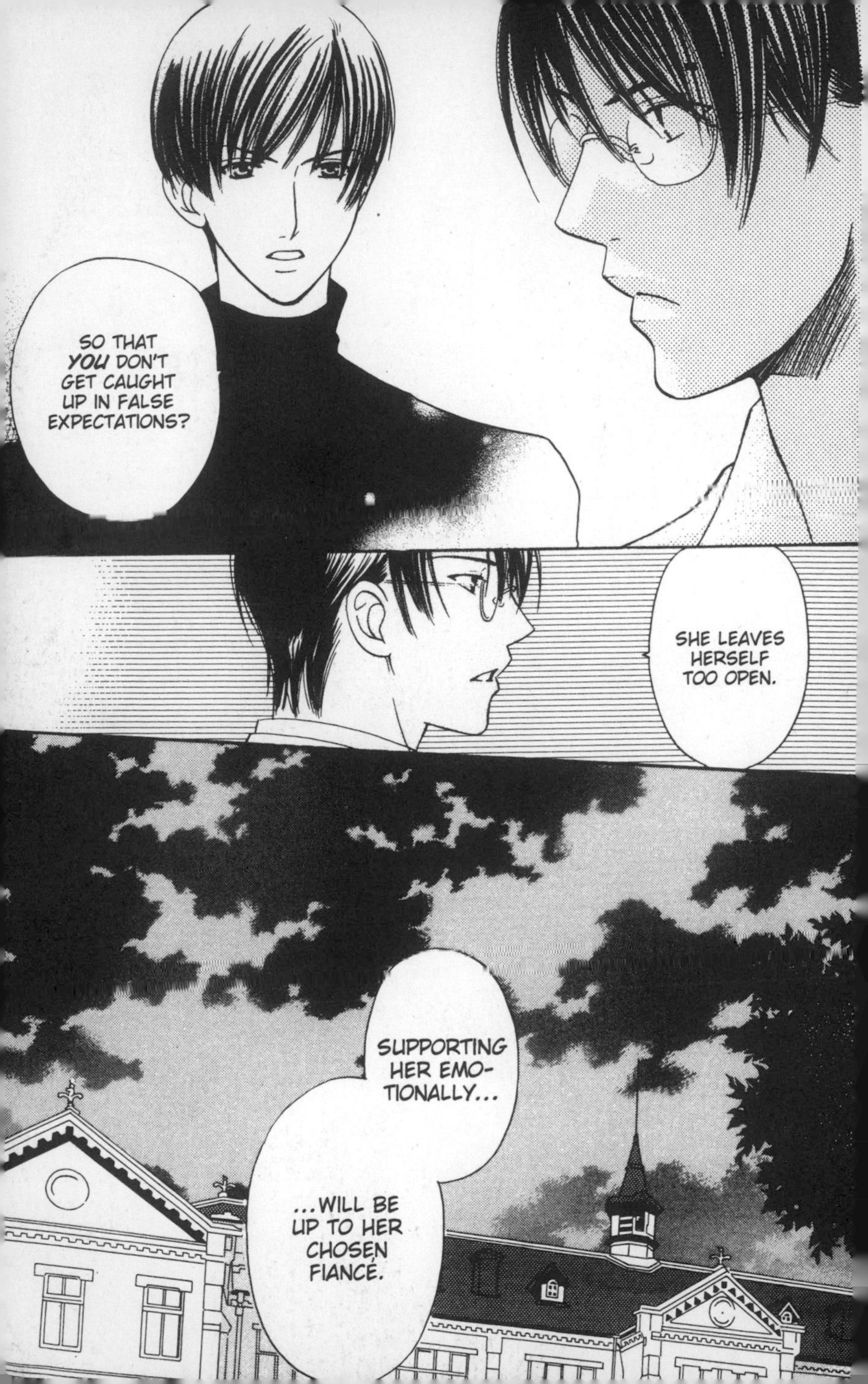
SO THAT *YOU* DON'T GET CAUGHT UP IN FALSE EXPECTATIONS?
SHE LEAVES HERSELF TOO OPEN.
SUPPORTING HER EMO-TIONALLY...
...WILL BE UP TO HER CHOSEN FIANCÉ.

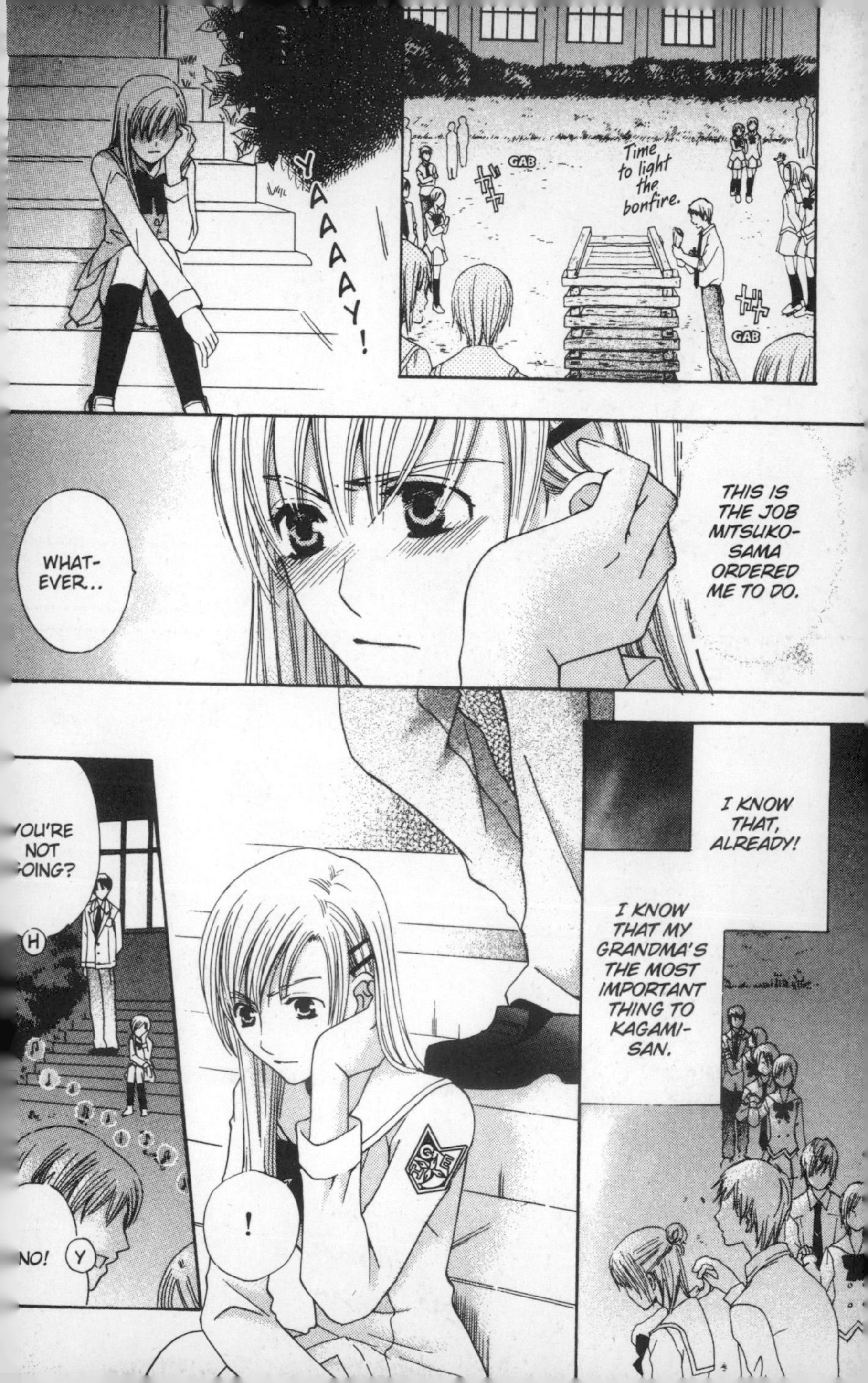
Time to light the bonfire.
GAB
GAB
YAAAAY!
THIS IS THE JOB MITSUKO-SAMA ORDERED ME TO DO.
WHAT-EVER...
I KNOW THAT, ALREADY!
I KNOW THAT MY GRANDMA'S THE MOST IMPORTANT THING TO KAGAMI-SAN.
!
YOU'RE NOT GOING?
H
Y
NO!

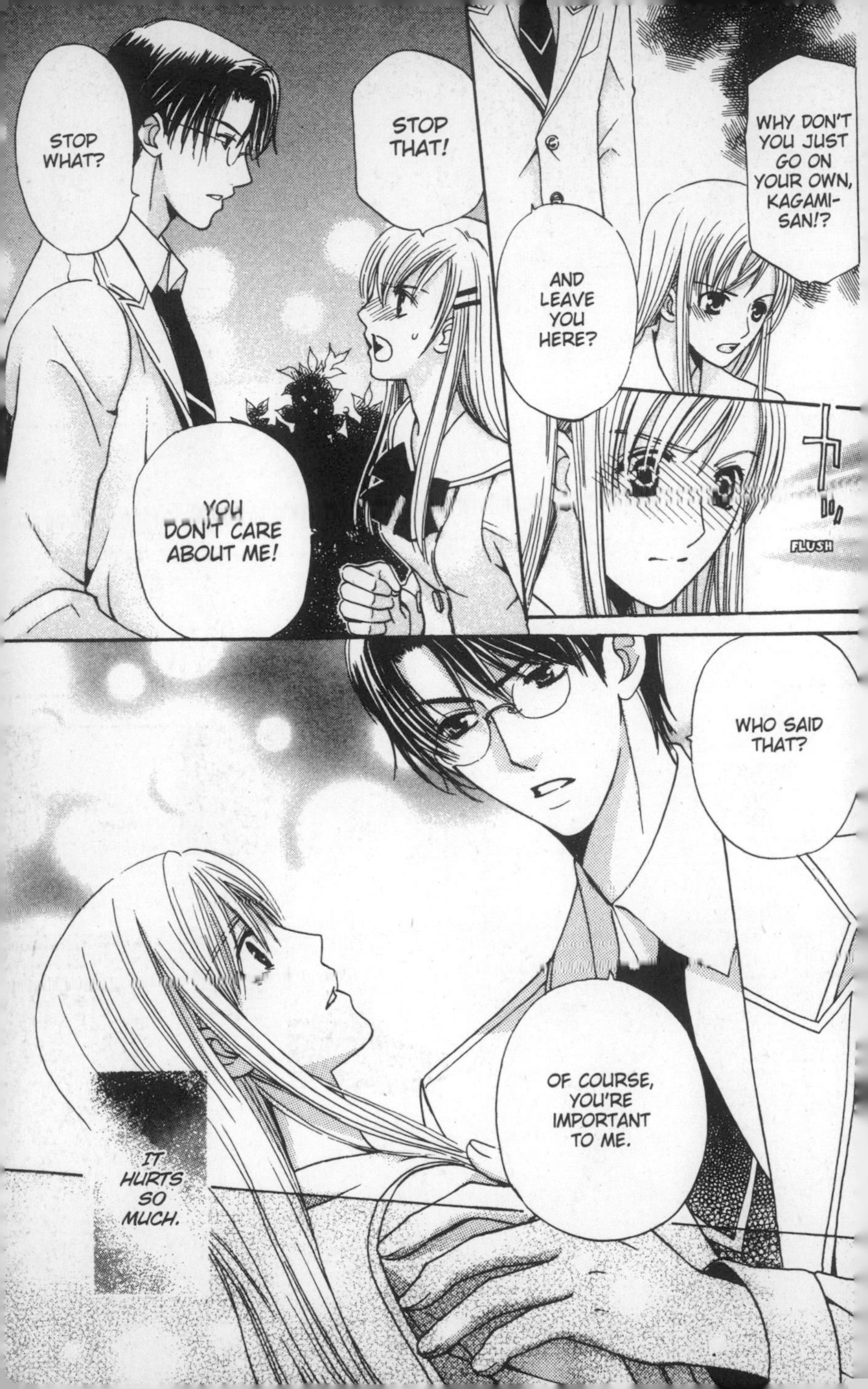
WHY DON'T YOU JUST GO ON YOUR OWN, KAGAMI-SAN!?
AND LEAVE YOU HERE?
FLUSH
STOP THAT!
STOP WHAT?
YOU DON'T CARE ABOUT ME!
WHO SAID THAT?
OF COURSE, YOU'RE IMPORTANT TO ME.
IT HURTS SO MUCH.

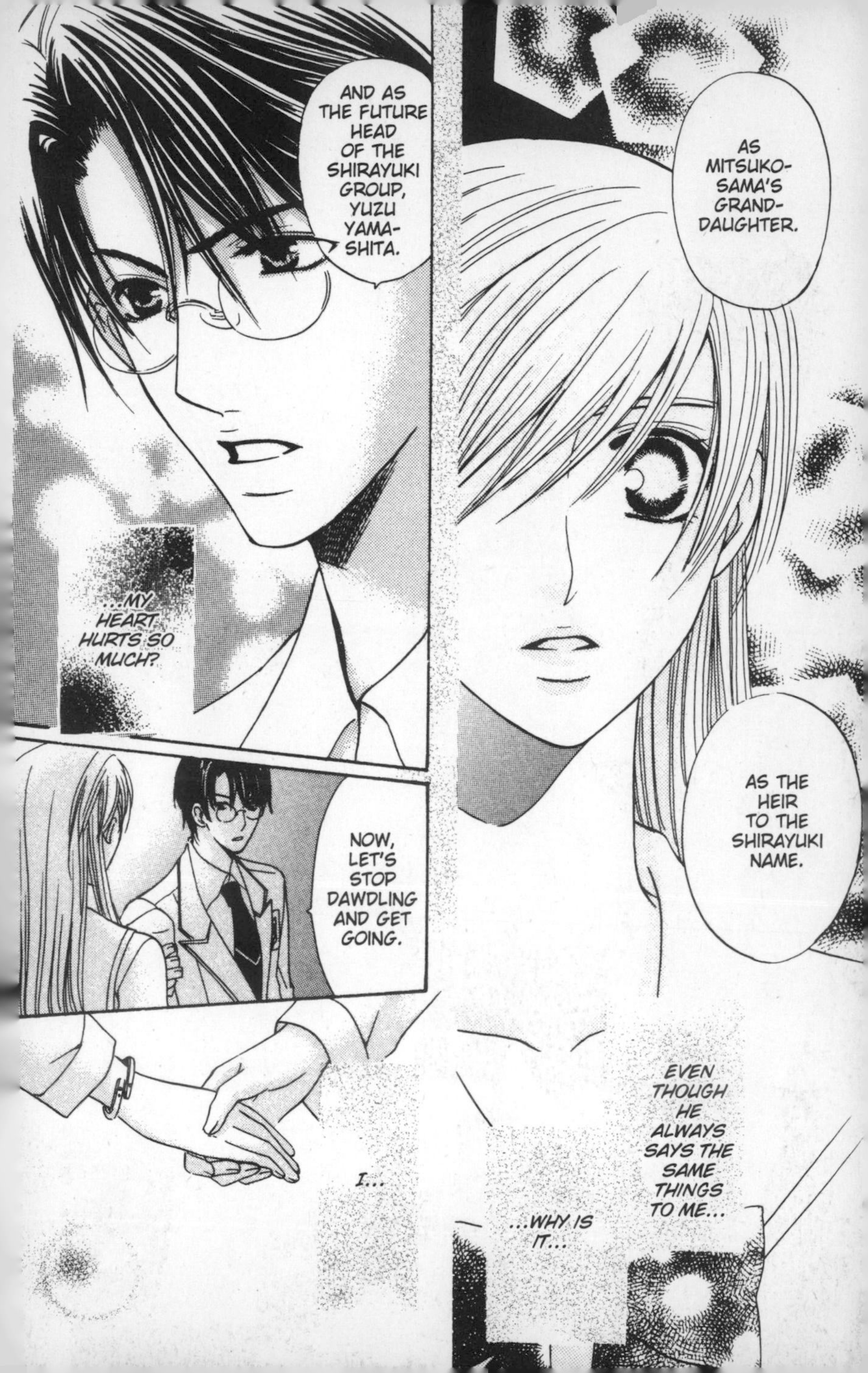
AS MITSUKO-SAMA'S GRAND-DAUGHTER.
AS THE HEIR TO THE SHIRAYUKI NAME.
EVEN THOUGH HE ALWAYS SAYS THE SAME THINGS TO ME...
...WHY IS IT...
AND AS THE FUTURE HEAD OF THE SHIRAYUKI GROUP, YUZU YAMA-SHITA.
...MY HEART HURTS SO MUCH?
NOW, LET'S STOP DAWDLING AND GET GOING.
I...

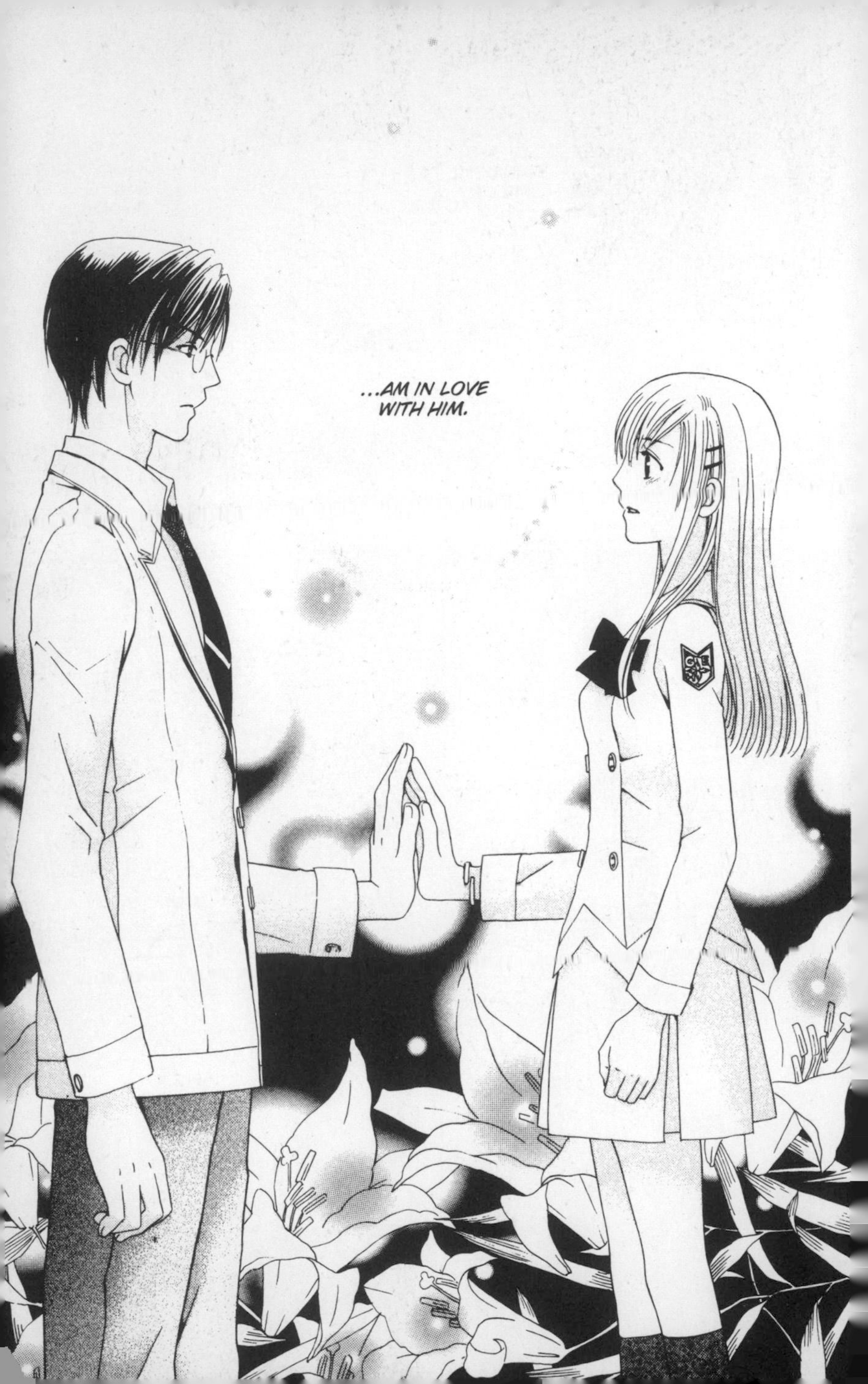
...AM IN LOVE WITH HIM.

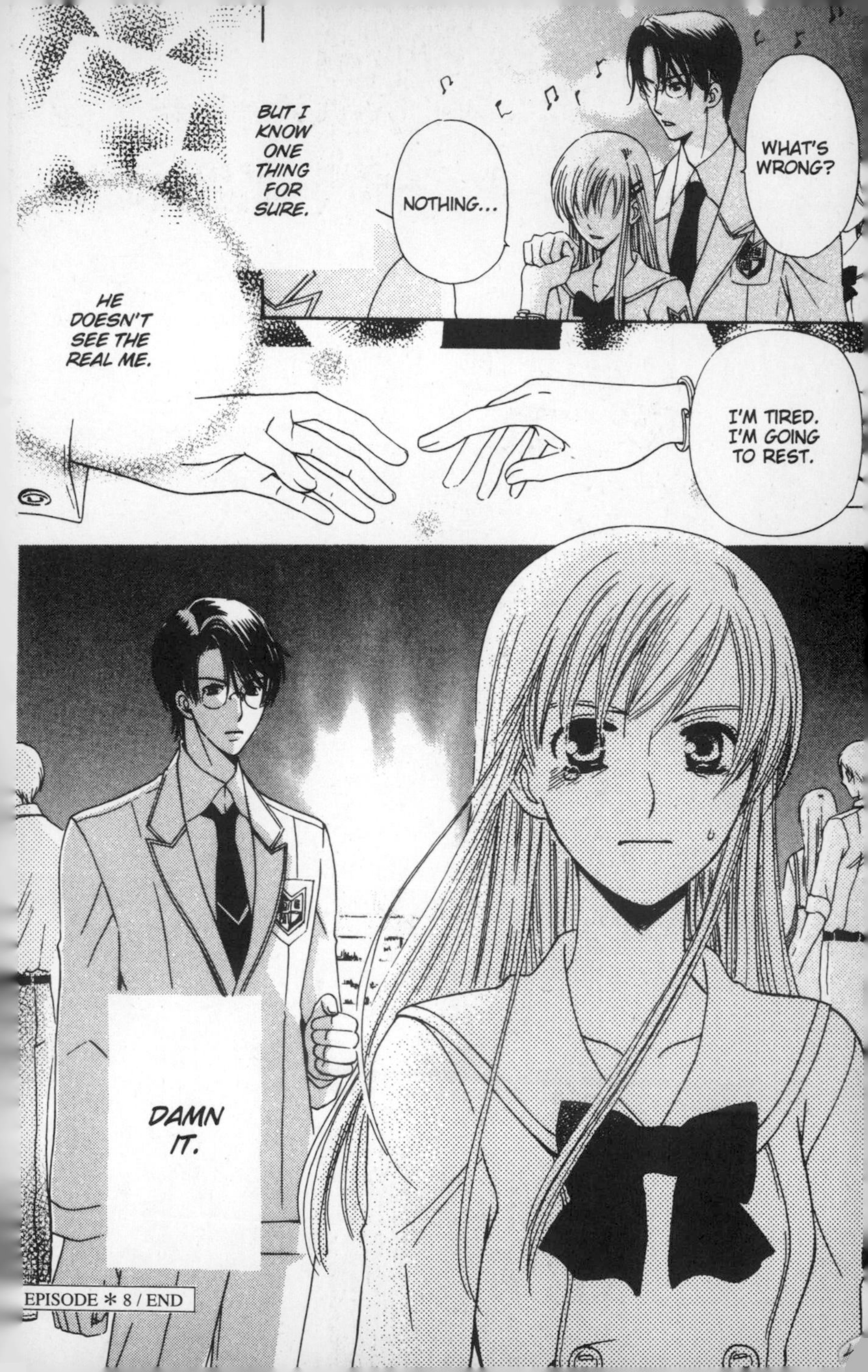
WHAT'S WRONG?
NOTHING...
BUT I KNOW ONE THING FOR SURE.
HE DOESN'T SEE THE REAL ME.
I'M TIRED. I'M GOING TO REST.
DAMN IT.
EPISODE * 8 / END

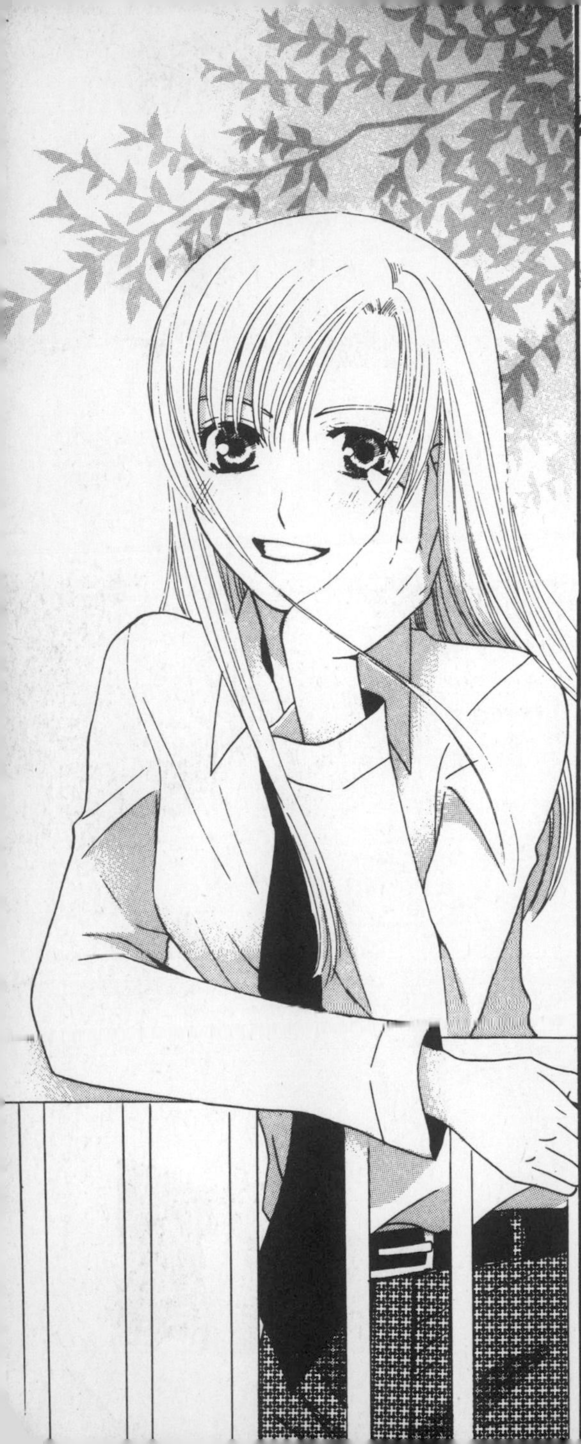

AFTERWORD & SPECIAL THANKS

Thank you so much for picking up volume 2 of Ultimate Venus. I'd like to extend my sincerest thanks to my editor Kishima-san, who always supported me. To Rosemary Tomoko-san, and Peppermint Kyoko-san who always helped me. I look forward to working with you, from now on, too.

March 25, 2007
Takako Shigematsu

TRANSLATOR'S NOTES:

g. 154 – ***taiyaki***

Japanese snack. These fish-shaped pancakes are filled with bean jam, served arm, and are the perfect snack for people on the go.

I'll be waiting for your correspondence.

Takako Shigematsu
c/o Go Media Entertainment
28047 Dorothy Drive
Suite 200
Agoura Hills, CA 91301

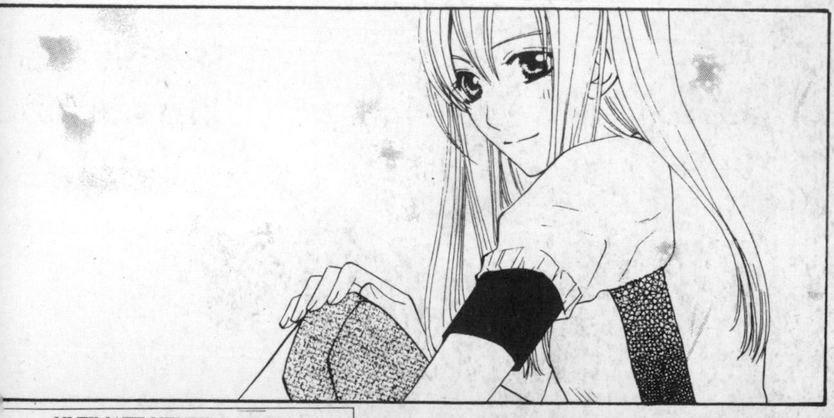

ULTIMATE VENUS 2 / END

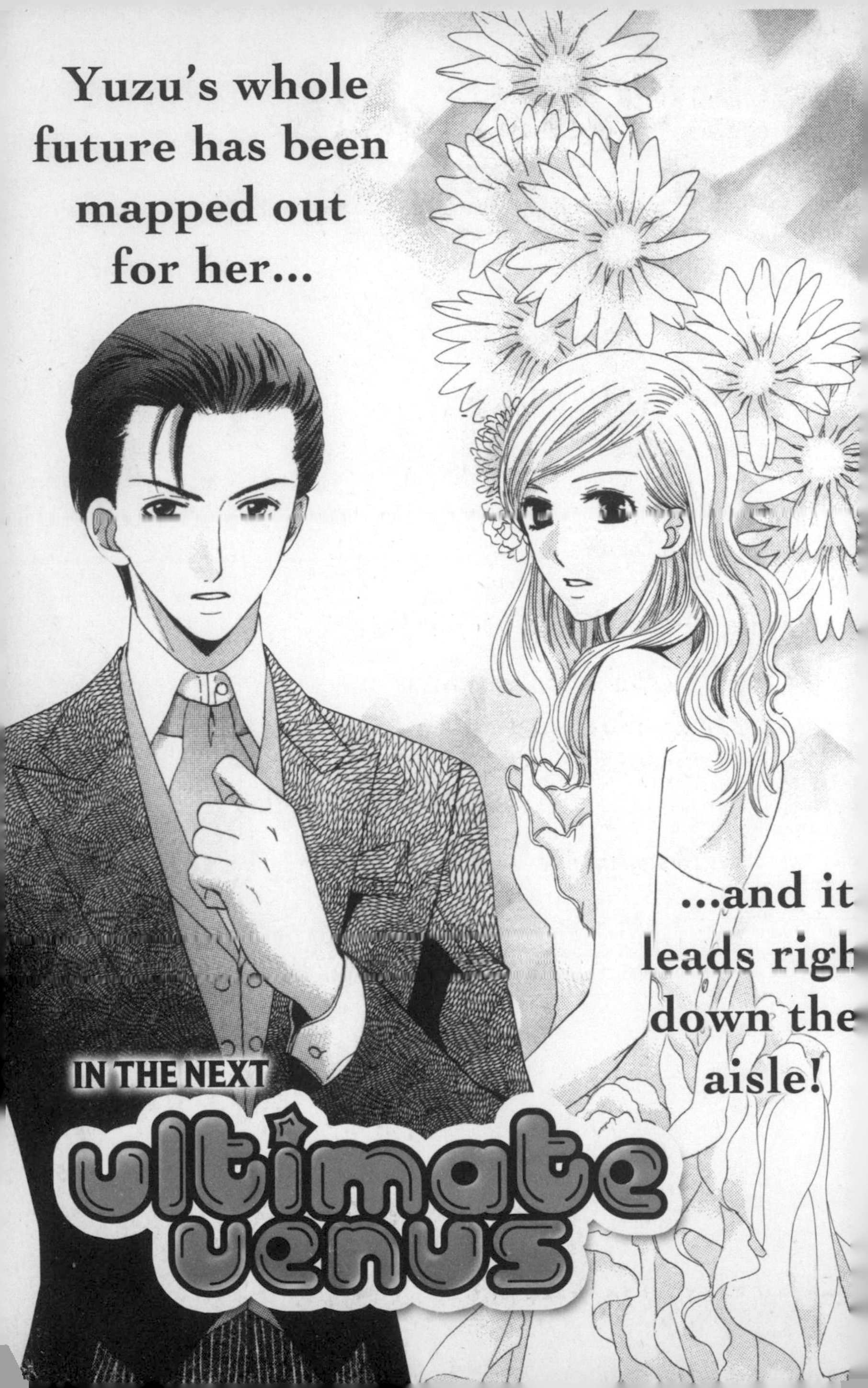
Yuzu's whole future has been mapped out for her...
...and it leads righ down the aisle!
IN THE NEXT
ultimate venus

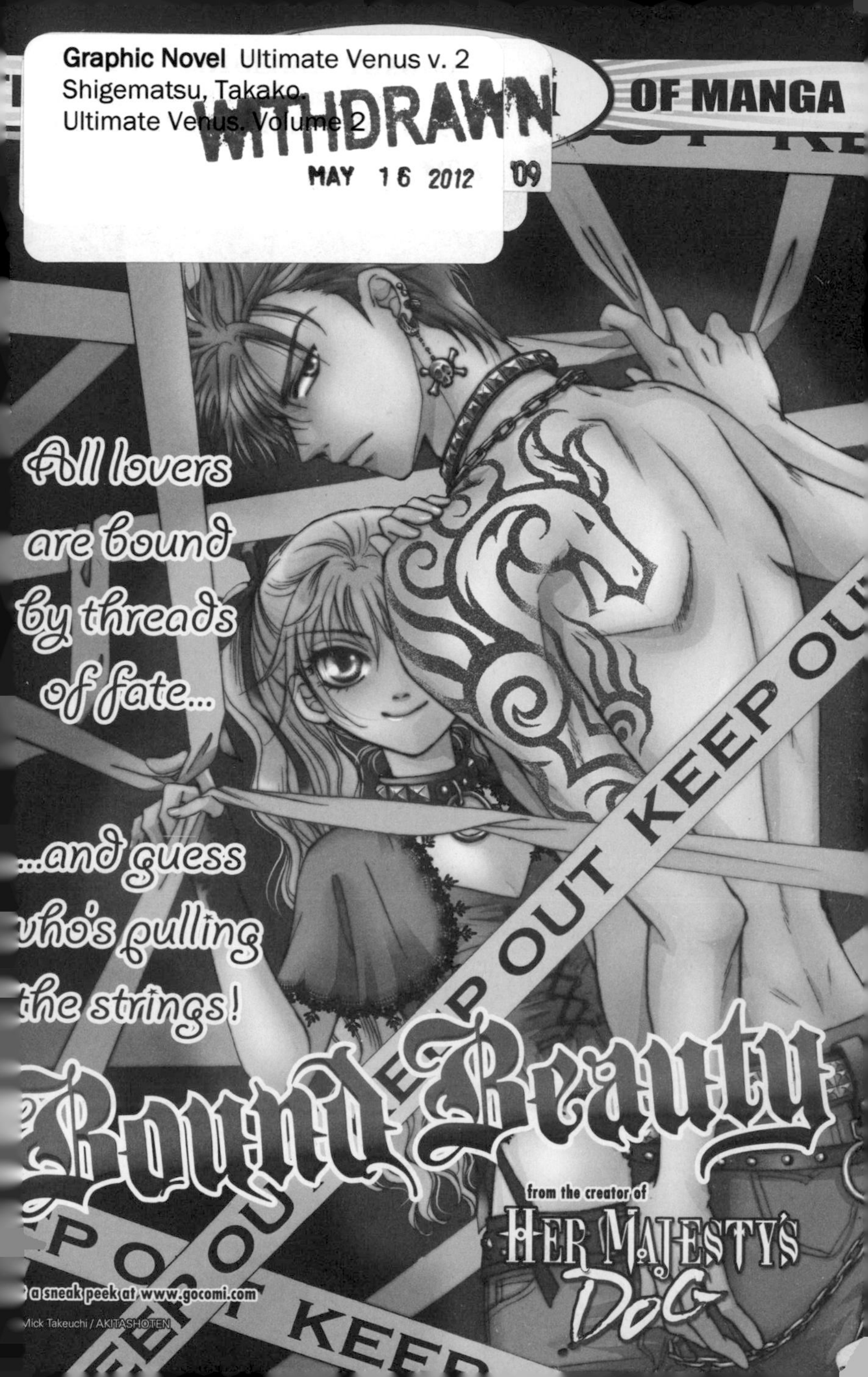
OF MANGA
'09
All lovers are bound by threads of fate...
..and guess
ho's pulling
he strings!
Bound Beauty
KEEP OUT KEEP OU
from the creator of
Her Majesty's Dog
a sneak peek at www.gocomi.com
Mick Takeuchi / AKITASHOTEN